JEWISH WRITING IN THE CONTEMPORARY WORLD

Series Editor: Sander L. Gilman, University of Illinois

# Contemporary
# Jewish Writing
# in Brazil ❧❧
# An Anthology

Edited and translated by Nelson H. Vieira

University of Nebraska Press : Lincoln and London

Acknowledgments for the use of
copyrighted material appear on
pp. 285–87, which constitute an
extension of the copyright page.

Publication of this
book was assisted by a
grant from the National
Endowment for the
Arts.

Library of Congress Cataloging-in-
Publication Data

Contemporary Jewish writing in
Brazil: an anthology / edited and
translated by Nelson H. Vieira.
p.   cm.—(Jewish writing in the
contemporary world)
Includes bibliographical
references.
ISBN 978-0-8032-4662-1
(cloth : alk. paper)
1. Brazilian literature—Jewish
authors—Translations into
English. 2. Jews—Brazil—Literary
collections. I. Vieira, Nelson.
PQ9636.J48C66   2009
869.08'08924081—dc22
2009029727

Set in Quadraat by Bob Reitz.
Designed by Mikah Tacha.

For Aaron,
*A son for all seasons*

# Contents

# Preface

This research project, the critical introduction, and the ensuing translations anthologized here represent the first panorama of twentieth-century Brazilian Jewish fiction available to an English-speaking audience. Although there have been several English translations of Brazilian Jewish fiction beyond the works of Clarice Lispector, whose own body of work has been translated into English and other languages (but for the most part has not been read within a Jewish context), none has been comprehensive. This volume aims to fill the gap with a broad, representative selection of modern Brazilian Jewish narratives—stories, chronicles, and excerpts from novellas and novels. Since this selection also represents the first extensive anthology of Brazilian Jewish writing in English as well as in Portuguese, one of the goals of this project is to provide a critical and sociocultural context for understanding these voices. Thus the introduction, which includes, beyond the analyses of the texts and their authors, a sociocultural and historical framework along with a theoretical focus on the concepts of diaspora and identity.

Recent critical studies continue to treat diaspora as a viable theoretical approach, but a study such as Sander L. Gilman's *Jewish Frontiers* (2003) introduces a new perspective by considering the intriguing concept of 'frontier' as a means of rereading Jewish history, an idea that can also be applied to literature. Reference to Gilman's study is important here because his idea of frontier seeks to go beyond the familiar Jewish experiential dilemma of center/periphery that theories on diaspora and borderlands customarily explore and develop. I agree with Gilman that his concept of the 'frontier' can be seen as an imaginary space of contestation and accommodation, of dispute and conciliation, where no group is privileged and there is no distinction between victims and oppressors, and I have applied this concept to several recent studies on Brazilian Jewish contemporary writing. Certainly Gilman's frontier tropes of negotiation, alteration, and construction are applied in this introduction. However, the theory of diaspora is especially enlightening within the sociohistorical context of this volume, which underscores the sense of dispersion, displacement, and disregard manifested in the texts of many twentieth-century Brazilian Jewish writers. The critical context of diaspora is also well suited to this volume in consideration of Jonathan Boyarin and Daniel Boyarin's findings in their study *Powers of Diaspora: Two Essays on the Relevance of Jewish Culture* (2002), which focuses on the idea of new diasporas beyond nation-states in light of today's transnational, global, cultural, and economic spheres. To underscore their argument, they focus on the paradoxical power and cultural consciousness of diaspora as primarily consisting of the two forces of 'contingency' and 'genealogy.' Such tension between the two forces of sociocultural contingency and Jewish genealogy (ancestral tradition) emerges in many of the Brazilian Jewish writings included here, thereby underscoring the need to read this literature within a diasporic context. On the other hand, recent studies on identity formation have explored the concept of not privileging any single identity in light of the fact that ethnicity does not necessarily shape destiny. As Amartya Sen, in his *Identity and Violence: The Illusion of Destiny* (2006), emphatically states, 'Life is not mere destiny.' This stance, which questions the potential violence embedded, for example, in fundamentalist postures, ultimately challenges the reality, ethics, or even authenticity of maintaining a sole identity. In this vein, the notion of community and concern for the other, involving interaction and dialogue, emerges as a new sociopolitical pathway for understanding multiple identities and changing circumstances, issues that many of these Brazilian Jewish writers dramatize in their fiction.

I began conducting research on Jewish writing in Brazil more than twenty-five years ago. This undertaking has resulted in several publications encompassing literary theory, criticism, analysis, and translation, all with the objective of interpreting the meaning and significance of this rich ethnic expression and its implications for understanding Brazilian culture. Although in existence for little more than half a century, modern Brazilian Jewish writing is notable because it not only contributes to the expanding corpus of ethnic literature in Brazil but also represents one of the most productive and enduring forms of that expression within Brazilian letters. Therefore, with the goal of presenting Brazilian Jewish voices in as coherent and accessible fashion as possible, this volume strives to inform as well as to draw an English-reading audience into a realm that manifests the New World experience of multiple migrations, not only in the Southern Hemisphere of Latin America but also, by extension, in relation to the migratory experiences in the northern universe of America and Canada. In other words, one finds in these pages the underlying motif about the ethnic Jewish experience of dispersion in Brazil, which can be applied to studies of a North-South dialectic, especially in our global and transnational world, where reimmigration is not uncommon. Consideration of this Jewish literature from the Southern Hemisphere will, I hope, lead to comparative studies that provide compelling analyses of Latin American Jewish writing within world Jewish literature and diaspora. Along these lines, the inclusion of Brazilian Moacyr Scliar's translated novel *The Centaur in the Garden* in the list of the 'Best 100 Books of Modern Jewish World Literature,' compiled by the National Yiddish Book Center in Amherst Massachusetts, attests to the potential role and impact that Brazilian and Latin American Jewish narratives can have on the global stage of culture and literature.

The Jewish Writing in the Contemporary World series by the University of Nebraska Press employs 'country' as the overriding means for categorizing and identifying the wide and rich cultural manifestations of the Jewish Diaspora in specific locales. Nevertheless, this volume on Brazil also alludes to the notable presence of Jewish writing in Spanish America, primarily in countries such as Argentina, Mexico, Peru, and Chile but also in other nation-states in Latin America. Latin American Jewish writing in Spanish and Portuguese is increasing as are the number of translations into English, so much so that, for more than ten years, I have been able to offer, with an ever-expanding bibliography, courses and seminars via English translation under such titles as 'Prophets in the Tropics: Latin American Jewish Writing' and 'Esthers of the Diaspora: Latin American Female Writing.' On the other hand, since Brazilian literature of Portuguese expression is often overshadowed by literature written in Spanish and in its English translations, this volume seeks to ameliorate this situation with, for the most part, first-time publications in English translation of narratives originally written in Brazilian Portuguese.

In addition to the critical introduction and its bibliography, *Contemporary Jewish Writing in Brazil* includes a previously unpublished 1998 interview with Brazil's most acclaimed contemporary Jewish writer, as well as twenty more Brazilian Jewish writers in English translation, each preceded by a brief biography and bibliographical information on the author. As mentioned earlier, the texts presented here were selected to provide the broadest possible sampling of Jewish narratives from Brazil. Certainly, many more Brazilian Jewish writings merit translation into English than those included in this volume. Within the limitations of a single volume, however, the selections presented here, I think, form a representative corpus of narratives reflecting the twentieth-century Brazilian Jewish experience.

Many individuals have contributed to the development of this volume over the last eight years. First of all, I wish to express my deep gratitude to Sander L. Gilman for inviting me to participate in this series and for his gracious patience, intellectual encouragement, and sterling scholarship. Second, I cannot adequately thank all the writers and their families who have given permission and have assisted me in this project. Moreover, my interviews and discussions with the authors themselves have enriched my own scholarship in this field. Although I take full responsibility for the translations, many of the authors have contributed directly by reading the translations and then making suggestions as well as graciously providing answers to my innumerable questions. The same goes for the family members of the deceased writers who have furnished invaluable input. I also wish to acknowledge the University of Nebraska Press for its generosity in financing my initial research on this project. I owe many thanks to my colleagues in two Brazilian academic units—the Program for Advanced Study in Contemporary Culture (PACC) and the Interdisciplinary Coordination for Cultural Studies (CIEC) in the School of Communication of the Federal University of Rio de Janeiro—for inviting me to conduct research as a fellow and colleague specializing in Latin American Jewish culture. I am particularly grateful for the assistance, encouragement, and generosity of my august colleague and dear friend Professor Heloísa Buarque de Hollanda and also to João Carlos Horta; they opened and continue to open their home to me and to extend themselves in numerous personal and professional ways. I also wish to thank my wonderful *gaúcho* friends Professor Regina Zilberman and Dr. Isaac Zilberman for their very warm hospitality, friendship, and professionalism. Although there are too many other individuals to name who have been supportive in this endeavor, I would like to recognize some Brazilian, American, and Israeli colleagues, friends, and acquaintances who have contributed in various ways to the development of this project: Anita Novinsky, Ilana Strozenberg, Beatriz Kushnir, Moacyr Scliar, Paulo Gurgel Lispector, Tânia Kaufman, Bela Feldman-Bianco, Jacó Guinsburg, Jerusa Pires Ferreira, Marcos Chor Maio, Rosana Kohl Bines, Mônica Grin, Teresa Cristina Monteiro, Edna Aizenberg, and Boris Schneiderman. Gratitude also goes to my colleagues George Monteiro, Luiz Fernando Valente, Onésimo T. Almeida, Leonor Simas-Almeida, Patricial Sobral, and Anani Dzidzienyo in the Department of Portuguese and Brazilian Studies as well as to all my colleagues in Judaic studies, in particular, Saul Olyan, David Jacobson, and Lynn Davidman. Thanks are also extended to Brown University for contributing to the support of my travel and research and to President Ruth Simmons and former dean of faculty Mary Finnell for their professionalism and inspiration. Finally, last but not least, I would like to express my deep gratitude to my perspicacious and loving wife, Nancy Levitt-Vieira, whose professional acumen, critical thinking, and personal encouragement and love have enabled me to complete this project.

Nelson H. Vieira

# Introduction

*In a land of brunettes, to have red hair was an involuntary act of rebellion.*
—Clarice Lispector, 'Temptation,' in *The Foreign Legion*

*Without the Diaspora the Jews would be form-impoverished; because of the Diaspora the Jews have a treasury of forms. . . . A primal concept of unity has garnered a universe of diversity.*
—Ellis Rivkin, 'The Diaspora: Its History and Significance'

## DIASPORA AND THE JEWS OF BRAZIL

Tropical Jews? Jews in the tropics? The questions suggest an oxymoron not only for those unaware of the existence of a Latin American Jewish Diaspora but also for others who tend to envisage all Jews within familiar U.S. and/or Old World historical contexts. How does one belong to a host culture or nation if one is also part of a diaspora and is thus obliged to live simultaneously within and between two worlds or more? Does the need for belonging induce a need for national sameness at the expense of diasporic ethnic difference? As the American Jewish painter R. B. Kitaj declares in his *First Diasporist Manifesto*: 'Life in Diaspora is often inconsistent and tense; schismatic contradiction animates each day.'[1] In other words, such a life may be problematic, unacceptable, and at times intolerable; these views perhaps may serve as a viable starting point for examining how diasporic people negotiate their identities in different cultural situations.

Framing the narratives in this anthology within the concept of diaspora is crucial for understanding Jews within the complex gestalt(s) of Brazilian culture and the conflictive and ambiguous social construction of its neocolonial existence as a New World nation, especially

regarding its historical, biological, and cultural experiences of contact
and mixing with other cultures and races via the processes of miscegenation, hybridism, acculturation, and assimilation. Added to this
reality is the phenomenon of modern-day immigration, the driving
force behind the formation of the modern Latin American Jewish
Diaspora. These are the cultural challenges that Jews face as they tread
the cross-cultural waters of Brazil and its Jewish Diaspora. Relevant
to this Brazilian Jewish experience is the observation on diaspora
identity made by Daniel Boyarin and Jonathan Boyarin: 'Diasporic
cultural identity teaches us that cultures are not preserved by being
protected from "mixing" but probably can only continue to exist as a
product of such mixing. Cultures, as well as identities, are constantly
being remade.'[2]

Within this diasporic context, this anthology strives to expand Jewish
literary horizons to an exciting part of the New World with narratives
that primarily evoke the cultural dynamics of Brazilian Jews, their
being on the 'outside' as well as on the 'inside,' via the gaze of Brazilian authors of Jewish descent. As 'prophets in the tropic of Brazil,'
these writers, principally immigrants or their descendents, harbor
'outsider-within' perspectives that provide the necessary distance for
assessing the host country's treatment of others and for previewing,
and even predicting, social inequities. Since this literature represents
the twentieth-century thinking and experience of Brazilian Jews, it
is not surprising to find many testimonies (fictional and memorial)
on immigration, the Holocaust, and cross-cultural conflict in which
the role of memory is paramount to keeping the past in the present.
As a burgeoning literature since the 1940s and 1950s, Brazilian Jewish expression in the modern era does not cover the voices of even
three generations.[3] Yet it exists and is growing, albeit sometimes in
nonmainstream publications. Commensurate with new or minority
expressions in other diasporas, one usually finds an emphasis on life
writing, memorial, and immigrant testimony as well as fiction. For
Jewish Brazil these forms of expression are plentiful, emerging in the
genres of the novel, memorial fiction, short story, memoir, testimony,
and the chronicle (crônica, a form combining fiction and nonfiction),
all represented in this anthology; this volume also includes innovative, realist, psychological, and fantastic narratives that refer directly
or indirectly to Jewish culture and identity. The literature included in

this anthology represents both the formative years of Brazilian Jewish expression and an evolving stage manifesting a more aesthetic literary style of sophistication and craft.

For purposes of an overall definition, Brazilian Jewish writing here refers specifically to narratives by authors who are Jewish or of Jewish descent. Although most of the narratives deal overtly with Jewish themes and characters, several narratives either suggest a covert, almost crypto-Jewish focus in their perspectives, approaches, and voices or dramatize unconventional stances and progressive issues often advocated by Jews and Judaism but not overtly identified as such. In the latter case, one could argue that such progressive issues are also taken up by non-Jewish writers, but here the issue relates not to what is autonomously Jewish but to what can be considered as authentic to Jewish culture. The autonomous stance invariably leads to the essentialism versus universalism argument, an unproductive line of reasoning because as Naoki Sakai states: 'Universalism and particularism reinforce and supplement each other; they are never in real conflict; they need each other and have to seek to form a symmetrical, mutually supporting relationship by every means in order to avoid a dialogic encounter which would necessarily jeopardize their reputedly secure and harmonized mono-logical worlds.'[4] Sakai's position is especially productive for understanding the cultural dynamics of our transcultural world, and especially of Brazil, where hybridism and mixing, since colonial times, have produced experiences and expressions across several cultural borders or frontiers.[5]

In this vein, some aspects of the Jewish experience are embedded in narratives that at first glance do not appear to have a Jewish impulse. In these cases, the impulse may be generalized under the themes of exile thinking, rootlessness, sense of belonging, social difference, solitude, and/or cultural alienation, due to various cultural and literary pressures suggesting that overt, visibly Jewish ethnic writing may be unwise, 'limiting,' and/or even dangerous in particular sociopolitical contexts in a culture. Thus we must consider this literature within the context of cultural anthropology as well as history, which suggests a cultural studies approach as a productive method to gain a more informed reading of Brazilian Jewish expression.

The example of Clarice Lispector immediately comes to mind because for the most part her writing is not referentially Jewish, yet it would be shortsighted to dismiss the Jewish impulse in her work. Her interest in gender difference along with her depiction of alienated elderly women have parallels with the transcultural dilemma of 'belonging,' a topic she articulates in her heartfelt and personal *crônica* 'Pertencer' (Belonging). Moreover, Lispector's writing cannot withstand an ethnic rubric because her narratives embrace situations and characters that transcend specific ethnic borders. Ethnic writing would indeed be 'limiting' for her because she understood the parallels as well as the differences across cultures. One might call her a visionary because her writing challenges the concept of advocating a single identity, an ever more common stance adopted by many in today's multicultural world of globalization. Nonetheless, the fact that she was primarily a Brazilian writer who happened to be Jewish does not preclude reading the Jewish impulse in her work. As a contrast, I have included in this anthology an author, Paulo Jacob, whose connection to Jewish ethnicity is ambiguous but who nonetheless writes about Jews in the Amazon with the cultural resources of an Orthodox Jew. Consequently, I am arguing not for an idealized, purist, or evenly balanced notion of Jewish or Brazilian Jewish writing, but rather for one that already harbors other cultural influences and that primarily, minutely, or covertly includes a Jewish impulse in its manner of presentation, its stance, or the selection of its themes and characters. Moreover, thinking about ethnic cultures in their 'pure' forms is unrealistic in the Latin American context, which, especially in the case of Brazil, despite its nationalist fervor and masked prejudices, already exudes, historically, biologically, and socially, a tense hybrid and fluctuating mosaic of multiculturalism. This approach to the narratives anthologized here will enable the reader to appreciate Jewish writing in other cultural contexts, and especially from the viewpoint of the continuity/discontinuity dilemma, which has plagued Jewish culture from time immemorial. With the memorial proclivity of keeping the past (not in its fullness) in the present, thereby responding to the issue of continuity (across different times), and with the diaspora reality of multiplicity (across different spaces), the postmodern politics of multiethnic identity offer alternatives for new cultural recognitions.

With a population of approximately one-half million Jews in Latin America distributed over such diverse nations as Argentina, Brazil, Mexico, Peru, and Venezuela, Jewish communities have begun to weave a distinct cultural pattern into the social fabric of these countries. Interestingly, Argentina and Brazil rank seventh and ninth respectively in world-Jewry categories. In Brazil the literary expression of this Jewish presence is notable, given the emergence of celebrated writers such as Clarice Lispector and Moacyr Scliar, who have garnered national and international renown, and the uniqueness of younger Jewish voices speaking via the Portuguese language and the Brazilian experience. Brazilian literature of Jewish expression offers the contemporary reader an opportunity to appreciate the articulation of a Jewish identity within the Latin American context, particularly within the frame of Brazil's multicultural and multiracial society, where 'to be and not to be' Jewish becomes not only a question of situational ethnicity and cultural negotiation but also a perennial dilemma for Brazilian Jews facing an ideology of nationalist assimilation that, on deep structural, social, and class levels, does not always accommodate expressions of cultural difference.[6] As a result, practices of social negotiation, situational ethnicity, cultural transformation, and sound acculturation surface as some of the many ways of being Jewish in Brazil.

    In terms of their simultaneous insider/outsider experience and their often complex makeup as cultural hybrids, today first- and second-generation Brazilian Jews (predominantly of Ashkenazi background) represent cultural identities originally shaped by displacement and difference. Or as Rey Chow in *Writing Diaspora* perceptively declares: 'Displacement constitutes identity, but as such it is the identity of the ever-shifting' (45). Consequently, the Jewish literary gaze may project myriad meanings and forms for issues such as identity, immigration, racism, ethnicity, nationalism, and memory as well as serve as a resource for debates on other stimulating topics such as cultural diversity, exile thinking, postcolonialism, and diaspora existence. Jewish writers in Brazil frequently comment on their own social history as a group and as individuals contending with the sociopolitical forces exerted by the dominant or host society. In this vein, their thematics invariably include issues of dislocation, alterity, difference, rejection, tradition, intra- and inter-cross-cultural conflict as well as negotiation, continuity/discontinuity, and anti-Semitism. In expressing these themes and questions, Brazilian Jewish writers also focus on the importance of language as a fount of endless interpretation, thereby manifesting an openness to indeterminacy and paradox along with a resistance to definitive closure, a stance so emblematic of Hebraic hermeneutics as opposed to the Western hermeneutical tradition that frequently manifests definitive interpretations and cultural universalism. The self-conscious, critical, and meta-critical proclivities in some writings also point to the interest in grappling with provocative enigmas instead of facile solutions. Thus as contemporary voices these writers challenge established nationalist norms and myths via unconventional and fantastic tropes. Their writings frequently point to the inadequacy of nationalist ideologies and nation building, which primarily define individuals according to a common national living space.

Interestingly, Brazilian Jewish writing, especially during its formative stage, often exhibits traits of traditional immigrant, memorialist, and nostalgic literature, but it also explores innovative forms and Brazilian themes while acknowledging the time-honored heritage of Judaic culture with the fresh eyes and voices of the Latin American experience. This hybrid form of expression manifests a partial affinity with the Brazilian ethos, which invariably finds itself 'in between' cultures; as Paulo Emílio Salles Gomes aptly stated: 'We are neither Europeans nor North Americans yet to us nothing is foreign because, deprived of an original culture, everything is foreign. The painful construction of our selfhood unravels itself through the tenuous dialectic between non-being and being other.'[7] While diaspora Jews may not be deprived of an original Jewish culture, they are frequently displaced from an original cultural homeland or nationalist ideology, which leads to their being considered 'other' and 'in between.'

What is the nature of Jewish identity in a country like Brazil, which professes liberal humanism yet has historically, despite offering social acceptance, manifested toward racial and ethnic others, especially non-European or those mistaken to be non-European, a chronic but subtle prejudice?[8] Prejudice evolved amid national animosities stemming from stereotyping but at the same time became partially mitigated by the powerful myths of racial democracy and of Brazil's cordial man, both ideologies promoting the image of social harmony. During the first half of the twentieth century, immigrants were often perceived as unable to assimilate and also as perpetrators of socioeconomic ills, a political tactic used by a national elite to steer blame away from its own abuses and to satisfy the suffering urban middle class by attributing unemployment to the free entry of foreigners, who supposedly contributed to social disorder and economic insecurity. Thus, affluence (mobility) went hand in hand with latent prejudice or racism. Here it is important to differentiate prejudice from the sustained and overt discrimination that occurred intermittently in the 1930s and 1940s. Although this prejudice also has roots in the colonial period and in the nineteenth-century founding of nation and national identity, its twentieth-century manifestations emanate from Brazil's modern history of immigration as well as from a state-oriented politics of nationalist social integration that, since Brazil's authoritarian, fascist, and populist New State of the late 1930s, clearly promoted an assimilation policy and doctrine of supposed social harmony in which concerns for the nation transcended and thereby masked issues of racial, class, and other differences. So how does one manifest one's ethnic identity when a rising socioeconomic nationalist homogeneity insidiously encourages ethnic demobilization? How does one mobilize a politics of ethnicity when institutionalized politics are primarily limited to parochial or national matters while ignoring or barely acknowledging ethnic particularity? Are ethnic politics even necessary in Brazil or in the rest of Latin America? In other words, should one protect or eject the hyphen between ethnic and national identities?[9] Or can the hyphen disappear and then reappear, that is, be negotiated according to specific cultural circumstances.

Another comment should be made regarding this hyphen. The use of the hyphen to call attention to nationality and ethnicity has not been a common practice in Latin America due to a variety of reasons such as nationalism but particularly the history of hybrid practices in many nations. This is especially true of Brazil, where ethnic and cultural mixing is common but not always comfortable and readily accepted. The hybrid proclivity ultimately leads one to consider a new positive awareness of *mestiçagem* (a form of miscegenation with cultural overtones; the term has no exact English equivalent) as a critical practice of cultural negotiation and translation. Anthropologist Néstor García Canclini expounds on this phenomenon in his essay 'No sabemos cómo llamar a los otros' (We Do Not Know How to Name Others), included in his study *La globalización imaginada* (1999/2000). Although Brazil has enormous socioeconomic inequalities and class fractures, sociologists and anthropologists such as Gilberto Freyre and Roberto Da Matta have nonetheless underscored the multiple cultural interpenetrations of the migratory contingents that have formed that nation, thereby suggesting a closer and a more cautious reading of race, culture, and ethnicity, of mestiçagem.

With a cultural and political legacy of nonpluralist ideology, despite the presence of a multiethnic population, the political and social national elite has contributed to the political passivity common among racial and ethnic groups in Brazil and, for that matter, in the Jewish Diaspora in general, where the status quo stance has often been the norm.[10] Moreover, in regions marked by political instabilities, weak democratic institutions, and authoritarian tendencies, which have driven the quest for national identity, it is unsurprising that a 'low profile' stance, calculated to ensure ethnic invisibility, nonconflict, and guardedness, continues to permeate the cultural politics of racial and ethnic groups. This position is especially understandable among groups such as the Jews, who, although rarely the target of overt discrimination in Brazil, nevertheless, represent a religious and cultural otherness that historically has challenged elite notions of national identity.[11] In a similar vein, the Brazilian folklorist Luís da Câmara Cascudo offers his general observation about Brazil's cultural attitudes toward Jews in light of an anti-Semitism traceable to early Christian societies: 'The populace [of Brazil] still sees the Jew with sixteenth-century eyes.'[12]

In Brazil the 'low profile' strategy to avoid making waves relates in part to what Sander L. Gilman calls the 'visibility of the Jew in the Diaspora.' In an essay thus titled he concentrates on body imagery and its cultural context, citing the Jewish nose as 'one of the central [constructed] loci of difference in seeing the Jew.'[13] Gilman's thesis may apply in part to Brazil, given that country's stress on appearance in general. For the Brazilian Jew, who may physically blend in or 'pass' vis-à-vis Latin 'swarthiness,' however, it is the overall cultural image of the Jew based on religious, historical, and social stereotyping that most influences the notion of 'visibility.' As Gilman observes in relation to discrimination or prejudice—real or imagined: 'It is the internalization of the negative image of the Jew, the desire not to be seen as a Jew, while retaining one's own identity as a Jew, that is one model of response to the sense of being seen as "too Jewish" or, indeed, being seen as Jewish at all.'[14] Given the historical 'bad' image of the Jew in countries where a history of Catholic prejudices and socioeconomic stereotypes and the resulting discrimination against cultural difference once prevailed, a 'low profile' strategy, be it in the form of situational ethnicity or cultural silence, ultimately aspires to cultural invisibility. A Brazilian example of this aspired invisibility, or low-profile stance, occurred when a component of the Brazilian Jewish community did not want to be associated with Carlos Heitor Cony's novel about a leftist Jew, *Pessach: A travessia* (1967) (Pessach: The Crossing), published during the beginning of the military dictatorship's most repressive period. Linking the Jews with the leftist practice of guerrilla warfare was tantamount to making the Jews visible as radicals opposing the military regime at a time when any form of leftist political mobilization was very dangerous.

The following comments by Gilman about ethnic visibility in the United States seem applicable to the Brazilian case, especially when one considers that the notion of ethnic identity is not overtly practiced in Brazil because, above all, everyone is first and foremost Brazilian, that is, except when differences become threatening: 'Ethnic identity—whether being Jewish-American or Asian-American or African-American—is validated as long as the general aesthetic norms of the society are not transgressed. For being too visible means being seen not as an individual but as an Other.'[15] In Brazil this visibility may take the form of being culturally incompatible (through word or behavior) with Christians in that nation.

With regard to a cultural and national scenario, the Jewish community of Brazil has frequently confused politicization with partisanship and appeared in the past to follow adaptive cultural strategies that for the most part resulted in group self-exclusion from visible political participation within the dominant society, the growing presence of individual Jews in high political offices notwithstanding. Furthermore, given the sporadic individual, artistic, and governmental manifestations of cultural diversity or multiculturalism emerging in the late 1990s, there appears to be an increasing but subtle, albeit superficial, acknowledgment of ethnicity. Nonetheless, with regard to an overall cultural strategy, Jewish survival in Brazil seems to replicate the millennial practice of maintaining discreet 'pluri-identity'—'ser um bom Judeu em casa e um bom cidadão fora dela' (to be a good Jew inside the home and a good citizen on the outside), which conveniently parallels the Brazilian paradigm of house and street, theorized by

the Brazilian anthropologist Roberto Da Matta. Here the home is
the confined, familiar space for assuming a cultural/ethnic/religious
identity, while the street is the arena for negotiating with the nation
and the larger society. But even on these two levels, one must ask how
exactly this negotiation takes place within Brazil's multicultural society? Interestingly, during Brazil's celebration of five hundred years
as a nation, in April 2000, the minister of tourism and sports, Rafael
Greca de Macedo, stated that Brazil was 'a land of ethnic peace'; yet
this statement begs the question of how one explains the concurrent
violent protests of Indians and other minorities. In a similar vein, we
might also ask, what are the ways of being and not being a Jewish
minority in Brazil?

## DIASPORA AND THE POLITICS OF
## ETHNIC IDENTITY AND EXPRESSION

As a point of departure for answering these questions, we might
consider a statement made by the Boyarins: 'Diaspora culture and
identity allow for a *complex continuation* of Jewish cultural creativity
and identity at the same time that the same people participate fully in
the common cultural life of their surroundings.'[16] I italicize 'complex
continuation' to accommodate in part the different manifestations of
Judaism—secular, assimilationist, cultural as well as religious—or
to paraphrase Jonathan Boyarin's assertion that Jewish continuity
should be grounded in some form of daily practice, be it religious
ritual or even the investigation of what it means to be a Jew. But it
is also important to recall that for diasporic behavior, according to
Rey Chow, 'the tactics of dealing with and dealing in dominant cultures' are 'the tactics of those who do not have claims to territorial
propriety or cultural centrality.'[17] These tactics become the social
reality of those who know they must negotiate their cultural identity,
albeit with potentially underlying insecurity. Negotiation becomes
the modus operandi instead of blind adherence to the violent myth
of consanguinity that demands absolute submission to one's ethnic
heritage. In other words, these negotiators cannot always fall back
on the politics of traditional nationalism.

As the Boyarins state so succinctly about maintaining one's cultural difference without controlling the land, implying that people and lands are not naturally connected: 'The genius of Christianity is its concern for all the peoples of the world: the genius of Judaism is its ability to leave other people alone.'[18] Consequently, Jews negotiate via their heightened exogenous tendency to know how to relate strategically to the rest of the world. In their conclusion, where they argue against the type of power that leads to domination over others, and thus renounce temporal power as the most effective mode to preserve difference and resist effectively, the Boyarins propose 'a privileging of Diaspora, a dissociation of ethnicities and political hegemonies as the only social structure that even begins to make possible a maintenance of cultural identity in a world grown thoroughly and inextricably interdependent.'[19] Although somewhat utopian in its conceptualization and charged with a critical eye on Israeli politics, this view is nonetheless based on historical examples of Jewish culture thriving in dominant cultures such as in Muslim Spain. On the other hand, while one may interpret the Brazilian style of no ethnic politics and the lesser recognition of ethnic identity as an example of the 'dissociation of ethnicities and political hegemonies' proposed by the Boyarins, one must consider that in Brazil powerful political hegemonies continue to exist and can exert pressure when differences transgress the norm.

Furthermore, it is important to remember that cultures are not fixed but are constantly being remade, circumstances that may be particularly relevant for the Jewish Diaspora of Brazil: 'While this is true of all cultures, diasporic Jewish culture lays it bare because of the impossibility of a natural association between this people and a particular land—thus the impossibility of seeing Jewish culture as a self-enclosed, bounded phenomenon. . . . In other words, diasporic identity is a disaggregated identity. Jewishness disrupts the very categories of identity because it is not national, not genealogical, not religious, but all of these in dialectical tension with one another.'[20]

This line of diaspora thinking also has much to offer the fields of cultural studies and postcolonialism because it entails an acute awareness of cultural border crossing. When one considers the notion of diaspora as part of the biblical story of Abraham leaving his own land to go to the Promised Land and Israel thus being born in exile, and the prophecies of the uprooted tribulations of the Hebrews in Genesis and Deuteronomy, one can appreciate how the embedded

Jewish experiences of deterritorialization and exile override having roots to the land.[21] Thus, we might say that the Jews have been telling us, for hundreds of years, about the pitfalls of nationalism. Within this history, it is evident that 'ethnocentricity is ethical only when cultural identity is an embattled minority.'[22]

In his mammoth anthology of approximately 150 Latin American Jewish writers, El gran libro de América Judía (1998), the Peruvian Jewish writer Isaac Goldemberg refers to this literature as a lens to focus on ways of being Jewish and Latin American without violating the aspects of Latin American Jewry's bifrontal personality or condition (11–18). Certainly his novels The Fragmented Life of Jacobo Lerner (1976) (La vida a plazos de Jacobo Lerner, 1978) and Play by Play (1984) (Tiemplo al tiempo, 1984) address this reality as a mestizo/hybrid condition, filled with tension, as does the work of other writers, such as Aída Bortnik's film Pobre mariposa (1992) (Poor Butterfly) and Mario Szichman's Argentine novel (about the Jewish Pechof family at the time of Evita's death) A las 20:25 la señora entró en la immortalidad (1981) (At 8:25 Evita Became Immortal, 1983). In so doing these authors also denounce the failures of authoritarianism, moral bankruptcy, and complicit acceptance via silence. In this way Goldemberg and writers like the Brazilian Moacyr Scliar challenge us to think of Judaism in Latin America as a counterexile, primarily in terms not of persecution, discrimination, alienation, and wandering but rather of transformation, ambiguity, valorization, recognition, and affirmation. Both of these writers, Scliar and Goldemberg, refer to Judaism as a process in constant renovation, citing Gershom Scholem's understanding of how each generation must redefine its Judaism.

In his discussion of the evolution of Jewish tradition in relation to continuity, Gershom Scholem refers to three paths as possible outcomes of its development: (1) the retention of continuity; (2) metamorphosis as a new configuration; or (3) a break, a rejection of the tradition. Scholem then asks, 'Is the break in a tradition really a break? Does the tradition not somehow manage to continue in new formulas and configurations even if metamorphosis is seemingly rejected? Is there anything that endures through all of this?'[23]

Scholem's views on cultural continuity underscore the central and mutable role of the continuity/discontinuity dilemma in relation to diaspora ethnicity as an arena for discussing the potential survival,

maintenance, or possible disappearance of Latin American Jewish
cultural difference. This is especially pertinent in light of the demo-
graphics provided by U. O. Schmelz and Sergio Della Pergola indicating that Latin American Jewish communities are shrinking at a rate
of 1 percent per year.[24] Along these lines two paramount features
intrinsically linked to the concepts of continuity and the maintenance
of cultural difference should be emphasized: on the one hand, the
idea of cultural identity as the sense of a continued authentic self and,
on the other, the phenomenon of belonging but not one necessarily
related to the traditional image of a safe haven.

In light of these features, let us return to the issue of what constitutes Brazilian Jewish writing by asking the questions: What is
ethnic discourse? Is it the overt treatment of ethnic themes, or is it
a literature manifesting a particular form of cultural thinking by an
author born into an ethnic family? Moreover, is there space for an
ethnic discourse in Latin America, a hemisphere or so of independent
countries still grappling with their respective senses of national identity?
What constitutes national, cultural, racial, or ethnic identity(ies) in
Latin America? What role does cultural memory play in this process?
Is individual memory different from collective memory? Does ethnic
memory construct identity as well as shape narrative?

While addressing Isaac Bashevis Singer's understanding of memory
and the temporary (amnesia) repression of memory due to trauma
and other factors, Sander L. Gilman in Inscribing the Other sees memory
as linked to identity in this way: 'To forget the Diaspora is the act of
forgetting the self.'[25] Furthermore, does a tension exist between the
memory of ordinary folk, that of marginal and/or ethnic groups, and
the public memory as seen and constructed by institutions committed to the ideologies of nationhood and citizenship (as articulated by
Homi Bhabha in his studies)? How do ethnic voices situate themselves
among these diverse memories? In Gilman's interview with Singer, the
novelist states this truism about Jewish memory: 'We are a very restless
people, and as I once said: we Jews suffer from many diseases, but
amnesia is not one of them.'[26] Gilman goes on to include the following observation, which characterizes the Jewish (and Singer's) stance
on memory: 'Jews are not supposed to have "amnesia," according to
Singer, but are supposed to be aware of their history, which is why
their holy book is a historical document rather than a philosophical

one.'[27] And finally does there exist an old, essentialist type of ethnicity as well as what Stuart Hall calls a *new* ethnicity, one addressing a wider variety of experiences across several cultural borders?[28] Many of these questions (drawn in part from Singh, Skerritt, and Hogan in *Memory, Narrative and Identity*) have contributed to the research and thinking that form the basis of this introduction to Brazilian Jewish writing in the contemporary world.

To reiterate, Brazil has often denied the existence of an ethnic politics or discourse because people in Brazil are first and foremost Brazilian, that is, they first identify with their Brazilianness. Yet why does there seem to be emerging in Brazil a series of new ethnic (Jewish, Arabic, Japanese) voices (young and old), otherwise practically unheard of fifty or even thirty years ago? On the other hand, within Brazilian literary history one finds a few earlier examples of German and Italian narratives written in Portuguese, but these did not constitute a current as in the case of Brazilian Jewish expression. Are the more recent ethnic groups and their writers questioning more the existential position of their ethnic identities in Brazil than other groups have in the past and consequently feel the need for more open ethnic expression? For instance, what happens when one's religious and ethnic identity and value system exist alongside the value systems of those of the dominant society as occurred with many Brazilian Jews and other Jews in the Jewish Diaspora? Moreover, are the younger voices emerging from these groups, expressing the same traditional sense of ethnicity, or is there indeed a manifestation of a new type of ethnicity, 'beyond ancestor worship,' perhaps less ethnocentric but nonetheless expressive of the need for some form of ethnic belonging?[29] Is there hope for a vital survival of Judaism in Latin America?

In his discussion of Amy Tan's *Joy Luck Club* and the Chinese American experience, Ben Xu does not portray the ethnic self as a 'higher form of self and self-awareness' but rather locates the existential position of ethnicity in a way that may in part relate today, or someday in the not-too-distant future, to some aspects of the Brazilian scene: 'The ethnic self, just like the existential self, is neither free nor self-sufficient, and therefore never an authentic or genuine self. Our ethnic experience, no less than our existential experience, depends on the mediation of others. We become aware of our ethnicity only when we are placed in juxtaposition with others and *when the priority of our other* identities, such as individual, class, gender, and religious, give place to that of ethnicity.'[30] Has the priority of these other identities, especially those of individual and class, yielded to that of ethnicity in Brazil and Latin America? Perhaps not yet to any great extent.

In discussions of issues of difference in Latin America and Brazil, ethnic difference for some groups may be underplayed or forgotten because the issues of class, economics, and politics often have a leveling effect since these concerns are representative of more important social priorities linked to issues of power, control, and survival. In her article 'Cultura e democracia no processo da globalização' (Culture and Democracy within the Process of Globalization), which addresses the questions of pluralist political representation as well as civil rights in Brazil and especially the difficulty of transforming the inequality of the popular masses or marginal groups and minorities into cultural difference or into a meaningful transcultural dialog of representation, the Brazilian scholar Paula Montero boldly states:

The criticism of nationalism may perhaps mobilize political groups in the direction of the suppression of social inequality, but it is unable to translate it positively into a new collective identity in which ethnic and cultural differences can live together. The individual seen as different is merely the individual who has no rights. In responding to the problem of civil rights, one loses the dimension of difference. In this sense, the nation's problem will perhaps be solved on the level of equal rights, but on the level of cultural differences it still remains an equation in search of a solution.[31]

Does this mean that the potential expression of difference, for Brazil and Latin America, may be overridden by the national ideological concern for class, economics, and politics, that is, at the expense of ethnic difference? These questions are raised here, not to answer them fully, but rather to use them to contextualize and not to essentialize the discussion of the fiction of Brazilian Jewish writers and how they portray the various ways of being Jewish in Brazil.

EARLY JEWISH EXPRESSION IN BRAZIL

With a population of approximately 120,000, or less than a quarter of the total number of Latin American Jews, Brazilian Jews represent the largest Latin American Jewish community after Argentina's. If one considers that Jews have been coming to Portuguese America since the early part of the sixteenth century, one can appreciate their experience as another avenue of the world Jewish Diaspora. However, since Portuguese Jews arrived as 'simulated' New Christians, thereby implying an absence of their original cultural heritage and religion, one can also begin to understand their eventual cultural disappearance during the colonial period via enforced assimilation. Yet, despite no direct link between the New Christian Jews of colonial Brazil and the Jews of the modern period, is it still possible that the expected notion of 'absented' difference continues to be manifested in diverse ways by contemporary Brazilian Jews and revealed in texts written by Brazilian Jewish authors? Does there exist in Brazil a neocolonialist proclivity toward the exclusion and/or subordination of Jewish writing in terms of its production and reception? Or are there diverse literary ways of expressing Judaism and Jewishness, just as there are different ways of being Jewish in Brazil? Does modern Latin American literature's recognized challenge to established genres and 'essentialist' mindsets, that is, its transgression of European textual models and ethnic nationalisms, emerge in Jewish expression south of the border? Do the Latin American literary strategies of transformation and resignification spill over into Jewish Diaspora experiences and expressions in Brazil? Does the Brazilian modernist concept of symbolic anthropophagy (cannibalism), of 'eating' and digesting foreign culture in order to produce something 'new' through cultural digestion, apply to Brazilian Jewish writing as well? Or does there already exist within Jewish writing an affinity with similar modes and innovations found in Latin American literature, in this case, Brazilian?

In light of these questions, it is also important to underscore that today's Jewish communities in Brazil are the result of immigrations occurring during the nineteenth and twentieth centuries and thus have no direct connection to the Jewish (Sephardic) population of colonial Brazil. Involuntary Jewish conversion had been enforced in 1497 by Portugal's King Manuel I and was carried out in the colony after Brazil had been 'discovered' in 1500. Except for the Dutch invasion and colonization in the Northeast during the seventeenth century (1624–54), when Jews were 'tolerated' socially and religiously, Jews never entered Brazil openly as 'Jews' for most of the colonial period. However, under the label of 'New Christians,' these Jews were certainly differentiated from the Old

Christians. Not until the latter part of the eighteenth century (1773) were Jews technically free from possible persecution and able to reside in Brazil as Jews after the obligatory 'New Christian' label and stigma were abolished. For Portuguese-speaking Jews the Brazilian colonial atmosphere of prejudice was based primarily on religion, politics, and then the ideology of purity of blood, directed primarily at crypto Jews and their descendants as well as other 'infidels.'

Forced to simulate Christianity, New Christians were often suspected of dissimulation, as if they were all secret Judaizers. In *Cristãos Novos na Bahia*, the Brazilian historian Anita Novinsky documents a picture of the history and treatment of Sephardic Jews during the Brazilian colonial era, when their status as New Christians never represented their full assimilation but rather pointed to a duality in which European questions of heresy and purity of blood always dictated their living between two worlds. Obliging many Jews to practice Jewish ritual clandestinely, the imposed conversion forced others to renounce their secret world and become 'true' New Christians, a renunciation that ironically only served to underscore their never being viewed as acceptable Old Christians. Although the Portuguese Inquisition was never formally established in the colony of Brazil, visits of the Holy Office to Brazil from the end of the sixteenth century created a climate of fear that frequently resulted in denunciations and imprisonment. Such was the case of Bento Teixeira (1561–1600), author of *Prosopopea*, considered to be the first notable poem written in the colony. A Portuguese New Christian as well as a diehard crypto Jew who was denounced in Brazil but interrogated in Lisbon for four long years, Teixeira was finally forced to renounce his Judaism in an auto-da-fé. Traditionally *Prosopopea* has been read as a Christian poem, celebrating the feats and tribulations of its Christian hero, while narrating some of the colony's growing pains. However, recent rereadings have pointed to the poem's crypto structure and theme, suggesting its dissimulating stance as well as its deftness at simulating the appearance of a Christian world. The poem's dual perspective and focus on persona and metamorphosis indicate that issues of alterity and difference have been experienced by Luso-Brazilian Jews since colonial times. Consequently, a reassessment of the socioeconomic and cultural activities of the New Christians in the colony will recognize further their important contributions to the colonization of Brazil.

From the beginning of colonization, the New Christians and their entrepreneurial spirit played a significant role in the development of the timber industry because they were involved in the first *feitorias*, or permanent trading posts, in Brazil and then later in the sugar cane commerce. But not all New Christians who came to the New World were secret Judaizers, traveling west solely for the purpose of practicing their Jewish faith. If this had been the case, they would have fled to other countries where they would have been free to practice their faith openly. Although their motivations were primarily economic and social, many did propagate their faith.[32]

Another New Christian whose work has recently been reinterpreted from a Jewish viewpoint is Ambrósio Fernandes Brandão, a contemporary of Bento Teixeira, who wrote in 1618 *Diálogos das grandezas do Brasil* (*Dialogues of the Great Things of Brazil*, 1986), a manuscript that was discovered in the nineteenth century but published only in 1930. Again, a crypto-Jewish reading suggests that the author infused his work with a Jewish perspective. The book is a series of six dialogues between two Portuguese, one recently arrived in the colony and the other an established immigrant, Brandônio (possibly referring to the author's name), who discuss the pros and cons of the new land. Rich in geographical and historical detail for understanding the relations between the Portuguese and the Indians and the African slaves, the *Dialogues* make no direct reference to the Jews except to suggest that the Indians were possible descendants of the Israelites from Solomon's times. Arguments for seeing the Jewish impulse in this work are also based on the text's constant reference to the Old Testament as well as on the paucity of Catholic icons and doctrine, the latter ordinarily cultural and religious staples in narratives of this sort. With the Inquisition casting its shadow over the colony of Brazil, it is no wonder that authors such as Brandão and Teixeira had to be cautious in their simulation as New Christians and their dissimulation as Jews.

The practice of dissimulation, which implied the presence of a different cultural perspective behind the simulation of the Christian mask, becomes in the history of the Jewish presence in colonial Brazil a telling manifestation of an awareness of being different, of being an 'outsider within' whose keen insights develop further an acute sensitivity to the many dimensions of difference. Perhaps one of the most noteworthy outsiders of the colonial period was Antonio

José da Silva, known as 'o Judeu'—the Jew. Born in Rio de Janeiro in 1705, da Silva was to become one of Portugal's most distinguished playwrights. However, before graduating from Coimbra in 1728, he was accused of practicing Judaism and later in 1737 denounced for the crime of heresy and apostasy. After professing his repentance to the Inquisitors, on October 18, 1739, Antonio José was garroted and then burned at the stake in an auto-da-fé. He was thirty-four years old. From that day Portuguese documents regularly refer to him as 'the Jew.' Furthermore, the declared founder of Brazilian Romanticism, Domingos José de Magalhães, wrote a play about this historical literary figure. Titled *António José, o poeta e a Inquisição* (1839), the play's central theme is dissimulation. The suspected disguise or mask of falsehood again becomes the characteristic most associated with New Christian behavior, thereby making impossible the intent of copying fully an Old Christian way of being. Thus an intended positive simulacrum ironically becomes a subversive one. Portugal's famous modern playwright Bernardo Santareno wrote a moving drama, *O Judeu* (1966) (The Jew), about da Silva's tribulations and fate within the context of Portugal's twentieth-century dictatorship and the New Christian dissimulation of its colonial past. More recently volume 1 of the mammoth biohistorical and literary treatment of the Portuguese Inquisition and the *converso* experience *Vínculos do fogo: Antônio José da Silva, o Judeu, e outras histórias da Inquisição em Portugal e no Brasil* (1992) (Bonds of Fire: Antônio José da Silva and Other Stories of the Inquisition in Portugal and Brazil), by the Brazilian Jewish journalist and writer Alberto Dines, serves as testimony to the enduring interest in this artist and his hybrid existence. Moreover, the attention to this historical and literary figure also indicates the renewed interest in the phenomenon of alterity, difference, and transformation accentuated in the New Christian and crypto-Jew/Judaizer experience. What impact did the New Christian experience have on the Brazilian ethos and culture? Is this behavior representative or evocative of the way non-Jewish Brazilians deal with difference in the modern period?

## THE JEWS IN POSTCOLONIAL BRAZIL

Interestingly, despite its problematic colonial history of discrimination and later the fascism of the 1930s and early 1940s, Brazil became known as a veritable haven for several waves of Jewish immigrants, especially during the modern period. In the early years of postcolonial Brazil, Jews began to emigrate more openly as Jews primarily after Brazilian independence in 1822, but by this time most of the New Christians of the earlier period through mixing and masking had lost their Jewish identity via assimilation. The early nineteenth century witnessed the settlement of Sephardic Jews from Islamic countries, but for most of the nineteenth century, non-Iberian Jews, the Ashkenazim, represented the majority of Jewish immigration in Brazil. During the 1800s these Ashkenazim first came from Holland, Alsace-Lorraine, and Germany, but during the last decade of the century, Jews from Russia and Eastern Europe became the primary immigrants. Moroccan Jews emigrated to several parts of South America during the nineteenth century and in Brazil to such regions as the Amazon. Other Sephardic Jews have been entering Brazil in relatively small numbers throughout the twentieth century, settling in many cities but particularly in Rio de Janeiro, São Paulo, and Porto Alegre. However, the Ashkenazim first began to arrive in Brazil in larger numbers with the initial wave of European immigration in the 1880s and specifically from Russia during the first decade of the twentieth century via the Jewish Colonization Agency's (JCA) efforts to establish Jewish agricultural settlements in the interior of Brazil's southernmost state, Rio Grande do Sul. (Several narratives in this anthology evoke various aspects of this historical experience.) Later waves came from Eastern Europe, Poland, and Germany during the 1920s, 1930s, and 1940s, but most of these twentieth-century groups of Ashkenazic immigrants came as refugees escaping the more modern forms of persecution—the pogroms and the Holocaust—documented in this anthology by memorial writing, illustrative of the importance of memory, of recording the past in the present, a well-recognized proclivity found in Jewish world literature. At the turn of the century Ashkenazic and Sephardic synagogues already existed in cities like Rio de Janeiro. Because most twentieth-century Jewish immigrants to Brazil were of Eastern European origin, the majority of the present Jewish population is Ashkenazic.

In a vibrant 1904 crônica of Jewish life in Rio, the famous Brazilian essayist João do Rio spoke of the 'density' of the Jewish community's almost ghettolike existence in Rio and of its colorful inhabitants, among them men of intellect and culture like the city's first hazan, David

Hornstein, a polyglot, professor, rabbi, and foreign correspondent. Many of the Jews in Rio lived in the famous Praça Onze (Eleventh Square), an area that during the 1920s became one of the first Jewish neighborhoods in the city, also known for its varied social activities and flourishing commerce. References to this neighborhood emerge in memorial and fictional narratives, which frequently have Praça Onze as the setting for their stories. During the early part of the twentieth century, in cities like Rio and São Paulo, there emerged the famous street vendors and door-to-door salesmen who sold on credit: the *clientelchiks*, *gringos de prestação* or *prestamistas* (as they were known in Rio), and the *russos à prestação* (as they were first called in São Paulo). Thanks to these Jewish immigrants, this type of commerce introduced a new form of business that made goods more accessible to the lower middle classes in Brazil under the installment plan. The early modern history and literary expression of the Jewish community in Brazil is linked to the travels of these men, who hawked their wares through the various neighborhoods of the city and introduced products not accessible to the population at large. Amid the many contributions of the Jewish culture's rich history to the Brazilian experience, it is their cultural legacy of tense hybridism from the perspectives of social alterity, identity, and negotiation that surfaces frequently in the expression of Brazilian Jewish voices.

A climate of intermittent discrimination, predominantly politically based, did surface much later and for a brief period during the height of Brazilian fascism in the 1930s and 1940s. Although its violence was more a threat than an actuality, the anti-Semitic atmosphere of the Vargas regime did show evidence of persecution as exemplified in the famous case of Olga Benário Prestes, the German Jewish political activist who participated in the 1935 Communist plot, led by her husband and leader of the Communist Party in Brazil, Luís Carlos Prestes. Seven months pregnant, Olga was deported to Hitler's Germany, where she died in a concentration camp gas chamber.[33] It appears that the anti-Semitism allowed by the Vargas regime was a means of appeasing right-wing militants such as Plínio Salgado and his nationalistic green-shirted political movement, the Ação Integralista Brasileira (Brazilian Integrationist Movement) (1932–38), and the fascist Gustavo Barroso, author of anti-Semitic titles such as *Judaísmo, Maçonaria e Comunismo* (1937) (Judaism, Masonry, and

Communism). The xenophobia reigning during this period had serious
implications for Jews, severely limiting their opportunities. Moreover,
Jewish immigration was officially restricted from 1937 to 1939, given
Vargas's authoritarian Estado Novo (New State) and its refugee policy
reflecting strong anti-Semitism. Nevertheless, many Jews managed
to emigrate to Brazil.[34]

The aftermath of the Second World War witnessed the growth
and upward mobility of many Brazilian Jews, who entered the liberal
professions as well as business. Today Jewish schools, synagogues,
organizations, clubs, libraries, student movements, press, and other
cultural phenomena flourish in Brazil. Much of this presence is documented in books such as Henrique Veltman's *A história dos Judeus no
Rio de Janeiro* (1998) (The History of the Jews in Rio de Janeiro). The
Jewish Federation also exerts a notable influence on the cohesiveness
of the various communities. However, an underlying issue for Jews
during the second half of the twentieth century was the place of their
ethnic identity. Although some studies such as Henrique Rattner's
*Tradição e mudança: A comunidade judaica em São Paulo* (1977) (Tradition
and Change: The Jewish Community in São Paulo) speak to issues of
assimilation and the ambiguous nature of Brazilian ethnic and racial
relations, others see this ambiguity as co-opting the legitimization
of Jewish culture in Brazil, since there exists no idea of the Jewish
group as a cohesive whole. The creation of social clubs and cultural
centers points to the attempt by some Jews to forge a space and a more
pluralistic conception of integration, emphasizing one's roots while
being part of the nation. Modern Jewish writing portrays this problem with critical insights; however, it was not until the last decades
of the twentieth century that literature dramatizing a more pluralist
approach to race and ethnicity began to appear.

## EARLY MODERN JEWISH WRITING IN BRAZIL

Driven by the flux of memory, most immigrant literatures, especially
first novels, draw on material very close at hand to the writer—personal
memories, the plight of emigration, adaptation to the new environment,
socioeconomic stability, and upward mobility. Ergo, one tends to read
such novels or short stories, especially early Brazilian Jewish fiction,

as semiautobiographical even when no direct evidence attesting to the authenticity of narrated events exists. Nevertheless, the historical stance and structure of the narration explain why this literature is considered to have powerful documentary value. Frequently narrated in the first person, these novels become a form of fictional autobiography or memorialism in which the narrator strives for historical verisimilitude or the illusion of authenticity. Furthermore, with its self-interrogation, first-person narration can serve as a signifier for the problematics of identity, representation, subalternity, hybridism, and transculturalization. The character of the testimonial text (fictional or otherwise) becomes a metonym for the complex and diverse cultural practices, mores, and institutions of a community or group. Brazilian Jewish literature of autobiographical immigrant fiction harbors these features but also emphasizes the visual and auditory aspects of Jewish memory and history as well as the importance of the viewpoint of the 'I.' However, this 'I' is no longer the elite patriarchal first person of modernist Brazilian memorialist writing, fictional or historical, which was preoccupied and 'identified' itself with the quest and development of a Brazilian national image. Autobiographical Brazilian Jewish fiction presents the memorial 'I' of immigrant fiction, examples of which are scant as Brazilian literary history attests.[35] The Jewish immigrant 'I' focuses on difference, thereby reintroducing the concept of ethnic alterity into the scope of Brazil's nationalist ideology at a point in time when modernist views of unity were beginning to be challenged. Although not always appearing in mainstream publications, Brazilian Jewish fiction emerges as the first notable current of ethnic discourse in Brazil.

As mimetic fiction presenting a realist vision of the Jewish experience immigrating to and living within Brazil, these narratives testify to a social history motivated by a deep expressive need to narrate and register the tribulations of the past as well as to dramatize the self-conscious comparison between being Jewish in the Old and the New Worlds. These retrospective novels become a form of living history of difference and consequently a bridge of memory between worlds as well as a means for their narrators to come to terms with their lives of struggle, conflict, and acculturation in the diaspora. Therefore, the reader soon recognizes the juxtaposition of Jewish cultural memory and individual memory as the fundamental elements shaping these

narratives. Although such novels tend to underscore the negative vicissitudes of their protagonists, their narrators position themselves
vis-à-vis individual and collective memory so that often the individual
memory and its trajectory of survival ultimately become the positive
forces in the narrative. When this occurs, the reader senses the beginning of what the Boyarins call a 'disaggregated identity,' of the narrator relating to different worlds and cultural spaces, despite conflicts
and tensions.

The first memorial novel to launch modern Brazilian Jewish expression is *Numa clara manhã de Abril* (On a Clear April Morning), published
in 1940 by Marcos Iolovitch. The significance of this novel lies not
only in its pioneering role but in its cultural value as a document of
immigrant and family strife in the early part of the twentieth century.
Moreover, due to the novel's semiautobiographical stance, the elements of documented memory (Jewish cultural memory of customs,
religion, and plight) become vivid testimony along with noteworthy
features such as the narrator's self-conscious and heartfelt account
of his feelings and philosophy of life. As a document the novel provides a heart-wrenching account of the failures experienced by the
*colonos* in their attempt to survive in the agricultural enterprise set up
by the JCA. In this regard the novel dramatizes in detail how, despite
the extent of these immigrants' hard labor to cultivate the land, they
ultimately failed. In a similar vein in Argentina, Alberto Gerchunoff's
much earlier novel *Los gauchos Judios* (1910), the first Argentine Jewish
narrative, also depicts Jews attempting to till the soil. The historical
value of Iolovitch's work lies in its reportage, narrated in episodic
tableaux of daily life amid the harsh conditions of farming in the
Brazilian interior.

The next overtly Brazilian Jewish work of ethnic significance is
also a semiautobiographical novel, *No exílio* (1948) (In Exile), by Elisa
Lispector (1911–89). Although narrated in the third person, the point of
view is first person, evident in the strategic use of interior monologue,
as a young woman narrator tells her story retrospectively. Another
pioneering novel of memory, this narrative focuses on the period
around the 1917 Russian Revolution, the pogroms, and the exodus or
flight of the narrator's family to Brazil; the years of World War II; and
the time of Israel's independence in 1948, which is the novel's frame
and the catalyst for the narrator's memories. Since the fictional family

of father, mother, and three daughters resembles the Lispector family and their actual flight from Russia, the reader soon becomes aware of the thinly disguised autobiography, evident in the slight changes of the first names of each family member. As in Iolovitch's novel, here the narrator develops an awareness of the need for independence. What makes this novel remarkable is the narrator's sensitivity to gender and her defiance amid the traditional values of Jewish family life. Elisa Lispector portrays the vicissitudes of the immigrant experience from the female point of view, thereby providing for Brazil an early picture of the role of women undergoing the drama of immigration.

The passages selected in this volume begin with the narrator's sensitive perception of her difference as a Jew, which becomes an early source for her anxiety and bitterness about the violent treatment of Jews, particularly during the pogroms in Russia. Peppered with Yiddish and Hebrew words, this fictional memoir also evokes a Yiddishkeit existence that reveals the hybrid experience of living in exile. The confessional tone sets the stage for her father's thinking about Israel and the Jewish condition, but Lispector also devotes a considerable portion of the novel to her own thinking about being a free spirit who nevertheless does not betray her heritage. The novel loses some of its literary value in the propagandistic dialogues with her father about World War II, Palestine, and Israel, particularly in the obvious didactic exposition on these topics.

Lispector captures not only the daughter's grief and abandonment but also the atmosphere of poverty and economic abandonment manifested in the shanties of Brazil. The young girl's spirited individualism in this novel is notable because it emanates from the voice of a Jewish woman who at a time of traditional social mores in a Latin culture already foreshadows the liberation that women will be striving for during the second half of the twentieth century.

Despite these beginnings the Polish-born Samuel Rawet (1929–84) is considered the actual precursor of modern Brazilian Jewish literature because he set the stage for a Brazilian Jewish literary discourse in 1956 with his critically acclaimed collection of stories *Contos do imigrante* (Immigrant Tales).[36] The 1956 publication date of Rawet's first collection of stories is considered the genesis of the uninhibited fictional expression of the Jewish experience in Brazil, despite the prior publication of the documentary-type memorial narratives about

Jewish immigration discussed earlier. Unconcerned with a semiautobiographical portrayal or a documentary perspective, Rawet stands as
the writer whose literary talents override reportage and yet provide an
insightful view of Jewish immigrant life in Brazil. Including several
collections of short stories, essays, and novellas, Rawet's work con-
tinually focuses on Jews and other marginal voices in Brazil. Rawet's
writing questions the attitude and treatment shown 'ethnic others'
and in general the other as someone who is socially and/or sexually
marginalized and thus does not represent Brazil's Catholic culture
and traditional mores. In short Rawet's fiction calls attention to the
difficulties of reconciling Jewish customs with Brazilian nationalist
norms. His portrayal of Jewish and Yiddishkeit culture in Brazil, as
well as the symbolic depiction of many immigrants and displaced
individuals, has led to his national recognition as the first publicly
acknowledged Brazilian Jewish voice in modern literature writing in
the Portuguese language.

Frequently set in the disadvantaged suburbs of Rio de Janeiro, many
of Rawet's stories depict Jewish protagonists struggling with their
identity in the context of social alienation and prejudice. Dramatizing
the bicultural conflicts that provoke social and psychological fragmentation, these stories question the absolutism of monocultural identity.
Issues of isolation, seclusion, and dislocation surface in many of his
tales and reflect in part Rawet's own experience in the initial cultural
desolation of life on the vast, lonely plateau of Brasília, where he
worked as an engineer. Travels to Europe and Israel inspired some
of his other story collections, but for the most part Rawet resided in
Brasília, where he died in 1984. Recognized by Alberto Dines as 'the
inventor of exile,' Rawet created fiction that manifests the tribulations
of displacement and the cross-cultural conflict of lives in dispersion.
In their diverse singularities, his protagonists become the prototypical
outsiders within. He developed the theme of Jewish immigration and
cultural conflict into the broader and universal issue of strangeness
and otherness experienced by all ethnic groups. In this sense he is
the diasporic writer par excellence.

Although Rawet's fame resides with his immigrant stories and
their depiction of the struggles with the dominant culture, he also
focuses on intracultural conflict, thereby underscoring the potential
dangers of rigid ethnocentrism. Moreover, with allusions to biblical

stories such as the *akedah* of Abraham and Isaac, Rawet also draws on the generational conflicts between fathers and sons as unending and irreconcilable. The use of inversion and irony also surface as modes for deconstructing the patriarchal and cultural myths that profess democratic harmony or racial democracy by attempting to cover up blatant prejudice, subtle discrimination, and socially rooted authoritarianism. These issues are incisively portrayed in his short story 'Christmas without Christ,' included in this anthology. In short these myths convey a false picture of the actual state of Brazilian race and ethnic relations. As overriding themes in all his prose, alienation, displacement, and marginality become vehicles for challenging social stereotypes, absolutist thinking, society's rigid norms, and the status quo. Above all, Rawet's outstanding contribution to Brazilian literature is his incisive understanding and vivid evocation of the Brazilian Jewish Diaspora. In our times of multicultural sensitivity, we may see how Samuel Rawet was indeed a prophet of difference.

LATER MEMORIAL NOVELS,
MEMOIRS, AND CHRONICLES

The continued production of Brazilian Jewish memorial fiction and memoirs along with the emergence of chronicles merit attention here because these publications reflect Brazil's ongoing fascination with life writing. As alluded to earlier, these immigrant narratives herald another type of Brazilian memorialism, not the canonical memorial voices emanating from the established Brazilian patriarchal families, who, from the start of Brazil's modernist phase, produced nationalist autobiographical novels and nonfictional memoirs such as the famous *Menino de engenho* (1932) (*Plantation Boy*, 1966), by José Lins do Rego, and his memorialist *Meus verdes anos* (1956) (*My Green Years*) as well as memorial works by authors such as Graciliano Ramos, Oswald de Andrade, Murilo Mendes, and Pedro Nava, among many others. Memorialism related to the immigrant experience became the other type of memorial expression that began to emerge in Brazil. In fact the Jewish contribution to fiction about immigrants in Brazil is significant because Brazilian Jewish immigrant voices represent the largest corpus of nonfiction and fiction related to a specific ethnic group.

During the first half of the twentieth century, except for the pioneering novel about German immigration *Canaã* (1902) (*Canaan*, 1920),
by the nonimmigrant writer Graça Aranha, and later Viana Moog's
*Um rio imita o Reno* (1939) (A River Imitates the Rhine), as well as the
pope of Brazilian modernism, Mário de Andrade, with his *Amar, verbo
intransitivo* (1927) (To Love, an Intransitive Verb), about a German
Fräulein governess in São Paulo, it is Italian immigration that makes
a mark in Brazilian literature, albeit the publication of a couple of
novels about Japanese immigration. Like Mário de Andrade in his
later stories about Italians in that city, another modernist, Antônio
de Alcântara Machado (1901–35), is the first Brazilian author to focus
consistently on immigrants in his stories, in this case, Italian immigrants in São Paulo. Nonetheless, beginning in the 1940s, Brazilian
Jewish writing provides a sustained and multidimensional focus on
immigration, despite the appearance during the 1960s and later of a
few more Italo-Brazilian novels as well as Arabic/Lebanese writing,
most evident in the acclaimed novels of Raduan Nassar. This large
production of literature, memoirs, and documents from the 1940s to
the present day, often appearing in the nonmainstream publications
of Jewish political, cultural, and religious organizations, is partially
explained by the high level of literacy among Jewish immigrants and
their descendants.

After Marcos Iolovitch and Elisa Lispector, the later Brazilian Jewish
immigrant memorial/testimony fiction, memoirs, and chronicles, for
the most part, emerge during the 1960s and continue to the early years
of the twenty-first century. While these publications are frequently
about Jewish immigrants adjusting to Brazilian culture, many focus
on the Second World War and the Holocaust.

Boris Schnaiderman, Russian born and a naturalized Brazilian, wrote
a very popular book about the Second World War and his experience
as a Brazilian soldier. In *Guerra em surdina* (1964) (War in Whispers),
Schnaiderman tells the tale, drawn from memory, testimony, and
fiction, of his narrator-protagonist's military service in the trenches
on the Italian front during the Second World War. Although the novel
does not focus on the immigration experience per se, it does provide
a unique opportunity to see the war from the viewpoint of a Jew who
immigrated to Brazil. Using a variety of narrative techniques such as
the diary, the soliloquy, and interior monologue, this novel written

in first and third persons stands, for its time, as one of the most innovative due to its style and structure. Later, Schnaiderman was to
become one of Brazil's foremost professors and translators of Russian literature and theory.

In terms of the continuation of Brazilian Jewish immigrant fiction,
Zvi Ghevelder's *As seis pontas da estrela* (1969) (The Six Points of the
Star) merits attention because it dramatizes scenes of the Jewish immigrant community of Rio de Janeiro populated by those who arrived
before, during, and after the Second World War. Born in Rio in 1934
of immigrant stock from Bessarabia, Ghevelder achieved his reputation foremost as a journalist, besides being a writer and political
commentator. With strong Zionist leanings, his memorial novel is
told from the viewpoint of a young Brazilian Jew whose parents were
immigrants. As an incisive observer of the people in his neighborhood
and of his father's adaptation to Brazil, especially during the 1940s,
the narrator introduces the reader to a variety of Jews, Ashkenazic and
Sephardic, whose tribulations center on dislocation, marginalization, and assimilation as well as economic and Holocaust survival,
Zionism, opportunism, and an array of problems that reveal the psychological states of the immigrant condition. Moreover, Ghevelder's
novel illustrates the difficulty of reconciling two worlds, the ways
of being Jewish and of survival in the new country, and the various
frustrations and situations that impact and shape immigrant lives.
As a novel depicting strong Yiddishkeit ethics, the story focuses on
the development of Favel Aterman from a nobody in the shtetl to a
well-respected mensch in the New World who becomes a community leader and assists Holocaust survivors who come to Brazil. The
novel represents a modern history of the Jewish community in Rio
de Janeiro from the 1930s to the 1960s. In the evolution of Brazilian
Jewish writing's search for a space in mainstream Brazilian publishing, this novel is significant because in 1969 it won special mention
in the national Walmap Prize.

Various nonfictional memoirs and chronicles continued to surface
during the 1970s, 1980s, and 1990s, attesting to the lingering presence of memorialism. Of note is Haim Grünspun's *Anatomia de um
bairro: O Bexiga* (1979) (Anatomy of a Neighborhood: The Bexiga), a
chronicle of the author's formative years as a young peddler in that
São Paulo neighborhood noted for its variety of immigrants. Born in

Rumania but arriving in Brazil in 1932, Grünspun, a medical doctor by profession, describes the Bexiga in the context of its urban setting of ethnic pluralism between 1933 and 1941. A more recent example is the autobiography *Carta aos meus netos: Uma autobiografia* (2000) (Letter to My Grandchildren: An Autobiography), by Anita D. Panek, who emigrated to Rio de Janeiro from Kraków, Poland, just before the Holocaust. Also in this vein is the voluminous memoir *Mulheres de valor: Uma memoria das mulheres que se destacaram na comunidade judaica do Rio de Janeiro* (2004) (Women of Value: A Memoir of the Women Who Distinguished Themselves in the Jewish Community of Rio de Janeiro), by Rachelle Zweig Dolinger.

Although various regions of Brazil are represented by fictional and nonfictional memorial writers, the southern state of Rio Grande do Sul, contiguous with Uruguay, has produced some of the most striking accounts of Jewish immigrants struggling in the two colonies, Filipson and Quatro Irmãos, sponsored by the Jewish Colonization Agency during the early part of the twentieth century. While this southern state constituted the earliest rural concentration of Jews in the modern period, Rio Grande do Sul is also noted for its strong regionalist *gaúcho* cohesiveness, a culture not unlike but also differing from that of the gauchos/cowboys of Argentina, memorialized early on in Alberto Gurchonoff's novel *Los gauchos judíos* (1910) (*The Jewish Gauchos*, 1955).[37] Thus a relationship between the Jewish immigrants and the local *gaúchos* was inevitable, producing a form of hybrid existence documented by various memorial writers and chroniclers. Two of the most interesting nonfictional accounts stem from a sister and brother born in Filipson, Frida Alexandr (1906–72) and Jacques Schweidson (1904–95), who wrote respectively *Filipson* (1967) and *Judeus de bombachas e chimarrão* (1985), the latter's title referring to the wide cowboy pants (*bombachas*) and gourd for maté tea (*chimarrão*), cultural mainstays of the local *gaúchos*. Although both narratives focus on the agricultural and cattle-raising colony of Filipson, each presents a different perspective. Alexandr's account, a series of chronicles, provides the reader with a faithful documentary narrative of the daily activities and relationships between the members of the colony. In the oral tradition style this narrative not only serves as an important historical document of a long-ago, forgotten experience, but it is also imbued with a feminine viewpoint that focuses on the domestic realm and poignantly demarcates the limited space for women at that time. However, Frida Alexandr's keen powers of observation, her individualism, and her proclivity for learning contributed to her writing a very informative narrative. As a microhistory of the colony's frustrations, the failure of the agricultural enterprise, and the eventual abandonment of the land, Filipson also offers a picture of the general conviviality between the Jews and the locals, given that the former were somewhat dependent on local know-how in order to survive. On the other hand, these chronicles also attest to the difficulties and tensions between the struggling 'colonizers' and the comfortable local administrators of the JCA, who for the most part regarded the immigrants with disdain. This personable and detailed narrative stands as testimony to that enterprise as well as to the power of memory and the need to document.

Jacques Schweidson, Frida Alexandr's brother, attests to the tradition of storytelling carried on by his ancestors and motivated by his daughter's pleas, by telling his story to his granddaughter in Judeus de bombachas e chimarrão. However, this autobiography not only focuses on the narrator, but it also attempts to depict the experience in the colony, with all its difficulties, in descriptive panorama and in less-negative tones. Although he was not inspired to write a hymn to the colony and Brazil, as critics have interpreted Argentina's Gerchnoff in his Los gauchos judíos, Schweidson nevertheless presents his Jews as robust and happy workers cultivating the land with success and being welcomed by hospitable Brazilian gaúchos. Interestingly, this view may be partially explained not only by the autobiographer's pride in his vibrant past but also by the fact that his story is told from a masculine point of view, which places Jacques beyond the realm of the house and among exciting activities such as horse racing. Nonetheless, a nostalgic tone permeates this narrative, and although memory nurtures the episodes, the overall tone of this account is one of homage to one's background and to an acceptance of the Jewish colony in a land unaccustomed to a Jewish presence.

Other narratives about the colonies continued to be published by such memorial writers as Adão Voloch (1914–91). His trilogy beginning with the novel O colono judeu-açu (1984) (The Great Jewish Colonist) about the colony Quatro Irmãos is notable for its strong socialist political flavor and its comments on the reciprocity between the Guarani Indians and the Jews, emblematized by the novel's title composed of the Portuguese word *judeu* and the Tupi word *açu*, 'great.'

Memorial accounts focusing on the urban scene can be found in the works of Samuel Malamud. Although the first part of his personal memoir *Escalas no tempo* (1986) (Stops in Time) chronicles his early life in Eastern Europe, his family's flight from the Ukraine to Rumania, and the flagrant anti-Semitism that motivated them to emigrate, this section also describes in rich detail the dynamic Jewish Eastern European culture. Here Malamud not only documents domestic activities and regional and religious rituals but also portrays the political situation and the impending threat to Jews.

In the second part, his memorial narrative chronicles his voyage to Brazil and his family's eventual settlement in Rio de Janeiro. The description of his sea journey and the family's train ride to the Brazilian interior offer the reader a vivid account of the immigrant's tribulations as a traveler. In spite of the discomfort, hardship, and frustration, Malamud's tale exudes spiritual optimism.

The diary-like narrative provides dates for most of the events and focuses on Malamud's personal development, cultural experiences, and education. However, perhaps the most singular factor of his immigrant experience is his early proclivity toward acculturation. Avid to participate in Brazilian culture and captivated by its spirited exuberance, Malamud describes how he negotiated his way to success in Brazil while maintaining his Jewish culture and participating in the Jewish cultural life of Rio de Janeiro. This work illustrates how many Jews operated simultaneously outside and within the Jewish community by being open and adaptable to the host culture but also being Jewish in thought and deed. This memoir along with Malamud's other famous work, *Recordando Praça Onze* (1988) (Remembering Eleventh Square), have archival value in their description of Jewish life in Rio. The latter is another memoir of Rio's first major Jewish neighborhood, almost a ghetto, and its communal life, told in prose and photographs that make up most of the publication. Appearing first in Yiddish, with a selection of Malamud's fiction and poetry that was omitted from the Portuguese translation, 'Remembering Eleventh Square' is a historical document from an eyewitness who chronicled its history as an indelible period in Jewish Carioca life.

In the genre of the urban *crônica*, one of the most enduring and prolific chroniclers is Eliezer Levin. With most of his writing spanning the

1970s and 1980s, his narratives, predominantly chronicles, are episodic
and anecdotal semiautobiographical accounts involving the various
colorful characters living in São Paulo's first Jewish neighborhood.
Even with his first episodic novel, Bom Retiro: O bairro da infância (1972)
(Bom Retiro: Childhood Neighborhood), characterized as a novel
told by an adolescent growing up in a close-knit Jewish community
during the 1930s and 1940s, the novel has a chronicle format, which
represents Levin's most natural form of writing. In this work the boy's
outsider identity vis-à-vis mainstream Brazilian society becomes his
struggle with self-identification. The chapters are interspersed with
news briefs about the impending Nazi terror in Europe in contrast to
the safe existence of the Paulista Jews. This novel provides one of the
most sensitive portraits of the impact of the Holocaust on Brazilian
Jews and their response to the annihilation of the Jews in Europe.

The stories anthologized here from his Nossas outras vidas (1989) (Our
Other Lives) capture the dual existence of Jews living in that metropolis,
especially the Yiddishkeit realm of their home and neighborhood;
these vignettes reveal the richness of Yiddish values, traditions, and
customs. As in all his books, Levin fills his narratives with Hebrew
and Yiddish words and expressions and provides a glossary to explain
their meaning. The juxtaposition of the Hebrew and Yiddish alongside
the Portuguese heightens the linguistic contrast but also recognizes
the hybrid existence in a multicultural and multilingual city. Of the
thirty-seven narratives, the five translated here evoke the viewpoint of
the adult voice as compared to the poor child, the adolescent student,
and the up-and-coming young man, the latter providing the perspective for the other stories. The Jewish humor in these chronicles/stories
recalls the comedy of a Jackie Mason whose Yiddishkeit potpourri of
characters immortalizes through mockery the seemingly irrational
cultural views of his people. As entertaining tableaux of daily Jewish
cultural life in São Paulo, Levin's works represent some of the most
vivid portrayals of that city's Jewish neighborhood.

## YIDDISH VOICES

Although Yiddish and Yiddishkeit culture are today waning in Brazil,
reference to that culture within the Brazilian sphere merits consideration because, as already mentioned, many writers use Yiddish terms

to lend a Yiddish flavor to their narratives written in Portuguese. Eliezer Levin is one of the many writers who continue to include a Yiddish vocabulary and glossary in the volumes of their chronicles and stories. Marcos Iolovitch and Elisa Lispector also sprinkled their narratives with Yiddish, and Samuel Rawet's stories evoke the daily Yiddishkeit existence of Jews in Rio de Janeiro. Even very contemporary writers draw on Yiddish for authenticity and ambiance when describing the past. While this *mameloschn* may still be spoken, it is certainly limited to the Jewish home and friendly relations within the community. An exception is the recent publication of stories/testimonies in Portuguese originally written in Yiddish by the São Paulo immigrant/resident Meir Kucinski (1904–76), *Imigrantes, mascates & doutores* (2002) (Immigrants, Merchants and Doctors), about Jewish community life in São Paulo.

In his book *Aventuras de uma língua errante* (1996) (Adventures of an Errant Language), Jacó Guinsburg traces the trajectory of Yiddish literature and theater in the world and describes the impact of Yiddish culture in Brazil. Guinsburg notes the Yiddish cultivated by Jews who settled in the great cities of São Paulo and Rio de Janeiro as well as in urban centers such as Porto Alegre and Curitiba, in addition to the agricultural colonies of southern Brazil, since the late nineteenth and early twentieth centuries. These immigrant groups and later ones from the 1930s through the early 1950s were responsible for introducing Yiddish as a *folkschprakn*. According to Guinsburg, however, today the maintenance of the language and culture can never be revitalized to the degree of its usage and practice during the first half of the twentieth century. Alluding to more than thirty poets, writers, and theatrical artists who published in Yiddish in Brazil, Guinsburg does note the small contribution of Yiddish and Yiddish culture to Brazilian letters. This literature focuses on the adventures of the urban *klientelchiks* (peddlers), tailors, merchants, craftsmen, workers, and families as well as the experiences of the farmer/colonists in the South. For both groups Brazilian Yiddish literature depicts the frustrations, struggles, and socioeconomic ascension; the cultural and literary limitations for Yiddish in the new country; the Yiddish press; the aura of the language's musical sound; the culture's cuisine; and its philosophical and poetic contributions as a 'language of the people' from the shtetl. The Jewish farmers and the city peddlers formed the basis for the maintenance of Yiddish culture in Brazil and were responsible for supporting and initiating Jewish cultural centers, clubs and associations, theater groups, new communities, in addition to other social, cultural, and religious institutions. Using Yiddish as a linguistic vehicle, they gave birth to schools, organizations, libraries, theaters, newspapers, magazines, books, and cultural events. In an article on Yiddish in Brazil, Guinsburg also mentions the miniscule impact of Yiddish culture in Brazil as used by women seduced into Jewish white slavery, a topic discussed later in reference to Esther Largman's novel *Polish Girls*.

Of the many Yiddish-oriented artists in Brazil, two other writers who capture Yiddish culture in a sustained fashion are Rosa Palatnik and Francisco Dzialovsky. As representative examples of authors working with this literary expression, they portray the 'slice-of-life' approach found in most Yiddishkeit literature of Brazil. Besides the encounter with the exoticism and sensual nature of Brazilian culture, these narratives center on topics such as secrets of intimate home life, Yiddish as a common bond, its loss of linguistic ground due to Portuguese's linguistic dominion, the encounter with other races and cultures, and the ambiguous attitudes toward Jews stemming from Brazil's New Christian past. These themes are depicted in order to manifest authentically Jewish-Yiddish culture as well as to contrast modern life in Brazil with the old culture of the shtetl villages of Easter Europe. Emerging repeatedly are issues concerning the ongoing moral and political arbitrariness in the New World. The predominant literary form is the anecdote with its folk morality and humor.

Although Rosa Palatnik continued to write in Yiddish after she emigrated from Europe, several of her works were translated into Portuguese. Represented here is the story 'Two Mothers,' which is emblematic of her narratives about Jewish immigrants living in Brazil. A Yiddish critic from Argentina, Schmuel Rojânski, quoted in Jacó Guinsburg's critical study, stated that Rosa Palatnik 'wrote in yellow colors' and her 'Yiddish is mixed with Polish localisms and with old Polish provincial familiar sayings and witticisms.'[38] This comment suggests Palatnik's anecdotal style of monochromatic narration of small domestic and community dramas. 'Two Mothers' uses contrast and bonding to tell the story of suffering maternal souls who occupy different socioeconomic levels in Brazil, due to the economic success and pretensions of the son of one of the women. The latter, representing the upward mobility and dangers of capitalist success that can wreak havoc on traditional Jewish family life and cultural values, is the catalyst for the drama in which the two mothers compare notes about their life in Brazil and how they are treated by their families.

Using the model of the suffering Jewish mother, these two characters, with typical Yiddish names, Beile-Guitel and Chaie-Sara, are portrayed expressing plangent and melodramatic cries and complaints frequently associated with Yiddish characters who are tragic victims of fate. On the other hand, these two characters also embody the plight of older immigrants who come to a land of more tolerance: 'This here is actually a country where Jewish rites are not kept, but whoever wants to maintain the tradition will not be killed for doing so.' The Yiddishkeit tone of the story, with the Yiddish intonations voiced by the two mothers, underscores the lasting and meaningful bonds of sincere family life and the overarching Yiddish theme of continuity, values, and tradition.

In Francisco Dzialovsky's novel *O terceiro testamento* (1987) (The Third Testament), the loss of valued traditions is also depicted alongside comic scenarios of Eastern European Jews adapting to the tropical climate and the porous nature of Brazilian culture. The central motif of the novel is the Yiddish radio program *The Third Testament*, which the narrator and his family listen to as they have their Sunday meal. This program serves as a cohesive element in the Jewish community of Rio since it covers a myriad of topics such as biblical stories, religion, history, and commentary about famous Jewish leaders and personalities. The young narrator becomes the observer of how he and his sisters contrast with their parents, who barely speak Portuguese, while the children have a passive knowledge of Yiddish, leading him to comment on the burial of a culture that began with the Holocaust and immigration.


## HOLOCAUST LITERATURE AND TESTIMONIES

One of the precursors of Holocaust literature in Brazil is the work of Jacó Guinsburg, the publisher, professor, and critic who did not live through the Nazi terror but at the age of three emigrated from Bessarabia in 1921 with his family. His short story 'O Retrato' (1946) calls attention to the Holocaust at a time when the subject was not yet a recognized literary theme in Brazil. This story registers the emotional impact of the Holocaust on Jews living in Brazil by using the photo of a lost cousin to evoke in the narrator the tensions created between his personal growth and the conflict in Europe from which his family escaped. Looking at the photo at different points in time prompts the narrator to delve more deeply into anxieties caused by the Nazi tyranny and the Allied victory, along with the eventual realization that the cousin did not survive. As will be noted later, Jacó Guinsburg continues to write short stories that still harbor many emotions related to the Holocaust. This is notable because, not having lived through the Holocaust, he nonetheless has been affected by its memory and tragedy, which have extended destruction and pain across oceans and continents. His writings are those of a survivor/witness via imagination and generational legacy.

The same power of imagination can be found in Moacyr Scliar, as manifested in his acclaimed story 'Na minha suja cabeça, o Holocausto' (1986) (Inside My Dirty Head, the Holocaust), about a young boy who cannot wash away the memories of a Holocaust he did not experience but has imagined based on his father's stories and activities to save survivors. As will be seen with the younger crop of writers in the 1990s, such as Roney Cytrynowicz, the extensive memorial force of the Holocaust penetrates the minds and hearts of those who only witnessed the horror through the tales and memories of survivors. These are indeed survivors/witnesses via generational storytelling and cultural imagination.

The Holocaust is an event that many Jewish and a few non-Jewish writers in Brazil draw on to relate their memory and understanding of genocide. The provocative 'pop' novel Hitler manda lembranças (1984) (Hitler Sends Regards), by the non-Jewish writer Roberto Drummond, juxtaposes the oppressive memories of a Holocaust survivor living in Brazil with the repressive authoritarian activities of Brazil's military regime (1964–85), thereby illustrating the Holocaust's symbolic power across cultures and the parallels with other authoritarian regimes.

Brazilian Jewish writers and survivors have published memoirs about the Holocaust, often after many years of forgetting, when they later gained the courage to remember their experience and to record it on paper. Writers such as Ben Abraham, Joseph Nichthauser, Malka L. Rolnik, Olga Papadopol, Sônia Rosenblatt, and others have published autobiographical accounts, frequently including photos and maps, or narratives that combine fact and fiction. There are also fictional works on the Holocaust by Jewish writers such as Américo Vértes, *Entre duas Evas* (1969) (Between Two Eves); and Alfredo Gartenberg, *O J vermelho* (1976) (The Red J). All these works deal with the persecution of Jews as well as some form of Jewish guilt, loss of memory, solitude, and faith.

Sônia Rosenblatt's account *Lembranças enevoadas* (1984) (Clouded Memories) combines all of these themes and offers a picture of the Holocaust outside the concentration camps, in Bessarabia, where persecution, brutality, lack of solidarity by non-Jewish villagers, the inhumanity of random assassinations, and the pogromlike plundering of the marauding conquerors also reigned. Scenes of the miserable conditions in the ghetto during the war are juxtaposed with others in which the Jews plan to fight back, albeit armed with brooms and shovels. Rosenblatt's story vividly captures the desperation generated by extreme hunger and thirst, thereby providing the reader with a realistic and disturbing picture.

Rosenblatt's narrative is also interesting because as an autobiographical account it deals with the problem of forgetting and the slippage of memory as well as the guilt expressed by those who survived. As a testimony filled with historical events, this narrative, told in a very simple and direct style, also reveals the emotional weight of loss, especially of loved ones. The vacuum created by this loss becomes even more devastating when Rosenblatt realizes that there are no graves for members of her family. The shocking scene, depicting a field of unrecognizable bones, including those of her family, evokes the lack of consolation felt by survivors such as Rosenblatt. Despite this and other scenes in which the Jews are treated as animals, Rosenblatt depends on the simple words of faith and blessings uttered by people such as her fiancé's grandfather in order to go on surviving. Her autobiographical account reveals the anguish of being a survivor and the enduring faith that sustained her.

## CLARICE LISPECTOR

As the premier Latin American woman writer of this century, Clarice Lispector (1920–77) deals with issues of psychological displacement by transposing her own sense of the uprooted and unfixed aspects of life in dispersion emanating from her experience as a Russian immigrant, a resident of Northeast Brazil and eventual migrant to Rio, and a diplomat's wife who lived abroad for many years. Via narratives involving the search for identity, she reclaims for herself and her readers an expression of the ontological struggle she experienced in trying to belong and to understand the human condition, resulting in compelling personal and feminine quests that border on the metaphysical. In such works as *A Paixão segundo GH* (1964) (*The Passion according to GH*, 1988), *Água viva* (1973) (*The Stream of Life*, 1989), and *A hora da estrela* (1977) (*The Hour of the Star*, 1986), her narrators frequently engage in internal discourses or quests on the phenomenon of 'being' and 'being other' simultaneously. As a Jewish writer of spirit and an independent woman open to mystical reception, Lispector weaves narratives that become spiritual quests struggling with the ineffable and the mysteries of life. Transcending the concrete sense of the written word, she frequently evokes silence or what words are incapable of saying—the ineffable or the unsayable—a concept also linked to Judaic philosophy and religion. In this vein the mystery of her writing reflects the hermeneutical idiom of the Old Testament, in which the imperfections of language and meaning are relentlessly seeking an answer, a hidden one that is unattainable for humans because it rests with the divine.

Clarice Lispector's spiritual universe partially stems from a Jewish sensibility that relates metaphors and motifs from biblical times in the desert to the modern-day displacement of migration and immigration, tropes frequently, albeit indirectly, linked to the Judaic Diaspora experience. Not exclusive to the Judaic experience, these motifs and images nevertheless evoke a culturally Jewish frame of mind within the context of dislocation, where personal search and incessant questioning flourish. Two works that illustrate this Jewish cultural propensity are Lispector's *A Paixão segundo GH* (1964) (*The Passion according to GH*, 1988) and *A hora da estrela* (1977) (*The Hour of the Star*, 1986), narratives manifesting the passionate process of quest for identity as well as the sentiments resulting from psychological, social, and cultural exile.

By using the desert as a trope for illustrating the sense of displacement and possible redemption, Lispector's GH subtly develops the question of cultural, social, and ontological otherness, frequently manifested in her depiction of the conflict between social and personal identity or social discourse/representation and self-knowledge. With images of the wandering Jew and the ineffable, GH's subjective and retrospective narrative alludes to the trials in a figurative desert and an individual's passionate struggle for answers. In turn GH's 'voyage within' dismantles her neatly constructed identity of immutable subjectivity and, especially, her well-ordered but false existential sense of self (her Sartrean *en-soi*, being-in-itself), which heretofore has never been challenged.

In 1976 Clarice Lispector returned to her northeastern roots in a short trip made one year prior to her death from cancer. She also made a metaphorical trip to this region via her unsophisticated, northeastern, and seemingly anti-Maccabean eponymous heroine, Macabéa, in her last publication, the novella *A hora da estrela*. In revisiting her Brazilian cultural roots by way of this very ironic narrative with its subtle Judaic motifs, Lispector was also returning more openly to her Jewish roots and to the various social classes she experienced in life. As a more evident coming-to-terms with her Jewishness and with her innate sense of social justice, this last work partially broke the author's public silence about her ethnic identity to reveal a complex voice that manifested a selective ethnicity transcending works of social realism and ethnic literature. As a writer interested in the metaphysics of the human condition, Clarice Lispector regarded ethnic literature as limiting and categorical. However, following the appearance of this novella, critical commentaries began to emerge about her oblique use of Jewish myths and motifs. This new way of reading her fiction stemmed from the novella's symbolic use of the apocryphal Maccabean legend, personified in her eponymic protagonist Macabéa. Inspired by the biblical Maccabeans and martyrs who resisted Greek oppression in their refusal to disregard Jewish law, this novella was especially motivated by an image of a poor, unknown girl who is displaced by migration and thus 'exiles' herself to Rio from the small and impoverished northeastern state of Alagoas. Here Lispector dismantles the Jewish archetypes of the martyr and the oppressed by using the nonheroic figure of the innocuous Macabéa. Without diminishing the reader's sympathy for this socially and economically oppressed character, Lispector avoids a facile picture of the protagonist's heroic idealization or glorification by depicting Macabéa's heroism as a form of dogged resistance: she simply endures and withstands. In readapting the Maccabean myth, Lispector underscores the results of displacement and disregard in the context of the sociopolitical injustice and repression afflicting millions of invisible others living in modern Brazil.

The two stories anthologized here and translated for the first time into English only recently appeared in published form in the collection *Clarice Lispector: Outros escritos* (2005), edited by Teresa Montero and Lícia Manzo. As very early 'forgotten' stories written before she became famous, these narratives already reveal Lispector's compulsion for social justice as well as her advocacy for women's independence of mind.[39] The significance of these stories also rests with their heralding Lispector's craft of narration, her deft use of interior monologue and the introspective first person to dramatize women's social issues. Criticized for not being an author whose work described social problems in broad strokes, Lispector always defended her approach as a method of engaging social justice issues reflected in the conflicts and introspection of her protagonists. In one of her chronicles, 'Literature and Justice,' she speaks about her defense of social justice and her perception of her northeastern childhood, a time of socioeconomic hardship. The Jewish cultural commitment to social justice and the golden rule affected many aspects of her life and writing. The Jewish painter Carlos Scliar remembered Lispector in the 1960s as socially committed, with a solidarity that was guardian-like: 'She was more than just a friend, she seemed to me to be a protective Jewish mother, generous, concerned.'[40]

During her years in law school and as a journalist, Lispector began to write articles and stories reflecting this sense of social commitment. Her articles discussed topics such as the question of capital punishment, women's right to join the work force, the plight of female orphans and unwed mothers, and of course the inferior status of women in Brazilian society and the world. Appearing in newspapers, family magazines, and student publications of her law school, these articles demonstrate Lispector's serious preoccupation with social ills and injustices. The story 'Trecho' (Passage) reflects this concern with social issues, in particular, the abandonment of unwed mothers, exemplified here by the insecure protagonist, Flora, who feels abandoned while waiting alone in a café for her lover. As she experiences the humiliation of being in a place socially unacceptable for an unaccompanied woman, her thoughts lead her to address the male-dominated society with the occasional 'gentlemen' as though to explain herself and to rebel against the insidious superiority men exert over women. Identifying emotionally with a frightened rabbit and a tiny fly, she nonetheless asserts her potential as a woman capable of being more than a mother and housewife, in her case, perhaps even a good poet. The self-consciousness so emblematic of Lispector's female protagonists is manifested here in her acute awareness of her female sense of self, underscored by such declarations as 'I do exist' and 'I am superior because I know that I exist,' statements made to affirm her sense of independence. Although her inner self protests against society; the government's disregard of women in her situation; her lover, who has kept her waiting; a cruel world going through war; Mussolini; and a murder in a fashionable Rio neighborhood, Flora appears to forget her rebelliousness, at least momentarily, when Cristiano finally does arrive.

Making several self-references to her ability to pretend, to play several roles, which Cristiano at first interprets as childlike, Flora recognizes her behavior as something more than mere role playing; she is a mystery that has yet to be discovered by others. Her feelings of insecurity, abandonment, humiliation, and inferiority are all manifestations of Flora's not 'fitting in,' of her being misunderstood by others, a state of mind akin to the sentiments evolving from the unjust treatment of women in a patriarchal society and to those feelings of alienation and double consciousness experienced by a diaspora self.

The story 'Eu e Jimmy' (Me and Jimmy) makes a bolder statement about freedom and equality for women and particularly about men's conception of women as mere accessories. The sociocultural dilemmas sparked by gender differences and the intimations of cross-cultural conflicts emerge in Lispector's writing as a preoccupation with social justice and the independence of the self. Her writing is a testament to the daily, subtle injustices that plague primarily women and, by extension, displaced individuals who struggle not to be appropriated by a dominant culture, be it sexual, social, and/ or national.

## OTHER WOMEN'S VOICES

Clarice Lispector's depiction of women in theme and form became the inspiration for many women writers. This section discusses women writers who focus on issues about the social condition of women in Brazil, including, again, Elisa Lispector, who, without imitating her sister Clarice, became a writer of stories and novels that depict women's inner struggle against insidious social obstacles. One of Elisa Lispector's later stories from the collection O tigre de Bengala (1985) (The Bengal Tiger), 'Out of Sheer Despair,' included in this anthology, exemplifies the desperation experienced by women as well as the type of literature that became the hallmark of Elisa Lispector's fiction. Interestingly, this story echoes many of the emotions articulated by the protagonist, Lizza, in the novel No exílio (In Exile, discussed earlier)— abandonment, isolation, despair, anxiety, loneliness, and the quest for self-liberation and independence. This short story of introspection, self-analysis, and alienation exemplifies the characteristics of the rest of Elisa Lispector's fiction, which is not overtly Jewish, except for occasional metaphors and symbols such as the peculiar feeling of terror symbolized by an allusion to the Inquisition. Her later fiction is very much in tune with the modern story's impressionistic and intimate portrayal of women, especially elderly women, who are cast aside by families, lovers, or society in general. In effect her later characters are still very much 'in exile,' but instead of a geographical and external exile, it is one of an interior and psychological state.

Although each female writer manifests her own unique style, the one who has been compared repeatedly to Clarice Lispector is Judith Grossmann, due to her re-creation of intimate female voices. However, Grossmann differs in her inclusion of an erotic aesthetic and her dense style, which frequently suggests a dreamlike state. In the past her narratives have delved primarily into the psyches of women characters. Highly regarded by critics and writers, her novels and stories apprehend states of being that plunge into the often unfathomable depths of the female heart. For example, in 1971 Samuel Rawet stated that in terms of self-conscious exploration, Grossmann's story collection O meio da pedra (The Middle of the Stone) represented for the short story what Clarice Lispector's Near to the Wild Heart represented for the novel. Grossmann's style is a labored creation of artistic language that often becomes powerfully evocative, thereby opening her narratives to myriad interpretations and earning her the reputation as one of the most suggestive and expressive storywriters of her time. Her work stands as original in part because it is at times deliberately inaccessible to facile readings.

Although most of Grossman's work does not focus openly on Jewish subjects, the themes of rootless beings and the continual emergence of suspicious foreigners indicate her subtle preoccupation with the themes of belonging, inconclusiveness, and ambiguity. This aspect of her work is exemplified in the story anthologized here, 'Mrs. Büchern in Lebenswald,' from the collection *A noite estrelada: Estórias do ínterim* (1977) (The Starry Night: Interim Stories). As the collection's title implies, it is the interim, the for-the-time-being, and the lack of closure that infiltrate her narratives, frequently resulting in ellipsis. In this story, which is included in the collection's section 'Livro hebraico' (Hebrew Book), Grossmann presents the story of a mysterious woman who comes to live in a small town. While there is a suggestion that she is a Holocaust survivor or related to such victims, she clearly cannot escape that horror even in the small town of Lebenswald. On a pilgrimage to atone for her sins, she performs acts of self-sacrifice and appears to be changeable; nothing about her disposition appears definite. As part of her atonement she initiates a young man into the horrors of her past experiences, which he finds to be almost unbearable. As she refers to him as dead and stillborn, the reader may assume that these states are representative of his intuition and initiation into the horrors of the world. When he 'escapes,' Mrs. Büchern encounters another lad, who is disturbed by his Jewish heritage and whose upbringing appears to be a holocaust of circumscribed behavior. The theme of survivor guilt emerges in his feelings about leaving his parents and 'surviving.' Labeled as the most alive, in his awareness, while the rest of the town is labeled dead in its petty existence, this lad eventually departs after Mrs. Büchern lacerates his heart, leaving him more dead than alive. One reading of the story may focus on the powerful emotional force of the Holocaust and how it transforms people's lives, even those who were not direct victims. Grossmann's contribution to Brazilian Jewish writing resides in her allusions to social and emotional dislocation and metamorphosis, conditions akin to cross-cultural ambiguities and transformations.

Amália Zeitel's first collection of stories, *Morangos com chantilly* (Strawberries with Cream), published in 1992, the year of her death, merits attention here because it is another interesting representation of the female Jewish voice in Brazilian letters. Active in the Jewish community of São Paulo and especially in Brazilian and Jewish theater, Zeitel did not focus overtly on Judaism or Jews in these stories. Nonetheless, her narratives dramatize the themes of exclusion and alienation and manifest a strong feminist proclivity in her depiction of the condition of contemporary women in Brazilian society. The title story of her collection is representative of these issues and, moreover, suggests a tie with the Jewish Diaspora condition in its treatment of the hazards of cross-cultural marriage, especially for women. Demonstrating a deft use of dialogue, a skill linked to Zeitel's literary development in the theater, this story exemplifies the miscommunication and misunderstanding that surface across different cultures. The development of the conversation between two old women friends, a Brazilian and a French woman who now lives in Brazil, is not so much due to cultural misunderstanding between the two women per se but rather to the schizophrenic result of the French woman's strict adherence to her Brazilian husband's wishes. Told from the viewpoint of the Brazilian woman, who observes the drastic change in Alícia's personality as well as the confusion about her name, the Brazilian Marília ponders Alícia/Julia's transformation that occurred after her marriage, from doctoral student to housewife. This story offers an extreme example of the difficulties and dangers of forced cultural assimilation and of the loss of culture and identity via the imposition of the mores of a dominant society. Zeitel's story thus provides another example of the potential social obstacles of a bicultural existence.

## POST-IMMIGRATION EXPRESSION

Contemporary Brazilian Jewish writing is also considered 'post-immigration expression' because the authors of this period are no longer immigrants but children of immigrants or Jews who arrived in Brazil at a very young age. Predominantly fiction, except for a few biographies, autobiographies, and memoirs, post-immigration expression stages its narrative plots primarily within the geography of

Brazil with a few allusions to the Old World. Moreover, while most of these works focus principally on Jewish characters, including immigrants, some also engage other issues and figures in Brazilian society. Topics such as hybrid existence and cultural difference are presented alongside inter- and intragroup conflicts. Besides the social dramas and historical realism expressed in immigrant fiction and memoirs, this literature also begins to explore other narrative techniques and strategies such as the fantastic realism found in Moacyr Scliar's stories and novels. Here the Latin American literary and cultural scenes become a powerful resource for writers already immersed in Jewish legends and parables.

It is appropriate to begin consideration of this expression with the best-known contemporary Brazilian Jewish writer, Moacyr Scliar, because he represents the most visible and sophisticated writer of his generation. Scliar is also the first Jewish novelist elected to the National Brazilian Academy of Letters. Moreover, he embodies the shift from a strictly realist approach toward fantastic realism and new historicism as opposed to other authors of his generation who continue to write, for the most part, from a strong social and memoir viewpoint. The innovations of fantastic realism in Scliar's work are evident in his tour de force novel *O centauro no jardim* (1980) (*The Centaur in the Garden*, 1984), about a Jewish centaur who must deal with being a horse and a man as well as a Jew, and in his Jewish Diaspora novel par excellence *A estranha nação de Rafael Mendes* (1983) (*The Strange Nation of Rafael Mendes*, 1987), about a Brazilian businessman who one day discovers that he is part of the 'dam(nation)' of Jews descended from the Iberian New Christians and earlier Jewish figures. Rafael's fantastic travel back in time via the power of the written word shows remarkable narrative ingenuity. However, sparks of Scliar's unique style already appeared in his first novella, *A guerra no Bom Fim* (1972) (*The War in Bom Fim*). Although inspired by his childhood memories of the Jewish neighborhood of Bom Fim in Porto Alegre, in the southern state of Rio Grande do Sul, this narrative also manifests technical innovations. Written from the viewpoint of the omniscient narrator, the novella's form is not memoir driven per se, but its content of reality and fantasy suggest a semibiographical tone based on memory. 'The War in Bom Fim' recalls the Jews' gradual adaptation to Brazilian society in the 1940s during a period of international turmoil.

In their homes the Jewish protagonists battle poverty, prejudice, and the issues associated with belonging to an ethnic minority, while, at the same time, the country is being bombarded by propaganda and news about the Second World War.

Scliar also uses allegory to represent the later period of repression carried out by the Brazilian military dictatorship (1964–85), especially during the dark years of the late 1960s and the early 1970s. As an allegorical tale this novella is also about ethnic belonging; as a young adult the protagonist is ultimately torn between his Jewish and Brazilian worlds. However, childhood fantasies and reality predominate in this novella, which spins a story of 1943 Brazil, a time when the young protagonist Joel attacks imagined Nazi Stukas and Messerschmitts while his sickly brother Nathan stands on rooftops playing 'A Idiche Mama' on the fiddle, in Chagall fashion. Despite the strong ethnic presence, the novella also undermines the notion of cultural absolutes with its gallery of Jews and non-Jews, blacks and Germans. This perspective becomes emblematic of Scliar's heterogeneous outlook and his pluralist stance toward cultural differences within and between groups, a view that continues to permeate his later works.

Other views of being Jewish in Brazil emerge in his acclaimed comic novel *O centauro no jardim* (1980) (*The Centaur in the Garden*, 1984). Here, Scliar depicts a neurotic and ambivalent ethnic who identifies himself as a Jewish centaur, evoking the tense hybrid nature of that cultural mixture, one that is, of course, not easy to reconcile unless you think that, as an assimilated centaur, hiding your hooves in chic cowboy boots will do the trick. The humor in this novel becomes key to understanding Scliar's wry depiction of cultural differences. Scliar's works present us with a variety of perspectives that demonstrate, via humor and imagination, how in some cases ethnic continuity and being Brazilian can coexist, albeit with tension, confirming a healthy affirmation of cultural difference and exchange that results in a dynamic expression of social inclusion, of allowing oneself to be lived through the other.

This stance of inclusion permeates Scliar's narratives, from the multicultural characters of *Os voluntários* (1979) (*The Volunteers*, 1988) to his more recent works such as the historical novel *A majestade do Xingu* (1996) (*The Majesty of the Xingu*), about a Jew who commits himself to living with and aiding the Brazilian Indians. This proclivity toward alterity is reminiscent of the Brazilian modernist Oswald de Andrade and his 'Cannibalist Manifesto' (1928), the rollicking treatise, alluded to earlier, that explains the anthropophagus Brazilian trait of 'swallowing' alterity, that is, absorbing and digesting the foreign in order to create something new. The Argentine anthropologist Néstor García Canclini, when discussing how Brazilians, compared with Argentineans, deal with the other, alludes to Brazilian spiritualism as a metaphor for the Brazilian tendency to 'allow oneself to be inhabited by the Other.'[41] Although this can be a very selective process and by no means eradicates the possibility of Brazilian racial or ethnic prejudice, there nonetheless exists what the Brazilian thinker Sérgio Buarque de Hollanda suggested when he commented on the Brazilian proclivity to 'viver nos outros' (to live in/through others), stated in his famous essay 'The Cordial Man.'[42]

Moacyr Scliar challenges notions of cultural coherence and makes otherness an insightful vantage point for understanding national diversity. Using humor and fantasy, he envisions alterity and difference as processes that defy rigid categories of identity. As agents of transgression, fantasy and humor oppose consensus reality and open up one's scope to difference, disorder, and possibility, thereby revealing aspects of cultures that would otherwise be bypassed. In much postmodern literature contradiction and questioning are phenomena of disorder that lead to liberating enlightenment.

In the story 'No seio de Abraão' (In the Bosom of Abraham), the reader is transported to a world of biblical parables and Jewish fables as well as Brazilian spiritualism as family members communicate with their deceased grandfather, who is now living literally in the left breast of the bosom of Abraham. As a fantastic and satirical comment on the Brazilian preoccupation with ghosts, mediums, and the other world, this story also uses Jewish humor to paint a droll and nonidealistic picture of eternity that does not hide human frailties but rather exposes them. The grandfather's good deeds in life are clouded by his marrying for economic convenience, that is, the abandonment of his first and true love, who now resides in the inaccessible right breast of Abraham. Moreover, reference to Abraham's hairy chest immediately dismantles the religious and cultural aura that makes this biblical figure lofty and in turn personalizes and humanizes the scenario, enabling the reader to relate to the frustrations and failures of the grandfather, who discovers that eternity has its risks and that our actions on earth do not disappear when one enters the bosom of Abraham. Describing a particularly Jewish conception of eternity as hardly idyllic, Scliar offers the reader an insight into a staple of Jewish cultural reality in which nothing is certain, perfect, or ideal.

A keen example of Scliar's take on alterity and cultural difference is to be found in his story 'Os filhos do andrógino' (The Children of the Androgyne). Here, the father/mother figure represents androgyny, which becomes a metaphor for gender as well as ethnic differences. One of the 'normal' children of this figure is the narrator, who attempts to grasp the family's unique and curious situation. The child observes that when the possibility of surgery emerges, the parental figure cannot decide whether to be a mother or a father, as though having to choose between two realities (cultural and/or sexual) would be unnatural and, by extension, unjust; the irony here lies in the dominant society's perception of the androgynous figure as unnatural. In terms of ethnicity the reader may perceive how androgyny serves as a metaphor for being 'in between,' a condition that refuses to choose.

The story 'Os necrologistas' (The Necrologists) is a comment on human vanity and differences as well as a clever statement on the egoism in art, academia, and culture. Scliar's stories draw the reader's attention to the potential tyranny of culture—dominant, egotistical, and ethnocentric—and to the need for social recognition along ethnic, racial, and national lines. As both nationals and strangers, Scliar's Jewish characters employ a postmodern language of margins and border crossings. Using the Jewish legacy of exile, Scliar transforms adversity, incongruity, transgression, and difference into dramas that unmask stereotypical nationalism. He focuses on a more in-depth view of Brazil, where diversity and difference may become affirmative expressions of enlightenment, liberation, and redemption.

As another example of post-immigration expression, Alberto Dines's publications reveal an interest in the relations between different cultures. His collection of stories *Posso?* (1972) (Can I?) addresses this interest, especially the title story, a surrealist narrative about the encounter between a Jew and a Catholic at Christmas, a meeting that leads to intimations about acculturation and the mutual acknowledgment of cultures. Advocating an atmosphere of reciprocal respect and brotherhood, the narrative nevertheless deals with the conflicts, prejudices, and misunderstandings between Jews and Catholics. This interest in the clash of cultures also surfaces in his trenchant biography of Stefan Zweig, the Austrian Jewish intellectual. Self-exiled in Brazil, Zweig and his wife committed suicide as if to make a statement about their feelings of estrangement in a different global world that no longer enabled them to reestablish their cultural and literary roots. Zweig's story is one of a self-exile who discovers he no longer 'belongs.' The passage anthologized here describes the shock of the suicide, the clash between the Brazilian Jews and the local authorities regarding Zweig's burial, particularly the ignorance of the state about Jewish custom and ritual, and the differences within the Jewish community. Interestingly, Dines alludes to Hitler's power and the subsequent atrocities when describing the authoritarian attitude of the Brazilian state regarding Zweig's burial. In doing so, he calls attention to the looming specter of the past nationalist/fascist tyranny in Brazil. Alberto Dines's contribution to Brazilian Jewish letters was enhanced with his epic and extensively researched study *Vínculos de fogo* (1992) (Bonds of Fire) about Antônio José da Silva, 'the Jew,' the famous colonial writer, discussed earlier, who was eventually executed by the Inquisition. Again the historical perspective surfaces in literature as another extension of Jewish memory.

Jacó Guinsburg writes brief tales of insightful psychology and pathos, even though his reputation rests primarily with his theater criticism and with his important contribution as a Brazilian publisher (of the Perspectiva publishing house) who also began the first Judaica series in Brazil. His commitment to the literary heritage of the Jews, including Yiddish literature, found its most expressive form in his extensive 1996 study, *Aventuras de uma língua errante: Ensaios de literatura e teatro ídiche* (Adventures of an Errant Language: Essays on Yiddish Literature and Theater), mentioned earlier in the discussion on Yiddish writing. However, Guinsburg has been composing short stories since the 1950s, and these brief vignettes often capture the viewpoint of the Brazilian Jew looking back at the immigrant experience. He has also published a collection of stories, *O que aconteceu, aconteceu* (2000) (What Happened, Happened). Because he came to Brazil as a child, Guinsburg looks at the Jewish Diaspora experience from the viewpoint of one who is well established in Brazil. Guinsburg's Yiddish and Jewish world was transplanted here by his family and later maintained by himself as a publisher and writer. His stories also manifest post-Holocaust reverberations and the generation gap across cultures. The stories translated here, 'Figuras na sombra' (Figures in the Darkness) and 'Miriam,' are narrated as brief moments of perception when memory and consciousness emerge to rattle the complacency and blindness of the present. In the first story Raquel's memory is suddenly sparked by a photo album that evokes a past that was once erased from her mind. The proverbial guilt and unreality felt by the protagonist once again convey the power of the specter of the Holocaust and its presence in the New World of the tropics. Another moment of epiphany appears in the second story when the mother, Miriam, gives a gold brooch to her daughter and becomes unhinged by her offspring's violent and possessive reaction upon receiving the jewelry. The mother recognizes for the first time that her daughter is not the carbon copy of herself that she thought her to be and that the child's sense of values is completely different. Troubled by this consciousness, the mother ponders how this transformation occurred. As a subtle commentary on the loss of values and tradition, this story stands as another example of the hazards of life in the diaspora.

Another intriguing phenomenon of the diaspora that has been the subject of fiction and study is Jewish white slavery, which spanned the last part of the nineteenth century and the early decades of the twentieth in Brazil. Dramatized in Esther Largman's novel *Jovens polacas* (1993) (Polish Girls), white slavery was perceived as a hazardous topic for the Jewish community, a taboo throughout the late nineteenth century and the early part of the twentieth. Only when Moacyr Scliar addressed the topic of Jewish prostitution in his novel *O ciclo das águas* (1975) (The Cycle of the Waters) did the subject become open for public discussion in Brazil. In fact, Scliar is considered the pioneer who broke the silence about Jewish prostitutes that had reigned in the Brazilian Jewish community, according to Beatriz Kushnir in her study *Baile de máscaras: Mulheres judias e prostituição—As Polacas e suas associações de ajuda mútua* (1996) (Dance of Masks: Jewish Women and Prostitution—Polish Girls and Their Associations of Mutual Assistance). This silence was motivated by the fear of social discrimination and group defilement. In his study on Jewish white slavery, Edward J. Bristow comments: 'The reluctance to deal with shameful subjects is grounded in the long tradition of *chillul hashem* (profanation of the name) or avoidance of actions that might disgrace or endanger the Jewish community.'[43] On the other hand, Kushnir's study documents how in Rio de Janeiro these 'excluded' women managed to maintain their original culture with their own associations of mutual assistance, cemeteries, and synagogues, thereby showing how social stigma led to a necessary sense of belonging and survival. The ultimate repression of the Zwi Migdal in the 1930s, the organization responsible for the white slavery, did not take place until after the *polacas* had left their mark in São Paulo and Rio de Janeiro.

As Esther Largman's novel reveals, the exotic pleasures associated with the *polacas* as well as that of other foreign 'women of the night' went hand in hand with the craze for being part of what was European, in custom and fashion—a tropical belle epoque. Largman's book, based on her own research and that of others, is written as a historical novel, a trend that surfaced during the 1980s and 1990s, especially after redemocratization and the historical revisionism that 'reconstructed' the past and pointed to its problems and injustices. The pages anthologized here cover the early part of the novel, when Sarah, a naive Jewish immigrant girl who was tricked into prostitution by the man she loved, visits her 'pure' immigrant and childless cousin Anita in the hope that the latter will adopt Sarah's child, for whom the 'impure' *polaca* wants a better life. With another character who researches the lives of these 'impure' women and tells the history of the *polacas* in Rio de Janeiro, the novel can be read as part fiction, part testimony, and part documentation. Another novel on the same topic by Maurício Eskenazi Pernidji, *A última polaca ou Sarah pede: Por favor, não tragam flores à minha sepultura* (1985) (The Last Polish Girl or Sarah Requests: Please Don't Bring Flowers to My Grave), attests to the rising interest in rediscovering this once hidden chapter of Jewish history in Brazil.

Other post-immigration contemporary writers hail from different parts of the country. For example, from Recife, in northeastern Brazil, Sara Riwka Erlich published the memoir *No tempo das acácias* (1978) (In the Season of Acacias), which combines her parents Eastern European past with her Brazilian Jewish biculturalism and her cultural link to Israel. Another example is Leão Pacífico Esaguy, who was born in the Amazon and writes about Jewish adaptation to the Amazonian culture in his collection *Contos Amazonenses* (1981) (Amazon Stories).

Another author from the Amazon writing about Amazon Sephardic Jews, who, in the modern period, began to emigrate to Brazil during the nineteenth century, is Paulo Jacob, who is considered to be non-Jewish. A prolific writer whose novels about the Amazon convey an ecological tone, Jacob has devoted one work to a Jewish theme. His novel Um pedaço de lua caía na mata (1990) (A Patch of Moonlight Fell on the Jungle), narrated in forty-six chapters, dramatizes the adventures of the Sephardic Jew Salomão Farah and his family, who find themselves isolated in the non-Jewish community. As an acculturated Jew who strives to maintain his heritage amid the many pressures of the Christian society, Salomão grapples with the insidious assimilation and the struggle to keep his family's ethnic consciousness. The Hebrew title of each chapter is named after some important date of the Jewish religious calendar as well as other cultural events such as bar mitzvah. These titles relate not only to Jewish culture but also to the novel's modern dramas of, for example, persecution, lament, and atonement experienced by the Jewish protagonists. The two chapters anthologized here, 'Tishá Beav' (Day of Lamentations) and 'Kidush Ha-Shem' (being a martyr for maintaining Jewish principles and identity), capture, respectively, the prejudice that Salomão's son experiences in school and the father's commitment to Jewish ideals and his ability to deal in assimilated fashion with the local gentry, including the local priest, who is constantly asking for Salomão's financial support. The direct reference to Salomão as a Jew by the local priest is both friendly and alienating, suggesting the fine line between acceptance and prejudice. Told in a Portuguese dialect of the region, the novel evokes the power of the jungle as well as a Jew's struggle to survive physically and culturally when resources are limited.

Biographies and autobiographies by other Jewish writers continue to be published, sometimes focusing not primarily on the Jewish community but on other aspects of Brazilian society. An example is Samuel Wainer's Minha razão de viver, memórias de um repórter (1988) (My Reason for Living, a Reporter's Memories). A famous journalist, Wainer narrates his activities in national politics and journalism, with allusions to his family's immigrant past. A more recent memoir, Negócios e ócios: Histórias da imigração (1997) (Business and Leisure: Stories of Immigration), by the Brazilian historian and political scientist Boris Fausto, traces the arrival of his grandparents from Turkey during the

1920s to the city of São Paulo, which at that time had a population of approximately 600,000 (35 percent of whom were foreigners) compared to the present-day 18 million. Besides offering a rare portrait of the Sephardim in Turkey from a Brazilian viewpoint, Fausto also tells the story of his Sephardic family and their successes as well as their cultural adaptation to Brazil while still preserving their cultural origins. In so doing he also paints a vivid picture of modern Brazilian history during the first half of the twentieth century, focusing especially on the ambiance of the city of São Paulo and the coffee industry and trade of that period.

Of curious note is Marta F. Topel's recent anthropological and ethnographic study *Jerusalém & São Paulo: A nova ortodoxia judaica em cena* (2005) (Jerusalem and São Paulo: The New Jewish Orthodoxy on Stage), an account of a four-year research project about liberal or hardly practicing Jews who transform themselves into *baalei teshuvá* (Jews returning to Judaism). The merit of this study is not only the Jewish author's suddenly finding her identity and her notion of the community 'strange,' but also how religious fundamentalism is sparked by present-day feelings of terror and xenophobia. Other studies, writings, and memoirs by immigrants and children of immigrants continue to surface, and more will likely be published during the twenty-first century.

## NEW VOICES SINCE THE 1980S

With the contemporary crop of Brazilian Jewish writers, who for the most part reflect a younger generation's experience with being a Brazilian of Jewish ancestry or who have been influenced by the local Jewish culture, we see the emergence of a more pluralist stance toward cultural and ethnic identity. As a contemporary writer, Moacyr Scliar clearly belongs to this current, especially given his multicultural approach to ethnic identity. However, this anthology also focuses on some writers in this group who are not fully established but are considered up-and-coming in light of the recognition afforded their first works. Their depiction of the identity of Brazilian Jews usually involves the acceptance of Jewish culture (at least its secular aspects) as well as a strategic cultural shifting, in other words, the use of situational ethnicity and selectivity, that is, social circumstances that dictate when it is convenient to be or not to be Jewish. Such behavior is considered not hypocrisy but rather a strategy of knowing how to live and negotiate in the diaspora. This perspective indicates a shift from an idealized cohesive but fragmented modernist sense of life to a postmodernist view that is multiple and polyvalent. Furthermore, although examples of Jewish self-hatred are portrayed in these author's works, they are often counterbalanced by strong ethnic allegiance. Although issues of conflict exist and prejudices still surface, these problems are primarily based on long-standing and, hopefully, waning stereotypes. Contemporary Brazilian Jewish literature still transmits primarily a more individual-oriented focus rather than one that includes a collective or community identity, except when issues of race and ethnicity are dramatized and are presented in comparison with other minority groups.

With five novels and a book of stories already published, Bernardo Ajzenberg leads the band of young Jewish writers publishing in today's Brazil. His works focus on interpersonal relationships in the grand urban center of São Paulo, with plots evoking the dramas found in courtroom or crime novels. His third novel, *Goldstein & Camargo* (1994), the first dealing with Jewish themes, also centers on a crime, but it is the psychological and inscrutable portrait of Goldstein, as told from multiple points of view, that lends this work a postmodern perspective. Ironically, in the search for his own identity, Goldstein breaks with his Jewish family and heritage, thereby setting the stage for the social and psychological conflicts that impact all the characters, who represent various backgrounds and ethnicities in the city of São Paulo. This pluralist scenario is already hinted at in the novel's title, a reference to the two protagonists, a Jew and a non-Jew, and their law firm. Told primarily from the supposedly objective perspective of the law partner Camargo, who investigates Goldstein's sudden disappearance, the novel relates the different versions of Goldstein's life according to family members and friends. With a *Citizen Kane* framework in which a narrator attempts to make sense from a variety of contradictory stories, the narrative becomes a conundrum, an almost unfathomable puzzle. Central to Goldstein's problems is his inability to deal with Jewish codes that are counter to those of the larger society. The drama of living in a modern city with all the ensuing disillusionment, impersonal relations, and insecure feelings, often covered up by a facade of normalcy, becomes acute when an event stirs up the past and questions the protagonist's sense of self.

In the chapter anthologized here, Ajzenberg has his narrator, Camargo, meet with Goldstein's sister, not realizing that she is his masseuse because she uses a different professional name. As the narrator explains: 'She used the pseudonym . . . because she thought her Jewish name likely to jeopardize her getting clients. . . . She feared discrimination fostered by competing clients.' The selective ethnic strategy employed by Miriam/Maura becomes another indication of an ethnic individual's use of a shifting identity. Ajzenberg is interested in the cultural traumas that cripple individuals who are unable to live comfortably in the diaspora. The sensitivity toward the Jew's plight in the diaspora is told by Ajzenberg with attention to the density and complexity of character as well as to the instability of modern life, where the coherent ties of the past no longer reign.

Roney Cytrynowicz, a historian by profession, has written a provocative and compelling collection of short stories, A vida secreta dos relógios e outras histórias (1994) (The Secret Life of the Clocks and Other Stories), that harbors fantastic elements. These stories treat diverse topics related to various locales—the Jews of São Paulo, the Jewish neighborhood of Bom Retiro, Israel, and Auschwitz. A comic story such as the 'A guerra das matzot' (Matzot Wars) is a humorous tale about the invasion of Korean immigrant merchants into the Jewish neighborhood and their competition in the manufacturing of matzo, the unleavened bread used at Passover. Other stories deal with the Holocaust, family life, and the condition of being Jewish. The tone of these stories is memorial, as if a zone of indelible painful memory has infiltrated the heart of each tale. Furthermore, in Cytrynowicz's stories the pain from the Holocaust does not dissipate over the distance of time and space. In the title story the narrator's grandfather has an obsession with clocks and time that becomes his way of giving meaning to a world that has lost meaning after the Holocaust. His veneration of the clocks and time become inseparable from his sense of Judaism. The correspondence between the 'tick-tock' of the clocks and the Hebrew, tikkun, for repair, tikkun olam, the repair of the world, evokes the pain of being Jewish after the Holocaust as well as the attempt to reveal the secret that will redeem the world. These stories of the Holocaust via imagination—Cytrynowicz is too young to have personally experienced the terror—are written from the point of view of a survivor(s). The survivor perspective is dramatized violently in the other story anthologized here, 'Shed II,' a tale of revenge and irony in which a Brazilian Jewish plastic surgeon, a survivor, is confronted with the Nazi camp executioner of his twin brother, who wants to alter his present facial identity. Cytrynowicz's collection represents an auspicious beginning for a writer with a profound sense for portraying what it means to be Jewish in the contemporary world, a diaspora world where the past lives on in the present.

Another *paulista* writer, Samuel Reibscheid, introduces a level of humor, sarcasm, and ribaldry in language that at times is bawdy but nevertheless succeeds in capturing the anger and frustration of being Jewish. The twenty-five stories in the collection *Breve fantasia* (1995) (Brief Fantasy), which at times border on the scatological, are a daring explosion of attacks on the conventional, hypocritical, and complacent aspects of society. A carnivalesque and Rabelaisian tone makes these stories enjoyable, provocative, and challenging. The humor and sarcasm used to unmask false virtue and automatic religious rituals contribute to Reibscheid's singular voice about Jews in Brazil. Furthermore, the Jewish elements in the stories are frequently sprinkled with Yiddish, thereby adding another comedic dimension of Yiddishkeit folklore. The refreshing spirit of not taking things seriously, identity as well as circumstances, permeates these stories and affords Reibscheid a provocative voice that opens up cultural boundaries to allow for cross-cultural 'trespassing.' The embedded pluralism in his stories again suggests the clever strategies used to survive in the Jewish Diaspora of Brazil.

As the last examples of the younger generation of contemporary Brazilian Jewish writers to be treated in this introduction, Jaime Lerner and Cíntia Moscovich, both from Rio Grande do Sul, narrate different ways of being Jewish, which in turn demonstrate what can occur with the coexistence of two or more cultures.[44] Jaime Lerner's collection of stories paints a picture of a repressive society in which individuals are always threatened by some force outside their immediate lives capable of destabilizing their sense of self. The insecurity felt by these individuals serves as a commentary on the oppressive codes that govern present-day society. Lerner's stories, told in ironic third- and first-person narration, always provide the reader with a distance that allows for a broad look at contemporary mores and the human condition. On the other hand, in 'Herança' (Legacy), from the collection *Entre quatro paredes* (1995) (Between Four Walls), Jaime Lerner deconstructs ethnic and racial borders in a story that clearly offers hope for the commingling of ethnic and racial others. In this story an invalid old man, Hirsch, contracts a mulatto as his male nurse and befriends a beautiful Afro-Brazilian woman, both of whom he eventually imagines as his 'children,' above his own son, who pays little attention to him. He immediately identifies with the social plight of prejudice experienced by these two blacks. In wanting to leave them a legacy, an inheritance, he decides to bring together these two 'children,' who are attracted to each other from afar. He also fantasizes about taking his adopted 'children' on a trip to Germany, and to Dachau, in order to acknowledge and share their mutual experience of persecution and victimization: 'The three would feel the same pain, the same indignation, the same bewilderment.' He dreams the following about his fantasy trip: 'He would go to Germany with João and Rita; the three of them would get satisfaction from parading around the streets of Berlin. An old Jew, a proud mulatto, and a voluptuous black girl without any inferiority complex to show.'

Lerner's story points to the richness of perspective gleaned from studying culture through the lens of alterity and socially marginal behavior. When we read such narratives by Brazilian Jewish writers, we are informed by perspectives emanating directly from alternative voices that envision a transformation of the nation's traditionally coded social behavior. Literature becomes the prophetic voice, predicting a social transformation that has yet to take place.

When interpreting diaspora as a prophetic discourse and model condition, Boyarin and Boyarin remind us of the following: 'Within the conditions of Diaspora, many Jews discovered that their well-being was dependent on principles of respect for difference, indeed that, as the radical slogan goes, "no one is free until all are free." Absolute devotion to the maintenance of Jewish culture and the historical memory was not inconsistent with devotion to radical causes of human liberation.'[45] Jaime Lerner's story speaks to the motivations for such human liberation.

Cíntia Moscovich is a dynamic young writer who does not shy away

from controversial topics. Her stories evince an independence of mind
that she transmits to her female protagonists. Her treatment of Jewish
themes is frank, bold, and incisive, often pointing to the problematic
generation gap and its misunderstandings. However, many of her
stories affirm a Jewish sense of culture and self that leaves space for
being both Brazilian and Jewish. With the story 'Os ímpio e os justos'
(The Unholy and the Just), from her collection *O reino das cebolas* (1996)
(The Kingdom of Onions), Moscovich presents a girl in mourning on
the day of her father's funeral. Irritated by the behavior of her uncle,
her father's brother, who exploits her vulnerability and grief by asking
questions about her father's will, the young girl immediately recalls
the generosity and tenderness of her father while she partakes in all
the rituals linked to the Jewish culture of death—washing her hands
in the temple's basin, the kiyor; the covered mirrors, a tribute to the
lack of vanity; and the Kaddish death prayer recited by the minyan,
the minimum of ten male Jews required for communal prayer. Here,
Moscovich constructs an atmosphere of cultural continuity within the
Jewish Diaspora via this daughter in mourning. In this way she dem-
onstrates how the maintenance of an ethnic space, via ritual, assists
the daughter in manifesting her great respect for her father, especially
in light of her uncle's falsity. While she evokes the memory of her
father, this Jewish girl identifies with him, a just man who is nothing
like his brother. The positive image of her Jewish father permeates
the narrative. This story commemorates the observation of ritual in
the diaspora and, above all, the ethnic continuity manifested by the
young girl, who honors the values of her heritage.

   In the story anthologized here, 'Sheine Meidale' (Pretty Girl), Moscovich depicts Jewish life in Porto Alegre in the 1960s within the frame
of a girl's coming of age. The story illustrates how children cross ethnic
and national identity borders much more easily than their parents and,
in doing so, develop a double consciousness of their ethnic heritage.
This cultural consciousness is manifested here when the young girl
realizes that her overly protective father becomes more lenient when
her first date turns out to be Jewish: 'I kept observing what could become a disaster. I prayed to God and to my guardian angel. Fortunately,
contrary to what I expected, my father lowered the paper and brought
up a subject, wasn't he [Mário] the son of Jacob, the doctor? He was.
I sighed because I knew my father liked familiar references.' This

young girl is cognizant of how different cultures are viewed, and her consciousness and openness announces her cultural sensibility.

Another refreshing episode, illustrating Moscovich's deft use of adolescent expression, humor, and irony, is the picture of this Jewish girl's introduction to sex with a goy. The boldness of the girl's language and the fearlessness within her self contribute to an affirmative statement about strong and positive gender and cultural identity, one devoid of the conventional and paralyzing trappings frequently associated with cross-cultural lives that reside in conflict. Furthermore, Moscovich's analysis of the roles disenchanted women are forced to play sets the stage for her sharp vision of the politics of difference in Brazil.


## FINAL OBSERVATIONS

All these narratives elicit the reader's attention to the potential tyranny of culture, dominant and ethnocentric, and to the need for social liberation along ethnic, racial, and national lines. Preserving a second culture and language not only results in what Pierre Bourdieu, in *Language and Symbolic Power*, refers to as an expansion of one's cultural capital, but also serves as a reminder of what Rey Chow implies—that a sense of belonging is never unadulterated because acculturation is always occurring in one form or another, especially in our global and transnational world.[46]

If in *Imaginary Homelands* Salmon Rushdie speaks of hybrid cultures in the context of what Stuart Hall alludes to as the drift toward globalization versus reassertion of localism, then Hall's observations are especially pertinent for Jewish Latin America: 'Although these tendencies appear to be irreconcilable, . . . cultural identities are emerging that are "in transition," drawing on different traditions and harmonizing old and new without assimilation or total loss of the past.'[47] Even though Hall associates the evolution of 'cultures of hybridity' primarily with the 'new diasporas' created by colonial experience and ensuing postcolonial migration, Rey Chow underscores the need to think beyond postcolonial paradigms and more toward diasporic existences. And whether or not one uses terms like James Clifford's 'traveling cultures' to refer to migration and the creation of diasporas, 'Diasporas imply multiple attachments. They accommodate to, but also resist the norms and claims of nationalists and traditional forms of identity. Diasporas are between nation states and traveling cultures.'[48] Brazilian Jewish literature evokes this stance in a more positive light with the second generation of contemporary authors. Silence and nonaffirmation appear to be the ways of being Jewish in the recent past—almost as if they were crypto ways of being Jewish—dissimulation as a result of socially and nationally imposed simulation. With the newer crop of writers we see the emergence of a more hybrid stance toward cultural identity, one that even challenges the concept of a single identity.

What does this literature tell us about the ways of being Jewish in Brazil? That cultural and social standardization or simulation, whether it be in the forms of nationalist assimilation, native allegiance, or cultural similitude, can and may still represent powerful social pressures as seen during significant moments in Brazil's twentieth-century history of immigration and nationalism. And while some of these social pressures may be on the wane in Brazil, as evidenced in recent fiction with doubly conscious and dual-allegiance protagonists, Brazilian Jewish writers of the past and present generations seem prophetic in their literary deconstruction of the tyranny of cultural similitude that thrives at the expense of difference. Moreover, by featuring in their fiction and memoirs criticism of the repressive social simulation in contrast to the meaningful role of cultural difference via positive images of ethnicity, Brazilian Jewish writers reveal, and sometimes purposely conceal, how ethnicity as a component of cultural identity and as a personal power resource has until recently remained relatively unexploited in Brazilian literature. Furthermore, by featuring simultaneously the themes of ethnicity and the question of belonging in their literature, Brazilian Jewish writers provide added dimension to the dramatization of being culturally the same as Brazilians but also different as Jews, implying that cultural ethnicity and identity are implicitly an in-between, an entrelugar, an ever-changing or altering condition and ironically so inherent to the modus operandi of Brazil's national cannibalistic identity and ethos.

Finally, Brazilian Jewish writers address the cultural and social blind spots prevalent in their country. They underscore issues of displacement, exile, fragmentation, alienation, prejudice, alterity, and disregard as well as those of quest, multiplicity, and change via innovative narratives that challenge unilaterally naturalist and mimetic dramatizations as well as the impossibility of maintaining one sole identity. Within their narrative quests, they claim a public space for the inclusion of difference by pointing to the gaps, fissures, and fractures related to cultural alterity. In this way, Brazilian Jewish writing reflects the much-needed sociopolitical principles of equity and ethics in the formation of ethnic identity and multiple identities.

# Notes

1. Kitaj, *First Diasporist Manifesto*, 37.

2. This quote is from the essay by Daniel Boyarin and Jonathan Boyarin titled 'Diaspora: Generation and the Ground of Jewish Identity.' This essay defines the Jewish Diaspora in an in-depth manner relevant to the Jewish experience in Brazil. It has served as one of the theoretical bases for my introduction.

3. See Vieira, *Jewish Voices in Brazilian Literature*, 1–18.

4. I originally discovered the reference to Sakai's essay in Rey Chow's *Writing Diaspora*, 5. The quote here is from Sakai, 'Modernity and Its Critique,' 105.

5. In *Jewish Frontiers*, while discussing 'frontier as a model for Jewish history,' Sander L. Gilman presents a strong argument for using the term 'frontier' over 'diaspora.' I agree with Gilman's concept and moreover believe that for literature 'frontier' may also be applied in the spirit of Mary Louise Pratt's 'contact zone,' an arena, imagined or real, for negotiating identities. Although the term 'frontier' may be applied to Brazil, the concept of diaspora is underscored in this anthology, since we are dealing primarily with Jewish identity and particularism in literature within the context of the Jewish Diaspora.

6. See Nagata, 'What Is Malay?' on situational ethnicity and selective ethnic identity and behavior.

7. This quote appears as an epigraph in Silviano Santiago's essay 'Apesar de dependente, universal' (Universality in Spite of Dependency), in *Vale quanto pesa* (Worth Its Weight). I refer to this quote later in the introduction to explain further the Brazilian proclivity to be 'in between.' A recent collection of Santiago's essays in English (*The Space In-Between*) contains this essay.

8. For an analysis of how Brazilian elites considered Jews to be the same as the Arab race and consequently non-Europeans, as well as how Jews challenged

elite notions of national identity, see Lesser, '"Jews Are Turks Who Sell on Credit."'

9. For a provocative treatment of this question and the uneasiness created by hyphens, see Sosnowski, 'Latin-American-Jewish Writers.'

10. For an overview of this notion on the status quo mentality, see Ages, *The Diaspora Dimension*, 33–41.

11. For an explanation of this 'low profile' stance, see Vieira, *Jewish Voices in Brazilian Literature*, 1–18.

12. Vieira, *Jewish Voices in Brazilian Literature*, 11.

13. Gilman, *The Visibility of the Jew*, 17.

14. Gilman, *The Visibility of the Jew*, 28.

15. Gilman, *The Visibility of the Jew*, 30–31.

16. Boyarin and Boyarin, 'Diaspora,' 720–21, emphasis mine.

17. Chow, *Writing Diaspora*, 25.

18. Boyarin and Boyarin, 'Diaspora,' 707.

19. Boyarin and Boyarin, 'Diaspora,' 723.

20. Boyarin and Boyarin, 'Diaspora,' 721.

21. For an understanding of how diaspora implies forcible dispersion, articulated in Deuteronomy (28:58–86), and how the homelessness of the Jews appears as a leitmotif in Jewish world literature, along with the appropriation of the figure of the wandering Jews, see Cohen, *Global Diasporas*, 1–29.

22. Boyarin and Boyarin, 'Diaspora,' 718.

23. Scholem, *The Messianic Idea in Judaism*, 49.

24. Elkin and Merkz, *Jewish Presence in Latin America*, 314.

25. Gilman, *Inscribing the Other*, 282.

26. Gilman, *Inscribing the Other*, 281.

27. Gilman, *Inscribing the Other*, 282.

28. See Stuart Hall's discussion of this 'new ethnicity' in his article 'Ethnicity: Identity and Difference.'

29. Elkin and Merkx, *Jewish Presence in Latin America*, 323.

30. This reference is drawn from Ben Xu's study 'Memory and the Ethnic Self,' 274–75.

31. Montero, 'Cultura e democracia no processo da globalização,' 112, my emphasis.

32. See Cohen, *The Jewish Experience in Latin America*.

33. For a biography of Olga Benário Prestes, see Morais, *Olga*.

34. For a detailed account of Jewish immigration to Brazil at that time, see Lesser, *Welcoming the Undesirables*, 19. Lesser argues persuasively that, despite strict laws, many Jews managed to enter Brazil.

35. For an overview of German, Italian, Jewish, and other immigrant narratives from Brazil, see Igel, 'Imigrantes na Ficção Brasileira Contemporânea.'

36. For more of Samuel Rawet's stories in English translation, see Rawet, *The Prophet and Other Stories*.

37. Of note are two recent publications in English translation of the original *Los gaucho judios*, one a re-publication, *The Jewish Gauchos of the Pampas*, translated by Prudencio de Pereda; and Edna Aizenberg's *Parricide on the Pampa? A New Study and Translation of Alberto Gerchunoff's 'Los gauchos judios.'*

38. Guinsburg, *Aventuras de uma língua errante*, 442.

39. These stories were 'rediscovered' and given to me by Teresa Cristina Montero Ferreira, a biographer of Clarice Lispector. Montero Ferreira found these narratives, which had been published in periodicals, in the archives of Lispector's law school in Rio. A copy of one of the stories, 'Eu e Jimmy,' is housed in the Clarice Lispector collection at the Casa Rui Barbosa in Rio. Both stories first appeared in book form in Montero and Manzo, *Clarice Lispector*.

40. Carlos Scliar's statement appears in the pamphlet *Perto de Clarice* (Near Clarice) prepared for the conference of the same name, which took place in Rio on November 23–29, 1987.

41. This symbol and the discussion about Brazilian hybrid practices appears in Canclini's essay titled 'No sabemos cómo llamar a los otros' (We Do Not Know How to Name Others), which has since been incorporated into his book *La globalización imaginada*.

42. This essay by Sérgio Buarque de Hollanda appears in his seminal *Raízes do Brasil* (Roots of Brazil) (1936).

43. Bristow, *Prostitution and Prejudice*, 7.

44. Numerous publications in the twenty-first century reveal the continued interest and richness of Brazilian Jewish fiction. Two works of note by emerging writers are Samy Wurman's novel *Olhos de céu* (Sky Blue Eyes), in which the female protagonist becomes a type of Messiah; and the Egyptian-born Alberto Moghrabi's collection of chronicles *Pequenos contos de enredo indeterminado: Crônicas* (Small Stories of Indeterminate Plot), about daily life in Egypt and São Paulo.

45. Boyarin and Boyarin, 'Diaspora,' 720.

46. Chow, *Writing Diaspora*, 24.

47. Rushdie, *Imaginary Homelands*, 394; Hall quoted in Cohen, *Global Diasporas*, 131.

48. Cohen, *Global Diasporas*, 135.

# Bibliography

Ages, Arnold. *The Diaspora Dimension*. The Hague: Martinus Nijhoff, 1973.

Bhabha, Homi K., ed. *Nation and Narration*. London: Routledge, 1990.

Blank, Paulo. *O tal do Judeu*. Rio de Janeiro: Editora Tikun Olam, 1989.

Bourdieu, Pierre. *Language and Symbolic Power*. Edited and introduced by John B. Thompson. Translated by Gino Raymond and Matthew Adamson. Cambridge MA: Harvard University Press, 1991.

Boyarin, Daniel, and Jonathan Boyarin. 'Diaspora: Generation and the Ground of Jewish Identity.' *Critical Inquiry* 19, no. 4 (Summer 1993): 693–725.

Boyarin, Jonathan. *Storm from Paradise: The Politics of Jewish Memory*. Minneapolis: University of Minnesota Press, 1997.

Bristow, Edward J. *Prostitution and Prejudice: The Jewish Fight against White Slavery, 1870–1930*. New York: Schocken Books, 1983.

Canclini, Néstor García. 'No sabemos cómo llamar a los otros.' In *La globalización imaginada*, 107–25. Buenos Aires: Paidós, 1999.

Chow, Rey. *Writing Diaspora: Tactics of Intervention in Contemporary Cultural Studies*. Bloomington: University of Indiana Press, 1993.

Cohen, Martin A., ed. *The Jewish Experience in Latin America*. Vol. 2. Waltham MA: American Jewish Historical Society; New York: Ktav, 1971.

Cohen, Robin. *Global Diasporas: An Introduction*. Seattle: University of Washington Press, 1997.

DiAntonio, Robert. 'Resonances of the Yiddishkeit Tradition in the Contemporary Brazilian Narrative.' In *Tradition and Innovation: Reflections on Latin American Jewish Writing*, edited by Robert DiAntonio and Nora Glickman, 45–60. Albany: State University of New York Press, 1993.

Elkin, Judith Laikin, and Gilbert Merkx, eds. *The Jewish Presence in Latin America*. Boston: Allen & Unwin, 1987.

George, Rosemary Marangoly. *The Politics of Home: Postcolonial Relocations and Twentieth-Century Fiction*. Berkeley: University of California Press, 1999.

Gilman, Sander L. *Inscribing the Other*. Lincoln: University of Nebraska Press, 1991.

————. *Jewish Frontiers: Essays on Bodies, Histories, and Identities*. New York: Palgrave Macmillan, 2003.

————. *The Visibility of the Jew in the Diaspora Body Imagery and Its Cultural Context*. Syracuse: Syracuse University, 1992.

Goldemberg, Isaac, ed. *El gran libro de América Judía*. San Juan: Editorial de la Universidad de Puerto Rico, 1998.

Gotlib, Nádia Battella. *Clarice: Uma vida que se conta*. São Paulo: Editora Ática, 1995.

Guinsburg, Jacó. *Aventuras de uma língua errante: Ensaios de literatura e teatro ídiche*. São Paulo: Perspectiva, 1996.

Gurchonoff, Alberto. *The Jewish Gauchos of the Pampas*. Translated by Prudencio de Pereda. Albuquerque: University of New Mexico Press, 1998.

————. *Parricide on the Pampa? A New Study and Translation of Alberto Gerchunoff's 'Los gauchos judios.'* Translated by Edna Aizenberg. Madrid: Vervuert/Iberoamericana, 2000.

Hall, Stuart. 'Ethnicity: Identity and Difference.' *Radical America* 23, no. 4 (1991): 9–20.

Hollanda, Sérgio Buarque de. *Raízes do Brasil*. Preface by Antônio Cândido. 10th ed. Rio de Janeiro: José Olympio, 1976.

Igel, Regina. *Imigrantes judeus/Escritores brasileiros: O componente judaico na literatura brasileira*. São Paulo: Perspectiva; Associação Universitária de Cultura Judaica; Banco Safra, 1997.

————. 'Imigrantes na Ficção Brasileira Contemporânea.' *Revista Interamericana de Bibliografia* 42, no. 1 (1992): 83–101.

Kitaj, R. B. *First Diasporist Manifesto*. New York: Thames & Hudson, 1989.

Lerner, Jaime. *Entre quatro paredes*. Porto Alegre: Secretaria Municipal de Cultura/Fumproarte, 1995.

Lesser, Jeffrey. '"Jews Are Turks Who Sell on Credit": Elite Images of Arabs and Jews in Brazil.' In *Arab and Jewish Immigrants in Latin America: Images and Realities*, edited by Ignacio Klich and Jeffrey Lesser, 38–56. London: F. Cass, 1998.

————. *Welcoming the Undesirables: Brazil and the Jewish Question*. Berkeley: University of California Press, 1995.

Lispector, Clarice. *The Foreign Legion*. Manchester: Carcanet, 1986.

———. *Selected Crônicas*. New York: New Directions, 1996.

———. *The Stream of Life*. Translated by Elizabeth Lowe and Earl Fitz. Foreword by Hélène Cixous. Minneapolis: University of Minnesota Press, 1989.

Lockhart, Darrell B., ed. *Jewish Writers of Latin America: A Dictionary*. New York: Garland, 1997.

Moghrabi, Alberto. *Pequenos contos de enredo indeterminado: Crônicas*. São Paulo: Editora & Livraria Sêfer, 2001.

Montero, Paula. 'Cultura e democracia no processo da globalização.' *Novos Estudos CEBRAP* 44 (March 1996): 89–114.

Montero, Teresa, and Lícia Manzo, eds. *Clarice Lispector: Outros escritos*. Rio de Janeiro: Rocco, 2005.

Montero Ferreira, Teresa Cristina. *Eu sou uma pergunta: Uma biografia de Clarice Lispector*. Rio de Janeiro: Rocco, 1999.

Morais, Fernando. *Olga: A vida de Olga Benário Prestes, judia comunista entregue a Hitler pelo governo Vargas*. São Paulo: Editora Alfa-Omega, 1986. Translated by Ellen Watson as *Olga: Revolutionary and Martyr* (New York: Grove-Weidemfeld, 1990).

Moscovich, Cíntia. *O reino das cebolas*. Porto Alegre: Mercado Aberto, 1996.

Nagata, Judith A. 'What Is Malay? Situational Selection of Ethnic Identity in a Plural Society.' *American Ethnologist* 1 (1974): 331–50.

Novinsky, Anita. *Cristãos Novos na Bahia*. São Paulo: Editôra Perspectiva, 1972.

Rawet, Samuel. *Contos do imigrante*. Rio de Janeiro: José Olympio, 1956.

———. *The Prophet and Other Stories*. Translated with an introduction by Nelson H. Vieira. Albuquerque: University of New Mexico Press, 1998.

Rushdie, Salman. *Imaginary Homelands: Essays and Criticism, 1981–1991*. London: Granta Books, 1991.

Sakai, Naoki. 'Modernity and Its Critique: The Problem of Universalism and Particularism.' In *Postmodernism and Japan*, edited by Masao Miyoshi and H. D. Harootunian, 93–122. Durham NC: Duke University Press, 1989. Originally published in *South Atlantic Quarterly* 87, no. 3 (Summer 1988): 475–504.

Santiago, Silviano. *The Space In-Between: Essays on Latin American Culture*. Durham NC: Duke University Press, 2001.

———. *Vale quanto pesa: Ensaios sobre questões político-culturais*. Rio de Janeiro: Paz e Terra, 1982.

Scholem, Gershom. *The Messianic Idea in Judaism and Other Essays on Jewish Spirituality*. New York: Schocken Books, 1971.

———. *On Jews and Judaism in Crisis: Selected Essays*. Edited by Werner J. Dannhauser. New York: Schocken Books, 1976.

Schwarz, Roberto. 'Brazilian Culture: Nationalism by Elimination.' *New Left Review* 167 (January 1988): 77–90.

Scliar, Moacyr. *A orelha de Van Gogh*. São Paulo: Companhia das Letras, 1989.

———. *O carnaval dos animais*. 4th ed. Porto Alegre: Editora Movimento, 1978.

Sen, Amartya. *Identity and Violence: The Illusion of Destiny*. New York: W. W. Norton, 2006.

Sheinin, David, and Lois Baer Barr, eds. *The Jewish Diaspora in Latin America: New Studies on History and Literature*. New York: Garland, 1996.

Singh, Amritjit, Joseph T. Skerrett Jr., and Robert E. Hogan, eds. *Memory, Narrative, and Identity: New Essays in Ethnic American Literatures*. Boston: Northeastern University Press, 1994.

Sosnowski, Saúl. 'Latin-American-Jewish Writers: Protecting the Hyphen.' In *The Jewish Presence in Latin America*, edited by Judith Laikin Elkin and Gilbert W. Merkx, 297–307. Boston: Allen & Unwin, 1987.

Spiro, Melford E. 'The Acculturation of American Ethnic Groups.' *American Anthropologist* 57 (1955): 1240–52.

Vieira, Nelson H. *Jewish Voices in Brazilian Literature: A Prophetic Discourse of Alterity*. Gainesville: University Press of Florida, 1995.

Wicker, Hans-Rudolf. *Rethinking Nationalism and Ethnicity: The Struggle for Meaning and Order in Europe*. Oxford: Berg, 1977.

Wurman, Samy. *Olhos de céu*. Rio de Janeiro: Garamond, 2001.

Xu, Ben. 'Memory and the Ethnic Self: Reading Amy Tan's *The Joy Luck Club*.' In *Memory, Narrative, and Identity: New Essays in Ethnic American Literatures*, edited by Amritjit Singh, Joseph T. Skerrett Jr., and Robert E. Hogan, 261–77. Boston: Northeastern University Press, 1994.

# Interview with Moacyr Scliar

This unpublished interview took place in November 1998 in Providence, Rhode Island, during Moacyr Scliar's one-month stay as writer-in-residence in the Department of Portuguese and Brazilian Studies at Brown University, sponsored by Brown University and the Brazilian Ministry of Culture. Scliar's many activities during his residence at Brown included presenting a series of talks on literature and Jewish writing in Brazil as well as conducting a Portuguese creative writing workshop on the *crônica*/chronicle genre, an essay form straddling nonfiction and fiction. This interview provides a cultural context for Jewish writing in Brazil from the viewpoint of Brazil's foremost living Jewish author.

N H V: What does it mean to be a Jew in your country?

M S: Well, that's a question I constantly ask myself throughout my life, and a question for which I don't know if I have a satisfactory answer. However, I have an answer that is at least the best response I could find. To answer that question, I think that one has to think of the possibilities in the practice of Judaism in today's world. Basically, the possibilities are the following: either a person is religious, and in that case Judaism is a religion, or a person is a Zionist and thinks Jewish existence can only be understood within Israel and so the person goes to Israel, or then the person is neither religious nor Zionist, such as in my case, and understands Judaism not as a religion, or as national life, but rather as a tradition, a culture, a history. So my approach to Judaism is basically that it's the idea of belonging to a group that had a common historical path and that along this historical path developed a common culture and that this culture has to be preserved as all things must be preserved that enrich human existence. What I see in Judaism is the equivalent to what people see in a family album. The vision of the past, therefore, the vision of our roots, and that vision helping us to comprehend the present.

NHV: And what does it mean to be a Jewish writer in your country?

MS: It means exactly to use as primary material for literature precisely that Jewish experience. I think that in Brazil that experience is important because Brazil is basically a country of immigration. In Brazil nobody is indigenous, except for the Indians, and even the Indians themselves came from other regions. But throughout the country's existence, groups from other regions kept coming to make Brazil their home and that accumulated experience is what forms Brazilianness. So the literature of the descendents of immigrants is an important literature in the sense of explaining, alongside other literatures, what Brazil is.

NHV: And in terms of Jewish immigration to Brazil, what are some of its principal characteristics?

MS: It is a very diversified immigration, which had already begun during the era of the discoveries, with the arrival of New Christians, and continues afterward with the arrival of the Jews from various parts of the world: Moroccan Jews at the end of the eighteenth and the beginning of the nineteenth centuries, Jews from Alsace-Lorraine, then Jews from the Arab countries, and, more related to my experience, the Jews of Eastern Europe, who began to arrive at the end of the nineteenth and the beginning of the twentieth centuries. These Jews first arrived via a movement organized by European philanthropic groups, who brought the Jews to be tenant farmers in Uruguay, Argentina, and Rio Grande do Sul, Brazil, and afterward we continued to grow in number with the Jews who fled the Nazi persecution or survivors of the Holocaust. I believe this experience of agricultural colonization is very interesting because it is not a frequent chapter in Jewish history and [is] different from other migratory waves. It [i.e., this wave of Jewish immigrants] did not go to the city but to the interior. Thus, they had a much more authentic experience of Brazil in the sense that they went to regions of Brazil where life was still very close to the country's reality during other eras.

N HV: In your recent book A majestade do Xingu (1997) [The Majesty of the Xingu], you describe different destinies for immigrant Jews in Brazil, besides the common experience of the arduous struggle toward upward socioeconomic mobility. Please comment on this.

M S: I think that the great conflicts of our time are reflected in the Jewish community. I mean, it's absurd to consider Brazilian Judaism or any other form of Judaism as one sole experience. In truth, it's a singular experience for anti-Semites or exaggerated apologists of Judaism. Because in reality there were different destinies and even conflicts within the Jewish community. In this book, A majestade do Xingu, I speak of two of these destinies. A geologist who dedicates himself to business, considered to be the classic Jewish occupation, and another Jew who will be a doctor, different from the classic Jewish occupation, however different from that of other doctors, Jewish or not, who dedicates himself to an extremely marginal group in Brazilian society, the Indians. So, what attracted my attention in the trajectory of this man's life, Noel Nutels, is that as an immigrant, he came from Russia, and in Brazil he identifies with a group with which he probably wouldn't have the least bit of affinity. Nevertheless, he identified with them exactly because of the suffering he noted within this group and that reminded him of the same suffering he himself had undergone as a child in Russia.

N HV: Generally speaking, do you have an idea of the image of the Jews in Brazil, among the non-Jewish population?

M S: Brazil is basically a Catholic country, albeit a Catholicism very mixed with, above all, Afro-Brazilian beliefs—syncretism is extensive in Brazil. But within this tradition, Brazil witnessed some of the more obvious anti-Semitic phenomena of the history of the Jewish people, for example, the Inquisition. The Inquisition was present during the first two decades of Brazilian history. It was not as drastic as it was in Spain, or even in the Spanish American countries. In any event, it was a presence that manifested an anti-Semitic tradition. One must say that this anti-Semitic tradition was never very strong in Brazil, where there never occurred anything comparable to the pogroms of Russia. But there existed the stereotyped image of the Jew as an exploiter, usurer, merchant, and that image persisted until not too long ago. But my impression, and I do not have statistics to support this, is that the image of the Jew in Brazil is changing. It's changing because, in the first place, the actual Jewish community changed a great deal, in the sense that today it is more integrated in Brazilian life and, in the second place, because the country matured, the very process of democratization during the last fifteen years brought a more tolerant view of groups that, within Brazilian society, were once discriminated against or even harassed. Today there exists much more room in Brazilian society for blacks, immigrants of various ethnic groups who in the past were marginalized. There exists a process of tolerance, of acceptance within Brazilian society.

NHV: You are part of a literary tradition that began in this century with, for example, Samuel Rawet and Jewish themes. As a Brazilian writer how do you see the maintenance of the Jewish tradition in literature, and afterward, what is your relationship with the rest of Brazilian literature?

MS: Now, I'm going to use this question to speak a little about this double condition of being a Jewish writer and a Brazilian writer. If I had to say what I am first of all, I would say that I am first a Brazilian writer because the language I use is the Portuguese language, which is the language of Brazil. The place where I was born was Brazil; the food I eat is Brazilian food; the landscape where I live is Brazilian. But this Brazilian experience was permeated by my Jewish experience, which resulted from my living within a Jewish household, not a religious one, but one in which Jewish history was somehow present from my reading Jewish authors, from my identifying with the Jewish people and Israel. And finally, from having nostalgia for the Jewish condition represented by the Yiddish language, by its history, by the literature of authors like Sholem Aleichem, I. L. Peretz, and many others. Another thing is something I feel in my own work, and that is Jewish humor. For me literature has to have humor—humor is an important component of literature. It's not a comic humor, not one to make people burst out laughing, but that Jewish humor, half bitter, melancholy, which represents a defense against despair and, at the same time, one that makes people smile—and not laugh, smile—that makes them think. Jewish humor is the great creation of Jewish literature.

NHV: More recently, other Jewish writers are emerging, a new generation, like Bernardo Ajzenberg, Cíntia Moscovich, Roney Cytrynowicz. To what do you attribute this new wave of writers?

MS: I believe the Jewish experience in Brazil has not run its course. There are no more incoming immigrants, but there are children of immigrants, grandchildren of immigrants, and for them that Jewish experience is still very important. Also, for Brazilian as well as other societies, there are other reasons: while the process of globalization and homogenization continues, while people make a given culture more and more global, [one] in which people are standardized by a certain type of culture, there exists the need to search for particularities, to seek out those things that characterize us as groups within the larger society or which characterize us as people. In other words, to search for our own identity. And to search for identity in the case of Judaism means to recover the past and for each writer to recover that past even within literature.

NHV: In terms of this past, one notices that in non-Jewish Brazilian literature, for example, there exists a tradition of memorialism beyond that of immigrants. Do you think this memorialist proclivity is going to continue within the Jewish community?

MS: I don't know. I think it would be a very difficult exercise in futurology [to speculate]. But my hunch is that this is a cycle, and like all cycles, it will have a peak and a drop—other cycles occurred in Brazilian literature and in Jewish literature as well. History is history; therefore, history will remain. But whether history is going to continue to inspire writers, for that I do not have a satisfactory response. My hunch is that the process of the Jewish community's assimilation into the larger society is going to continue—it's a rapid process—and that Judaism, as uneasiness, will no longer be so strong in the coming years. I mean people will no longer suffer with their Jewish condition; the Jewish condition is no longer a motive for suffering, for anxiety or turmoil. It is something that is going to be part of people's lives; just as people root for a soccer team or have their favorite authors or like certain films, they are also going to have that vestige of Judaism, which is going to be part of their lives, to enrich them, but it is not going to be such a transcendent force as it was in the past. For example, in Europe to be or not to be Jewish was a question of life or death.

NHV: How do these young Jewish writers see themselves ideologically or politically? In other words, in relation to assimilation into national life or toward acculturation by maintaining some distinction as part of a minority culture?

MS: Judaism is going to always be a reason for being different, but [it is becoming] more and more attenuated. Jewish intellectual life is more and more integrated into national life. For example, a Brazilian Jewish journalist, when he or she writes for a newspaper, he or she writes as a Brazilian, seeing Brazilian reality. It's clear that there exist traces of Judaism in his or her attitude, for instance, that value that Judaism places on the written word, on intellectual debate, and even on a certain prophetic tradition from biblical times, of saying what is right and what is wrong. When I see Brazilian Jewish journalists in action, I always have the impression that in some way they are heirs of that ethical and cultural tradition.

NHV: In present-day Brazil, how would you characterize the socio-economic progress of Brazilian Jews?

MS: They have improved their lives very rapidly, even though there still exist Jews who are poor, and it's an error to think that the Jewish community is a rich community. It is basically a middle-class community, and the children of merchants, artisans who came from Europe are doctors, lawyers, and executives. It's not a state of wealth that stands out. Of course there are very wealthy Jews, and it's also obvious that, compared to the Brazilian population on the whole, the situation of the Jewish community from the economic point of view is better. However, that is not an absolute, because as far as the actual quality of the middle class, the Jews suffer the same problems that the Brazilian middle class suffers, that of losing during the last few years their consumer power, which they suffered and continue to suffer with the economic crisis.

NHV: In another vein, what would be the position of many Brazilian Jews toward Israel and the question of Palestine?

MS: I have no statistics, but my impression is that the vast majority of the Jewish community identifies with Israel. The vast majority of the Jewish community was thrilled with the creation of the State of Israel, supports the State of Israel, and would even be capable of making sacrifices for Israel. Now, support for the State of Israel does not mean automatic support for the government of Israel. So, many people within the Jewish community make that distinction very clear, in saying that Israel as a state has to survive; this represents not only a victory for the Jewish people but also a victory for humanity. But the politics developed by the government of Israel is another thing. The Israeli government is a government, and as such it is more like other governments than it is like Judaism. Thus many people say, and in my way of seeing as well, that there exists no 'why' about automatically supporting the attitudes of the State of Israel, of the Israeli government, above all, with reference to the question of peace. I also have the impression that, for the majority of the people in the Jewish community, as for that matter the very people of Israel, the question of peace is a fundamental one. And peace at this time signifies establishing a way of living together with the Palestinians, a people with whom Israel shares the territory.

N H V: When you were younger, there were many Zionist movements, for example, there exists a Brazilian kibbutz. Did you participate in any of those movements, or did your family or friends? How was Zionism regarded in Brazil?

M S: The question of the State of Israel, founded in 1948, was closely followed, with extraordinary emotion, by the Brazilian Jewish community. Suddenly Zionism began to be an ideal for many within the Jewish community. Above all for the youth, and above all for those young people who had socialist ideas, because for us Zionism meant not only living in Israel, but living in a kibbutz and to live a collective life, a life of equality, of social justice. In that sense, we were heirs of the Jewish reformers of the nineteenth century, many of whom became leaders of the socialist movements and the communist movements, which during the 1950s were still a great impetus to mobilization for young people. Therefore, the idea of the kibbutz was really one that represented for us the realization of utopia. It's clear that, like all youth movements, it was very sectarian, and since we maintained a rather closed group, the exchange of ideas also was not very well developed. It is evident that, at some point, the movement in this form really came close to fanaticism. And our parents paid a heavy price for that. But I think that it was an extraordinary experience, very rich. And I would say that this experience did not restrict itself to the idea of going to Israel, of going to live on a kibbutz. I did not go to live in Israel, I did not go on a kibbutz, and yet I do not feel that I threw away the ideas of the youth movement. I think when I went to work in public health, even when I dedicated myself to writing, in some way, I was providing another outlet for the ideas of the youth movement.

NHV: Speaking of the past, did you ever attend any event of the Yiddish theater in Brazil? Did your parents talk about it?

MS: I not only went to the Yiddish theater; I actually participated in the Yiddish theater because in Porto Alegre, the Yiddish theater was very funny. We also had our own theater. But what people really enjoyed was when the 'troupes' of actors came from abroad and above all from Buenos Aires. However, the 'troupes' were really a couple, an actor and an actress. For example, Max Spellman and Guita Galina were famous. And as such it [the troupe] was very poor, without resources, without money. So it didn't even have costarring actors. When they arrived in the city, they had to recruit young people to be part of the play. They would quickly explain to the young what they had to do. I remember a play—it was very ingenuous—that took place in a kibbutz, and so there were Max Spellman and Guita Galina and there were young people who had to sing and dance, and I was one of those youngsters, singing and dancing there on the stage.

NHV: Did they perform in Porto Alegre's famous São Pedro Theater?

MS: Yes. And everybody went when there was Yiddish theater, but it was a curious thing because their greatest anxiety was to know what time the play was going to end, because it couldn't end after the last streetcar, because they had to catch the last streetcar in order to return to the Jewish neighborhood of Bom Fim. And there's a story that one time they ended the play in the middle because it was the hour to catch the streetcar and so everybody got up and left the theater. [laughter]

NHV: Since there no longer is a Yiddish theater, but there is Jewish literature, what are the basic cultural elements that contribute to the maintenance of Jewish traditions in Brazil?

MS: Well, it's not Yiddish. Yiddish is no longer spoken, or if it is spoken, it is very limited. My fear is always that this maintenance may be seen as a curricular activity, as a course of study, with exams, homework, things that the young detest, you have to take an exam, and so on. I'm afraid that they're capable of developing this attitude in relation to Judaism, especially if Judaism is transformed into a curricular activity. Judaism is more than an intellectual experience; it's an emotional one. So I don't really know what is being done, but I believe that this recent tendency of recovering the Jewish past is happening. For example, in Porto Alegre it is very visible, via organizations like the Marc Chagall Institute. I think this kind of activity is happening or is going to happen in other cities of the country.

NHV: So for Jewish intellectuality, not being necessarily religious does not represent an obstacle to cultural maintenance?

MS: I have a position in relation to Jewish religion. I think that Jewish religion is more religion than it is Jewish. What I mean is the following: I think that religions are more similar among themselves than different. All religions have a series of rituals, practices, penance, self-punishments, celebrations, and, in some cases, these rituals help non-religious people as well. That is, the death of a beloved person would be very difficult if there didn't exist the ritual of the funeral. The same for weddings, which become more emotional with the component of the religious ceremony. Now, the bad side of religion, in my view, is when religious people try to force other people to do what they don't want to do. And in this sense, Jewish religion has its fanatics who assume a hegemonic position and who want to control Jewish life. This is a very disturbing phenomenon, especially because it's a very disseminated phenomenon, that is, religious fundamentalism is on the rise. It would even be paradoxical that, with the greater amount of technical progress, archaic beliefs return. But I think it's exactly on account of this, that the ascension of fundamentalism is a response to modernity, to a modernity that destroys, very rapidly, traditional structures. Thus, for those people, those groups, those nations that are marginal to the process of modernization, religious fundamentalism is a response. If they do not have access to the consumer goods that modernity imposes, sometimes violently, they flee to the past to escape, in some way, the anguish of witnessing modernity and not being able to participate in it.

N HV: Now returning to the topic of Moacyr Scliar, what was your own Jewish upbringing like? In your memory, which factors actually contributed to your cultural formation?

M S: My parents were not religious. My father was a man even somewhat hostile toward religion, but he was hostile not for any ideological issue; he was hostile because he was actually polemical. It was part of his quarrel with his parents and so forth to be against religion. I studied in a Jewish school, but again I did not attend Yiddish classes, and that's because my mother was a teacher and used her influence to spare me from Yiddish. Naturally, I think that was a mistake, well intentioned, but in any event a mistake. And moreover I lived in a very Jewish neighborhood, Bom Fim. I took part in youth movements, I traveled to Israel, so Judaism was something very present in my life. And such a strong presence that there were only two or three things one could do: either to negate it completely, to say, no, I have nothing to do with this, I do not want to know about these things, which was Samuel Rawet's attitude at the end of his life; or [to] pretend that it doesn't exist, which was Clarice Lispector's attitude; or to accept it, and I opted to accept it. I don't know what led me to this, but I think it was the most honest attitude and, above all, the most positive, because each time we reject something that is part of our past, our culture, we pay a price, and I preferred to pay the price of really accepting my Jewish culture, my Jewish origins, than to pay the very high price of repelling that origin.

N HV: Taking into consideration the difference between prejudice and discrimination, did you as a Brazilian Jew ever have such an experience?

M S: Yes, I had experiences like that of having to confront discrimination and frankly, sometimes, harassment. I studied in a Catholic school; I was one of the few Jews, and at a time when anti-Semitic ideas were still very present. So for me the idea [was] that I not only was part of the group that had killed Christ but that I had killed Christ; I personally was responsible for the execution of poor Jesus. And that was a nightmare during my childhood, especially because many of my classmates were constantly reminding me of my Jewish condition. It was a very curious thing because I had a teacher at that time who was fanatically Catholic, and afterward he joined the Catholic movement of social commitment, and he wrote me a letter, saying that he recognized the errors that had been committed and he apologized. It's a phase we have overcome in Brazil because the majority of the Brazilian population discovered that the Jews are not bogeymen. And, between parentheses, one of the elements that gives me more satisfaction in my work is to discuss with young people the Jewish aspects of my literature, and to see, with pleasure, that for them many times what I write is a revelation. I don't write for them in order to propagandize Judaism, but I am content that they can discover other sides of Judaism via my books.

NHV: Why then do you write in the first place?

MS: That's a good question. I write because I cannot not write. I have another profession; I'm a medical doctor. If Jehovah materialized before me and said you can choose but only one thing, literature or medicine, I would choose medicine. Medicine is a much more direct experience. The experience mediated by words is inevitably solitary, always leaving the person with a sensation of abandonment. I understand why there are so many writers who drink, who feel despair because actually it is not an easy life. It's very exciting to have an idea, to transform it into words, but the moments of excitement in the life of a writer are relatively few. Whereas in medicine, perhaps it's even an idealized view of medicine, which I haven't practiced in a long time, the contact with the patient, the emotional exchange, this is an experience that at every instant renews one's confidence in what one is doing. Of course, medicine also has many frustrations; many times I saw my patients die, and that caused very deep despair. I really miss the time when I treated patients.

NHV: As for literature, who is your reader, to whom do you direct your prose?

MS: I don't know, I . . . when I had few readers, I knew who they were. [laughter] Today, fortunately or unfortunately, the number of readers [has] increased greatly; I no longer know how to characterize the group of people who read me. But I think I know . . . the reader for whom I write is a person who likes to hear stories and who has a sense of humor and who is sensitive and intelligent. And this reader has to have money to buy books. [laughter] But that goes without saying.

NHV: Would you say there exists a link between your prose and the Yiddish tradition as in writers like Peretz or Singer?

MS: Well, I won't dare to say that I am a continuator of that tradition, but I would like to be. Yes and no. I think in Singer's case, he resented that transplanted Judaism; I think Singer is a displaced writer of Eastern Europe. If one is to talk about Jewish writers in the Diaspora, then I am more a Michael Gold, for example. And I am even more Phillip Roth during his early phase, prior to his intellectualization. To that tradition, I am assuredly bound.

NHV: In our times of feminism and postfeminism, the image of the Jewish woman is often a traditional one. How do you portray women in your books?

MS: Well, in this case, you have to remember that I am a gaucho as well. I grew up in a culture that—not so much now—was very macho. It's a patriarchal culture; the man is the principal figure, the patriarch. In my head, along with that figure was the figure of the Jewish mother, the overprotective mother, nurturer, and I had a model in my own house because my mother was a very typical Jewish mother. I believe that the image of the woman in literature has evolved greatly, to such a point that I would say that today literature in large part deals with feminine issues. Of course, women are present in my literature, but I am obliged to admit that the figures more present in my work are masculine. Sometimes I [have] tried to construct fiction around feminine characters, but in truth the masculine experience continues to be very strong in my case.

NHV: Do you believe that the theme of the Holocaust is going to continue to be a main theme? You have treated this topic in your work, and, interestingly, some of the new generation of writers, who did not experience the Holocaust directly, write about it as well. What implications does the Holocaust have for a country like Brazil?

MS: I had the not very sensible idea that fifty years after the end of World War II the theme of the Holocaust was going to lose much of its potency. It's a surprise to me that the Holocaust is so present, but it's also explainable. The truth is that it was a transcendent experience, because of its drama, because of the horror it inspired. I believe my generation is one marked by the Holocaust. It's a generation that endured the Holocaust, had some proximity with it, but the images of the Holocaust and the accounts of the Holocaust profoundly marked my generation and I think that appears, albeit in indirect form, in the literature of Jewish writers of my generation. And this leads to the question about how one deals with the Holocaust—one deals with the Holocaust by talking about it in literature. Many people ask themselves, and I think, up to a certain point, it's a relevant question, whether words authentically represent what the Holocaust was, and, for the survivors of the Holocaust, if perhaps the most dignified response would be silence. I don't know how to say anything about this, I only know that the Holocaust inevitably implies a mission and that mission is not to let this happen again. Not only in relation to Jews, but in relation to all the groups that, in one form or another, are massacred.

N H V: In your early books, you used allegory a great deal. Do you still feel the need to use allegory today?

M S: No longer. This shows that writers evolve. Allegory was very current, not when I began to write but when I began to get published, especially because of magical realism and fantastic realism. Also, I was very influenced by writers who used, if not allegory, at least metaphor, or the parable, as is the case of Franz Kafka. However, as a writer matures, he changes, and in my case, maturity meant, paradoxically, a return to realism. Today I do not need to create characters who fly in order to write fiction. I believe one has to search for supra-real elements within reality, the elements that one would be able to synthesize within circumscribed situations that especially speak about the human being.

N H V: In the 1970s, that period many times dictated a bent toward allegory, isn't that so? For example, The Carnival of the Animals is a political book.

M S: Yes, exactly, I had forgotten to mention that. Censorship, the rejection of the freedom of speech, many times conditions the use of the metaphor, symbolism, and literature between the lines. Borges summarized this very well when he said that the dictatorship is a stimulant for the nation. In fact, during a period such as the military dictatorship in Brazil, there existed a tendency to resort to metaphorical literature.

NHV: You said that you're no longer very interested in creating allegorical characters, but the fantastic, at least during the 1980s, did not disappear, because we have novels such as your *Centaur in the Garden*.

MS: Yes, it's true. Afterward, I wrote another book, *Scenes of the Miniscule Life*, in which the characters are miniscule. But curiously, in my recent *Majesty of the Xingu*, no longer is there any of that. However, there are the character's fantasies, and these fantasies provide this supra-real element, which in the other books were an integral part of the plot.

NHV: Leaving the fantastic element aside, in *The Centaur in the Garden*, one of the main themes is hybridity, in socially ethnic terms and so on. Would you comment along these lines? Why a hybrid figure such as the centaur?

MS: It's very hybrid; it's hybrid in the way it's portrayed; it's a creature half human, half equine, but it's hybrid because it's an element of Greek culture, introduced into other cultures, and in my case, Jewish culture. It's really very hybrid. The figure of the centaur addresses something very present in people's lives, which is the conflict between two natures. With the centaur it's the animal and the human natures. However, I used the centaur to speak of other conflicts, the conflict between Jewish culture and Brazilian identity, the conflict between the condition of the well-behaved middle class and the character's impulses to free himself, even sexually. I appropriated the figure of the centaur because it's a very powerful one.

NHV: By the way, I think that this novel is a very useful example of a multicultural Brazil, and I am also referring to your novel *The Volunteers*, in which you have diverse ethnic groups, diverse voices. Do you see Brazil as a multicultural country?

MS: I don't have the slightest doubt that Brazil is a multicultural country. Now for a long time the majority of cultures within Brazil were stifled cultures. For example, when one thinks that *capoeira* (the Afro-Brazilian bodily assault and dance form) was prohibited by the bourgeoisie, that *maxixe* could not be danced, that Afro-Brazilian cults were persecuted, that immigrants were treated with disdain, that women had no place in society, one realizes that there were many stifled voices within Brazilian culture. I think one indication of Brazil's maturity is this democratization of culture, which allows all voices to be heard.

N H V: At some point you stated that the Jewish presence is important to Latin America literature?

M S: I think that the Jewish presence is important in Latin America. Not quantitatively but above all for what it represents. When one thinks that the Jews were present since the first moments in Latin American history, as Latin America and not Indian territory, and if one sees the importance of the Inquisition, of the importance the Jews had in various sectors of the culture, one notices that it really is a human group whose expression far exceeds the actual number of people. It's a group of small size but one of much repercussion. So it is not strange that the Jews be represented in Latin American literature in much greater proportion than their number.

N H V: Regarding Jewish thematics, I notice how, for example, in the works of Samuel Rawet or Clarice Lispector, the theme of belonging or exile frequently reappears. Are you concerned with this notion of belonging?

M S: I used to be preoccupied with that. The young person has the need to belong and to be a part of a group. Maturity is a process in which one can learn to live with oneself. Young people are very conscious of their own precariousness as people, ergo the need to integrate oneself within a group, a religion, a people, a party. Now, in the case of Judaism, as in other groups that were persecuted throughout history, the notion of belonging, to be part of a group, was a very important one because one had to know whom one could trust. And at times that stance was accompanied by some degree of paranoia with regard to the stranger, the goy, in the Jewish case. In Judaism the meaning of the word *goy* is very interesting, for it's a much more frightening word than the word *gentio* (gentile) in Portuguese. By definition, goy is an enemy, a threatening creature. So it was crucial to know who was a goy—them and us. But as the Jewish community matures, this notion is losing its importance. Thus the goy is no longer so threatening, so one's daughter can now marry a goy, which in the past was a catastrophe, a betrayal, and it is not surprising that many religious

Jews considered the son or daughter who married someone outside the group as having died. They would say the prayer of the dead for them. But today this is no longer happening. Of course, this change is going to dilute Judaism, but I also think that it opens a door, in terms of human relations, which is a very great improvement.

NHV: One last question: Would you like to make one final comment on the question of the Jewish writer and the word, language, the importance of the word?

MS: This is exactly the comment to finalize this interview. What I want to say is the following: after so many years of writing, what I value most is the word. Suddenly I realize that words are very precious, that a word is not only a series of letters one puts on the computer screen or on a sheet of paper. Behind every word there exists a whole history; that word, while it was being pronounced or written by millions of beings before us, in some way it summarizes all those experiences, all those emotions. I have a very great affection for the word. To say things with the right words, right in the intellectual sense, is the great feat for the writer. Today what bothers me most in a text is the fact that it is badly written. On the other hand, what I most value in a text is the fact that the words are transmitting exactly the ideas and the emotions. In other words, this means [that the words] give value to the poetic dimension of literature. I am not a poet; for a long time I was indifferent to poetry, but I now read poetry more and more because I am moved by this search, at times painful, for the word that is going to say precisely what one wants to say.

# Marcos Iolovitch

Marcos Iolovitch was born in Russia in 1907 and emigrated to Brazil with his family, under the auspices of the philanthropic Jewish Colonization Association (JCA), during the early part of the twentieth century to work on the Quarto Irmãos farm in the southern state of Rio Grande do Sul. Very little detail is known about Iolovitch's life except the semiautobiographical events dramatized in his novel, *Numa clara manhã de Abril* (1940) (On a Clear April Morning). Considered to be the earliest fictional account of this emigration, which took Jewish immigrants from Russia to the harsh interior of Rio Grande do Sul and then later to their final settlement in the capital city of Porto Alegre, this novel stands as an invaluable documentary narrative according to Moacyr Scliar in his preface to the novel's 1987 second edition. The confessional tone of this narrative reveals the extreme hardships and trials suffered by the narrator and his family—hunger, poverty, death, hard labor, family conflicts, social pressures, and alienation. The sincerity of the narrator's voice gives credence to the memoir/memorialist nature of the novel and at the same time critically conveys the immigrants' frustrations with the JCA. The excerpts translated here from the early part of the novel dramatize the heartrending departure from Russia, the struggle on the farm, and the early days of their settlement in the city.

# Marcos Iolovitch

EXCERPTS FROM *On a Clear April Morning*

# I

On a clear April morning in the year 19 . . . when the steppes had begun
to turn green with the happy coming of spring, in Zagradowka, a small
and cheerful Russian village in the province of Kersan, very pretty
circulars with colorful illustrations were scattered about, describing
the excellence of the climate, the fertility of the land, the richness and
the variety of the fauna, the beauty and the exuberance of the flora,
of a vast and faraway country in America, named—BRAZIL—where
a Jewish colonization enterprise, titled the Jewish Colonization Association, better known as the JCA, owner of a large parcel of land
called 'Quatro Irmãos,' located in the municipality of Boa Vista do
Erechim, in the state of Rio Grande do Sul, offered settlements of
land, by means of advantageous propositions, to whomever wanted
to become a farmer.

In the wintertime, when the waters of the Schisterni River were
transformed into a thick and polished mass of ice, the youth of the
village used to ice-skate there. Situated on the left bank of the river,
Zagradowka rested far from civilization, forgotten by the world, abandoned by the government, and entrusted to its own fate, as were other
innumerable settlements of the extinct czarist empire that found themselves dispersed across the immeasurable vastness of the steppes.

Its inhabitants, simple people, unlearned and of primitive customs,
made their living peacefully from commerce and agriculture.

A large main street, cut by various cross streets, divided the place
in half. Almost at the end of the road, at the point where it separated
into two roads that proceeded to the different borders, there arose a
small church in the center of a circular garden. At the entrance to the
settlement, and on the right-hand side for one coming from the river,

stood my father's store. And on the same side, at the other end of the
street, next to the church, stood the store belonging to his stepfather,
the oldest and the richest merchant of wheat in that region, whom my
grandmother, in a second marriage, wed three years after the death
of her first husband.

Orphaned when he was eight years old, my father began to work
in his stepfather's establishment, behind whose counter he spent his
adolescence, obtaining in exchange some savings. At nineteen he got
married and opened, on his own, a modest store.

Of frank disposition and very kindhearted, he enjoyed wide esteem
among his countrymen, leading a practically carefree life. When his
shelves began to empty, he would go by sleigh to Krivgorog to shop in
order to replenish his establishment. And in this manner his life glided
by placidly, always within the same rhythm, without surprises.

But as the years went by and with the arrival of children, he began
to worry about their future.

Upon reading the circulars, the populace awoke from their customary quietude, causing the most absurd commentaries about the
truthfulness of the information and the geographic location of Brazil. On that day, and during the next, one didn't talk about anything
else. It was the obligatory topic of conversation everywhere. In the
pharmacy, in the stores, in the synagogue, and mainly at the weekly
Friday market.

Some of Zagradowka's inhabitants were not unaware of the existence
of a free and fabulously rich land called America, of which they had
a very vague and nebulous idea. But they had never heard of Brazil,
and for that reason it appeared to them as nothing more than a mere
legend, created by the imagination of some adventurers.

Father also had little education; however, he had no doubts about
what the announcements said. He possessed an unlimited belief in
the good faith of men. He had this faith because he read and reread,
with growing interest, the propagandistic pamphlets. And he ended
up becoming joyfully enthusiastic about the description of the new
land. Especially because of the colorful illustration on the cover.

The cover of the circulars displayed a simple landscape of Brazilian rural life.

Beneath a clear and distant sky, of a very soft blue, a farmer, in a
wide-brim hat, a white shirt with rolled-up sleeves, bent over, grabbed

the handles of a plow, pulled by a yoke of oxen, turning over the virgin land. A bit in the distance, in the background, the vegetal gold of extensive ripe wheat fields. But beyond, bluish in the distance, coconut and palm trees and mysterious forests. And at the forefront, standing out in bright and robust colors, an orchard in which orange trees predominated and under whose shade pigs were eating beautiful oranges that had fallen to the ground.

This small picture had impressed him profoundly.

He didn't like the business of exploiting naive peasants. However, agriculture seduced him. He deemed it to be one of the cleanest and most honorable professions. Therefore, he wanted his children, who were all he-men, to follow this path. In this way he thought he could assure them a splendid future by making them into farmers. In time, he thought, they would marry. They would become a large family. They would all live together, leading a happy life in a tranquil corner of a virgin world.

In Brazil he saw the providential land for the realization of his plans.

He spent some time intimately caressing the beauty of this dream. He wasn't inspired to reveal it to anybody. He would spend his spare time pondering the colorful pamphlet cover and the orange trees.

The oranges in Russia were imported. They'd come packed in boxes and wrapped in tissue paper like the California apples that arrived here. And they were very expensive.

He would gaze at the wheat field, symbol of abundance. And he imagined himself a farmer, tilling the land with his children, far away, very far away in a distant country called Brazil.

Finally having decided to change his life, he shared with his wife his resolution to leave Russia in order to become a farmer in America.

Mother protested vehemently, invoking sentimental reasons. She wasn't going to leave her parents, relatives, and friends to go seek adventure in a country whose existence she doubted. However, her objections did not dissuade him from his decision. And to make his decision irrevocable, he announced, a little later, the selling of his establishment. He took stock of what he had. And set the date of departure.

On the designated day, the whole village turned out to give us their wishes for a safe journey and to say good-bye.

I and my brothers were placed in a wagon filled with baggage, while my parents said good-bye.

With great difficulty they managed to disengage themselves from the long and sentimental embraces of their friends and relatives. With their eyes filled with tears, they held close to their heart each one of the people present, trying in vain to hide their premonition that each of those embraces was the last one they would ever give in their lives.

Having said good-bye, they sat down on the front seat of the wagon, which began to move slowly.

The repressed sobs burst forth from the bosoms of those friends. The lament became widespread. Men and women lowered their heads, drying their eyes. And a bunch of handkerchiefs and hats waved in the morning light.

Some relatives began to accompany us at a distance, while the vehicle very slowly moved away, leaving behind two parallel grooves on the straight and seldom-used road, which stretched like a dark ribbon until it could no longer be seen on the flat, open plains.

Only many, many years later did I come to understand the meaning of two parallel lines . . .

After having gained a fair distance, Papa turned his gaze for the last time upon his native village.

The multitude of friends and relatives had dispersed. The village stayed behind in the distance.

Chimneys unfolded slow batches of feathery smoke in the chilly morning air. The cadence of a distant motor and the unhurried fall of a hammer on the anvil synchronically accompanied the sluggish rise of the day, which the sun was flooding with the joy of its light. Only one handkerchief, like the wing of a wounded bird, was slowly moving in the air.

Who would have remained there, waving repeatedly from the same place?

He squinted his eyes a little to see better.

It was a handkerchief, left by someone, stuck on a bush that the wind was moving, giving the impression that the steppe itself, which had seen him born and now was seeing him depart toward an uncertain destiny, was saying to him, in the silent eloquence of its sad gesture, its final good-bye . . .

# III

From the Island of Flores we proceeded to Erebango, district of Boa Vista of Erechim, the final point of our destination.

Of this last stage of our voyage, for me no other remembrance remained except the cold and rainy night of our arrival in Erebango, where we were picked up by a settler who gave us shelter in his home until the day the shed for the immigrants, under construction, was finished.

One of the first visitors we received in the new land was Death, which took away forever the youngest of my brothers.

My parents had gone to visit a family that lived at some distance, and they took him with them. Returning home, they took a wrong turn and got lost in a forest, where they were forced to stay overnight. On the following morning when they arrived home, the child was feverish. A few days later he passed away.

I still remember well the day of his death.

In the backyard, seated on a pine log, Mama was crying. Near her, in silence, letting his heavy tears fall on the boards he was nailing, Papa was making the coffin for his dead son. Each nail he banged into the wood was as if he were burying it into his heart. A little farther ahead, I and my brother Daniel contemplated that painful scene without really understanding.

Mama called us. Hugged us. She squeezed us tightly against her heart, caressing us. And after covering us with kisses mixed with tears, she raised her eyes toward the serene and clear sky, begging God in ardent prayer that he spare us.

The coffin completed, they placed the cadaver inside. Luiz, the oldest of my brothers, mounted a horse, and my father brought him the casket in which a piece of his life was going to be buried.

On the way from the cemetery, which was very far away, Mama's lamentations exploded. She called for her son in loud cries, exclaiming: 'Don't take my son . . . Beijinho, my dear Beijinho, why are you leaving your poor mother?'

Papa hugged her and led her inside the house. Both of them took off their sandals, sat on the hard ground of beaten clay, and moving their chests back and forth, they began to pray, chanting in Hebrew

the saddest lament I heard in my life, the old funereal chant of the
Jewish people.

Once the sacramental days of mourning of the Jewish funerary ritual
ended, we moved to the lodgings for immigrants. It was a wooden shed
that housed under its uninsulated roof about eight families. It didn't
have walled rooms. The 'rooms' were made with sheets, which the ten-
ants extended like walls in order to have a pale illusion of privacy.

Communal life in the shed was not always sad.

A little baby, more or less one year old, awakened one night by
hunger, began in the dark to search for the breast of its mother, who
was sleeping by its side. And by mistake it brought its avid little mouth
to the breast of a young girl. Feeling the voluptuous pressure of the
lips on her bosom, she let out an instinctive cry, waking up everybody
in the shed.

That mistake conveys the size of the space that separated the ten-
ants at night.

We waited many months for the demarcation of our settlement. And
while we waited, we went on using the remainder of the scanty savings,
since the voyage from Russia had been made at our expense.

When the day arrived for us to take possession of our land, we boarded a wagon pulled by a pair of horses and started on our journey.

The day was somber, with the threat of rain.

As we reached the main road, a strong downpour fell, drowning
in a pail hanging in back of the vehicle a brood of chicks we were
bringing with us.

Papa was at the front of the wagon driving the animals. At his side,
withdrawn and silent, sat Mama.

When the rain stopped, the clouds dissolved, showing a glimpse
of washed pieces of the sky. And the sun reappeared, spreading a
restorative joy over the wet fields.

After many hours of travel, we entered a forest through a recently
hewed trail. At a certain point in the road—I don't know why—the
horses got frightened and began to run wildly, threatening at each
moment to overturn the wagon, which miraculously maintained its
balance.

Mama threw herself toward the back, grabbing us, while Papa pulled
the reins, yelling: hold on, hold on . . .

Terrified birds fled. Once in a while, a reptile rapidly crossed the road and disappeared into the woods. Tree branches hanging out over the road whizzed by, beating us on the face and head.

On the opposite side of the woods, when we got to a small incline in the middle of the countryside, the horses were forced to stop. During our flight we had lost a basket with sweet bread brought from Russia. Later we lamented this loss a great deal because the bread the settlers gave us was very bitter . . .

We rested a bit and continued our march, arriving at our destination a little before nightfall.

Seated around a campfire with some burning pieces of firewood, several men were drinking maté tea.

Not knowing how to speak Brazilian, Papa greeted them with a timid nod of his head, to which all responded. Next, a backwoodsman with a raspy gray beard, olive skin, and a gentle manner that inspired confidence got up and came over to shake our hands.

Papa handed him a letter from the administration of the enterprise, which introduced the bearer of the letter as the proprietor of the land he occupied.

After reading the letter, he pointed us to a place near the fire. The circle of men around the fire squeezed together to give us room. And the men resumed the conversation interrupted by our arrival.

A farm hand unhitched the animals and transported our baggage to the shed.

Night was falling.

In the sanguine sunset the afternoon was in decline. The first shadows from the valleys and the meadows dragged themselves over the slopes and slowly covered the mountains. A great silence, broken only by the gurgling murmur of a nearby creek, by the sorrowful peeps of lost birds, and by the harmonic dissonance of the buzzing of insects and the croaking of frogs, raised itself from the land, spilling a soothing, sober, and deep peace over the melancholy solitude of the fields.

Finally we were in possession of our land.

Some days later, the occupant of this land gathered his men and goods and left in search of another resting place.

The farm hands went ahead, prodding a herd of swine and cattle. He was the last to depart, leaving us a beautiful dog as a souvenir.

In the settlement colony we spent three years of great hardship. A rough life of effort and failure. And we were vanquished in the fight against the land, each of us experiencing his or her baptism in blood.

On account of a fall from a horse, Davi fractured an arm. Solon cut himself in the foot with an unfortunate stroke of the ax. Papa was wounded by a steer. I was almost torn to pieces by a diamond-shaped grating with iron teeth when I was steering a team of oxen, reducing the tilled soil into clumps of dirt. Today I still have on my left shoulder an enormous scar. It's an indelible souvenir of this accident.

We neither knew how to tame the cattle nor how to treat the land. And the result was a real disaster.

But my saddest memory of our lives as failed farmers was the loss of another little brother.

It was a warm afternoon in the summer.

I was in the cattle chute, collecting the horsehair that the animals left on the barbed-wire fence, and with which I braided reins for my little wooden horses.

Since evening I had been awaiting the return of my parents, who had gone by wagon with their youngest to the district headquarters to visit our neighbor who was sick in the hospital.

Suddenly in the distance I saw two figures walking, followed by a wagon. Despite the distance, I recognized them right away. I dropped my toys and ran to meet them. But as I approached, my joy was transformed into a sad presentiment.

Held up by my father, and with indecisive steps, Mama arrived, crying. And both of them were completely wet, with their clothes sticking to their bodies.

'You lost one more brother,' said Mama, sobbing, without hugging me.

Only then did I notice the absence of my brother.

As Mama came closer to the house, she was losing her strength. Climbing the hill, she fainted. Papa carried her into the house in his arms. He put her down in the room. And sprinkled her face with water and vinegar.

As she regained her senses, she became delirious, calling for her son.

That was when I learned how the accident had happened.

As they were returning from the clinic, when they were crossing the last bridge, the oxen became startled and tipped over the wagon. Mama, with her son in her lap, fell into the river. It happened so quickly that Papa barely had time to jump out of the vehicle to see his wife and son being devoured by the waters. That vision left him for a few seconds on the bridge completely petrified, immobile as a statue.

Feeling herself being dragged by the water, since the current was strong underneath the bridge, Mama, in an instinctive gesture of self-defense, raised her arms, grabbing onto one of the tree branches grazing the surface of the river. Seeing her struggling with death, Papa threw himself into the river and managed to save her half-dead body. When they regained their senses, they noticed the absence of their son.

They searched in vain, desperately. The impetuous current of the river had dragged him far away, very, very far away.

In view of Mama's mounting delirium and hallucinating cries demanding her son, my older brothers went to the scene of the disaster to attempt another search. And for many hours they looked in vain for their drowned brother, turning upside down, in every sense, the area around the bridge and combing the course of the river. Finally, downhearted, they returned home.

Mama was sleeping. By her side, with his elbows buried in his knees, his head in his hands, Papa kept vigil. Nobody said a word. Everybody understood just by simply looking.

Luiz decided that we should go to sleep in the shed.

It was a warm and clear night. Through a wide gap in the wall of the shed, I saw emerging from the woods, edged with a pale golden halo, a semicircular light, rising and growing slowly, until it formed the shape of an enormous reddish disk.

It was the moon.

'Look how beautiful the moon is!' I exclaimed in Yiddish.

'Today no one must find anything beautiful,' Luiz admonished me.

Nevertheless, I couldn't take my eyes off the moon. And I stayed there contemplating it until I fell asleep.

Very early on the following day, my brothers returned to search for the body.

Under the fateful bridge and in the surrounding area, the bed of the river was probed without any result whatsoever. Seeing that their efforts were fruitless, they called off the search. And the waters kept forever in their treacherous bed my little brother's body.

But to console Mama, Papa and Luiz convinced her, days after the accident, that they had by chance found the body floating on the surface of the river, lost in a remote forest, when they were laying barbed wire in that spot. And since the cited place was very far from home and the body was already in an advanced stage of decomposition, they had buried it near the river.

It was necessary to invent this lie in order to console her. She could not resign herself to the painful idea that, even after his death, her son would not find rest and would be dragged perpetually through the waters, serving as nourishment for the fish and the vultures.

I also was naive to presume that there was no greater suffering than that. But when I became a man, I proved to myself that I was wrong.

And, in truth, O Mother, how small is your suffering compared to the suffering of those unfortunate mothers who, defeated by misery, see the live flesh of their daughters devoured, many times with impunity, by the vultures and sharks that fill the grand river of life! . . .

# IV

Depressed by these setbacks, defeated by the lack of experience in tilling the land, we reached a point of extreme destitution. Our remaining provisions had been reduced solely to manioc flour and sweet potatoes.

Hunting remained the last recourse for us. But this activity is forbidden by the Jewish religion, which only allows for the consumption of meat following the rigorous observance of the ritual prescribed by its laws. The food prepared according to its dietetic prescriptions is called 'kosher.' And tref is what one obtains with the violation of said laws.

As a matter of fact, my father, like generally all the Jews of the old generation, was religious. He had preferred, therefore, to endure hunger rather than to transgress one of the precepts of his multicentury faith. But in order not to allow his children to suffer the doleful consequences of his religious feelings, he decided to abandon farming and become a day worker, a job in which he was accompanied by his oldest son.

In the beginning they earned their bread as members of a road gang constructing a railroad line. Afterward they went on to work for the Jewish Colonization Association. They fenced in the settlements with barbed wire. They made holes in the ground. Set the stakes. And nailed the barbed wire.

They drew a salary, if I am not mistaken, of one penny for each excavation of sixty centimeters in depth and twenty-five in diameter.

They left for work in the early morning on Mondays and only returned late on Fridays in order to spend the Sabbath, a day of observance for the Jews, at home.

With their tools on their shoulders and on their backs knapsacks, which held a teakettle, bread made from manioc flour, a bit of coffee as well as sugar—provisions for the whole week of arduous labor— their legs bound in gunny-sack cloth, and their feet wrapped in sacks of the same material, they would leave their home, wife, children, and brothers and depart for the brutal victory of a piece of bread, like two men condemned to harsh labor. Carrying in their souls the resigned sadness of the vanquished and in their hearts the uncertainty of their return, they disappeared into the woods, sloshed around in the grassy marshes, and opened holes in the hard ground of the fields.

They worked from sunrise to sunset, exposed to the bad weather and sleeping in the open. They returned always exhausted, dirty, with their clothes soiled by red clay, their shirts torn, and their hands callused.

They looked like Volga boatmen. But instead of boats filled with cargo, they dragged the heavy weight of their misfortune, hitched to the train of misery.

And then Papa began to drink.

Oh! Volga, Volga, how ample your river banks . . .

# V

I don't know how or where Papa managed to get money for the journey. I only know that one cold wintry night we arrived in Porto Alegre.

The passengers on board the same train, after exchanging embraces with friends and relatives, began leaving the inside of the station. We were the only ones who had remained in the deserted station. We didn't know anyone, nor did anyone know us.

A railroad worker came to tell us something.

'I no understand Brazilian,' my father stuttered, complementing his thoughts with gestures.

The railroad functionary gave a discreet smile, making us understand by mimicry that it was time to close the doors of the station.

We hurriedly grabbed our baggage and left the station, then stopped indecisively on the pavement, not knowing which direction to take.

Couriers immediately drew near offering their services. Papa said no with his head, looking dazed at the busy traffic on Voluntários da Pátria Street.

Streetcars passed by filled with people. Automobiles were driving by rapidly, impatiently honking their horns. Youngsters were running around hawking the evening newspapers. Men and women, in pairs or alone, were walking briskly on the sidewalk with a somber air, worried, swelling the immense human wave that was coming and going at an uneven and accelerated pace.

A Jewish wagon driver, after a brief talk with us, saved us from that distressing experience of abandonment, taking us to his home, where he generously offered us his modest hospitality.

This merciful man still lives in Porto Alegre. However, he is almost blind. For seeing the suffering of others, God, who is infinitely good, almost took away his vision . . .

Without money and without an occupation, with a large family in a completely strange environment, Papa realized that the only course left to him was to begin his new life by way of the old one he had left behind: through the door of commerce.

He picked the occupation of fishmonger, the only one he could practice, given the conditions in which he found himself. It didn't require much capital nor any knowledge of the language.

He bought two baskets, strung them together with a large leather strap, went to the market, filled them with fish, and came back peddling his wares: 'Feeesssh . . . Feeesssh . . . Fresssh-vater feeessh . . .'

Mama, who had been waiting impatiently for him since early on, recognized his voice and ran to the window. Upon seeing him from afar, carrying the two baskets and advertising, in loud cries, his merchandise, she turned her back annoyed.

A little later, Papa arrived. He came in pleased. He removed the strap from his neck and dropped the load on the floor.

'Well,' he said, rubbing his hands and straightening up his back, 'I have already earned my keep for today. Tomorrow, God will help us again.'

Seeing his wife dejected and guessing her deep-seated disappoint-ment, he offered this justification: 'We are in America, woman. And here, any occupation serves. Honest work is not dishonor.'

And taking out a fish, he ended by changing the subject: 'Take this and prepare a good lunch. It's getting late and I still have to make a few rounds in order to sell the rest of the fish.'

Grabbing the fish unenthusiastically, Mama murmured with a sigh: 'Nice, nice exchange you made. You left your store in Russia in order to become a fishmonger in America.'

Papa didn't answer. He lowered his head, placed the strap on his neck, lifted the baskets, and, casting a reproving look at her, left the house.

His wife's complaint had hurt him deeply. He was to blame for the situation he had reached. He had made the exchange with the best of intentions. By choosing farming, he thought he was giving his children a good future. He couldn't live by exploiting others. His conscience rebelled. He wanted a productive life.

He swept away the thoughts that saddened him with the litany of his livelihood.

'Feeessh . . . Feeessh . . .'

And everyday, almost at the same hour, he would fill the streets of that neighborhood with the same refrain: 'Feeessh . . . Feeessh . . .'

# Clarice Lispector

Clarice Lispector was born in the Ukraine in 1920 and died in Rio de Janeiro in 1977. Fleeing from the pogroms in Russia, her family arrived in Brazil in 1921. After a Yiddishkeit childhood and early adolescence in the Brazilian Northeast, the family moved to Rio in 1934. Lispector resided there until 1944, when, after marriage in 1943, she traveled with her diplomat husband to the north of Brazil, then Europe and the United States until 1959. Lispector received her law degree in 1943 but never practiced as a lawyer; she had already been employed as a journalist since 1942. It is uncertain when she began her first novel, *Perto do coração selvagem* (1943) (*Near to the Wild Heart*, 1990); an auspicious literary event for Brazil, according to the critic Antônio Cândido, this work is considered today to be a watershed for women's literature in Brazil. The author of nine major novels and eight collections of stories, in addition to hundreds of *crônicas*, Lispector was also a translator and the author of four children's books. Most of her major titles (see introduction) have been translated into French, Spanish, and English. Her famous collection *Laços de família* (1960) (*Family Ties*, 1972) questions the conventional role of middle-class women and unmasks the insidious coercion to conform exerted by family and society. Epistemological, existential, and metaphysical queries permeate her work and often lead to a woman's quest for self-knowledge and self-expression, frequently achieved through writing. Although Lispector's narratives are not overtly Jewish, her texts manifest a preoccupation with the word and its power, reminiscent of Judaic hermeneutics, very evident in her last novella, *A hora da estrela* (1977) (*The Hour of the Star*, 1986). The two stories anthologized here were published only recently in a collection titled *Clarice Lispector: Outros escritos* (2005) and have never before appeared in English translation. 'Trecho' (1941) (Passage) and 'Eu e Jimmy' (1944) (Me and Jimmy) address respectively the plight or place of single mothers in society and the battle of the sexes. These tales demonstrate Lispector's insight into the female condition and point the way to her reputation as Brazil's and Latin America's premier woman writer.

# Clarice Lispector

# Passage

Actually nothing happened on that gray afternoon in April. Neverthe-less, everything predicted a grand day. He had let her know that her coming would constitute the big moment, the greatest event of their lives. For that reason she entered the avenue bar, sat down very close to one of the small tables by the window in order to see him as soon as he appeared at the corner. The waiter wiped the table and asked her what she wanted. This time in particular, she need not be timid and afraid to commit a gaffe. She was waiting for someone, she answered. He looked at her for a moment. 'Is it possible that I have such an air of being abandoned that I can't sit here waiting for someone?' She said to him: 'I'm waiting for a friend.'

And by now she knew that her voice had sounded perfect: calm and nonchalant. (Well, it wasn't the first time she was waiting for someone.) He wiped a nonexistent spot on the corner of the marble table and, after a calculated delay, replied without even looking at her: 'Yes, ma'am.'

She makes herself more comfortable in the narrow chair. She crosses her legs with a certain elegance, which Cristiano himself had said was natural to her. She holds on to her purse with her two hands, sighs calmly. Fine. It's just a matter of waiting.

Flora very much enjoys living. Very much so. On that afternoon, for example, despite her dress pinching her waist and her waiting in horror for the moment she would have to get up and cross the length of the establishment with her too tightly fitted skirt, despite all of this, she thinks it's good to be sitting there, in the middle of so many people, having a cup of coffee with some pastry, like everyone else. She has the same sensation as when she was little and her mother gave her 'real' pots and pans to fill with food and to play 'housewife.'

All the small tables in the café are full. The men smoke fat cigars and the young guys, snug in their ample jackets, offer each other cigarettes. The women have soft drinks and bite into the sweets with the daintiness of rodents, so as not to smear their lipstick. It's very hot inside, and the fans on the walls are buzzing. If she weren't dressed in black, she could imagine herself in an African café, in Dakar or Cairo, in between palm-leaf fans and dark men discussing some illicit business, for example. Even among spies—who knows?—wrapped in those Arab sheets.

Naturally it was somewhat absurd to be thinking playfully, exactly on this afternoon. Exactly when Cristiano had promised her the greatest day in the world and exactly, oh! exactly when she was afraid that nothing would happen . . . simply due to Cristiano's absence . . . It was absurd but always when 'things' happened to her, she inserted between those things perfectly futile and preposterous thoughts. When Nenê was going to be born and she was in the hospital, lying down, white and deadly afraid, she obstinately followed the flight of a fly around a teacup and in a general way got to thinking about the accidental life of flies. And in truth, she had concluded about those tiny beings that there are great studies to be done. For example: Why is it that, possessing a beautiful pair of wings, they do not fly higher? Are those wings impotent or not ideal for the flies? Another question: What's the mental attitude of flies in relation to us? And in relation to the cup of tea, that sweetish, warm, and big lake? In fact, those problems were not unworthy of attention. It is we who are not yet worthy of them.

A couple entered. The man stopped at the door; he leisurely chose the place, in order to make his way there with his wife on his arm, the ferocious air of one who prepares himself to defend a right: 'I pay as much as the others do.' He sat down, cast a look of defiance around the room. The young girl was timid and smiled at Flora, a smile of class solidarity.

Well, the time is flying. The waiter with the blond moustache approached Flora, acrobatically holding a tray with a dark drink in a sweaty glass. Without asking her anything, he sets down the tray, places the glass near her hands, and goes away. But who ordered a soft drink, she thinks anxiously. She remains quiet without moving. Oh! Cristiano, come soon. Everybody against me . . . I don't want a soft drink; I want Cristiano! I feel like crying because today is a big day, because today is the greatest day of my life. But I'm going to contain within some small, hidden corner of myself (behind the door? how absurd) everything that worries me until Cristiano's arrival. I'm going to think about something. About what? 'Ladies and Gentlemen, Ladies and Gentlemen! Here I am ready for life! Ladies and Gentlemen, nobody looks at me; nobody notices that I exist. But, Ladies and Gentlemen, I do exist; I swear that I exist! Very much, indeed. Look, you who all have this air of triumph, look: I am capable of vibrating like the stretched string of a harp. I can suffer more intensely than all of you. I am superior. And do you know why? Because I know that I exist.' And what if I drank the soft drink? At least that woman who is looking at her as though she weren't there, as though she were a small, empty table, would see that she is doing something.

She carefully selects a straw, unwraps it with nonchalant gestures, and slurps the first gulp. It's a good thing that Nenê didn't come. The drink is ice cold, and everything that Nenê sees she wants to taste. When Cristiano shows up, will he ask her first about herself or Nenê? Cristiano said that both of them were children, that in the group he was the only adult. But that doesn't sadden Flora. Once, right at the beginning, he left her seated in a corner of the room and began to walk from one side to the other, rubbing his chin. Afterward he stopped in front of her, looked at her for some time, and said: 'But you are a little girl!'

Nevertheless, afterward he got used to it and Flora always pleased him. Precisely because, since she was a little girl, she knew how to play at everything. With Ruivo she pretended to be a soldier who kills; with the neighbor downstairs she was a wagon driver; at school she pretended to be an Indian who has many children, and even a teacher, a housewife, a bad neighbor, a beggar, a cripple, and a street vendor of sweets. With Ruivo she pretended to be a soldier, forced by circumstances, because she needed to win his admiration.

In this way, it was not difficult to play at being Cristiano's lover. And she played so well that, before leaving, he told her: 'You know, kid, you are worth more than I thought. You are not a little girl, no. You are a woman full of sense and independence.'

She liked Cristiano's compliments, as when he had complimented her on her new dress. Or when the French teacher had said to her: 'You weel bee yet a goood poette!' Or when her mother said: 'When "that one" grows up, she's going to catch anyone she wants!' Well now, of course, she knew how to do different things and even very well. But she wasn't any one of those personalities who played a role in order to have a good time or out of necessity. Flora was something else that no one had yet discovered! There's the mystery.

The soft drink disagrees with her horribly. Her stomach becomes queasy. For a moment she closes her eyes and sees the dark liquid in rising waves, flowing and flowing again, roaring. And Cristiano doesn't show up. She's been there for an hour. If Cristiano were to arrive at that moment she would have him order something bitter, and her nausea would disappear. Afterward, he would proudly say: 'I really don't know what you would do alone. You come up with things exactly at the inopportune time.' And why suddenly this taste of coffee in my mouth? She waves to the waiter. 'Ice water,' she orders. After the first swallow, she perks up.

'What kind of soft drink was it?'

'Coffee flavor, miss.'

Ah, coffee. Oh, she felt worse. The waiter looks at her curiously and ironically.

'Are you feeling better, mademoiselle?'

'Yes, of course, I didn't feel anything.'

'Drink a cup of hot coffee and everything will go away,' he said tenaciously.

'Bring me some, please.'

'Cristiano where are you? I am small, Ladies and Gentlemen, down deep I am Nenê's size. You don't know who Nenê is? Well, she is blond, she has black eyes, and Cristiano says he isn't surprised when he sees her little face very dirty. He says that in our messy room the fresh flowers, Nenê's small face, and my air of being a 'poor dear' are indivisible. But there is something in my stomach. And Cristiano doesn't show up. What if Cristiano doesn't show up? The landlady of the house where we live, Ladies and Gentlemen, swears that the abandonment of young unwed girls with children is common. She even knows three cases. What are you saying? Oh, don't smoke now.'

The waiter comes with the coffee. He has a beautiful blond moustache.

'If I were you, I'd try to get rid of the soft drink. All you have to do is place two fingers in the roof of your mouth. The "toilette" is on the left.'

Flora returns from there humiliated and doesn't dare to look at the blond moustache. She leans back against the chair and feels miserably well.

A fresh breeze comes through the windows. 'Mussolini's Declarations. Suicide in Leblon! Here ye, the evening newspaper!' Faraway sounds of car horns. Cristiano missed his train, or he abandoned me forever.

The café became familiar in her eyes. The waiters are after all foolish and very busy men. They are arranging the chairs on the stage for the orchestra, wiping the piano. Customers from another class, from the class of those who, after their bath and dinner, 'need to enjoy life while they are young; and why does one have money anyway?' install themselves at the small tables.

'This means that I'm a lost woman,' Flora thinks.

At first she hears some small, muted beats, cadenced, singular, and mysterious, coming up from the stage of the orchestra. In mounting effervescence, like little animals popping up in an unknown environment, the beat is being accentuated. And suddenly from the last Negro in the second row, a wild and prolonged cry rises, until it dies in a sweet lament. The mulatto in the first row twists into a spin; his instrument points up to the air and responds with a husky and childish 'boo-boo.' The small beats seem like men and women swaying at an African voodoo ritual. Suddenly, silence. The piano plays three spontaneous and solemn notes. Silence.

The orchestra in soothing tempo, almost immobile, cowering, floats a blue, pianissimo fox trot, as insinuating as a fugue.

Some couples were leaving arm in arm.

I have been here for so long, so long! Flora reflects, and she feels that she must cry. This means that I'm a lost woman. She presses her forehead with her hands. What's going to happen now? The waiter feels sorry for her and comes to tell her that she can wait as along as she wants. Thank you. She sees herself in the mirror. But is she the one who's sitting there? Is she that girl with the expression of a frightened rabbit, who is thinking and waiting? (Whose little mouth is that? Whose small eyes are those? Hers; don't bother me). If I don't try to save myself, I'll drown. After all, if Cristiano doesn't show up, who will tell all these people that I exist? And if suddenly I were to shout at the waiter and ask for paper and ink and then were to say:

Ladies and Gentlemen, I'm going to write a poem! Cristiano, dear! I swear that I and Nenê belong to you.

'Just imagine: Debussy was a poet-musician, but such a poet that just one title of his suites makes one want to lie down in the backyard grass, arms under one's head, and dream. Just imagine: Bells in the trees. Perfumes of the night . . . Just imagine . . . A thin woman shouted at the neighboring table, banging the backs of her hands on the table, as if she were saying: 'I swear to you, now it's nighttime. Don't argue.'

'Nonsense, Margarida,' retorted one of the men coldly, 'nonsense.' Well, poet-musician . . . Just look . . .

Flora would ask for paper and would write:
'Silent trees
astray along the road.
Quiet refuge
of coolness and shade.'

Cristiano will not be coming. A man approaches. What's up? 'Huh?'

'I'm asking if you want to dance,' he continues. He blinks his myopic eyes in a silly and strange manner.

'Oh, no . . . Really, no . . . I . . .' He continues to look at her.

'Frankly, I can't . . . Oh, maybe later . . . I'm waiting for a friend.' He still standing. What to do with that rubble? My God, it's my eyes.

'I don't . . .'

'Please, madam, I already got the message,' said the offended man.

He goes away. What happened, after all? I don't know, I don't know. If I don't lower my face, they see my eyes. Silent trees astray along the road. Oh, surely I'm not crying because of the myopic man. Also, it's not because of Cristiano, who will never, ever come. It's on account of that quiet woman at the next table; it's because Nenê is beautiful, beautiful; it's because those flowers have a lingering perfume. Quiet refuge of coolness and shade. 'Ladies and Gentlemen, exactly now that I have so much to say, I don't know how to express myself. I am a grievous and serious woman, Ladies and Gentlemen. I have a daughter, Ladies and Gentlemen. I could be a good poet. I could catch whomever I wanted. I know how to play at everything, Ladies and Gentlemen. Right now I could get up and make a speech against humanity, against life. Ask the government to establish a department for abandoned and saddened women who will never, ever have anything to do in the world. Ask for some urgent reform. But I can't, Ladies and Gentlemen. And for that same reason, there will never be any reforms. It's that instead of shouting, of protesting, I only feel like crying very softly and remaining quiet, speechless. Maybe it's not just because of all that. My skirt is short and tight. I'm not going to get up from here. In compensation I have a small handkerchief with little red dots, and I can very well dry my nose without you, Ladies and Gentlemen, who don't even know I exist, ever noticing.'

At the entrance a tall man appears with newspapers in his hand. He looks all around, looking for somebody. That man is coming exactly in Flora's direction. He presses her hand, sits down. He looks at her with his bright eyes, and she confusingly hears . . . 'Honey, you poor thing . . . the train . . . Nenê . . . darling . . . ?'

'Nonsense, Margarida, nonsense,' says the man at the next table.

'Do you want something?' Cristiano asks. 'A soft drink?'

'Oh, no,' Flora answers. The waiter smiles.

Cristiano, completely happy, lightly squeezes her knee underneath the table. And Flora decides that never, ever again is she going to forgive Cristiano for the humiliation she suffered. And if he hadn't shown up? Ah, then all that waiting would have a reason; it would make sense. But, this way? Never, never. To rebel, to fight, that's for sure. It's important that Flora, unknown to everybody, finally emerges.

'Flora, I missed you so, so much.'

'My dearest . . .' Flora says sweetly, forgetting her short and tight skirt.

# Clarice Lispector

# Me and Jimmy

I still remember Jimmy, that boy with disheveled brown hair covering the elongated cranium of a true-born rebel.

I remember Jimmy, his hair, and his ideas. Jimmy thought that nothing exists as good as what's natural. That if two people like each other, there is nothing to do but to love each other, simple as that. That everything else in men that moves away from that simplicity at the beginning of the world is showing off; it's froth. If those ideas came from some other head, I wouldn't stand to even listen to them. But there was the excuse of Jimmy's brain, and above all, there was the excuse of his bright teeth and his clean smile of a happy creature.

Jimmy used to walk around with his head held high, his nose up in the air, and when crossing the street, he would grab me by the arm with a very naive intimacy. I became troubled. But the proof that I was already at that time imbued with Jimmy's ideas and, above all, with his bright smile, is that I would chide myself for feeling troubled. Discontent, I thought that I had developed too much, distancing myself from the standard—animal. I told myself that it was futile to blush on account of an arm, even less a sleeve of clothes. But those thoughts were diffuse and presented themselves with the incoherence I am now transmitting on paper. In truth, I was merely looking for an excuse to like Jimmy. And to follow his ideas. Little by little I was adapting myself to his elongated head. What could I do, after all? Ever since I was small, I had seen and felt the predominance of men's ideas over those of women. According to Aunt Emilia, before getting married Mother was a spitfire, a tempestuous redhead with her own ideas on freedom and equality for women. But Papa, very serious and tall, also came with his own ideas on . . . freedom and equality for women. The bad thing was the coincidence of the subject. There was a clash. And today Mother sews and embroiders and sings at the piano and makes little cakes on Saturdays, everything on time and with joy. She still has her own ideas, but they are summarized into one: the wife must always follow the husband, like the accessory follows the essential (the comparison is mine, the result of my law classes).

For that reason and Jimmy, I also became natural little by little.

And that's how one beautiful day, after a hot summer night, in which I slept as much as this moment that I am writing (these are the antecedents to the crime), on that beautiful day, Jimmy gave me a kiss. I foresaw that situation, with all the variables. He disappointed me, it's true. Well, 'that' after so much philosophy and delays! But I liked it. And from that time on I slept restfully; I didn't need to dream anymore.

I used to meet Jimmy on the corner. I would give him my arm very naturally. And later, very naturally, I would caress his disheveled hair. I felt that Jimmy was amazed by my improvement. His lessons had produced a rare effect, and the student was diligent. It was a happy time.

Afterward we took our exams. The actual story begins here.

One of the examiners has soft, deep eyes. Very beautiful hands, dark. (Jimmy was white as a baby.) When he spoke to me, his voice became mysteriously rough and warm. And I made an enormous effort not to close my eyes and not to die of joy.

There were no inner battles. I slept very well. I would meet with the examiner at six o'clock in the afternoon. And his voice charmed me, speaking to me about ideas absolutely non-Jimmiesque. All that enveloped by the twilight, in the silent and cold garden.

I was at the time absolutely happy. As for Jimmy, he continued to be disheveled and with the same smile so that I had forgotten to explain the new situation to him.

One day he asked me why I was behaving so differently. I answered him cheerfully, using Hegel's terms, gleaned from the mouth of my examiner. I told him that the original equilibrium had been broken, and a new one with another base had been formed. It's useless to say that Jimmy didn't understand anything because Hegel was subject matter for the end of the syllabus and we never got to that point. I then explained to him that I was very much in love with D . . . , and, in a marvelous moment of inspiration (I was sorry the examiner didn't hear me), I said to him that, given the situation, I would not be able to unite the contradictions, reaching a Hegelian synthesis. Useless to digress.

Jimmy looked at me dumbfoundedly and only knew to ask: 'And me?'

I got irritated.

'I don't know,' I responded, kicking an imaginary stone and thinking: well, that's your problem! We are simple animals.

Jimmy was nervous. He made a series of insults, that I was nothing but a woman, inconstant and a butterfly like all the others. And he threatened me: I was going to be sorry for that sudden change of behavior. I tried in vain to explain myself with his theories: I loved somebody and it was natural, only that; that if I were 'cultivated' and 'thoughtful' I would begin to make everything complicated, displaying moral conflicts, civilized silliness, things that are absolutely unknown to animals. I spoke with admirable eloquence, all due to the dialectical influence of the examiner (here's Mama's idea: the woman must follow . . . etc.). Jimmy, pale and destroyed, told me and my theories to go to the devil. I shouted to him that those crazy ideas were not mine and that, in truth, they could only have been born from a disheveled and elongated head. He shouted even louder to me that I had not understood anything that he had explained to me before with such kindness; that every moment spent with me was lost. It was too much. I demanded another explanation. He again told me to go to hell.

I left confused. In commemoration I got a bad headache. From the little bits left of civilization remorse appeared.

My grandmother, a lovable and lucid old woman, whom I told of the situation, leaned her little white head and explained to me that men are in the habit of constructing theories for themselves and other ones for women. But, she added after a pause and a sigh, they forget them at the moment they act . . . I replied to Grandmama that I, who applied with success Hegel's law of contradictions, had not understood a word about what she said. She laughed and explained to me in good humor: 'My dear, men are animals.'

In this sense, have we returned to the beginning? I didn't think that was an argument, but I consoled myself a little. I slept somewhat sadly. But I awoke happy, purely animal. When I opened the windows of my room and looked at the cool and still garden with the first rays of sunshine, I was sure that there really is nothing to do but to live. Only Jimmy's change of behavior continued to intrigue me. Theory is such a good thing!

# Elisa Lispector

Elisa Lispector was born in the village of Sawranh, Ukraine, in 1911 and came to Brazil as a little girl. She died in Rio de Janeiro in 1989. She spent her adolescence in Recife in Northeast Brazil and the rest of her life in Rio de Janeiro. She became a naturalized Brazilian and entered the Federal Civil Service, working at the Ministry of Labor as international conference coordinator; she once represented Brazil at an American conference held in Peru dedicated to the study of the female workforce in Latin America. In 1947 she also worked as a journalist and studied sociology at the National Faculty of Philosophy and art criticism at the Brazilian Foundation of Theater. Elisa Lispector was the first writer to receive the José Lins do Rego Prize for her novel *O muro de pedras* (1963) (Stone Wall). The author of seven novels and three collections of short stories, Elisa Lispector began her career in 1945 with her novel *Além da fronteira* (Beyond the Border). Lispector is recognized as a writer who deals with the themes of solitude and incommunicability; her introspective narratives reveal fearful, angst-ridden characters who suffer in the face of an indifferent world. The two pieces translated here are respectively from her semiautobiographical novel, *No exílio* (1948) (In Exile) and from one of her collections of stories, *O tigre de Bengala* (1985) (The Bengal Tiger). The excerpt dramatizes the coming of age of a young Jewish girl living in Northeast Brazil, and the story exemplifies one of her existentially 'lost' women characters.

# Elisa Lispector

EXCERPT FROM *In Exile*

She turned back to the first source of her bitterness, to the first warning that the Jew is a separate being, someone who has a reason for struggling and suffering. To suffer always, even in his worship of God. In church, where Eudóxia had taken her one afternoon, the atmosphere was festive: the icons on richly decorated altars, the organ, incense, the peasants wearing bizarre and multicolored clothing. In the synagogue, not even bells or images. No decoration, no joy whatsoever. Men and women wearing dark clothes, seated on hard and long benches, men and women in separate sections. Up on the pulpit, only the Torah and the menorah. The service, severe. The men, praying in contrition; the women, raising their voices, mixing their lament with their prayers. They shed tears as if they were bemoaning all the evils and imploring redemption for all men.

In school, which she attended for a short period, the difference continued. Every morning, before classes, the ceremony took place in the music room. The *Pop*, the priest, came in sacerdotal vestments, the long white beard illuminating his face, crucifix in hand. The children and the adolescents, in blond or brunette braids, rosy cheeks, stood up serenely and chanted melodious sacred hymns to the sound of the grand piano.

Together with other classmates of exclusion, she stayed timidly to one side, very quiet and very sad.

She was different. She didn't understand yet if that was good or bad, as she felt neither honor nor guilt. She only knew that she didn't belong in that milieu.

Oh, how she hated them later. She felt their hostility, even when they seemed indifferent. In her heart she knew that she loved them. She loved them despite the hate they themselves incited in her. At times she had managed to love them even more than the Jews, since

with them everything was so much more simple. It was only a case
of loving them, nothing more. First of all, one needed to understand
them. To suffer with them, in order only then to reach them.

'A girl must not stay unmarried for a long time. She must marry, form
a family. That's what tradition ordains.' And Pinkhas wanted this
ardently, given that God had not bestowed on him a male child who
would continue his name for the next generations and, after his death
and his wife's, would say Kaddish.

Lizza contemplated the photograph, dumbfounded, her heart beating irregularly.

'This is your cousin Benny, my brother's son. I don't know if you
remember him; I don't think so. When he was in our house, both of
you were still very small. Now he is a man raised according to Jewish
precepts.'

Facing the mirror, on the day that she had adjusted her first dress
as a young woman, when she smiled coquettishly at her slim figure
of burgeoning curves, on that day she loved for the first time. Love
and marriage existed, yes, each day she was aware of that, but they
were facts alien to the kind of love she had conceived.

'He's one of our sons,' her father went on, 'not like the many others
who walk around here and who don't know a word of the Torah. I am
going to send for him.'

Lizza continued to stare at the photo; she looked at it as if through
a fog, her eyes brimming with water, and it was hard to understand.
In the meantime, her father continued talking, persuasively.

'And what if I don't like him? Since I hardly even know him, how
are you going to send for him from such a distance? What's to be
done afterward? What's to be done if I really don't want to marry him?
Moreover, I really don't want to, nor do I want to get married.'

While she was speaking, more and more was she strongly convinced
that she would be incapable of facing that situation.

Pinkhas heard his daughter with sadness and understood a lot of
what she had not been able to tell him. In the meantime, she still
pondered: parents are more experienced than their children and only
want what's good for them. That's how it has been in all times.

That parents always wanted their children's happiness, Pinkhas
knew. However, as to whether the road would always be the same, he

now had his doubts about this reasoning. His honor warned him, and his respect for individual freedom stopped him, hesitantly. The present times were really something else, he had to agree, and he himself should keep up, if he didn't want to remain behind. These were the precepts, yes, but he had to temporize, be discriminate, concede.

Withdrawing to her room, Lizza sat down on the edge of the bed, bent over, her hands abandoned in her lap. She stayed that way for a long time, her thoughts agitated.

'What do you want to be?' Her father had asked her. 'What are you saving your life for?' And she hadn't known how to respond. She hadn't dared. Now she felt the ground underneath her feet slip away from her, as if she were playing with ghosts, mere ghosts, her crazy dreams.

Marim's death imposed a hiatus on the flow of everything.

In the lapse of a few hours, Lizza made advances beyond her very self, experiencing life and death. She was no longer that tender and blind tree branch, but a heavy trunk of pain and knowledge.

For a whole night long, they kept vigil by Marim's bedside, hearing her painful gasps and trying to capture the meaning of words as flimsy as her breath. Afterward, the sounds of the funereal prayer, uttered amid the lament of friends who had gathered, reached Pinkhas's and Lizza's ears. Lizza began to feel her heart hurting a great deal, like a pain lacerating her to her marrow.

When she saw her mother again, she was already placed on the bier, shrouded by *takhrikhin*. Her first reaction was a cry so acute as though with it she wanted to split the sky. But the sky remained blue and distant; the sun, shiny yellow, the murmuring persisting all around. Next, she fell into a stiff silence, not seeing anything or anybody anymore. From afar arose within her a vague memory of something terrible and irremediable, in view of her father's decomposed face, in listening to his laments.

'Why did she abandon us? What will become of us now? Lizza, Marim died. What are we going to do without her? What will become of us?'

Afterward, men came to close the coffin and carried it outside, while someone approached Pinkhas and made a cut in his lapel, in practice of the *keri'ah*, and he cut the neckline of Lizza's dress.

Only during shivah did Lizza begin gradually to come out of the fog of her tormented thoughts, to understand, and to assess how much had taken place. And the more she advanced, the closer she came to the chaos.

'When I die, don't cry,' she still heard her mother say. 'It will be such a big relief for me.'

Meanwhile, she couldn't think of her mother without abundant and ardent tears running down her face. She couldn't accept the idea of death. She suffered for her dead mother, and she suffered for her father and her orphaned sisters. Everybody had become orphaned. And when she thought about her own self, she felt more than orphan-hood. She was simply adrift. For everything else that wasn't the care she had provided for her sick mother, she felt inadequate in her daily life of family bonds and personal interests.

On the other hand, a new thought beckoned her. The moment had come to be free, to embark upon the great inner experience, to take possession of her own self. But at the time she didn't understand the voice of this calling. It seemed to her to be devoid of meaning.

'Not now,' she said to herself, 'not yet.'

When her sisters had returned from the house of the friends who had taken them in on the day of Marim's death and during shivah, Lizza greeted them with a pallid face, her black dress covering her thin body. They embraced in tears; then they sat down seriously and fearfully in the easy chairs of the living room, bathed in cold and faint sunlight, and spoke about the deceased.

They spoke timidly, afraid of disturbing the silence and the absence of their dead mother, fearing that their weeping and their words would reach the wilderness and the pain of their deceased mother. They felt for her such great pity. They felt the actual injustice of death.

'How could this have happened? And why had it happened to her, given that she already had suffered so much?' That was what they questioned, in their naiveté, hurt by the brutal event.

Mourning dresses, visitors, and household duties were, little by little, imposing a kind of deadening routine on the habits and impressions of Lizza and her sisters.

When he arrived home, their father would start pacing the long cor-ridor. He didn't speak about Marim. Actually all of them avoided making a reference to her; as a tactic they would bypass the topic, omitting her name, because she was present in all their thoughts and actions.

They had to move. Each time they passed by the room that had been hers, it seemed to them that Marim was calling out. They heard her weeping, they continued to feel the presence of her suffering.

Levi was the son of pious parents, old Hassidic stock, and he himself a veteran student of the Yeshiva.

And this time Lizza did not manifest opposition.

That she was adrift, empty, and that she accepted him only because she wanted to end that torment once and for all—that she hadn't told her father or anybody else. She had simply accepted him, without weighing the consequences or the sacrifice of her life and the one she was dragging along, like a fall from a high cliff. But the antagonism and the sensation of anguish from their first encounter did not disappear with her fiancé's subsequent visits.

Levi's myopia, his slightly bent back due to his long vigils over the Talmud, his awkward and meek manner, far from bringing him close to her, instilled in her an unbearable feeling of flight and regret. She felt she was betraying him because she understood that something strange and entirely new was developing within her. Without being able to translate it into words, she realized that a new strength undermined her will of submission, driving her toward other plans for her life.

It was like this, many times; while everybody else was sleeping, she would sit up in bed and continue to look into herself, terrified with her own sense of self. Her imagination was inflamed, pushing her far away from the life that insisted on wanting to annihilate her. In the morning she felt worn out, her nerves tingling just under her skin, trying uselessly to abate the violence in her heart.

The closer each day came to the marriage, the more she understood the impossibility of carrying it to a successful conclusion.

One rainy morning she got up with a heavier and saddened heart. She dressed, and without telling anybody at home, she left for the cemetery. When she arrived there, it was still raining, the lead sky threatening to cave in on her. The way to the cemetery was muddy and slippery; the miserable shacks were immersed in the slimy marshes, the squalid and disheveled women and children who appeared at the broken doors and windows sunken into that darkness of desolation and ruin. She passed through the rusty gate, which opened with a long screech, and walked among the grave stones until she reached her mother's. She lingered there for a long time, contemplating the block of marble, in a complete state of intellectual and emotional stagnation. Death was marked by that block of stone, but the stone told her absolutely nothing. In that tomb, and in all the others, there was absence and silence—silence on the ground and in the sky. A broken headstone up ahead, wounded her sensibility. Something stirred within her, and Lizza attacked herself and the brutalizing behavior that had taken hold of her.

'Underneath this ground lies my mother's body—her eyes, her voice, her tenderness, and this means nothing to me? Nothing?'

With this outcry, she began to let go, little by little; tears appeared in her eyes. But the assurance for which she had come she didn't find. No, her mother's tomb didn't mean anything to her, except that life is ephemeral and death the forgetful finale.

'All merely a dream, but a bad dream, disturbing. So, is life only this?' she went on. And to arrive at this point, so many wounds, so many frustrated hopes, so many lies. Her tears were now abundantly running down her face, tears of revolt. The gray sky lowered even more; the rain fell copiously. Now she truly felt the tomb's wilderness and the desolation of her dead mother lying under the soggy black ground. The cold began to take hold of her, climbing from her feet and reaching her throat. Then she retreated. She returned by retracing her steps, already seeing with other eyes the huts deep in the quagmire, the disheveled women peeping out of their shanties, the dirty sky, the ground wet and sad.

She entered the house frozen, feeling her limbs swollen and worn out, but a great calmness within her. She had made her decision. Inside the house, she found everything quiet; her sisters had gone to school, her father to work. In the kitchen the maid was absorbed in her household chores. And the tinkling of the dishes and the utensils brought a mood of sweet and familial pleasantness. She took shelter in this. She went to her bedroom, took off her shoes, and stretched herself on the bed. Gradually, in the silence and the shadow of the room, she began to fall asleep, dragging her body and mind to a deep and healing forgetfulness.

Her father's voice was tranquil, deliberate. He asked his daughter to repeat what she had said. And when she did, he still pondered for a while. Then he tried to dissuade her from her proposition. He spoke about the mission of women and of their duty in matrimony. But to himself the words were no longer convincing. He felt that his daughter had her own reasons and that he could not dissuade her. Father and daughter talked to each other for a very long time, with suffering and understanding. As she went on, Lizza felt like drowning her initial impulse and retreating, acquiescing, such was her grief caused by her father's pain. But now it was necessary to go all the way.

Pinkhas contemplated his daughter with amazement. 'What times are these that are occurring?' As for his daughter, he simply didn't know her. What was in store for the fate she had chosen? She said she wanted to continue to study. But what good would come to a woman of much knowledge? On the other hand, how not to concede, if, through her, he relived his own frustrated dreams? With confessing it, he was proud of Lizza.

Certainly this had not been the way he had devised things. When he visited his friends and saw them with the sons of their sons, continuing themselves through memory and generations, he also wanted to see his daughters married, and grandchildren, so that his pure and overflowing happiness would brighten his days in old age. Nevertheless, he agreed. At the moment he only saw his daughter's intentions.

The following day would be one of a splendorous sun. Lizza awoke when it was still dawn. The roosters were challenging themselves, clamorously awakening creation.

She went to the veranda; she pushed the windows wide open.

'Maybe in this way the day will not take long in arriving.'

Next she washed herself in the shower turned on to full force, stretching her limbs in a bird's delight in spreading its wings. Free, at last. She laughed happily under the water running coolly on her clear face. She dressed herself hurriedly, went to the kitchen, and made coffee. She burned with impatience for the whole household to wake up, so that the day might begin once and for all. She yearned to set her course on the long, long road that she still had to traverse.

'But freedom is also slavery.'

Now she could follow her own road. But how not to detain oneself in view of the torment that was increasing, and how not to approach her father, given their conflicts? How to betray her own past that had come with her since infancy via the current of vicissitudes and terrors in which she had grown up? That ancestral heritage, she couldn't drown it in one unique, liberating impulse; she couldn't in a burst of emotional intuition isolate herself from the fatality of the events occurring in such a disturbed world, despite her knowing that, as a lone human being, she was impotent to act.

Elisa Lispector

# Out of Sheer Despair

You know, Doctor, I like these therapy sessions because they're completely informal. None of that lying down on the couch, your sitting behind me with a pad of paper and a pen in hand, calling to mind an envoy sent by the Holy Office in search of a heretic who will justify the flames of the Inquisition. With us it's different. Seated like this at your writing table, one facing the other, the game is more honest, albeit not always friendly. As a matter of fact, I'm the one who talks more; at times I realize I'm quite verbose, now lying a little, or better yet, dogging issues, then going on with stories that have nothing to do with what's important.

But I swear all that I have been telling you in these last sessions consists of an honest search for something I sensed is hidden behind what I was saying but which I hadn't figured out.

'. . .'

'Wait, I'm not going to tell you right off what it is—and not because I'm unsure of my discovery—for it's a truth so incandescent that at the moment it occurred to me, it almost blew me away. For months now, I have been going around in circles, until all of a sudden I woke up this morning with the idea, so clear, so logical, so . . .'

It cost me a lot to arrive at this conclusion, but, before telling me if I'm right, try to remember how I told you about my astonishment as I was regaining my senses while I was lying down on a stretcher in a dark corridor of an emergency hospital, without even knowing how I got there. Let's recapitulate, and see if it's not what I'm thinking.

At the beginning, on the operating table, wearing a horrible hospital gown, a stained sheet covering my legs. The cold room, the assisting nurses (two) going from one side to the other. Time is passing. I cannot focus my thoughts on anything. If I hadn't felt the hardness of the operating table, I would say that I'm floating in space, and little by little a pain, at first annoying and vague, gradually becomes so sharp and so overwhelming that it's difficult to pinpoint where it is.

I feel sorry for myself, and at the same time I'm actually angry at myself for being there, in that situation. As a matter of fact, I feel more anger than pity, as if I were suffering a well-deserved punishment. 'Doesn't this already tell you something?'

Finally, one of the assisting nurses, skinny, pale, tiny, nothing more than a bird, pulls a small stool near me, sits down, leans her face really close to mine, takes my hand—my inner strength gives in; I'm relenting—she asks my name, smoothes my hair. She asks if I am alone or do I have someone with me in the hospital—and by now I do not feel so alone. She wants to comfort me in my sorrow, and in a short time she begins to enumerate her own problems. Imagine, she was sick for two days; she even got a shot (she showed me her skinny arm marked with a red blotch); and the institute didn't even want to cover the days she was out, she, of all people, who never misses a day and who works in two hospitals, doing a full shift in each hospital, and also studies at night, because she has a widowed mother and six little brothers to support.

I forget my own worries, and even my spreading pain, and begin to offer advice: Don't do that, young woman. Don't overwork, because it will ruin you. Afterward, nothing left for you or for your six little brothers. I tried as well to work above my capacity, for other reasons, and the result was a beautiful hole in my right lung, and there was no pneumothorax that could remedy it. And since I had no choice, I abandoned my studies and continued only to work, and in the beginning even that was hard for me to endure. Imagine that just two weeks after the phrenicotomy, with the bandage still on my neck, I had to return to the typewriter. But I'm tough. As you can see, it's hard for me to die. Even after an accident like today's, I'm speaking to you as if nothing had happened. Take care of yourself, young woman, I again added.

A mist blurs my vision, I feel as if I were vanishing. I come back to my old self.

'But where is this surgeon who doesn't show up?'

'The delay is not with the surgeon,' responds my little bird almost in a whisper. 'It's the anesthesiologists, who are very busy. At this moment, they're operating in three different rooms, all critical cases.' She goes back to smoothing my hair. 'Be patient, it won't take long.'

It didn't take long. All of a sudden various men appeared, wearing white surgical masks, aprons down to their knees. I don't know whose idea it was that I was suffering from heart problems; I didn't even have the strength to contradict them. They decided I couldn't have general anesthesia. And I who wanted so much, so much to fall asleep.

First, they turned me on my back and gave me a painful and drawn out spinal injection, which, like an electrical current, kept on spreading its pain through my womb and my hips; next, a thick needle rapidly penetrated the vein above my pulse, for the intravenous; they tied my wide open arms to wooden boards, transforming me into a pathetic image of the Crucifixion after Good Friday. There were two anesthesiologists: while one was taking my blood pressure and my pulse, the other was firmly fastening an oxygen mask on my face, but so tightly, that I was suffocating more than I was breathing.

I closed my eyes, and I surrendered. I didn't want to see them cutting me up. It didn't hurt much, but in anguish I followed all their movements.

Finally, it was a relief to feel the surgeon take great care in the work of sewing up my body, as if I were a witch doll made of cloth. I even felt the needle penetrate and the thread go through my flesh.

In the dark infirmary, dimly lit only by a light coming from the corridor, they put me on a bed among other beds lined in a row; some, I noticed right away, were occupied; others were not. Afterward, the stretcher carriers left. I remained in the shadows and in solitude.

With eyes wide open transfixed on the ceiling, I remained until dawn, thinking without stopping, trying to understand. It was astonishment mixed with panic. As much as I tried, I could not grasp how that happened to me. It was difficult to believe. Above all, it was ridiculous, gratuitous, because, in truth, I hadn't had any need to come to Rio at that time of the night. How did that happen to me? I kept asking.

Little by little, I began patching one memory to another, albeit a bit confusingly. I felt a chill as I recalled the cold on the mountain range. The bluish afternoon coming through the window panes that secretly watched the empty road. I, alone in the house, coming and going from one window to the other, without knowing what to do with myself, hesitating between continuing my translation work or catching up on my correspondence. Suddenly, out of sheer despair I seized the car key, and before I knew it I was traveling down the road.

It was still early morning in the infirmary, and at times I was distracted from my thoughts as I heard outside the starting up of cars and motorcycles and the happy hubbub of young people laughing and singing. I figured out that in the proximity of the hospital there must be some bar or nightclub. And it consoled me to realize that carefree life continued to go on.

By midmorning, I took care to identify my companions in the infirmary. To my left an old woman with skin the color of wax was resting, so quietly, so still that, even though one conceded that she was sleeping, she had the total appearance of a cadaver. To my right another woman in the very same condition: same age, the same appearance of a cadaver ready to be buried. A nun was watching over this second woman, a mother superior, as I learned afterward; I asked her to see if the woman to my left was still breathing. She was breathing, she assured me, after having completed her inspection. The attendants were already coming into the infirmary, some bringing trays, others pails and brooms. Gradually I began to hear a wheezed crying, like that of a child, so weak and heartfelt and which was to be repeated at intervals during the nights I spent there. I looked at the row of beds in front of mine, and I saw there from the angle of the room: a really horrible thing to describe, Doctor. It's enough to say that she was in a cast from the waist down and was lying there in the dirty and messy bed like a broken doll; at the extreme opposite end of the pavilion, there was another young girl lying down with one leg suspended from a pulley in the direction of the ceiling. No, no I'm not going to tell you about everything I saw. I'm so tired.

Ah, but Sunday at the hospital was beautiful! A flock appeared—I was going to say of white herons, but no, herons are much more graceful, delicate, subtle—and pigeons are fat and chubby, fidgety, and how they coo! Well it was a flight of pigeons, the Sisters of Charity who came to visit the mother superior in the bed next to mine, all of them wearing immaculately white habits, starched, the pleats unfolding over their high busts and wide rumps, their round and smiling faces framed by white veils that fell almost to their waists. It was obvious that they were not reclusive nuns, the kind that lived incarcerated in the convents, praying for the salvation of humanity. Even though they also took care of men—men as well as women, of course—but they did so in one of those so-called rest homes, where the exacerbated fits of human despair are repressed with sedatives in high dosages, when not with electrical shocks. A hardly pleasant task, let's admit. Perhaps because of this, in their visit to the mother superior, the nuns felt like high school girls on vacation. But the kitchen of the 'rest home' must be pretty good, judging from the roly-poly and healthy appearance of the solicitous and charitable nuns.

The black girl there in the corner who used to wake up crying in the middle of the night, and who had a mother in the state of Espírito Santo, and who had come to the big city to work as a domestic, and as soon as she went outside was hit by a car and picked up from the street by who knows who and thrown in that hospital, also received her visitor. One could see it was her lady employer. A young white woman, elegant, well dressed. She stayed at the foot of the bed for about ten minutes, if that much, and, if in her 'doctor's visit' she didn't read the patient's chart hanging from the bed, she also didn't pay much attention to the condition of the person in it. Upon leaving, as a gift she left for her an enormous soiled straw bag and a pair of very high heels with the sole already worn out. And the visited girl became happy, and boasting, showed her beautiful presents to her roommate from the extreme end of the room, the one with the foot raised to the ceiling, who, in turn, retorted that perhaps not even a year from now could she get to wear the high heels, which had the effect of throwing cold water on the fervent happiness of the girl with her feet in casts.

The girl with the raised leg received her visitor as well, but at night. The masculine visitor, who had not worn the visitor's badge on his chest, certainly enjoyed the good graces of somebody at the hospital's reception desk: the girl asked the attendant to turn off the light in the pavilion, that the light from the corridor was enough. The visitor stayed quite a while, and a kiss sealed his departure. The girl became happy, and I was happy for her.

Ah, but I also had my visitor, who was very different from hers. It happened very early in the morning, as soon as the infirmary began to perk up; I'm not going to say who it was. I will only say that it brought me a good smile, one of those from the heart, a friendly handshake, and it gave me much strength, really a lot.

I see, Doctor, that you are squirming in your chair. Don't be impatient. I am not going to tell you everything that happened between the episodes in the hospital up to the revelation I had this morning. And look, nearly three months of being confined inside my house, like in a prison. In much the same way, I'm not going to speak about the painful bandages, neither about my apprehensions and doubts over whether I would one day still manage to walk again.

Agree with me that I couldn't convey to you just like that a discovery I made after torturing myself for such a long time. Now decipher this: the fact that I had gone out driving at night without any destination and had not stepped on the brakes in time, wasn't that a subconscious act of self-destruction?

'It was.'

Prolonged silence.

'So long, Doctor. I'll be back tomorrow.'

Time passes.

'Good afternoon, Doctor.'

'Good afternoon.'

'Today is yesterday's tomorrow. Do you know what is happening to me, Doctor? From the way they operated on me, I have come to feel the strange sensation of having been mutilated. But, after you made me understand . . . You know? I am harboring within me a feeling like one who has gone to war, returned with scars, but nevertheless came back.'

After all, wasn't it a kind of war that I had with my very self? 'So, if I am here, nothing else matters. I am alive. No, don't say anything. I promise you that from now on I will be sensible.' Why am I alive? I swear I'm not going to ask. I swear that I will never again ask for what purpose one lives, why one lives, what one lives.

# Jacó Guinsburg

Jacó Guinsburg was born in Bessarabia in 1921 and at the age of three, along with his family, disembarked in Santos, São Paulo, Brazil. After several years in the interior of the state of São Paulo, his family moved to the capital city of São Paulo in 1930, where he remains today. Literary critic, publisher, and professor, Guinsburg is credited with writing one of the first short stories about the Holocaust from the Brazilian point of view, 'O retrato' (1946) (The Picture). With a doctorate from the University of São Paulo, where he is a professor of theater aesthetics and theory of theater, Guinsburg is considered to be a pioneer in writing about Jewish literature in Brazilian literary supplements. As a speaker of Yiddish, Guinsburg is also famous for disseminating Yiddish literature in his role as publisher, essayist, and translator of Yiddish fiction and theater into Portuguese. His synchronic study *Aventuras de uma língua errante: Ensaios de literatura e teatro ídiche* (1996) (Adventures of an Errant Language: Essays on Yiddish Literature and Theater) represents the first comprehensive study on this topic written in Portuguese. Director for thirty years of the prodigious publishing house Perspectiva, Guinsburg has among his own critical titles *Stanislavski e o Teatro de Arte de Moscou* (1985) (Stanislavsky and Moscow's Theater of Art), *Vanguarda e absurdo: Uma cena de nosso tempo* (1990) (Avant-garde and the Absurd: A Scenario of Our Times), and *Semiologia do teatro* (2007) (Semiology of Theater). As a writer of very short stories since the 1940s, Guinsburg composes short narratives of indelible moments in people's daily lives. The two stories anthologized here, 'Miriam' and 'Figuras na sombra' (Figures in the Darkness), reflect the tone of Guinsburg's collection *O que aconteceu, aconteceu* (2000) (What Happened, Happened). Respectively, these stories treat a mother's shocking awareness of her own daughter's difference and the impact of the Holocaust on a woman whose family perished under the Nazi terror. The stories present glimpses of generational, cultural, and psychological dislocation.

# Jacó Guinsburg

# Miriam

Miriam leaned over her mother's shoulder. She couldn't manage to contain her emotion. A quiver ran through the little girl's body. Oh, how good it was to have a birthday and to get pretty things! And on top of everything that brooch . . . Ever since the day she had seen it for the first time, she had dreamed about it. And today . . . it would be hers! The young girl's black eyes brightened with redoubled intensity beneath her thick, dark eyelashes. Her pale face acquired a slight coloring. She bent over even more, hugged her mother from behind, squeezing her tightly. But her gaze was fixed on Rachel's hand, which was stirring inside a small safe.

The mother felt the girl's eagerness. And urged on by it, she hurried to find the sought-after object. Nervously she emptied the contents of the small safe. The jewels scattered all over the top of the vanity. Rachel cast her eyes over the small treasure. Some of the stones glittered cruelly, hurting her eyes. She looked away. But soon afterward she continued with her search. Suddenly, she picked up a small gold object, sighing with relief. Miriam, whose impatience was increasing by the minute, as soon as she saw the brooch couldn't hold back.

'Let me, Mother! Let me see!' she exclaimed anxiously. Her arms let go of her mother's neck; her hands lunged forth greedily, grabbing the gift. Her face was already transformed. She gasped . . . How beautiful it was!

That small pagan god, arms open wide, all gold, with the sensual expression on its face, had always fascinated her. But now she felt aglow. All her nerves, all the cells of the young girl, seemed to vibrate with her taking possession of the object. She wanted to clutch it tightly against her chest, to cover it with kisses . . . It was hers; it had always been hers!

Rachel, a bit startled, observed the violent reaction of her daughter.

She had never thought that a simple object could provoke such emotions . . . But, after all, she was only a girl . . . And, besides, her age
. . . Sixteen years old . . . Everything becomes violent, uncontrollable.
Yes, at this age nothing should surprise her, more so with a sensitive
child like Miriam.

Miriam, who was turning the small brooch over and over, looking at
it with unrestrained passion, had completely forgotten her mother's
presence. She saw nobody; nothing else was important to her. She
looked like a devout woman of ancient mysteries in the ecstasy of
her adoration.

The late afternoon light filtered through the curtains, populating
the room with shadows. The twilight swallowed all the details and
all the decorative touches, leaving only, in its nakedness, a huge bed,
also adorned with curtains, which seemed more like a shrine. A ritual
halo enveloped the room. And in the middle, the immobilized girl,
sacrificed to the golden god . . .

Suddenly, Miriam, as though awakened from a dream, looked around,
encountering Rachel's amazed look. Mother and daughter looked at
each other . . . The girl's arms, until then outstretched, dropped. A
sensation of shame invaded her. It looked like she was blushing. It
was as if she had committed . . . a crime. She was mute and paralyzed.
All of a sudden, in an abrupt move, as though uprooting her very self
from the spot, she ran out.

Rachel made a gesture as if she were getting up. But she let herself
fall again into the same place. She needed to reflect a little. In all that
business there was something strange. Her age, for sure, explained
. . . But that ecstasy for a simple adornment . . . It was so strange. A
piece of jewelry always attracts . . . undeniably. Few women escape
its enchantment. She herself, when her husband had brought her the
gold brooch, she had felt flattered . . . And even happy and vain. She
had worn it many times. She liked that beautiful golden god. And on
the day Esther, her friend, stared for a while at the cameo, she had
even felt a kind of tenderness toward it . . . But she had never shown
any special preference for it. It was an ornament like so many others. So when her daughter had manifested her wish to receive it as
a birthday present, she hadn't vacillated even for an instant. It was
a present like any other. But Miriam's attitude . . . Perhaps it was
merely emotion . . . No . . . No . . . That rapture she had witnessed

was something more . . . There, there were sparks much too alive, an unrestrained impetus of passion . . . It wasn't merely the ardor of a young girl. That adoration revealed something different, strange . . . another world, a world unlike hers . . .

Another world. She had never suspected this. Miriam was her daughter, fruit of her womb, nurtured with the milk of her breasts, and lulled to sleep by the warmth of her bosom. She had always considered her to be a new version of herself. The small differences she sometimes noticed . . . Ah, this was from her father . . . But the rest, the main part, Miriam was . . . Rachel, a most faithful copy. She had always thought in this way. And now she saw in her daughter another being, another valorization of things, another mentality . . . No, she couldn't understand. It was inconceivable . . .

Her gaze began to wander restlessly. She was looking for something to settle upon. But the twilight had already changed into darkness . . . And it was nightfall. Rachel saw herself alone, surrounded by thick darkness—a black wall, smooth and uniform, impenetrable and without any point of support. Her repelled gaze became feverish. A shiver ran through her body. She wanted to shout . . . But her lips only let out a suffocated moan.

Jacó Guinsburg

# Figures in the Darkness

Rachel brusquely folded the pages of the newspaper. Below her very white forehead, her eyes withdrew into their dark, light-spotted depths. On her oval face, framed by black curly hair, two lines that radiated at an angle, on both sides of her slightly aquiline nose, creased even more, in apparent contradiction to her voluptuous lips, to the animal whiteness of her teeth and to the sensual curves of her body, which in middle age had not changed. An air of absence, of a present that became undone at each invocation of memory, was enveloping her being.

Suddenly, she got up from the small sofa where she had been lying and made her way to the bedroom. It was an ample apartment in which quadrangular furniture and large mirrors suggested a modern style; its clear geometry of crossing reflections were dimmed by the semidarkness of the cold and gray afternoon that filtered through the curtains, affixing more gloom to the two oriental daggers that decorated the wall.

Approaching the vanity, Rachel cast her eyes on the faceted bottles of perfume and the porcelain accessories on display in front of her, stopping at a small easel on which one saw, delicately outlined, almost in miniature, the figure of an old Jew with his tallith over his shoulders and his eyes raised in fervent prayer. She lingered a few seconds contemplating it. A slight shiver passed through her body. A tinge of anguish clouded her gaze.

In a nervous gesture she opened a small drawer built into the piece of furniture from which she took out an album of photographs. She touched its surface as if reconnecting with an old friend and fell upon the vanity's little bench. Opening the album at random, she began to leaf through the pages without stopping. As though cast under an enchanted spell, she began to transport herself in images that were coming to her, not from the album but from inside her very self. From the lost folds of her memories, there appeared figures frayed by time, images of a life erased by the past.

How much had changed! Who was seated there, in the midst of all that luxury and comfort? Was it really her? The question, as a dissonant note of objectivity, disrupted her self-absorbed invocation. Almost instinctively her attention turned to one of the photos in the album. Who would have said? Twenty-three years had passed. Nevertheless, she was that shriveled adolescent. It really was her. That little girl with long braids, a poorly fitted dress, wide-eyed, and a frightened expression, a family picture.

Father, mother, those brothers and cousins who were there in that yellowish sepia of old photograph paper, seemed to jump back into their lives, circling her, entwining her, touching her, screaming, crying and imploring, in mute voices that agonized in their silence—figures of the darkness who had been and stopped being.

Rachel felt that she was suffocating. She seemed to be drowning in a feeling of deprivation and impotence. She wanted to scream her despair. Everything around her had plunged into indistinctness, leaving her all alone, released to the spectral solitude of her memory.

# Samuel Rawet

Samuel Rawet was born in 1929 in Klimontow, a small Polish town and shtetl near Warsaw that was destroyed during World War II. He emigrated to Brazil at the age of seven along with his family and settled in the northern lower-class suburbs of Rio de Janeiro. His first collection of stories, *Contos do imigrante* (1956) (Immigrant Tales), marks the notable beginning of Brazilian Jewish fiction. This collection was followed by another, *Diálogo* (1963) (Dialogue); *Abama* (1964), a novella; *Os sete sonhos* (1967) (The Seven Dreams), winner of the literary prize Prêmio Guimarães Rosa; another collection, *O terreno de uma polegada quadrada* (1970) (The Land of One Square Inch); *Viagens de Ahasverus à terra alheia em busca de um passado que não existe porque futuro, e de um futuro que já passou porque sonhado* (1970) (Voyages of Ahasverus to a Foreign Land in Search of a Past That Does Not Exist because of the Future, and of a Future That Has Already Passed Because It Was Dreamt), a novella; *Que os mortos enterrem seus mortos* (1981) (Let the Dead Bury Their Dead), a collection of stories. In addition to three unpublished plays, Rawet has published several books of essays: *Consciência e valor* (1970) (Conscience and Valor); *Homossexualismo, sexualidade e valor* (1970) (Homosexuality, Sexuality, and Valor); *Alienação e realidade* (1972) (Alienation and Reality); *Eu-Tu-Ele* (1972) (I-Thou-He); and *Angústia e conhecimento* (1978) (Anguish and Knowledge). In addition to being a prolific writer, Rawet was also one of the engineers who worked with the architect Oscar Niemeyer to build Brasília. The two stories that follow, 'Christmas without Christ' and 'Moira,' are respectively from his second and last short story collections. The first evokes the 'low profile' but seething position of the Jew as stereotyped in a Catholic household; the second challenges the idea of one absolute identity via the interior monologue of a troubled actor.

# Samuel Rawet

# Christmas without Christ

Tear a man away from his peace, his silence, his routine of cutting a slice of meat or taking a sip of ordinary wine on an extraordinary day, raise his criminal face stigmatized by who knows what habits, leave his body exposed inside-out in visceral nudity, a new buffoon fondled by the scourge of bruising caresses, chase the simian tail in his coccyx, chop off his ankles and in a burst of laughter split his capric skull, block his scintillating and ubiquitous eyes, root out his generating mass of ideas, conflicts, and sometimes feelings, amputate his sex and offer half to each one of the two mouths that stare at him with obscene grins, and from the ashes of his bones consumed by an unjust holocaust no vestiges are allowed, neither in the air, nor on the land, nor in the water, nor in the fire that precipitated them, nor in the remembrance of the one whose bones made these ashes. But then where to disperse them, where, if beyond the infinite there is another much bigger infinite? Thoughts? A speech made enthusiastically by the half drunk who suddenly recuperates his clearheadedness? He wouldn't know how to articulate it. Only the surge of feelings as a reaction to what he had heard, and the figure of Nani in front of him, at the head of the table opposite him, the glass of wine held by tremulous and wrinkled hands, the head of an old woman connected to black shoulders of silk, her wrinkles stirred by a ravenous decrepitude, her rumpled complexion in the half shadows of candles and the dim lights of the wall fixtures, her greedy fixation upon the amount of wine allowed. It is Nani who becomes the object of Nehemiah's, Nehemiah Goldenberg's gaze, while the others go on chatting as if nothing there had changed, and it is in Nani that he tries to catch a glimmer of support, some approval, if there is approval, a response, if one is forthcoming. It is Nani, remote, doting, alien to any logic whatsoever, fixated on the wine, seeking unconsciously to revive

emotions, to warm nerves of buried dreams, but yet still dominating
the table completely; it is in Nani that he wants to catch her total hatred,
without subterfuges, within the truthfulness of her dementia. From
what is now being said and from what will soon be said, he will not
retain one word. His intention is the opposite. To retrace everything.
To restore the sentences he heard the instant they were pronounced,
and to reweigh them within their static context, without the usual
connectives, without the purpose of communication. It is in Nani
that he seeks to stop time, to stop it until it becomes immobile, so
that, once inertia is surmounted, he will be able to invert the flow of
time. Never to go against the current, but to contain its impetus, to
subdue it, and to turn its course upstream. They were talking about
Jews during that Christmas supper when Nehemiah, at first feeling
constrained, was overcome by his sudden awareness of being the
intruder invited there by his friend, and even more brusquely came
the other conclusion: there was the whole universe, the others and he,
experiencing the same clichés and the same unsolvable contradiction.
Only Nani had asked for more wine. Nani, Ana Castanheira de Miranda
Campos, with her seventy-five years of physical energy ruling over her
ten subjects at that far end of the dining room of a modern residence,
with its gray and blue walls, its motley easy chairs, its anatomical
benches, its ameba-like vases, its immense picture window with its
low sill overlooking the bay at Urca, the mountainous crests and the
reflection in the calm waters of the bay, and the contrast between the
meter-and-a-half pine tree, already divested of the holiday gifts, and a
baroque Christ halfway up the wide mural on the wall facing Nehemiah,
in back of Nani. They were talking about Jews during that Christmas
supper, near the multicolored pine tree and facing the Christ eternal-
ized in the spasm of his last terrestrial pain. And there they were to
Nehemiah's left: Albino Fontoura, Nani's son-in-law, importer and
representative of various state industries; Lenita, a brunette sports-
woman of seventeen, green inconsequential eyes, daughter of Albino;
another son, already married, Luís (a successful politician in his very
first election, a vest adjusting a roly-poly body, temples and forehead
radiating an eternal calmness), and his wife, Vera, daughter of a career
senator, a thin, angular, and melancholy face, straw hair, a slender neck
boxed in the two burrows of her small décolletage; Sílvio, brother of
Lenita and Luís, Nehemiah's friend, and fellow teacher in the same

junior high school, a neutral face, brown hair always in place, timid, self-absorbed. To the right: Mrs. Miranda Campos Fontoura, Nani's daughter, fifty-five years of calmness in the apathy of a not-too-aged face, of successful childbirths, of serene emotions, with the indefinite glow of one who always wanted to operate on the outside but who never thought of taking a step toward the door; Eneas, her son, and Albino, her oldest, the thirty-five spry and victorious years of a prosperous lawyer with a lucrative practice of abundant lawsuits, and his wife, Malu, Marta Cavalcante Fontoura, a placid, domestic expression as she inclines her head, a woman who only asks for a pillow or a kiss in order to fall into an indifferent sleep; Labieno de Miranda Campos, another of Nani's sons, suspiciously forty, a deliberate and serious voice, but somewhat satiny, teeming with emphatic modulations, a critic of the plastic arts and the secretary of a professional magazine, almost bald, manifesting obesity in his rounded chin and gestures, one who spends the day walking on thick rugs; Vânia Fontoura, sister of Albino, forty years old, dirty blond hair, skin from the indolence of sunbathing at the beach, legally separated, pretty, uninhibited. Facing him, Nani, with her wineglass between her fingers and her lips drawn back in the anticipation of pleasure. And he, Nehemiah Goldenberg, thirty complex and troubled years, history teacher, nonconformist, restless, bearing in his actions the despair of obscure causes and the serenity of those already lost; neither light nor dark hair, two eyes, a forehead, a nose (an illusion, the straight and classic line from the bridge of his eyebrows down to his lip?), a mouth, a face, two hands, two legs, a torso, and a chest, and a member in his groin. By dint of constant abstractions, Nehemiah had already immobilized all of them even though nothing at the table reflected the process of capturing their previous state. Amid hands that spread, that crisscross knives and forks, that lift greenish glasses, or that dab the napkin on their lips—here is the static group of his design. His own organism keenly feels a bit of the effort squandered, inasmuch as he had not deprived himself of drink, but his determination infuses him with vital juices and internal stimulants, enlivening his arteries and muscles, leveling two tensions. His left hand holds the fork; his right hand stopped the cutting of the knife and let the blade stay carved in the slice of pork roast. And acknowledging his impulse, he is ready to go ahead with the inversion of the facts, with the capture of lost fluxes, with the reconquest of one instant, that alone will make it possible for him to weigh cumulative arguments.

'Jews are very charming, very charming. And an extraordinary political sense. Marx and Rothschild, Disraeli, and Bernard Baruch . . . An extraordinary political sense. They have the world in their hands.' In the mouth that now chews, in the juxtaposed lips, oscillating in the periodic contact with molars, Nehemiah reviews the primitive expression and rethinks Luís's eloquent gesture. The ceremonious tone, the clearly articulated sentence, the vacuity of the traditional resources (is this how nations govern themselves?), the 'highfalutin' use of tongue-twisting names, that's the level of comprehension. The smooth caress with the taste of an ironic slap but which, at the moment for decisions or for positions in jeopardy, will come crashing down like a harsh blow.

'Great financiers, entrepreneurs!' In what lucrative ventures were they useful to you, or in what swindles did you manage to outwit them? If by chance, Albino, if by chance you one day suffer a setback in that game that is the same for you as it is for them, and if by chance one of them benefits from your loss, somebody always benefits, will you say the same thing? Or will you look deep down, or not even so far, for the crudest expression, the clear-cut, decisive invective with the implication of a final verdict without appeal.

'And what shrewdness? Admirable!' To what shrewdness are you referring, Eneas, to the one most familiar to you, to the one you practice on a daily basis, by offering an eternal subversion of facts, ideas, concepts, proofs, to the one you manage, under the impact of well-planned rhetoric, to obfuscate the truth of some mistake, without the need for any metaphysical speculation as to whether to own up to this truth, to the one that by artful means eliminates the evidence, to the one that brings tears to your eyes in proportionate abundance according to your revenue or to your reputation, to the shrewdness that creates doubt, and from this doubt you extract the yes or the no, according to your interests, to the shrewdness that draws adequate subtleties from these bulky treatises that decorate your shelves, to the one that, in the name of some ethic or logic, represents the negation of these; is it to that shrewdness, Eneas, you are referring?

'But weren't the Jews the ones who killed Christ, Papa?'

Lenita was not able to repress the question that for her externalizes

the unpleasantness of that presence; she manifests her reaction of
antipathy that is caused by who knows what. Something in his eyes,
in his mouth, in the movements of his hands, in the awkwardness of
his helping himself to the food, in the lack of assurance with which he
lifts the platter or fills his glass. She had already seen him several times
in discussion with Sílvio, and she was turned off by her brother's sub-
servience, always agreeing, incapable of offering opposing arguments
that wouldn't be demolished by four or five harsh, cutting remarks; so
in her head she mulls over thoughts in search of one that appears to
her to be decisive. And what surfaced was the summary of millennia,
the gross but effective crystallization of so many doctrinaire philoso-
phies. The embarrassment causes a brief hiatus in the conversation.
Everyone bent forward awaiting some aside, some gesture that would
serve as pretext to make the response magically disappear. And the
yes or the no answer could be said by anyone of them, even by him,
Nehemiah. Would it be worth it? Atavistic reminiscences of frightful
feelings befall him as he contemplates the Holy Week procession of
the old country. The day condensed into hatred, the idea made into
word, yes, and action. Perverse alchemy, intending to redeem the
body while showing the claws that *all of us* have already clenched at
one time. And in that phrase all theological arguments end; there the
consequence of piles of ethical propositions is summed up; there the
greatest soritical logic comes to a close: blood.

'And what works of genius did his death not inspire. Michelangelo,
Rouault . . .'

Ironic or evasive? The smooth tone of the sentence fills the atmosphere heavily with tinges of hidden sordidness. Labieno stares at
Nehemiah as if expecting some gesture of gratitude for the finesse
used to get around the sudden silence. Laughter and the clinking of
silverware attest to their relief at the somewhat improper but spiri-
tuous 'out.' Nehemiah looks straight at Labieno and confronts him
with his undisclosed intention. The crease in his lips maintains the
half-concealed smile, full of implied meanings that did not escape the
other man's thoughts. Hence the greater repulsion. Names thrown
out like that, under what pretext? He didn't want to go around gen-
eralizing, but for some time he was already bothered by those names,
or similar ones, stated with nervous ecstasy. More than representing
enthusiasm he saw the shell of erudition covering the same identical

end: sordid and brutish. Crazy mannerisms in the face of a phenomenon that didn't go below the epidermis; feverish agitation without
the true feeling of solemn emotions, without the stroke of drama felt
in the most audacious attempt; merely an external vibration to mask a
marginal, sterile, cynical, hardly ambiguous, plan. Useless to debate
his theory when the other's face becomes blank and Labieno's hand
presses the napkin to his mouth.

'Mister Nehemiah, you don't even seem Jewish. You enjoyed the
roast pork so much.' Malu smiled at him with the indulgence of one
who comes to the aid of the needy, while Eneas, approves of his wife's
good sense in what he would call a *tactful move*, inspiring the stranger's
admiration. But the smile disappears when in Nehemiah's expression
there is no perceived reception for the praise. A bit more polished,
and he would have made some gesture of gratitude. But the assumption about the ethos of those people coming-from-who-knows-where
takes away the pleasure of being so courteous. Anything else would
not be expected.

'Oh, . . . Oh, Mister Nehemiah, you've become broadminded, isn't
that so? The essential thing is being true to one's spirit, faith . . .
tradition.'

On another occasion he would have answered her with different
gestures and, with different feelings, he would see her beautiful profile, her sunburned skin, her tender eyes, the vertical line of her neck,
and the natural curve of her shoulders. Her hair radiating natural
highlights, her mouth a little wide, slightly aggressive, but sincere
in the modulation of hidden conformities. And in an undertone, he
could whisper to her an affectionate: 'nonsense.' Urges and words
still lingered inside him. However, why bother now? Vânia emerged
amid the ordinariness of clichés, automatic affection in a dimly lit bar,
her three daily thoughts mulled over and over prior to floundering in
some corner. He felt her momentary interest. There was something
exotic about him, a variant amid the monotony of identical types. He
noticed her graceful way of placing her hair at the back of her neck
and her hand resting gently near his. He controlled himself.

'A little more wine, my daughter!'

Nani was asking for wine. It is Nani who becomes the object of
Nehemiah's gaze while the others continue to chat as if nothing there
had changed; it is in Nani that he tries to incite a spark of support,

some approval, if there is approval, a response, if one is forthcoming. It is Nani, remote, doting, alien to any logic whatsoever, fixated on the wine, seeking unconsciously to revive emotions, to warm nerves of buried dreams, but yet still dominating the table completely, it is in Nani that he wants to unleash total hatred, without subterfuges, within the truthfulness of her dementia. In her he sees the historical continuity that doesn't acknowledge any form of adaptation, that consciousness already formulated, inflexible, not making room for readjustments or doubts, insensitive to the most concrete sign of her failure because she possesses the absolute truth. There exist in her fingers reminiscences of medieval intolerance and the determination of the most rigid of contemporary politics; there exists in her thumb the impulse of tetrarchs facing the vanquished lying in the arena. Nehemiah knows that words will mean nothing when the thumb is turned upside down. And Nani sips her wine.

On the wall the crucifix. The half-opened eyes, a serene shadow under the eyelids, the lips almost closed. The arms and the legs stretched and nailed to the cross. The shriveled belly, furrows along the line of the hips, and the hard muscularity of the thighs. Nehemiah looks at the long hair covering the forehead, the curly beard split into scrolls in the middle of the chin.

Would the answer come from you? Human or divine, you die repeatedly for our lives, and we always die your death. Your greatest apostle had an inkling of the eternal symbiosis, when, wanting to justify and save us, perhaps, planted the seed of our degradation in our simple presence as witnesses and pawns at the moment of global forgiveness. You and I live perpetual death and resurrection throughout the centuries. When your most dedicated servants, and even more dedicated are they to other inspirations, strive to do the best in their zeal: we die. When others more gentle, whose tenderness does not shun the hyena or the criminal, receive us with benevolence: we live as marginals, hated and feared, even though in our hand no other weapon is left except the last coin of some booty stamped and approved by somebody who gave it in your name. Prophet, they extracted from you the quintessence of your world vision, and with it forged the greatest era of exuberant thought: the Middle Ages. But of your life, they kept the moment in which you now exist: agony. Based on your agony they staked out the universe and wove banners in its name, and when the ire of so

many crowns begged for a palliative, there we were. And why are we
to blame, if when they seek you out in your most simple form, in your
earliest belief, they always find us? If Jeremiah's lament anteceded the
Sermon on the Mount, if Amos's indictment preceded the response
to the rights of Caesar? And afterward came the new belief, and even
those who no longer remember that agony, upon seeing us, remember
that many times that's why we die: and so they kill us. And from this
age-old confusion, procreated over a thousand years, when will we
be released, you and I?

Sílvio serves him a little more wine. Nehemiah thanks him, turning
his attention to his plate. He drives the knife in, cuts the slice, and
bites into it, followed by a swig of wine. Facing him, Nani gulps the
glass down and stretches out her authoritarian arm.

'A little more wine! Today is Christmas!'

Samuel Rawet

# Moira

What shadow recrudesces around him? What bitter rebellion builds up into distorted moments and nullifies any perception whatsoever of objects as objects? Suddenly he identifies himself as a receptor of adulterated images, incapable of a concrete, singular, immediate encounter with the other. There were men all around him; his daily life was everybody's daily life, seemingly; it had its moments of exaltation and fury, but there was solid and stratified time, and it was painful when a fickle impulse of flux manifested itself. He opened the window onto the small side patio. It was raining. And like all rainy days are gray, and gray was his sentiment when he woke up, he once more packed the past into a solid block. The morning had started a little while ago. From the Machado Plaza noises from vehicles. In the house still the silence of the night. He drank his coffee and lit a cigarette. He knew that a certain bitterness framed his features or should have. He still hesitated in recognizing expressions that revealed nothing or thoughts not articulated in form and meaning. What role was he playing? He went to the bathroom, urinated, washed his hands; in the mirror of the cabinet he still saw traces of his makeup. He could go to sleep. What was he looking for in sleep? What was he looking for on the stage? A way of being in the world, a way of being in the face of death? WORLD. DEATH. WORDS? He clipped his fingernails too much; he tightened the belt of his robe, lit another cigarette. What kind of comfort or liberation was he looking for in the idea of suicide. Some kind of blackmail that he was actually doing to himself? An irruption of the famous death wish? Did it really exist? Death wish oscillating between creation and destruction, binding the deepest depth of his condition, or the condition? He crossed the room several times, looked at the closet, the bed, the rugs. He opened the closet, looked over his clothes. Once again in the bathroom. The sink. The shower. The towel. The soap. A daily routine. The eternal routine. A sentence. The eternal sentence. The time. The flux of time. An instant. A fraction of what? Between the past and the future, the present, suffocated, compact, almost absent. Childhood. What was there of beauty in his childhood? Why now imagine what didn't even come to be? The comparison. A dream that one could have dreamed, and which comes by way of what is seen? Or the nostalgia for a simple opening, the longing for a form pregnant with possibilities. If . . . if . . . if . . . Irresponsibility? The purely playful sense? Or the infinite responsibility of being in the world that offers itself to an agony in perpetual amplification? Would it be possible to capture the despair of a child in the face of the saturation and opacity of things? Would it be possible to imagine the contraction of the senses in the face of an organism's pure fruition that affirms itself in its genesis? Of an organism larger than the epidermis? Of an unsatisfied epidermis in search of its form? He again becomes upset over the trouble during last night's performance. The fatigue with the role was beginning to weigh him down. Four months playing the same guy by Albee, four months as the husband of the dean's lover, four months of hearing the same tune. *Who's Afraid of Virginia Woolf?* In the middle of his lines he had become silent and began to stare at the audience. He wanted to see the audience. He wanted to become the audience. Actor and a man of the public at the same time. A symbiosis. An unreality produced by two beings in collision. Irony. To go the way of humor. To go the way of what? To be what one is, what one wants to be, and what one must be. Two realities? Three. The photograph album updated. A taste for order, for regularity, from time to time, a pleasure in following his career. To review an ascension or a fall. And the difference? He noticed that he was beginning to notice an ambiguous situation forged by observation. And he became afraid. In order to distract himself he sought refuge in his day-to-day life. And he ascertained that there was the place of his vocation. Not on the stage. Acting was spontaneous. Being something always ended up in artifice. The simulation of getting along with others. And the director? The author? The set designer? The lighting man? The makeup artist? The costume designer? The prompter? A destiny? The destiny? God? A name, a reality, a possibility, a concrete being in his image and likeness, hearing and wanting to hear? A You? The horror came to him upon seeing himself again in the photographs of Creon, Oedipus. A name. The discharge blasted through his body; he feels immense, immense in his greatness and horror. Upon raising his hand he notices a slightly hieratic tic, a certain pomposity in the gesture. The tumult stabilizes. Now, he was acting for whom? Was he acting or being? Who was he? I? He changed his clothes. He looked at himself in the mirror. He opened the door to the street. The street. The perfect role.

# Rosa Palatnik

Rosa Palatnik was born in Poland in 1904 and died in Brazil in 1979. Well-known internationally in Yiddish literary circles as an accomplished short-story writer, she left her native land in 1928 and went to Paris, where she lived for ten years, publishing her first collection of stories in the Jewish press. Her tales center on two major themes: life in the little city in the interior of Poland, its Jewish customs, poverty, popular figures, and the daily dramas and existence that were obliterated with the Nazi occupation; and Brazilian Jewish life and the cultural transformations of living in the Jewish Diaspora of Brazil. Winner of many literary prizes from Brazil, Europe, Israel, and the United States, Palatnik wrote not stories with complicated plots but rather narratives filled with strong powers of observation and folkloric types who convey a culture wounded by immigration. She often focused her stories on the cross-cultural conflicts and changes arising between Jewish values of the Old World and their transportation to the New World, in this case Brazil, where she settled, in Rio de Janeiro, in 1937. During this period the majority of the Brazilian Jewish community cultivated Yiddish; two daily Yiddish newspapers were published in Rio and São Paulo and read from the north to the south of the country. She published in Brazil in Portuguese translation: *Krusnik-Rio* (1953); *Ante o turbilhão do Atlântico* (1957) (Facing the Whirlwind of the Atlantic); *Treze contos* (1961) (Thirteen Stories); *Contos escolhidos* (1966) (Selected Stories); *Arca de veludo* (1972) (Velvet Ark); and *Dois dos justos* (1975) (Two of the Just), which contains the story that follows, 'Two Mothers.' This soulful, at times comic, story is a lament on the generation gap widened by immigration and also about family values frequently sacrificed in the name of upward mobility. Framed in a Yiddishkeit simple world that is disappearing, Palatnik's story is reminiscent of Sholem Aleichem transported to Brazil. The story not only captures the poignant points of view of two mothers, but it gives a Brazilian dimension to what is known as a Yiddische mama.

# Rosa Palatnik

# Two Mothers

At Eleventh Square, near the Jewish butcher, next to the narrow steps that lead to a large church, sits Chaie-Sara on a stone bench, impatiently waiting so long for her good friend Beile-Guitel, who comes almost every day from distant Ipanema so that, according to Chaie-Sara's words, the two women would unburden their suffering maternal hearts, each one with her own story.

It's the time of the Jewish Easter. The heavy tropical heat cooled down a little. Fresh autumn breezes already begin to blow from the rebellious sea, and as a result of the frequent rains, the nearby hills seem melancholy, tearful.

Chaie-Sara is seated bent over in her old coat, her long face wrapped in a black silk kerchief. Her eyeglasses are blurred by a cold mist.

Chaie-Sara didn't stop thinking: 'Strange, how Beile-Guitel is so late today.' Suddenly, she feels a slight tug on her sleeve: 'Oh, my dear,' exclaims Chaie-Sara, 'you're coming at me from behind?' Beile-Guitel's clear and delicate face seems very agitated. Her silver hair, combed in a page boy, is disheveled, undone. With contained anger she says in a low voice: 'All the trouble on account of the good-for-nothing black chauffeur who submissively takes his hat off to me, bows to the ground, but to take me downtown, nothing. He says that he doesn't have orders from Mister Oscar . . . Rascal! To take the boss's mother somewhere he needs an order?'

Chaie-Sara gives a wink with her red and sickly eyes, which seem to spit photographic flashes behind her thick glasses. She gives a dry cough and interrupts Beile-Guitel:

'Well now, poor fellow, why is it that the miserable chauffeur is so guilty anyway? I think that if your children don't always give him permission to take you anywhere, he's forced to obey . . .'

While she spoke, Chaie-Sara made room for Beile-Guitel to sit down.

She observed in Beile-Guitel's mournful look a small, radiant spark and for that reason deduced that it was better to wait until the abundant wellsprings of emotion flowed by themselves, and thus she kept waiting, quietly. Ever since they met, this was the first time that a muffled cry was heard, coming from the hidden depths of Beile-Guitel's body . . . Chaie-Sara let her cry as much as she wanted and finally said: 'Now that's enough! Let's hear what happened . . .'

Chaie-Sara and Beile-Guitel became acquainted on board a ship that brought these two Jewish mothers to the arms of their children, in Brazil. Between the sky, the water, and the rising waves, they opened their hearts and began to tell their stories.

'I had a wonderful husband,' Chaie-Sara said, 'a religious and studious man. I had wonderful sons. But earning a living was a problem. We suffered eating farina of the worst kind, rotten macaroni, and on Saturdays, it was that hard, roasted dough taken from what one scraped off the bottom of the street vendor's tray. And even like this, we lived. Until the children began to scatter. The oldest went to Argentina, the second one went to Mexico, and the middle one went to Australia, two to Brazil. And when we realized what had happened, we were only grandfather and grandmother. Soon after, my husband began to wail: "This is a futile world. The real world is the one of the beyond . . ." And it wasn't long before he left for it . . . Then my sons began to write: "Why do you keep warming yourself by a cold hearth? Is it to watch over the dead in the cemetery? Come stay with us. This here is actually a country where Jewish rites are not kept, but whoever wants to maintain the tradition will not be killed for doing so." I didn't have much to pack: the tin menorah for the festival of Hanukkah, the silver container for the aromatic herbs, a copper grinder, a cast-iron frying pan. This is the inheritance I am taking to my children . . .'

Beile-Guitel, who had listened with a shrewd smile to Chaie-Sara's tale, finally spoke: 'What a tragedy, hm? With mine I suffered my best years . . . He was self-centered. He used to say: you can't sit here, don't stand up over there, and his mommy was exactly like him: "Don't knead macaroni sitting down, one doesn't grate plant roots standing up . . ." I had two commanders . . . so that my life between the two of them became very restricted, and so we ended up going to the rabbi. But when the holy rabbi looked with disapproval at the top of my stomach, he turned up his hooked nose right away: "I do not grant divorces to pregnant women."

'When my son, Oscar, came into the world, the rabbi kept saying: "No, he's very small, poor thing, he needs his mother's breast, and when one breast-feeds, one doesn't know how one stands in terms of religious purity. In short, you can go back home."

'Since I saw that this situation had no end, I separated from my husband, and when I got the divorce, the boy was already in school. And what didn't I do to educate my only son? I sold green pears, apples out of season; I washed floors . . . And when the first hair on his narrow chin appeared, he felt out of place in his mother's house and went away, got married, and had a son. But his mother bore up under all of that through his letters. There he became rich, a millionaire, and wrote to me: "Come, Mother, you're going to like it . . . but remember you must come well dressed. The main thing is a beautiful hat."'

Beile-Guitel burst out laughing in the midst of her narrative and continued: 'Worker's hands, pains in my feet, backaches, and a hat on top of my head. And where was I going to find a hat? The tiny hamlet only owned one straw hat, for the summer as well as the winter, and when a girl needed to meet her fiancé, she would ask one or other to borrow the hat. For that reason, I went specifically to Lublin; I bought a man's velvet beret, which looked more like a frying pan, and I went off to Brazil.'

On a warm day of a tropical summer, the two mothers stepped off the ship. Chaie-Sara in a satin dress, with pleated hips, wavy wig, and reddish face. She looked like she was returning from the synagogue on Saturdays. Her two sturdy sons immediately surrounded her, accompanied by their pleasant and plain Jewish wives. Half a dozen grandchildren came closer.

'Grandma, Mother-in-law, Mama!' All together they were happy about the visitor; they kissed, hugged, boasted, nothing different from her old household.

Tranquil, with measured steps, an elegant man of medium height with a Panama hat, wearing sunglasses with gold frames around his blue eyes, approached Beile-Guitel, bowed very gentlemanly, and said in a low voice: 'Hello, Mama! So, don't you recognize me anymore, Mama?'

'Oh,' Beile-Guitel began to tremble, 'it's you, my son, I swear I did not recognize you.'

Beile-Guitel wanted to throw her arms around his neck, cry, laugh, shout, but his stiff composure made her lose some of her enthusiasm.

Mister Oscar gave his mother a gallant kiss and cast an unsatisfied look on her unfashionable hat. He pointed to a radiant automobile that gleamed from a distance: 'Pepina and Georgy are waiting over there,' and he pointed with the finger that had a big, sparkling diamond.

'But how come,' asked Beile-Guitel with a laugh, 'don't they have permission to get out?'

Mister Oscar asked her first of all to get rid of that frying pan of a hat; he shook the dust off her wrinkled dress and calmly directed her toward the car, where a black chauffeur respectfully opened the large door.

The sun at high noon splashed rays of silver and threw light upon a fat Jewish woman in a blue hat with white feathers. 'Hello, Mother-in-law. Come in,' Dona Pepa requested in a refined voice.

'Hello, Grandma.' Little Georgy ceremoniously kissed Beile-Guitel's hand.

Beile-Guitel felt a little uncomfortable. 'So, it's like this,' she thought, 'meaning they are rich like princes.' She already began to envy Chaie-Sara.

In the elegant neighborhood of Leblon, in a marvelous house, surrounded by a garden full of flowers, the first thing she encountered the large dog, Boliek, that jumped forth and greeted her with such an unusual barking that her heart shrank. 'Go away!' and she began to run from the dog. 'Oh, my God, a mad dog,' and she thought . . . 'Oy, such a beautiful reception.'

When they entered the flourishing garden, the tropical sun was already painting the tops of the trees with rosy hues. White flowers were already beginning to curl up for sleep, and the angelic lilies intoxicated the air with their sweet aromas. Upon seeing a marble palace in the middle of that fragrant garden, Beile-Guitel was as careful as if she were stepping on glass . . . She had the impression she was about to slip and fall . . .

In the grand reception room, heavy bronze statues slept on high columns. There were so many valuable oil paintings on the walls, almost one on top of the other . . .

'So, Mama, why are you so confused? Make yourself at home, Mother,' and Mister Oscar tried to awaken her from her bewilderment.

'I swear I don't know what's happening to me.' Beile-Guitel raised her thin shoulders, moved her gray head from side to side, and didn't stop being amazed. 'What immensity . . . what riches. Rothschild . . . like Rothschild.'

Over and over again, Dona Pepa rang the bell. Each time another maid would appear, listen submissively to the orders, and then disappear.

From little Georgy's room came many voices. 'The boy, poor thing, doesn't want to eat anything.' Dona Pepa was explaining Georgy's whining. 'You have to insist; if not, he won't eat,' and with her intelligence from many hard years of life, Beile-Guitel interrupted with a smile: 'I don't remember Alter having a bad appetite . . . On the contrary, most of the time there was nothing that would satisfy his hunger . . .'

After the lavish dinner, they began to show their mother the whole immense house: luxurious carved furniture, Persian rugs, heavy silverware, so crammed in the drawers that these even shook, and finally, they went out to show her the large garden, the backyard and even the pretty little doghouse, which had a little bed, a special plate for eating, and even a small bathroom . . . Beile-Guitel said very little; she looked at everything in an astonished manner, as in a dream, but finally asked silently: 'What is it that you did, my dear Alter, to be able to attain all of this?'

'What is it that I didn't do?' Mister Oscar answered questioningly and pensively conveyed: 'Knocking on the doors of Brazilians in order to sell on the installment plan, climbing the hills, sleeping in the Israeli Benefit Society, eating beans and rice, what misery . . . Until, Mama, well, it's a very long story . . .'

From the small window of the little doghouse, one could see the sky, enormous; you could hear the croaking of the frogs and the echo of the Brazilian carnival . . .

Dona Pepa appeared at the door, looked discreetly at her diamond watch, and said in a low voice: 'It's already late; we have to take Mother so she can go to bed . . .'

Something had burst inside Beile-Guitel's heart . . .

'Take me?' she asked with a frightened voice and veiled anxiety, 'Why take me? By chance is my bed too far away from here? . . .'

Mister Oscar rapidly unbuttoned his collar . . . He felt very hot; he wanted to explain . . . but Dona Pepa intercepted: 'Far away? Who said it was far away? It's right there, on the other street . . .' In this interim Mister Oscar took hold of the conversation: 'You, Mama,' he began in a muffled voice, 'like your silence, tranquility, calmness, in order to pray, to eat kosher and . . .'

Beile-Guitel began to let out a sharp laugh . . . 'But, Mother!' Mister Oscar retorted, 'but it's only for your own good, understand . . .' Beile-Guitel wasn't able to stop herself from laughing, and laughing like this, with one hand she covered her son's mouth, and with the other she dried her 'laughing' tears.

'It's all right, it's all right; it doesn't matter, dear Alter. We Jews understand each other.'

The enormous dog, Boliek, threw itself suddenly on its little bed, showed its pointed teeth, and without any apparent reason began to bark wildly. Beile-Guitel was startled, cast an envious gaze at the clean little doghouse, straightened her rumpled dress, and repeated once again: 'It's all right, it's all right; it doesn't matter where one sleeps. Over there, I'll definitely find what will serve me.'

In her new bed Beile-Guitel began to go over the exotic impression of her first day in Brazil. Her feelings of oppression, ever since she stepped off the ship, she tried to drown in her tears . . .

A white moon, round, like a great silver medallion, hung sadly in front of her window; she stared at it, and as if trying to console herself: A mother cannot be angry . . . a mother has to understand . . . forgive . . .

Beile-Guitel stirred about in the strange bed for a long time, moaning in a low voice, hearing the old mattress springs accompanying her moans, and, when it seemed that the full moon was coming closer to her window, almost touching her hands, she suddenly saw that it wasn't the moon but rather the dog, Boliek, which, stretching its long teeth and growling like a lion, pulled off the bedspread and wanted to swallow her . . .

Bathed in perspiration, Beile-Guitel awoke from her nightmare and saw the moon entwined in a black cloud. From the dark sky came a small rain:

'What luck that dog has,' Beile-Guitel spoke into the night. 'What luck . . . he lives like a prince in the palace of my children and still comes to bark at their mother, damn dog.'

When Beile-Guitel met with her shipboard companion, Chaie-Sara, for the first time, the latter's wrinkled face was already smooth, as if she had passed through a steam roller. Also her ugly shoes had been replaced by light sandals. And she herself was feeling fine and content. She grabbed Beile-Guitel by her arm.

'My dear, why so dejected? Your children have the reputation of being millionaires . . . What's your life like with such rich children? Tell me.'

There at Eleventh Square, where Chaie-Sara lived, the Jews got together in the noisy corner bars and talked about their records of sales on the installment plan. Some praised their customers, while others cursed the damned swindlers. When Beile-Guitel appeared, with her graceful walk and healthy look, everybody turned around: 'That's the mother of the millionaire, a grand person.' The Jewish women looked out their windows and offered a thousand opinions: 'Beautiful, but sad, she has an elegant manner as if born to be a princess.'

With her typical laugh, Beile-Guitel provided an answer for Chaie-Sara right away: 'All goes very well . . .' and added laconically, 'rich children, right?'

'I am also doing very well,' Chaie-Sara began to boast, 'and almost to the contrary, I am doing too well. My children don't leave the house without saying good-morning to their mother, and my daughter-in-law serves the first dish of macaroni to her mother-in-law. My grandchildren as well do not stay away from me, but, poor things, they don't understand what I say. They chatter in a semiharsh language, my dear. Here the adults do not understand what the children are saying. This is my home,' and she opens the door to an old house with many windows. 'Look, my dear, a bright room, familiar pillows, dishes, and new pans . . . You know, when I don't trust their kosher food, I cook for myself.'

In Beile-Guitel's clear eyes a slight luster sparkled. With a contained calmness and, apparently, laughing, she asked: 'And don't your children have a dog?'

'A dog?' Chaie-Sara asked seriously. 'That's a good one; my children are simple door-to-door peddlers; they knock on doors, poor things, on the hottest days, in the hills; they bathe themselves in rivers of sweat, and they go on living . . . But a dog? Where would they keep the animal? Only if it were under the bed,' Chaie-Sara concluded with a laugh.

Beile-Guitel felt that she would end up crying out loud . . . And with effort, she said in a low voice, 'Well, I'm going, because in a little while it will be difficult to find even standing room on the streetcar.'

The sun was already bending over the window of Chaie-Sara's bright room as if it wanted to cast one last gaze on that happy household.

'Fiddlesticks!' exclaimed Chaie-Sara. 'The streetcar and look who it's for! The mother of the millionaire! Can't your son send his chauffeur with the car?'

Chaie-Sara got very peeved with that situation. Beile-Guitel ground her words between her teeth as if she wanted to go over them well, detain them so that they didn't come out too strong.

'My son, Alter,' she began to justify, 'is always very busy, poor fellow; so much responsibility is not funny. Why then will I go and bother him?'

Chaie-Sara thought: 'She is shutting me up; OK, let it be.' On the other hand, on her way home, Beile-Guitel also thought: 'Could it be that Chaie-Sara is also hiding the truth? Who knows?'

That's how the two of them thought they were fooling each other, and they began to meet almost everyday, to tell the things that were in their hearts, except that Beile-Guitel's greatest disappointment had not been mentioned, until . . . until their last meeting . . .

'Speak up, my dear Beile-Guitel, open up your heart; I won't let you leave until you say what's on your mind,' and Chaie-Sara wouldn't stop insisting, at the side of her friend, who remained seated as if petrified. Her clear eyes looked into the distance; she rocked her covered head, and her straight back accompanied the movement.

'So?' Chaie-Sara did not stop. 'Let's hear it; speak, you're going to feel better.'

From the nearby synagogue, where some religious Jews were saying their afternoon prayers, one heard the sounds of their murmuring prayers. From the big church came the chords of 'Ave Maria.' And in the cloudy sky there suddenly appeared a one and only star.

Beile-Guitel trembled, as if she had awakened from a nightmare;

she made a gesture of resignation with her hand and spoke like a sleepwalker: 'To feel better? Who? Me? I know . . .' and she let her face drop, crying on Chaie-Sara's wide shoulder, and for the first time since they met, she cried in a loud voice, sobbing on her neck, as if she were her sister, and then she began to pour out her stifled, accumulated bitterness.

'I can't take it any longer.' Beile-Guitel's voice became more hoarse. 'I knew that my grandson, Zalman, was going to have a birthday; I heard that they were preparing a big party; from a distance I saw them washing the windows, taking care of the garden . . . Well, since I am the grandmother, I also prepared myself, quietly . . . A new dress, new shoes, a black purse because to tell the truth, my Alter does not deny me any money. But,' and Beile-Guitel began again to cry, 'why do I need their money if there isn't one drop of love from the heart? Because the "golden calf" dazzled their minds. They became blind and deaf; they forgot respect for their mother,' said Beile-Guitel shouting. 'Today, when I go out,' she began again, 'I see a line of automobiles up to their house. My God! I began to tremble. Today? Is Zalman's party today? They didn't even tell me? I'm going there, ready to choke them, and my daughter-in-law starts coming in my direction. "Mother-in-law, darling," she begins in her refined voice, which doesn't even go with such a "developed" body, "here there will be important businessmen, manufacturers, industrialists; they don't understand one word of Yiddish. Why should you behave like a mute? It's better if you . . ."

'I didn't let her finish, because I knew that her words would be a sin. I only looked at her, controlled myself so as not to faint, and left without saying a word. From far away, I stayed watching the birthday party of my grandson, Zalman, and I implored: "Do not punish them, my Lord, because of their blindness for wealth; after all, they're my children, even though it really hurts my heart." You know, Chaie-Sara, these sins are planted in the heart of a person; they stay there hidden for a long time, but one day, when a small screw loosens, the sins jump out like assassins and keep tormenting people.

'I was far away and I saw the chauffeur arrive with the shiny town car. He faced me as if he hadn't recognized me. "Can you take me downtown?" I asked. He turned his head mumbling that he did not have any order to do this. He certainly had orders to go and fetch some highfalutin lady for the party, who doesn't speak Yiddish. Oh, money!

It makes people deaf, dumb, and blind. Do you remember, dear Chaie-Sara, there in our city, a grandmother was an adornment, she would be seated in the most important place at each party, but here a dog is more important. Just look at their disgusting dog. One of them shows him affection, the other washes him, my grandson kisses him, but nobody has respect for the mother, not even the chauffeur.'

Chaie-Sara, who had also begun to cry, embraced Beile-Guitel, looked at her with great respect, as if she were looking at something sacred. She dried her tears and, finally, gave a secret praise to God. A praise and an exaltation for the kindness he bestowed on her. And Beile-Guitel felt that all the doors of justice would be opened for her when she emptied all the evil that had accumulated within her. She placed her two hands on her knees, rocked herself as she used to do when reading the Yiddish translation of the Bible, and said: 'I suffered my whole life; I dedicated all my life to my only son; I yearned for a ray of light; I thought I would be treated with honor, as I was in my home, which I left. But it's that they became rich, princes, and so I have to announce myself to the doorman before stepping on the threshold of their house. If I go to the garden, the dog attacks me right away. Oh, that dog, dear Chaie-Sara, that dog! He'll certainly be at my grandson's birthday party. And the daughter-in-law, is she by any chance better? From a distance, she makes a gesture with her hand: "Excuse me, Mother-in-law; I'm going to a fashion show." And my Alter always has a meeting. Always looking for honors, but for his mother there is not one honor left. They kiss my hand, my forehead; they whisper, just like in the movies. Only to close their eyes. Why is that? Let them give me a little of their heart, my own little nook in their palace. The rest is foolishness. It would be better if they founded a Jewish school so that my little grandson would understand what his grandmother is saying.'

Beile-Guitel smoothed her wrinkled blouse, dried her tearful face, and said softly: 'In the end, who knows if we also would be like that if we were in their place? Well then, does there exist a limit to the savage power of the blindness for riches? I remember that there, in our old little city, my Alter was a socialist. And here? I can't even recognize him. But remember, dear Chaie-Sara,' and Beile-Guitel extended her tremulous hand, 'this stays only between the two of us.'

'Well, my friend.' Chaie-Sara embraced Beile-Guitel tenderly, kissed her tearful eyes, and began to walk hurriedly, as if she wanted to run away from the evil that, may God save us, could also touch her. 'Don't you worry,' she shouted from a distance. 'God is the Father.'

With a fear hidden in her heart and a silent joy in her eyes, Chaie-Sara entered her home quickly; she saw her children seated at the table, waiting for her to have dinner. She then raised an expression of gratitude and a praise to God for being the object of the great filial love she possessed.

# Judith Grossmann

Judith Grossmann was born in the state of Rio de Janeiro in 1931 and is the daughter of Rumanian immigrants to Brazil. Educated in Anglo-Germanic letters, she received her degree from the Federal University of Rio de Janeiro in 1954. She studied at the University of Chicago under a Fulbright fellowship. In 1974 she became professor of literary theory at the Federal University of Bahia, where today she is professor emerita. In 1959 she published her first collection of poems, *Linhagem do Rocinante: 35 poemas* (Rocinante's Heritage: 35 Poems); in 1970 a volume of short stories, *O meio da pedra* (The Middle of the Stone). In 1976 she was awarded the Prêmio Brasília (Brasilia award) for *A noite estrelada: Estórias do ínterim* (1977) (The Starry Night: Stories of the Interim), a collection of stories that established her as one of Brazil's most compelling short-story writers. Another collection of poetry, *Vária navegação: Mostra de poesia* (Varied Navigation: Poetry on Display), was published in 1996. Grossman has published four novels: *Outros trópicos* (1980) (Other Tropics), *Cantos delituosos* (1985) (Punishable Songs), *Meu amigo Marcel Proust romance* (1997) (My Friend Marcel Proust Novel), and *Fausto Mefisto romance* (1999) (Fausto Mephisto Novel). Another collection of stories and chronicles, *Pátria de Histórias* (Homeland of Stories), appeared in 2000. Recognized as a writer of deep psychological states, Grossmann focuses primarily on childhood and women, often in an introspective manner that has led to comparisons with Clarice Lispector. Although Jewish themes do not pervade her work, the themes of rootlessness and memory emerge repeatedly. 'Mrs. Büchern in Lebenswald,' from *A noite estrelada*, is one of the twenty-two stories from the section titled 'Livro hebraico' (Hebraic Book), which evokes the guilt and trauma related to Holocaust survivors and how they cope with that past horror.

# Judith Grossmann

# Mrs. Büchern in Lebenswald

Nobody in Lebenswald knew for certain who Mrs. Büchern was. Where she had come from. How she had come. Why she had come. Since her youth Mrs. Büchern was on a pilgrimage to atone for her sins. She had not been in Buchenwald. But she had not escaped Lebenswald. There she was. She had come with little baggage, some books, a few adornments. She had set herself up in a small apartment, which she tried to transform into a wonder of beauty. The living-room window faced the sea, where there was always a white ship that at night exploded into pink, blue, and yellow lights. On top of a small wrought-iron table, always one red solitary rose in a green bottle, a candlestick of blue agate, a heavy key, an ashtray of thick glass encircled by a metal rim. Mrs. Büchern kept her books in a lid-covered pine box upon which sat a Victrola and a pile of records. Mrs. Büchern ate very little. She nourished herself almost exclusively with fruit and tea. She was a vegetarian for practical reasons—the smell of beef would spoil the ambiance. On a small plate of blue glass, Mrs. Büchern always had raisins, pastries, walnuts, but these things were exclusively for her guests. As part of her atonement, Mrs. Büchern didn't eat delicacies. Mrs. Büchern didn't work. Nobody knew where her means of support came from, and though she lived frugally, it was obvious that she had the means, for she always had enough to pay for the rent, the laundress, the fruit, the tea, and the roses.

The neighbors were the ones who were most intrigued by Mrs. Büchern. By Mrs. Büchern's age, because Mrs. Büchern was ageless. Some days she seemed radiant, talkative, resplendent like a girl; other days she seemed gray, fearful, bent over like an ancient person. By Mrs. Büchern's past, because she had no past. In the meantime, there was talk about the picture of a certain child, which sometimes appeared on top of the glass surface of the small table and at other times disappeared. By Mrs. Büchern's disposition, because she didn't have a definite disposition. At times she greeted everybody with a smile that was like a kiss; then other times she snubbed everybody. By Mrs. Büchern's appearance, because it was the most changeable. At times she appeared extremely elegant, her brown hair impeccably set, her long fingernails painted; other times people saw her appear almost shabby, her hair messy, her fingernails bitten. Mrs. Büchern was an enigma in the apartment building, but as an enigma they respected her. Inasmuch as she didn't define herself, it was impractical for them to define her, and so they left her in peace.

They respected Mrs. Büchern so much that they respected the tall and thin lad with the look of a frightened bird, who visited her on a daily basis. On the agreed-upon number of rings of the front-door bell, because she would only open the door for him, she hurled herself to receive him. They laughed a lot, and she used to run her hands through his hair, because that's exactly what he needed. He devoured her 'nutritions,' as he called them, there on the blue plate, and they stayed together until dawn. Within one month, they had already talked through several eternities. Only to him, practically a child, had Mrs. Büchern chosen to confide her past experiences. At times it was too terrible for the lad. He shuddered, shriveled in horror, but he understood, with no need for explanation, why Mrs. Büchern told him those things and why she had selected him as a repository. In truth Mrs. Büchern, also as part of her atonement, occupied herself with the initiation of the young sage of Lebenswald. The lad was the only dead man in Lebenswald. All the others were alive, very much so, frenetically immersed in their little lives, their little things, their little matters, their little plans, their little assaults.

The lad was the only dead person around, and that's why he was so sad. He loved life, he would like to be alive, but he recognized that it was impossible. However, for that very reason he could contemplate life from afar, love it more than everybody else, and whisper it into everybody else's melodious ears. Mrs. Büchern was the first to recognize what everybody would recognize later, and thus with all her dedication and loyalty she busied herself with his initiation. The lad had been brought up by parents who didn't know how to immediately recognize his stillbornness, and therefore every moment of the day they exacerbated it even more. His teachers didn't recognize it, and his classmates didn't recognize it either so that, in the beginning, he became more and more unrecognized. Oh! If it hadn't been for Mrs. Büchern, what would have become of the stillborn from Lebenswald? But what too would have become of Mrs. Büchern if it hadn't been for the stillborn? She would have been left without an activity, without a role. That's why she was finally repudiated by the lad on the day she recognized herself to be the most genuine accomplice in his still-bornness. And having been crucified by everyone, parents, teachers, classmates, he implacably crucified Mrs. Büchern, who was there for that reason, so that he could leave from there resuscitated.

Having fulfilled her mission, Mrs. Büchern got ready to leave Lebenswald in search of a more advanced position, in continuation of her atonement, when, on a brisk and breezy morning, suitably gray, she understood, on a given corner, at a given crossroad, whose asphalt was wet from the night dew, that there was still something she had to do in Lebenswald. In front of her stood a young man, long, silky, honey-colored hair, satin eyes, two topazes, two suns on that lead morning, who smiled and beseeched her. Mrs. Büchern didn't have the slightest doubt as to what was happening; she smiled in return and acquiesced. She would stay a little bit longer. Ready for her second mission, Mrs. Büchern prepared herself carefully for the initiation of the saint of Lebenswald. The first night was spent without sleep, because the young man did not stop talking, wanting to give her, on that first day, the complete story. Which was completely unnecessary since Mrs. Büchern already knew about everything. Because Mrs. Büchern knew about everything without anybody having to tell her a thing. Mrs. Büchern took his hands and let him melt into words. Nevertheless, not even this was enough, because in the end he asked her for an Equanil, a substance she didn't even know about, let alone have in the house.

It appears that Mrs. Büchern had inordinate confidence in her own resources. The lad told her about how he was the son of Jews and about how all that stuff about Judaism bothered him. How, at five years old, he stayed around to contemplate his nanny in her bath, which they took together, lying down afterward on her bed, to watch the rest of her hygiene. How his mother never let him get dirty when he was a little boy. How he had been motivated to be crafty, to dupe, developing from that time on nausea for the process, which almost prevented him from surviving. How at five in the afternoon, he was walking home from school, his tears running down his face, out of fear that his beneficent parents might have run away from him. How all women were prostitutes. How he detested his work, without any other objective but material gain. How, up until now, he still tried to help his very rich, beneficent parents, who had never helped him, out of gratitude for the good teachings they had transmitted to him. How nothing he provided for them still seemed enough to them and how he felt guilty about having left them in another city, in search of better possibilities to help them. How his friends propositioned him. How his own beauty bothered him. How his own sensitivity bothered him, making him deny it and try to replace it with some kind of brutality, which he evidently did not achieve, making him feel even more devastated. How he was ashamed of everything, of everybody, of being naked, of his own voice, of what he said, of his feet, of his perspiration. And how he was ashamed that everybody was alive, and how, in collusion, he too was alive, this being the greatest of his shames.

Mrs. Büchern had confirmed then what she had known since the beginning, that the lad was the only man alive in Lebenswald. All the others were dead, really dead, inexpugnably, submerged in their little daily deaths, their familiar little tombs, their little shrouded apparel, their little four-wheel biers, their little chairs of four little legs, their little tables of four little sides. The lad was the only one alive and for that reason he was so sad. He loved death, he would like to be dead, but he realized that it was impossible. But because of that he could contemplate death from afar, love it more than everybody else, and blow it into everybody's waxed ears. This was the destiny of the young man of Lebenswald—to blow skeletal words into everybody's waxed ears. Mrs. Büchern did not quibble, and even though her second mission might be more difficult than the first, in tempering that explosion of sun, blood, nerves, life, in order to make the lad more apt to survive in that mortuary labyrinth, she did not hold back. Having to transform the external smile into penitence from the soul's lips, having to remove a bit of the luster from the eyes and from the golden hair, Mrs. Büchern also had to die inside several times in order to carry out her mission successfully. And in this task, of continuously ordaining the lad, Mrs. Büchern busied herself for months and months, composing, at last, the mask that tore his heart.

Understanding that along with his, Mrs. Büchern's heart was also torn, he realized, at a glance, that she was the most genuine accomplice in his vitality, not hesitating as such to sacrifice her with the greatest possible speed. And having been sacrificed by the maid, by his mother, by his father, and by the oceanic multitude around him, so much practice in the execution of that task had made it so that this didn't take him more that a few seconds. And having sacrificed Mrs. Büchern, who was there for that reason, he left that place more dead than alive for ever and ever.

This time Mrs. Büchern did not have any doubt about packing her bags and leaving Lebenswald. In fact, there couldn't be any more possibility of her staying, because she had already taken care of the two most important residents of Lebenswald. And besides the two most important residents, what else would there be? And despite Lebenswald not yet knowing about any of that business, in due time it was certainly bound to know.

# Alberto Dines

Alberto Dines was born in Rio de Janeiro in 1932, his parents having immigrated to Brazil from the Ukraine. Journalist, biographer, short-story writer, screenplay writer, and film critic, Dines began his studies in the city of São Paulo. During his formative years he enrolled in Jewish schools, and when he was a student at the Escola Popular Israelita-Brasileiro Sholem Aleichem, he caught sight of the famous Stefan Zweig, then a political refugee in Rio and who was to become the subject of one of Dines's successful works. Early on he became involved in a socialist-Zionist youth organization. This was the first of his many contacts with Israel. As a journalist and editor he later became editorial director of the nationally known daily newspaper *O Jornal do Brasil*, a position he maintained for twelve years during the height of the military dictatorship. At the time he also was appointed affiliated professor of journalism at the Catholic University of Rio de Janeiro. He spent the academic year 1974–75 at New York's Columbia University as a visiting professor of journalism and international affairs. After he returned to Brazil, he was awarded a fellowship to Portugal to conduct research on his book *Vínculos de fogo* (1992) (Bonds of Fire) about the Portuguese Inquisition and the life of José Antônio da Silva, the Jew. During his stay in Lisbon, he also published *O baú de Abravanel* (1990) (Abravanel's Trunk), tracing the genealogy of the Jewish Abravanel family. In 1972 he published a collection of stories, *Posso?* (Can I?), which treats the themes of dislocation and acculturation and, in the title story, the need for mutual respect between Catholics and Jews. Besides his active journalist career, he is particularly well known for his bestseller biography, *Morte no paraíso: A tragédia de Stefan Zweig* (1981) (Death in Paradise: The Tragedy of Stefan Zweig). Another edition appeared in 1982, and an expanded version (596 pages) was published by Rocco Publishers in 2004. In the excerpt that follows, Dines tells of the events immediately following the discovery of the suicide of Zweig and his wife. This scenario illustrates the clash between Jewish and Catholic rituals and what it means to be a Diaspora Jew in the tropics.

Alberto Dines

EXCERPTS FROM *Death in Paradise:*
## The Tragedy of Stefan Zweig

## [Chapter 10] The Buried Candelabrum

*Everywhere I go I am a foreigner and, under the best of circumstances, a guest.*
The World of Yesterday, introduction

*The everlasting menorah . . . , like all of God's mysteries, rests in the darkness
of the ages. Who can tell whether it will remain so forever and ever, unseen
and mourned by its people, who go on wandering from exile to exile; or
whether, one day, it will be discovered when Israel once more comes into its
own, and the resplendent menorah will shine in the Temple of Peace.*
The Buried Candelabrum, end

'I entered the bedroom and remained there I don't know how long without
raising my head. I couldn't or I didn't want to look. On the two modest
beds, pushed together, lay the master with his handsome face slightly
altered by its paleness. The violent death had not left any visible signs of
violence; he was sleeping without his eternal smile, but with enormous
sweetness and even greater serenity. It appears that he died before she
did. His wife must have seen the end of that life; she held him by his
head with her right arm, and all of her face was hidden by her husband.
On being separated from his body, her arm and hand had remained
twisted and rigid; it was necessary to use force on that fragile and hard
little body in order to place it into the coffin. The woman's face was
deformed. Nothing will be able to wipe away this image.'[1]

[. . .]

On the veranda their close friends assembled, devastated. Some of them
completely crushed and withdrawn: Feder, Agache, Mistral, Strowski,

Koogan, Malamud. Others who had shown up persisted in the silly talk that fools make to get themselves through important moments. For instance, there was Stern, who kept assuring a reporter from the *Revista da Semana* that among Zweig's projects was a biography of Santos Dumont, precisely the same information that, a week earlier, had so deeply irritated Zweig, the friend he was now mourning. To *O Jornal* the very same Stern bragged about writing the final chapter of Zweig's autobiography. And Stefan hadn't even said good-bye to him before committing suicide. Claudio de Souza kept up the endless task of dealing with the authorities. Both of them by that time had already perpetrated the hasty translation of his *Final Statement*, which, as Zweig's last words, had taken several days to write.

As he did every Monday, the tailor Henrique Nussembaum had gone to Rio to buy cloth and supplies. He had returned at five in the afternoon to find an odd commotion in the store. They were waiting to tell him about Zweig's death. As the leader of the small Jewish community in Petropolis, he felt obliged to do something for his coreligious friend. He went to Gonçalves Dias Street, but the house was off limits. A policeman blocked his way, but the little man was brazen:

'I stuck my finger right under his nose and said: "According to the deceased's religion, you're the one who doesn't belong here!"'

Since the authorities knew him, they let him go inside. Later, during the vigil, when the bodies had already been transferred to the head-quarters of the Petropolitan Academy of Letters at the Pedro II School (on November 15 Avenue), Nussembaum made another scene, and it wouldn't be the last one: he demanded that Jewish ritual be respected— the flowers and wreaths were to be placed in the other room and the coffins closed. Only those who wished to do so could open them.[2]

The early morning was cold. In the photos published by the *Tribuna de Petrópolis*, the groups of strangers who kept vigil over the suicides were well bundled up. The icy gust of the European winter had finally reached paradise.

On Tuesday, February 24, the country awoke to the tragedy of the suicide. The morning newspapers, unmoved, maintained their rigid practice of reporting only international news on the front page. In Zweig's circle, the suicide was being interpreted as another casualty of war; however, from the viewpoint of the morning papers, this was not war news and so was noticeably relegated to the inside pages. The evening newspapers, on the other hand, covered their front pages with dramatic headlines about the tragedy.[3] Summer would only officially end on March 20, but the euphoria had petered out, the season of pleasure and joy finished. Just one week after carnival and here was another day of ashes: a poet had fallen. The sinking of two Brazilian freighters, the patriotic feelings kept at bay by the militaristic state, the will to fight for grand causes, all converged upon that solitary death. The feelings of regret blew into the quivering leaves of the trees. The news that Stefan and his wife, Lotte, were to be buried in Petropolis at four in the afternoon caused many people, very early on in the day, to organize enormous caravans of vehicles at Mauá Square in Rio. Special buses were chartered. Paulo Rónai, representing the Hungarian PEN Club, remembers seeing taxis being fought over by groups of people anxious to pay their last respects to the suicidal couple.

A palpable tragedy.

Alfred Gartenberg, who a year earlier during the proceedings of the Conference of the Brazilian-Israeli Association (ABI), had so persistently demanded of Stefan that he take a stand on the persecution of the Jews in Europe, went as far as Mauá Square.

'I turned around; I didn't have the courage; my conscience was hurting me on account of that earlier demand of mine.'[4]

One of the groups that went up to Petropolis was indeed different. Long beards, some wearing long coats and black hats in spite of the summer: a delegation of Orthodox Jews. The Eastern European shtetl that Hitler was destroying was surviving right there in the middle of the tropics. They all belonged to the funeral society for the dead, Chevra Kadisha, the traditional holy congregation headed by the chief rabbi of Rio himself, Rav Mordechai Tzekinovsky.

The Chevra Kadisha met early on Tuesday morning to discuss Stefan Zweig's death. In those days the rules were very strict about Jewish ritual and who could be buried according to the law. There was much discussion. Rabbi Tzekinovsky was in favor of sz being buried alongside the Jews, despite the reproachable circumstances surrounding his death by suicide. *Adonai natan, Adonai lakach,* God gives, God takes. Even though Stefan had transgressed against such strict doctrines, the rabbi confessed that he was influenced by the writer's work, above all, by his marvelous story *The Buried Candelabrum,* a painful fable about the heritage of the Jews.

'The problem cannot be faced by the way he died but by the way he lived,' said Tzekinovsky, a pale, thin man with deep, dark eyes who spoke little and always softly. The epitome of outward fragility and inward strength. Whoever knew him would be unable to link him to the tense dispute that was going to develop that afternoon.

'We decided to go to Petropolis to claim the body of that Jewish writer so that he would be buried alongside his people. I don't remember exactly which member of the authorities received us. It could have been the mayor or someone else, but whoever, he was the highest authority present at the time. We were received courteously, in the best Brazilian tradition. However, when we mentioned the reason that brought us there, the man's face turned somber.

'"Did Stefan Zweig leave a will stating the place of burial?"

'"But is there some indication in his will that he did not wish to be buried in a Jewish cemetery?" asked Rabbi Tzekinovsky in true Talmudic dialectic discourse. "It's a basic assumption that a man is to be buried alongside his people. There's no need to be specific."

'The man in authority was not convinced.

'"But the writer never manifested his Judaism."

'"Whether or not he manifested his Judaism, that is a discussion for the heavenly tribunal. Nobody knows what happened during his final moments."

'"But the honor of Petropolis will be deeply wounded if Zweig isn't buried here."

'"Sir, if he is to be buried in a public square, we shall step aside; really it will be a great honor for Petropolis. But if he is to be buried in a cemetery, then there is no reason for him not to come to ours."

'The man in authority was visibly irritated.

'"If you keep on insisting, we shall be so obliged to bury him. But you should know, the population will feel frustrated. This could create a lot of anger. Impossible to foresee the consequences. In this case the blame will be all yours."

'Nothing more, nothing less: a threat. At the exact moment when Hitler was lighting the ovens of the Holocaust, in delightful Petropolis, in order to pay homage to the celebrated writer, the specter of the pogroms was being unleashed.

'The rabbi realized that there was nothing to be done. He said his good-bye, and followed by the delegation, he departed.'[5]

Koogan remembers: when they told him that the suicides were to have official funeral rites and were to be buried in Petropolis, he didn't mind. At that point in history the Brazilian government's homage to a recognizably Jewish writer was interpreted as a political gesture. Koogan came across Rabbi Tzekinovsky during the vigil and remembers having heard from him the following: 'It doesn't matter; wherever a Jew is buried, it becomes sacred ground.' That was Zweig's own idea in The Buried Candelabrum—no matter where the surviving relic of the Second Temple was buried: wherever it was, so was its message. But Tzekinovsky, according to the very same document, neither approved of the other rabbi, from the reformed movement, Dr. Lemle, who was already in Petropolis, nor of his action of having accepted the task of burying them in a non-Jewish cemetery.

Henrique Nussembaum saw the two rabbis at the school building, one leaving, the other entering. The tailor, in his own way, had also tried to rescue the Candelabrum. On that morning he had asked Claudio de Souza to take him to the Rio Negro Palace in Petropolis to speak to President Vargas. Claudio acquiesced. Vargas received him standing up and hurriedly.

'President, he belongs to us . . .'

Claudio de Souza reminded me that I was speaking to the president of the republic. Vargas didn't seem to mind the informality and calmly said to me: 'It's the people of Petropolis who want him here.'[6]

At 3:50 in the afternoon, Carauta de Souza made a speech before the two coffins in the name of the Petropolitan Academy of Letters. In the mourning chamber the Firemen's Honor Guard stood in line at attention; the black coffins with dark handles were taken to the hearses. Carrying Stefan's coffin: a military officer, representative of the federal governor Admiral Amaral Peixoto, the mayor Cardoso Miranda, Leopold Stern, D'Almeida Vitor, Professor Clementino Fraga (representing the Brazilian Academy of Letters), Abrahão Koogan, and as envoy of the Israeli organizations of Rio, Israel Dines.[7]

All businesses in Petropolis were closed. Five thousand people accompanied the bier on foot. The church bells rang; on the flagpoles the Brazilian flag at half-mast. On the sidewalks and on the balconies, people waving good-bye.

In the cemetery, in obedience to Jewish ritual, the coffins were placed on wooden planks so that the bodies would be close to the ground while Rabbi Lemle read a passage from Zweig's own *Vision of the Prophet*.[8] Cantor Fleischmann chanted a passage from the Psalms and the Kaddish prayer for the dead. About a meter away stood the tomb of the imperial family with Hapsburg princes and princesses.

In Stefan's house one of the wicker baskets that had been rummaged through in search of the poison was stuffed full with torn bits of paper. Here a reporter found a piece of writing that described the miserable life of the Jews in Germany, enslaved, tortured, murdered. It also confirmed Stefan's not being unaware of the lack of attention paid to him in Berchtesgaden, where he was considered a dangerous intellectual enemy of Nazism. 'Nevertheless, Thomas and Heinrich Mann are of greater worth than I . . .'[9]

'I cannot say very much about the National Socialist government's reaction to Stefan Zweig's suicide. All I can remember was that his death was greeted with much joy and that the party considered it to be a well-deserved end for that enemy of National Socialism. (signed) Albert Speer.'[10]

FINAL STATEMENT
'I, overly impatient, am leaving ahead of time.' Stefan Zweig.

# Notes

1. This beginning to chapter 10 is a fragment of a letter by the poet and then reporter Gabriela Mistral to Eduardo Mallea, literary director of *La Nacion*, Buenos Aires. This appears in Raul de Azevedo, *Vida e Morte de Stefan Zweig*, special addition of *Aspectos* (Rio), no. 40, April 1942, p. 91.

2. Statement by Nussembaum to the author. The majority of the people during the public vigil opened the lid of Stefan's coffin in order to pay their last respects. This explains the version given at the time about Lotte's coffin being sealed due to the strong odor.

3. In spite of the morning papers' habit of including only international news on the first page, several times a week the newspaper published front-page pictures of its owner, Assis Chateaubriand, christening the airplanes used for training in his war campaign Wings for Brazil.

4. Paulo Rónai, information given to the author, October 1980; Alfred Gartenberg, statement given to the author on May 13, 1981.

5. The statement was written by hand in Hebrew by a member of the commission who went to Petropolis and does not wish to be identified out of respect for Rabbi Tzekinovsky, who was still alive, residing in Israel, and who had consciously infringed on religious commandments and Jewish ritual by trying to bury a man who had committed suicide. The newspapers of February 25, 1942, register the presence of a delegation of rabbis who had appeared prior to the burial on Tuesday afternoon.

If by that time the letters left by Zweig to Koogan had been opened, the question would have been settled differently; in the document written on February 20, Stefan specifies that he wishes to be buried in Rio. In one of the notes he left a few days later for his friend who was a publisher in Petropolis, Stefan reiterates his wish for a simple funeral—which can be interpreted as an alternative to the Jewish ritual he expected he would be denied. Cardoso Miranda, in a statement to the author, denies his participation in the meeting with the rabbis, alleging that he wasn't even present at the funeral. However, in the photos and articles from the newspapers, the mayor appears holding one of the handles of the coffin.

6. This episode was first printed in the *Jornal Israelita* (Rio), May 8, 1980, in a statement made by Nussembaum and taken down by Egon and Frieda Wolff. On January 11, 1981, in Petropolis, Nussembaum repeated to the author, in the presence of his wife and son, the same story. The only difference is that in the first version he indicated Carauta de Souza as his escort, and in the second, Claudio de Souza.

7. According to the newspapers, Admiral Amaral Peixoto was representing the federal government. The military chief of staff, representing the president of the republic, General Francisco José Pinto, showed up during the vigil. Getúlio Vargas, in spite of spending the summer in Petropolis and of knowing about the official funeral rites, did not appear.

8. A passage from *Jeremiah* (theater), originally translated into Portuguese by Candido de Carvalho.

9. Azevedo, *Vida e Morte*, 73.

10. Albert Speer, letter to the author, October 30, 1980. The last survivor of Adolph Hitler's cabinet and the architect responsible for the Nazi public spectacles and several buildings of the period. Later put in charge of the war effort and the labor camps. Found guilty by the Nuremberg tribunal, he completed his sentence and was set free. He lived the rest of his life in Germany. He died on September 1, 1981, in London, when he was about to take part in a program sponsored by the BBC.

# Sônia Rosenblatt

Sônia Rosenblatt was born in Bessarabia and as a refugee fled to Brazil, where she settled in the northeastern city of Recife, capital of the state of Pernambuco. Her memoir, Lembranças enevoadas (1984) (Clouded Memories), is significant because it is one of the few Holocaust memoirs of a Jew residing in Brazil. As she states in her preface, the memoir was written not only as testimony of the Holocaust and to denounce its horrors, but also as a challenge to the insidious process of forgetting, thus her title. Inspired to write her narrative after listening in 1977 to the Israeli minister Simone Weil, who spoke against silence, Rosenblatt offers in a direct style the details of one horror and indignity after another. Having personally known this agony, she is marked forever by its inhumanity, and yet she attempts to transcend this with a book filled with human compassion. Another factor that affords this narrative special attention is Rosenblatt's picture of the victimized Jews as nonpassive, striving to participate in uprisings that were ultimately defeated. Instead of the image of the passive and persecuted Jew, one witnesses the rage and the will to fight back, albeit in vain. The drama portrayed in these excerpts paints a vivid picture of the tribulations of the Jews during the war and of how, despite the obliteration of her family, this woman still found the faith and the strength to survive.

# Sônia Rosenblatt

EXCERPTS FROM *Clouded Memories*

## [Chapter 6]

In 1939 the Germans had already occupied Poland, and the small state of Bessarabia, where Lipcani was embedded, was claimed by Russia, which had wanted it back.

The small state of Bessarabia remained in the control of Rumania from the end of the First World War until 1940, even though it was always coveted by Russia.

So in 1939, with the Rumanians being one of Germany's allies, there was an uneasiness in the air.

On behalf of the Rumanian government, on a Thursday night in 1940, a laconic 'communiqué' was transmitted over the radio to the population, informing them that on the next day, Friday, the Rumanian army would be withdrawn from Bessarabia and that, by nightfall on this same Friday, the Russian army would occupy the state. And that's what happened.

The nightmare experienced on that Friday is indescribable. The crazed population ran through the streets buying everything so that later they would have something to exchange for food.

In that one day the stores became empty. Leather was a scarce item in Russia, and shoes were purchased, in all sizes, by everybody in the hope of afterward being able to exchange them.

Although being very much in the control of the Rumanians for twenty-two years, the population of Bessarabia knew what awaited them from the other side of the Nistru River, in spite of the border being rigidly guarded.

Unfortunately the unexpected occurred: from the first day of the occupation there no longer was any bread.

The region of Bessarabia was the second largest producer and exporter of grain in the world for the other countries of Europe, exceeded only by the Ukraine.

In a land so rich in wheat, not to have bread became unimaginable.

The best cakes and other goodies were prepared in the region. Having to stand in line the whole night through in order to get a black bread was almost unbelievable.

Nevertheless, on both the population of the city and that of the country, which beforehand had at their disposal their own wheat, the identical torture was imposed.

The Russian forces gathered all the grain from that region for Russia itself.

# [Chapter 7]

Without delay the Russian government initiated the program of nationalization and monetary devaluation.

When Rumanian money was exchanged for Russian rubles, the banks only gave three hundred rubles to each person. Even those who had a lot of money were left with nothing.

The peasants, who, as a general rule, kept their savings buried for a 'rainy' day, upon receiving merely three hundred rubles for their capital became uninterested in money and decided not even to sell their products.

That attitude caused the 'famine,' which spread rapidly. The grocery stores ceased to exist under the recently implemented Soviet system; moreover, the cooperative system had not yet been adopted.

Obviously, the solution found by the people was the return to the old system of barter.

People would buy used clothing from city establishments, and the peasants would be willing to exchange food products for these. Such food was then sold in the city for money. With this money the people would again buy used clothing, reinitiating the cycle of exchanges. Only perishable food products were brought to the city by the villagers: tomatoes, red peppers, and eggplants, which the people used to call 'tri-colored' for representing the colors of the Rumanian flag: red (the tomatoes), yellow (the peppers, which when ripe turned yellow), and blue (the eggplants).

For the rest of the food products, such as butter, chicken, and so on, only the old system of trade worked.

# [Chapter 8]

My parents' grocery store was closed up and no longer belonged to them.

They let them live in only one room of their own house, and they also had to pay rent. That was only during the winter.

Afterward my father would be sent to Siberia, the place reserved by the Russians for the 'bourgeois.'

'Statiá 99' was the name given by the Russians to the document listing all those designated to be deported to Siberia. And they were many.

Once the panic among the population was rampant, many people fled to the neighboring city, the prosperous Tchernovitz. Among them, me, my husband, and our little son.

That was the first time I was separated from my parents. Due to the irony of fate, my father had been classified 'bourgeois,' a pejorative designation given by the Russians for his having worked for forty years in a grocery store in order to support his family of five children.

It was difficult to find a roof in Tchernovitz because of the large number of Russians who had already invaded the place and the inhabitants of Lipcani, who had already taken refuge there.

A kind of underground place was rented by my sister, and that was enough for us not to fall into the claws of the Communists.

Even the clothing we wore was laundered in Lipcani, in my parents' home. We lived in the hope that everything was going to become normal shortly. For us the war had not as yet represented an immediate threat.

The newspapers reported news about the German invasion of France. The commentaries were ironic about the haughtiness of the French in their self-satisfaction with their refined pastry and their giving in at zero hour.

Immediately the Russians drafted a general mobilization, and my husband was included.

The chiefs of the Ministry of Finance, where my husband worked, had already sent their families back to Russia and promised to help me. When the time came and I appealed to them for help, they ignored me.

The Jews went out into the streets in search of transportation to escape when the news arrived that the Germans would be occupying the city of Tchernovitz.

My oldest brother was with me on that occasion, and he was the one who got us a place, but without our baggage, on a wagon filled with people, pulled by two horses.

I was separated from my only suitcase. That was the beginning of leaving everything behind and of the hunger.

On the road the distressed villagers gave my little son a boiled potato.

# [Chapter 9]

That's the way we returned to Bessarabia. We became perplexed at no longer finding Russians over there.

All that powerful Russian military apparatus that had occupied all the cities of the territory of Bessarabia had disappeared as in a dream.

In the cities that we passed through, we did not stumble across even one Russian soldier.

The people commented that the Russian generals would have probably 'sold' themselves to the Germans.

So, traveling, I, my brother, and my little son—who wasn't yet three years old—arrived at the home of my brother Michael who lived in Securoni and where the rest of the family had already taken refuge.

Michael worked as inspector in the Russian National Bank, which obviously there were no reasons to defend during the Russian occupation, since nobody possessed any private resources.

The joy of our reunion didn't last very long.

The Rumanians came back to occupy the territory of Bessarabia, now as allies of the Nazis.

The initial mandate given to the Christian population was always the same one: to do what they felt like doing to the Jews, for three days.

The pogrom began. It lasted two weeks. It was executed with all the levels of the perversities that characterized it: pillage, stonings, rape, killings, and so forth.

## [Chapter 10]

Our house was not spared. My brother Michael, under the influence of the great poet H. N. Bialic, who had condemned the nonresistance of the Jews in the pogrom of Kishinev—capital of Bessarabia in 1905—incited us to fight.

We armed ourselves with brooms, shovels, and other domestic tools, and we stayed inside our house waiting for the aggressors.

The Rumanian peasants arrived. They surrounded the house and gave the first shot, aimed as a warning sign, at the window.

They hit the owner of the house, who died on the spot.

They knocked down the front door and then advanced with their firearms pointing in our direction. They had on their side the Rumanian soldiers.

My father stepped in front of us and begged that they let us live.

We fled without any destination, and the infuriated multitude advanced, initiating, with exaltation, the plundering of all our belongings, even destroying them in the fray and in their hurry.

We found refuge in one of the poorest hovels in the city, where there were only two single beds, without mattresses.

Even so, avid peasants, howling like wild animals, invaded the place and went for an old briefcase that was lying in a closet with no door, thinking they would find some money in it.

Next we went to the pharmacy where my sister-in-law Ita had been working as a pharmacist for the Russian army.

The horde of wild Rumanians had also already passed through there. All the merchandise was destroyed, including medicines, and so on . . .

There we took shelter for a few days. From my wise father I still remember the words: 'A life like this is not worth living,' because we would have to steal potatoes from some garden to satisfy our hunger.

Our sense of hopelessness was even greater when we heard the new mandate: expel the Jews from the city.

## [Chapter 11]

On that occasion it seemed to us to be a mandate without any objective, the fact of our being expelled from the city.

We didn't know, but the Rumanian army was waiting for us on the roads with whips and firearms.

Our father refused to leave because Mama, already more than seventy years old, did not feel strong enough to travel.

I remember his comment: 'What else can happen to us? They are going to shoot us.'

But that's not what happened. They found them and forced them to leave.

The system adopted by the Rumanians was different from that of the Nazis. Without gas ovens, they sorted the Jews in line.

They would shoot one line. They ordered the other line to walk, letting them 'live.'

The scene was so Dantesque that the executed ones had their 'luck' envied by those who remained. Their suffering ended right there and then.

The objective of leaving one part of that population alive was to finish them off by fatigue, famine, thirst, cold, since we traveled on foot day and night for months at a time, whipped along by the soldiers.

In the beginning they still allowed us to drink water. But those unfortunate, starving, and exhausted Jews, when passing by the Nistru River, ended their own lives by voluntary drowning.

We were allowed to walk only through the small woods and forests. In the heat of the summer of 1941, we refreshed our brows with a dry leaf, and we even licked it for want of a drop of water.

I realized that thirst is even worse than hunger.

# [Chapter 12]

That painful journey by hundreds of thousands of Jews revealed, in its tragic elements, all the resignation of those who, on their backs, carried their disabled loved ones.

Nevertheless, despite all the suffering that the caravan manifested, not one peasant from the villages we passed dared to show any gesture of solidarity.

Even a priest, who was asked permission for the use of a barnyard so that one of the foot travelers could give birth, excused himself.

We covered her with a sheet, the only resource we had to lessen the villagers' ridicule aimed at her. And on the dirty ground the act of birth took place.

In the Ukraine an identical scene had as its stage a stable. But, unfortunately, with a sad outcome: the woman died in labor; any medical assistance for us was forbidden.

From these painful reminiscences flows the memory of the birth of Nicinha's child. She was my companion in Ustia, and in 1944 I went to the village of Lúgova with her, by order of the Germans. There, also in a stable, she gave birth to her child.

This time, in spite of my inexperience and aided by an elderly lady, I had the opportunity to help a child to be born, in order to live in such a cruel world, but one which we love so much.

Life, come what may, we all wanted and we want to live, until the last moment.

A touching example of this deep-rooted love of life I witnessed when Sunia's aunt died. She was only skin and bones, the poor woman, on the brink of death. Totally drained of all her strength. Before emitting her last breath, her fingers twitched on her husband's arm and she babbled: Doctor!

# [Chapter 23]

With the defeat of Stalingrad, the Rumanian soldiers allowed us to leave the barnyards, and then we could live in shacks, in the village. Four of us lived in a room that once had been a storage shed for firewood: me, a couple, and an old man. Together we had the resources to pay the rent.

In the spring I, along with another woman, mashed clay and spread and applied it to the walls and the ground. After we applied a little whitewash, it seemed like a palace to us, our room.

Firewood for our consumption we used to get by going into the forest, after the guard retired. We gathered some fallen branches and carried them on our backs.

Once when we came back a bit early, he caught us and forced us to return our bundles of wood, besides giving us a vigorous beating.

Another time, it happened that we failed to meet up with each other. On that day only I and Nisinha, my roommate from Britsheve in Bessarabia, went to look for our fuel.

We agreed on our meeting place in order to return together, and then we left, each one to an opposite side of the woods. In that search for firewood we went further and further away from each other.

We tried to find each other by shouting, but the echo made it even more confusing.

Like a miracle, there appeared before me a villager, who guided me correctly to my village because I was actually going in the opposite direction and moving further and further away.

Afterward it wasn't easy to put up with the malicious gossip that arose from their having seen Sonia coming out of the woods in the company of a villager with a physical deformity.

Good humor was our sustenance. Good people helped us. I got flour from the boss at the mill, Julião, who was one of my customers for used clothing, when I was in the business of exchanges. And there were many others like him.

# [Chapter 24]

In Trans-Dniestria those who were directed to the line of those to be shot were envious of those who weren't.

Before being shot those wretched souls were forced to dig their own graves. Only God knows the agony they felt.

For the others all that would be left was the affliction of collapsing from hunger, thirst, and cold.

Many of these others died in Ústia and were piled up, during the winter, in front of the barnyards and stables where beforehand they had managed to survive.

With the coming of spring and the thaw, the rural police ordered the survivors to carry the thawed skeletal cadavers to a distant wood, in order to clear the fields so that there would be better conditions for a new planting.

The thousands of corpses were thrown into common graves.

Months later, in September, at the religious period for visiting the graves—a time that precedes the Day of Atonement—we, the survivors, went to the aforementioned wood to carry out the traditional religious ritual.

The horror of the scene we witnessed was appalling.

We saw, on an interminable extension of land, on the surface of the ground, bones from human bodies in the open. Some of them had already been eaten away by animals.

Despair took hold of all of us. Astonished, we ran in one direction and then another, without knowing what to do and without having any idea of where to find the mortal remains of loved ones.

The rite of the prayers for the souls who had left this world was carried out in front of those collective remains.

Faith continued burning in our bosoms, and not even that mortifying scene would dissuade us from honoring the memory of our deceased, who, parting from this world, returned to eternal rest.

We asked God, in his clemency, to remember the souls of our dearly departed, who were put to eternal sleep.

Even today I deplore not having any gravestone for my close family members who departed, so that, when I need to, I am able to cry and get things off my chest. On those occasions I remain inconsolable.

# [Chapter 25]

Meanwhile, I was visited by the husband of my childhood friend, Inda Vaidergon. He took me to where their family was gathered in the city of Bershad.

In that place the Jews stayed in a 'ghetto.' Some ancient alleyways on the periphery of the city, with old, broken-down houses.

I found hundreds of them living in only one room, on the ground, in the cold, in that year from 1941 to 1942, in the most chaotic conditions. The majority died from hunger and the cold.

For the rest who miraculously survived, the physical space in which they lived became more comfortable.

Without having the right to leave the 'ghetto,' the Jews found ways of exchanging clothing for food with the local population.

As they approached a certain square where the exchange took place, the Christians were harassed and dispersed by the soldiers with whips and violence.

In the beginning my friend still owned a fur coat, and thanks to it, they were allowed to stay in the city, and her husband kept on 'working' in the sugar factory.

She and her sister, Tziupa—who lives today in Israel—'bartered.' I didn't have anything to do there, not even knowing how to begin, so I returned to my village.

# [Chapter 26]

The prayers for the souls of our dearly departed are always said at the end of the religious holiday and especially on the Day of Atonement—Yom Kippur.

There isn't a soul who does not lament the loss of love and affection from those beloved beings who have departed forever. Their goodness and devotion remain indelibly outlined in our own existence.

We ask God for their souls and we ask those souls that they ask God for our lives.

We ask God that the memory of those dear souls be a perennial blessing for us and for the future generations.

As a rule we appeal to the souls of those beloved beings that they protect us and guide us on the roads of life. And we do this consciously and unconsciously.

In certain circumstances my dreams help me to survive.

At the end of my potato provisions, after the typhoid fever, I dreamt I was in my parents' home; I was getting ready to straighten up the beds when my mother and my sister appeared. They told me: 'You go; the rest of us will do the job.' I left, and having gone up to the village, in good time I managed to do what was necessary to earn my subsistence.

I dreamed again prior to my decision whether I would go to Barshad to stay close to my friend.

In that dream my oldest brother appeared and warned me not to go, alleging that I wouldn't find people who could truly help me at that time.

Not taking into consideration the advice I had received in the dream, I went to Barshad. In fact, it was not a favorable time for me, and so I returned.

From the time of that experience, my understanding and faith deepened regarding what the help of my vanished relatives and their protection meant for me, especially during my greatest difficulties.

# [Chapter 28]

In my history of blessings one that occupies a prominent place is the one I received—when I was still young—from the grandfather of my future husband.

He was a very religious man with a long beard, eighty-four years old, and he came to know me prior to the last trip he made, to Israel, affecting me deeply with his kindness.

Placing his hands on my head, he prayed, blessing me.

The prayer he uttered was the same as that of the ancient rabbis of the temple of Jerusalem:

'May God bless you and keep you;

May he turn his face to you and care for you

In all the pathways of your life.'

That prayer is the same one that today still blesses the people of Israel in their celebrations, uttered by the descendents of those rabbis. The emotion I felt at receiving the blessing from the grandfather of my fiancé was equal to that feeling of not having known my paternal and maternal grandparents, who had all already passed away at the time.

As I recall all these facts, it becomes evident that the value of all those spiritual protections must have contributed to my having saved myself.

# Samuel Malamud

Samuel Malamud was born in the Ukraine in 1908 and emigrated to Brazil with his parents in 1923. He died in Rio de Janeiro in 2000. He received his law degree in 1932 from the Federal University of Rio de Janeiro. Following his arrival in Brazil, he dedicated himself to the local Jewish community, taking on the roles of founder and director of various Jewish cultural, beneficent, and educational organizations. In addition to practicing law, Malamud was also an active journalist and lecturer. In 1930 he was invited to be secretary of the newspaper *Iidiche Presse* and in 1939 became one of its correspondents; from 1939 to 1942 he wrote articles in Yiddish about the dangerous international situation in Europe. In 1997 these articles were translated into Portuguese and published as *A segunda guerra mundial na visão de um Judeu brasileiro* (The Second World War in the Eyes of a Brazilian Jew). He was also one of the writers and editors responsible for the collection *Biblioteca de Cultura Judaica* (Library of Jewish Culture). In recognition of his services, the Israeli government appointed him first honorary consul in Rio de Janeiro from 1949 to 1952. His memorialist writings about the history of the Jewish community in Rio include his personal memoir, *Escalas no tempo* (1986) (Stops in Time), and an intriguing view of the old Jewish neighborhood in Rio, published in Yiddish and Portuguese as *Recordando a Praça Onze* (1988) (Remembering Eleventh Square). In the excerpt that follows from *Escalas no tempo*, Malamud recounts his arrival in Brazil and the first months of adaptation with detailed comparisons about the Jewish cultural life of his native land. These pages provide a rich view of both cultures and especially of a Rio de Janeiro that no longer exists. As a type of diary this book delves with keen insight into the process of acculturation.

# Samuel Malamud

EXCERPT FROM *Stops in Time*

## Emotion in Guanabara Bay

At dawn on the thirtieth day, creaking with fatigue, the *Desirade* began its approach to the entrance of Guanabara Bay. During the night nobody in third class had slept, almost all being immigrants on their first voyage. Brazilian soil was near, and those whose destination was Rio were packing their suitcases. They were buoyed by the emotion of beholding and greeting the New World.

The early morning was somewhat rainy, and a dense fog hid the contours of the Ocean Mountain Range. At six in the morning the ship received permission to enter the waters of the bay, and as it slowly glided by, it passed a row of warships decked with flags, discharging shots of dry gunpowder. The calendar registered the fifteenth of November 1923. Only after we disembarked did we learn that this had been the celebration of the proclamation of the republic of this country. That daybreak reminded me of the night in December 1920 when we crossed on foot the frozen Dniester River, fleeing my hometown, the city of Mogilev. What a difference!

After the functionaries of the maritime police had arrived on board, while the ship was still outside the barrier, and examined the documents of those whose destination was Rio de Janeiro, the steamship was able to dock. On the pier warehouse number 1 and Mauá Square were bubbling with people of all origins. The majority were waiting for the immigrants who were going to disembark. Others were there in hope of finding some compatriot or taking advantage of the national holiday for an outing to the pier. At customs we were received with much goodwill, except for a long wait due to the large number of passengers. Our baggage was unloaded without great difficulty, and the porters took charge of delivering it to the designated address.

We were met by our fellow countryman, neighbor, and old friend of my parents Nathan Roitberg. He came from Ouro Fino especially to meet us. We were going to depart for that town on the same night. Also there were Max and Lola Brand, the uncle and aunt of the girl who had embarked at Le Havre and who had been in my mother's care during the crossing. With them was their son Salo, the first young Brazilian Jew I met as I disembarked. Our initial interaction was difficult due to the absence of a common language. His Yiddish was very weak.

Mr. Luís Scheinkmann also came to wait for us, a man my parents knew only by name. His sister and brother-in-law, Liuba and Falik Roizman, were friends of my parents in Oknitza. We spent the day in his house in Rio until it was time to leave for Ouro Fino. In the meantime, our friend Roitberg took advantage of his stay in Rio to visit friends and to participate in the meeting taking place that very day in which the weekly publication *Dos Iídiche Vochenblat* (The Israeli Weekly) was founded. As a veteran social activist and ardent Zionist, he was happy to take part in that historical event.

Our host lived on Silveira Martins Street in a two-story house whose windows faced the garden of the Catete Palace. After learning about the importance of November 15 in Brazilian history, I was emotionally gratified to be, right on the day of my arrival, looking so closely at the beautiful garden of the Presidential Palace.

While my parents were engaged with our host in animated conversation, sharing with him news about his relatives and recalling common friends and acquaintances from Secureni, the hometown of the Scheinkmann family, I stood there not knowing how to spend the time. In the house there was a girl, our host's stepdaughter, about twelve years old, quite delightful and very well behaved—but where was the language for us to communicate? I spoke Russian, German, Hebrew, and Yiddish. She knew Portuguese and French, since her mother was French. I tried to avail myself of the scant knowledge of French I had learned in school, but my vocabulary wasn't adequate to carry on a conversation. The time passed without any great problems until lunchtime. We maintained a conversation with our gestures, interspersed with French words here and there and the very few Rumanian words still in my memory and which seemed similar to Portuguese.

This first luncheon was plentiful and delicious, with a touch of French cuisine—the seasoning was European. For the first time, we also ate rice and beans—a very Brazilian touch. Once our meal was finished, they brought our luggage. I helped put our suitcases in order. Our train would be leaving at seven o'clock at night. There still remained several hours to be filled. I thought about solving my communication problem with the girl by drawing or painting watercolors, things I had liked to do since I was a small child. She didn't have any paints or brushes. I asked for paper and pencil, and so we passed the time talking by drawing pictures. It was a challenge to see who would make the best drawings of landscapes, birds, trees, and so on.

At nightfall Nathan Roitberg came to get us, and we went by taxi to Central Station, today called Don Pedro II, where at 7:00 p.m. the train would leave for São Paulo. We had to go as far as Cruzeiro, the first transfer stop on our way to Ouro Fino.

We arrived in Cruzeiro after midnight, and the train of the South-Minas line, on a narrow-rail gauge, was to depart at five o'clock in the morning. The train left after considerable delay. It went to Soledade, where there would be a second transfer, on a railway of an even narrower gauge that went as far as Ouro Fino. We reached Soledade around four o'clock in the afternoon, but at that point there was a small traffic accident. Probably the railroad switchman did not turn the switch with the necessary dexterity, and so two cars in our string of railroad cars jumped the track and ended up on three lines, which interrupted all the station's activity. Fortunately, there were no grave consequences, not even panic among the passengers, although the train was full. There was only a loud racket. The derailment caused another delay in our trip, and we left Soledade at night. To our surprise we were subjected to a third and unexpected transfer stop: a freight train had tumbled over between the next-to-the-last station and Ouro Fino, and we had to change trains in the middle of the countryside in complete darkness, carrying our baggage for about two hundred meters. A special string of trains from Ouro Fino came to pick up the passengers. It was already past ten at night.

I remember that starry, cool, and fragrant night in the south of Minas when we traveled on foot by the railroad bed, content, peaceful, free, and without fear. The delays and the unforeseen events did not cause any annoyances or uneasiness. Our friend Roitberg was worried only about not being able to communicate with his family. In those days the means of communication were unreliable. But the railroad station had at its disposal information about delays via the telegraph, and those who were waiting could get news about the time of arrival.

The only problem during this long train trip was the food. We had coffee with milk and mineral water; we ate sandwiches of cheese and fruit. Traditionally, my parents as well as our friend Roitberg ate kosher food. The dairy products and the fruit did not cause any problems. But they did not eat chicken or meat that wasn't butchered according to Jewish religious prescriptions. As for pork, it was categorically forbidden.

At the station in Ouro Fino, all the Roitberg family was waiting for us. The reunion was emotional. It had been four years since we last saw one another in Mogilev. After we settled into our lodgings, even though we were exhausted, we enjoyed the lavish dinner that had been prepared.

During our journey my father as well as I had been learning with our friend Nathan our first words of Portuguese and the most common everyday expressions. Thus, on the following morning, when my father greeted our neighbor, a genuine Mineiro, with a bom-dia, he was extremely surprised and immediately spoke to the rest of the neighbors about the intelligence of these foreigners who learned with such speed the language of the country.

Roitberg had established for himself a shoe and clothing store, and his children were street peddlers. They ran through the streets of Ouro Fino, selling small gems, accessories, and costume jewelry. I hung around with them during the time we stayed in Ouro Fino, keeping them company and improving my vocabulary. I spoke Yiddish with them.

The city of Ouro Fino was like a real garden. All the houses had large yards with fruit trees and small vegetable gardens. Business was limited to the main street and to the area surrounding the cathedral. The style of the buildings was typically provincial. It reminded me a lot of Mogilev. The architecture was different. The streets had not yet been paved. The wagons and the few automobiles kicked up the dust. I liked the oxcarts with their typical screeching wheels, which could be heard from a distance, announcing their arrival.

It was there that I became aware of the lepers who lived isolated in special sanatoriums outside the city and who once a week would come mounted on their horses to get some assistance from the local population. The population would keep their distance. They feared any direct contact with them. Years later I again saw the same scenario in Pouso Alegre. It seems that at that time all the cities in southern Minas had these weekly visits because there were many isolated leper refuges in that region.

We stayed in Ouro Fino for about a month. The climate was magnificent. The nights, pleasant. Even the daytime heat was very bearable, and there was always a refreshing breeze in the shade. But my father was getting worried. He needed to begin to think about our accommodations and employment. He did not have the resources for a long period of inactivity. He had brought some money, and we had received some financial assistance from his family in the United States. But depending on others displeased him profoundly. He was always a man of action. Very grateful for the Roitberg family's hospitality, we returned to Rio de Janeiro, where we lived temporarily in the home of Arie Coslovsky, another friend and neighbor from Mogilev, on Caromina Méier Street, in front of a small square at the Méier Station. Their house was too spacious, and for that reason they sublet a few rooms. Christmas was already approaching, and afterward they informed us that carnival would come. My parents had then decided that it would be better to rent a house once this hectic period of festivities had passed. By then my father should already be working, and our house would be chosen according to the situation of the moment.

In Rio de Janeiro my parents met relatives and friends from the Ukraine and Bessarabia. Some of them, already settled in the country for quite some time, were well established. All of them volunteered to help us find a place to stay, but based on the sole criterion that was the general plan for every immigrant Jew without a definite profession: that my father become a peddler. My father tried to convince them (all of them) that he could experiment by trying his regular branch of work, trading wood and grains. Actually, he did not know the market or the language, but he would make contacts with the firms connected with this business to see whether it was possible to get involved. The negative response was unanimous. Everybody, including those who had already established themselves with stores for furniture, textiles, shoes, or clothing, had begun their business venture as street peddlers, hawking from door to door in the city's neighborhoods that were in full development and which offered all the conditions favorable for this type of commerce. They also recommended that I help him in this work, even though I intended to continue my studies.

My father would go out in the company of some of his peddler acquaintances to see how this mercantile activity worked. He would return home in a bad mood and discouraged. He could not see himself as being very successful. Out of curiosity I also went out, approximately two times, in the company of an adolescent peddler who was introduced to me as an excellent professional. I found nothing at all attractive in this kind of activity, even though I could attest to his managing to make a good wage. That business did not attract me at all. I had other ambitions. The company of this young guy helped me to become familiar with the Méier neighborhood, recognized at that time as the most developed suburb. Actually it had tranquil and bucolic spots that were beautiful, with lovely homes. The real-estate fever had not yet caught hold.

Of my childhood friends and schoolmates from Mogilev and Secureni with whom I became reacquainted, some lived in the surrounding neighborhoods, others at Eleventh Square and in other neighborhoods. The first classmate from Mogilev who came to visit me right away in Méier was Manuel Bronstein. My childhood friend Germano (Grischa) Coslovsky, grandchild of Arie, was with me every day. He lived nearby. The majority of my old classmates whom I was rediscovering and the young guys I was meeting were already enrolled in the Pedro II High School and got to wear uniforms. I definitely felt a certain envy and longing to go to school.

It was around the end of December. It would be the first Christmas we would spend in a completely strange land. The shopwindows were very decorated, and everywhere the preparations for the commemoration of the great Christian holiday were evident. It reminded me of the Christmas festivities in the city of Mogilev and even in the small village of Oknitza, in Rumania. The middle of winter. The snow covering everything with its radiant whiteness. The cold reaching twenty degrees below zero. In the streets, groups of people festively dressed and at times with masks, carrying stars made of colored fabrics, going from door to door, chanting beautiful Christmas carols, ringing sleigh bells to announce the birth of Christ, and asking for presents. All the homes, without exception, were visited. The population of Poltavskaia Street was made up entirely of Jews. I recall that my maternal

grandparents and my parents would already be preparing with anticipation the sweets, the money, the presents, and the refreshments
they would be handing out. Normally these groups went to sing on
the doorsteps of the people they knew. Nevertheless, I cannot refrain
from emphasizing that the evenings of Christmas, like that of Good
Friday, represented a traditionally sad memory for the Jewish communities, especially in czarist Russia and in the various neighboring
countries of Eastern and Central Europe. It was on these dates that,
from time to time, the pogroms took place, instigated sometimes
by the actual authorities, sometimes by the anti-Semitic clergy, who
accused the Jews of being responsible for the crucifixion of Christ.
That's why, Christmas Night, called *di blinde nacht* (blind night) by the
Jews, engraved itself in my memory. Meeting in one of the homes, our
neighbors spent the night wide awake, playing cards, conversing, or
reading aloud some stories from the flourishing Yiddish literature of
that time. The housewives participating in the gathering prepared delicious dishes: roasted chicken and duck, hot goose pastrami, borscht
from very hot beets with meat and potatoes, *varenikes* (thin dough filled
with potato or Saracen wheat very much like our fried turnovers), all
this accompanied by pickled cucumbers, tomatoes, and watermelons,
and for dessert, fruit preserves and various sweets. We stayed awake
until dawn.

On the first Christmas I spent in Rio de Janeiro, I missed that folkloric celebration of the Ukraine and Bessarabia, where the Orthodox
Church reigned, and I also found it strange that the Christmas decorations had European characteristics, with Santa Claus all bundled
up, traveling by sleigh, and Christmas trees decorated with snow. I
attributed this to the European immigrants, who maintained the traditions from their countries of origin. With the passing of time I came
to know the typically Brazilian folkloric Christmas commemorations,
like those of the Northeast.

What made me happy was the tranquility that prevailed in the bosom
of the Jewish families. The atmosphere was of love and peace, without
tensions, and everybody felt joined together in view of the Christmas
preparations, without any fears whatsoever of prejudice or violence.

In Brazil of the 1920s, the majority of the population did not know
what a Jew was. For the less cultured, the Jew was confused with Ju-
das, and they imagined him not as a common man but as something

similar to the devil, with horns and a tail. The Jews with whom they maintained daily contact, whether as peddlers who sold them clothes, bed and table linens, jewels and chattels, or even as the already-established merchants in diverse businesses, were treated as Russians, Poles, or simply 'gringos,' a word designating any foreigner. For the Jews 'gringo' was the same as *griner* (green) in Yiddish, which they used to call the recent arrivals to the country: they were green before they were acclimated and settled. Be that as it may, the immigrant Jewish element felt free and at peace during the Christmas festivities, and the tradition of the 'blind night' in Brazil lost any meaning whatsoever. It was only remembered to stress and to rejoice in the freedom and equality they enjoyed in this hospitable country, where no discrimination based on race or creed prevailed.

After Christmas and the New Year, we began to hear the first musical sounds that announced the coming of carnival. Yes, this holiday was totally unknown to me. Carnival in the twenties was really a popular festival of the street, lasting two months. From the beginning of January there were, every night, confetti battles in various neighborhoods of the city. Some of them, like the ones in Méier, became famous. Méier was made up of a rather large population and had good commercial stores. Access was easy by train or by streetcars, which trafficked both sides of the railway in various directions. The transportation on the right side, for those who came from the city to Méier, went via Arquias Cordeiro Street and continued on ahead to Cascadura, extending by transfer at the Jardim, up to the suburb of Cachambi or Inhaúma. In that area during a certain period of time, the streetcars drawn by donkeys were still operating. On the left side, the streetcar came by the Twenty-fourth of May Street, took Dias da Cruz Street and continued to the far side of the Engenho suburb. Thus for the confetti battles of that suburb, people from all sides flocked together, from the Northern Zone of Vila Isabel and Tijuca, Lins de Vasconcelos, and Boca do Mato (a bucolic neighborhood in Méier) and even from Downtown Rio and the Southern Zone, at that time still in the stage of active development.

My first carnival confetti battle left me euphoric from the joy, the mixture of colors, the music, the ecstasy of the dancers, the movement of the crowd, the democratic nature of the fraternizing and conviviality, and the effusion of feelings and enthusiasm of living life to the fullest.

Without knowing the language and still without knowing how to move about in my own neighborhood and in the surrounding neighborhoods and suburbs, I became a fan of carnival. As a mere spectator I became a participant in all the confetti battles of the area, such as those on the Twenty-eighth of September Avenue, a haven for the composer Noel Rosa, and those of Dona Zulmira, the Baron of Bom Retiro, and the Engenho Novo, and the many other battles that were announced. The closer we came to carnival, the more confetti battles took place, sometimes several on the same night. It was fun to ride the overloaded streetcars standing up or on the running boards of the head car or hanging along on the back. The streetcars crawled while the merrymakers gave vent to their joy. The streetcars of Rio were appropriate for the climate—completely open, with long benches on which at least five passengers fit. When it got tight, seven or eight people squeezed in, besides those who managed to stand within the scanty space between the benches. When it rained, the situation became difficult. On one side of the streetcar a protective canvas was lowered. On the ends of the cars, the situation was worse, because sometimes there were leaks due to the poor upkeep.

On the three days of carnival, the celebration was concentrated on Rio Branco Avenue, known at that time as Central Avenue. There on the avenue passed the line of open automobiles, decorated and filled to the brim with costumed and masked people. The parade line took place on Saturday night. On Sunday began the parade of clubs and samba schools. The three main carnivalesque clubs of that time—Democratics, Fenians, and Lieutenants of the Devil—paraded their allegorical floats on Fat Tuesday.

But what was worthwhile in the carnival of the twenties was the huge participation of the masses with their disguises, the uninhibited nature of those who considered themselves frustrated artists, those who gave expression to their creativity and to their imagination, during that popular, free, and spontaneous commemoration. The joyful and contagious songs engaged everyone with their rhythm and captured the multitude who sang them with all the strength of their lungs.

That first carnival postponed for two months the problems of our adjustment and gave my father time to decide about his means of livelihood. It was really very good to have this time. After some contacts and exchanges of ideas regarding a solution with his friends and relatives, he had to opt for the traditional route, that of the peddler, with a slight variation: he would go out into the street in the company of a trained peddler, paid as an employee, in order to help him sell and communicate with his customers. Also his friends were going to give him a loan to help him acquire an established clientele, with credits to be received. The acquisition was arranged with a 30 percent discount on the securities to be collected, and the seller was responsible for the integrity of the debtors. That form of contract facilitated the work because the purchased clientele represented potential future customers for new purchases, either while they were still paying the existing debt or after this debt was liquidated.

We rented a house with two living areas, two bedrooms, a kitchen, a bathroom, and a small yard in a village of houses at 210 Souza Barros Street, very close to the Engenho Novo station. There were five houses in a dead-end street. The construction of the house was very primitive, the wooden boards of the floor uneven. We lived in that house for more than two years.

Across the railroad tracks, on the corner of the Baron of Bom Retiro Street and the Twenty-Fourth of May, in a two-story house above a corner bar, the Jewish families who lived in the surrounding area had set up a synagogue, which my father attended on Saturdays. I used to accompany him. Since few adolescents attended, and the leaders recognized that I knew how to pray and to chant the melodies of the readings from the Haphtarah (the biblical passage read after the chapter selected from the Pentateuch) and the respective blessings, they frequently honored me with this responsibility. It was a special distinction that pleased my father and filled him with pride.

With the beginning of the academic year and to start my learning of Portuguese grammar, I began to attend the Freitas Course, which operated in a house at the beginning of Senator Eusébio Street, near Eleventh Square. The teachers were the Freitas couple, owners of the school. The primary and the beginning of the secondary levels were taught there. I had already arrived from Rumania with the fourth level of middle school completed. I took this course of study for a very short period of time to familiarize myself with the language. The students were all younger than I, the majority Jews. I actually learned the language via my companionship with friends I rediscovered and new ones I made.

By the end of 1924, under the system of external preparatory courses, I took at the Pedro II High School the exams for mathematics and geography, two subjects I knew well and in which I was always a good student. I passed mathematics without any difficulty. In geography I experienced the first and only failure in my life as a student. It occurred not on the written exam but during the oral. Part of the geography exam was on cosmography, which I had never studied. That subject was required only for the oral exam, and the teacher who examined me was Honório Silvestre. He was the terror of the examining board. He had the physical appearance of a Slav. He wore wire-frame glasses, which rested at the tip of his nose. He spoke rapidly and in a low voice. Ever since my first years of schooling, I have been very sensitive about exams. I even managed to get gastric problems. There I was, facing a situation in which I neither completely understood nor clearly heard the formulated questions about a subject totally new to me. I simply became mute. I flunked.

While I had been preparing myself for the first preparatory exams, for practical reasons of gaining employment, within three months I passed the typewriting course at the Velox School, which operated at San Francisco Square. I already was more than decisive about continuing my studies, but I had to work to help my parents. I didn't want to think about the family income. Our financial situation was very unstable.

# Francisco Dzialovsky

Francisco Dzialovsky was born in Rio de Janeiro in 1952. He completed his undergraduate studies in geography and environmental Studies and his graduate studies in contemporary philosophy at the Catholic University of Rio de Janeiro. He worked in the business field and is currently a high school teacher. He began his literary career with his well-received novel *O terceiro testamento* (1987) (The Third Testament), about the Jewish and Yiddishkeit experience in Brazil. The title is taken from a Yiddish radio program of the same name within the novel. The radio program broadcasts information about Jewish history, religion, culture, personalities, and the Bible, providing the narrative with a phenomenon that lends cultural cohesiveness to the Jewish community. The radio show becomes a barometer for measuring the level of assimilation from Yiddish to Brazilian language and culture, thereby pointing to the gradual effacement of Yiddish culture in the New World. The novel also offers a view of what it is like to live in the Jewish Diaspora in general. Using humor to depict comedic cross-cultural clashes, Dzialovsky makes several outrageous cultural references that appear in the excerpt that follows. However, it is the issue of belonging that overrides all other themes in order to demonstrate the power of assimilation, which in the end dominates the younger 'Brazilianized' generation.

Dzialovsky's second novel, *Devoração* (2001) (Devoured), depicts the life of a well-dressed, handsome, and meticulously clean man from Rio whose past life of brutal violence and sexual consumption continues to manifest itself in his self-image as a contemporary Lothario. The novel discusses issues such as materialism and capitalism, morality and religion, the bourgeois Left, and the current-day ideology of the young.

# Francisco Dzialovsky

### EXCERPT FROM *The Third Testament*

## I

Whatever is revealed in confidence sooner or later ends up in the public domain, especially when keeping secrecy pertains not to one or two people but to the entire community. Therefore, it is impossible to explain how, for years at a time, our neighborhood kept the secret.

Treatises have already been written on the subject of the secret or on its violation; sociologists wrote theses; psychologists explained its workings; historians researched its origins. The malicious ones, in order to shorten the story, say that the secret only has value when it is shared by many, and would rush to point to our neighborhood as a typical case. But how would they explain the secret's rigorous boundary within the physical borders of the neighborhood? The river that ran abundantly and poured forth bubbling with life, just like an Amazonian river stream suddenly dries up to the point that, a few meters away, nobody conceives of its existence?

Scholars would shrug their shoulders and between being resentful and surprised would say that our situation was merely the exception to the rule.

After all, just like coffee, carnival, and soccer, gossip is a national institution, and what our neighborhood never lacked was gossiping busybodies, ready to blab about everything: there isn't a soul who doesn't know how many lovers the owner of the bakery, Mr. Paiva, keeps; or that Dona Terezinha's daughters are not really such virgins; or that Pedrinho, the sales clerk at the grocery store, fooled his boss by passing behind his back first-class merchandise to the fiery Solange, under the complicit eyes of her mother, Dona Teodora, who insisted on accompanying her daughter everywhere, since it did not look good for an adolescent girl to walk the streets alone. One suspects that Pedrinho was sleeping with both of them, in collusion with Mr. Rodrigues, husband and father.

That's merely malicious gossip, a field in which our busybodies possess a know-how that would make anybody else envious. All the same, the secret was another story. It was born and it died within the neighborhood, maybe because it was a secret of life and death. The lives of some people began to have new direction, the death of others a certain meaning.

Imagine if in some way the secret leaked out and the newspapers got wind of it! Pandemonium would break out in the neighborhood; our lives would be transformed into a hell with the invasion of strangers and adventurers, who would certainly take advantage of the situation. One of the last peaceful spots in Rio de Janeiro would become a stage for disorder and chaos.

But each of the inhabitants was perfectly conscious of the problem, of the delicate character of secrecy. Precautions were taken, the four cardinal rules were checked before making any commentary, always in a low, whispering voice, and when one noticed the presence of a stranger, the discussion of the subject ended.

Not even relatives, no matter how close they were, lovers, childhood friends, who unfortunately lived beyond the borders of our select neighborhood, suspected that we were maintaining such well-guarded secrecy.

So why not let the subject die right there? Why not act pragmatically and pretend that the impenetrable doesn't exist? Seeing that what is obvious and calling our attention is not always detected, imagine a secret that by definition is something hidden, covered with mystery.

It so happens that our secret had substance; it was palpable; it would conform to the greedy hands that caressed it. It had color, and what a color! Yellow, specifically a golden yellow.

Gold. That's the secret. Our neighborhood was swimming in gold.

It is known that we Brazilians have a very special inclination for this noble metal. A paternal tenderness, an unselfish love that makes us protect and keep it safe every time we fondle it in our hands. A constant and unshakable fidelity that gives us a feeling of spiritual superiority and makes us feel better as we accumulate it.

This passion has roots in our childhood; in school we learn to revere those who destroyed our jungles in search of brazilwood; those who razed our forests gathering medicinal species; those who tore down our woods, imprisoning and enslaving the Indians; those who burned our vegetation, corralling our animals, exterminating them and selling their pelts. But the greatest adoration, the most gripping belonged to those who with great sacrifice and unequaled heroism abandoned their families and took leave in search of gold and precious stones.

And our neighborhood, in shameless debauchery to the suffering that the early pathfinders experienced, in derision to their epic bravery in unknown dangerous territory, ridiculed the high ideals of the nation's pioneers, the discoverers of Brazil, by brazenly accumulating gold. And the most aggravating: there was no need in the least to dig, to prospect, to sift. Just like the dew, which in the dead of night condenses and accumulates on cold surfaces, gold would emerge resplendently and invitingly to whoever was walking unhurriedly, paying attention to the spaces in between the cobblestones, next to the garbage dumps, against the light posts, under the park benches, in between the magazines displayed at the newsstands, at the door of the grocery store, on the school's wall, and in so many other places that to describe them, it would take a long list.

But the forefathers of the nation would have another reason for envy, beyond the ease with which gold was found: this metal did not emerge in the coarse form that nature offered, mixed with gravel and other impurities; neither did it come in those obnoxious and anti-aesthetic gold bars traded by governments, nor those round and tinkling gold coins so pleasing to the robbers of banking establishments in cowboy films. It came already finished for the consumption and happiness of whoever encountered it. Finished products of the finest gold craftsmanship and the greatest art of jewelry: elegant watches so that workers would not lose their time, gold and silver bracelets studded with precious stones to adorn the wrists of genteel ladies, necklaces to decorate the necks of all sizes, widths, and colors, from the whitest Lusitanian to those of ebony of the unsullied descendents of the ancient coastal lords of Nigeria and Senegal, which go so well with the strings of pearls, a delicious contrast and effect, hanging from all shades of miscegenated necks, which would be made even more attractive if caressed by the fruits of the abundant collection.

The newlyweds were not forgotten; shiny wedding rings decorated with care and exoticism in order to clutch the vein that links the ring finger to the heart, always guaranteeing the couple's union and happiness, were not difficult to detect by careful inspection, which, in turn, would discover elegant rings to decorate and dignify the other fingers, exorcising the natural jealousy they feel for the ring finger.

And the earrings! They always appeared in pairs, identical twins, each pair more beautiful than the other. There were many, from austere semicircles, cheerful, dangling designs to the complicated and artistic arabesques. Big-eared ladies, girls with ears sticking out like fans, no longer had to hide their auditory shells beneath traditional hairdos; all they had to do was to hang one of those pairs of earrings from their ears in order to transform them into sensual receptacles for the most obscene invitations and confidences.

There was somebody who found a tooth. It's true that such a discovery never repeated itself, but it was a gold tooth to make any smile whatsoever envious. Not one of those common and commercialized incisors, but a modest and honest molar. One suspects that it was even a wisdom tooth, one of those that erupts at a mature age, conferring to the mouth responsibility and seriousness, controlling horselaughs, and giving more weight to one's words. An ancestral tooth, proof of our heroic and carnivorous past, a rare piece disputed by brave conquerors, yanked from an enemy killed in combat in order to decorate the chest with a necklace of honor for the boldest warrior.


## 2


While the race for gold continued in the streets, at home life followed its normal path, given that the standards of normalcy are not defined.

Today there is talk about the abyss between generations; technology advances at a rapid pace; customs change so quickly that notions of right and wrong for the parents become unacceptable for their children. That's one problem we didn't have, because my parents spoke another language. Not in the figurative sense, but in the more real sense of the word: while I and my six sisters spoke Portuguese, the language of Eça de Queiroz and Machado de Assis, my parents spoke the language most widespread in the countries of Eastern Europe until the outbreak of the Second World War, not in the number of actual speakers, but whenever we met someone who knew it—Yiddish.

While the geometric proportion of the speaking population of official languages increased, the speakers of Yiddish would decrease in the same proportion, leaving behind the increasingly older survivors of a universe that existed before the great war and whose glory seems to be recognized only by the overworked Dumah, the angel of death, and the other inhabitants of the Yenne Welt, the other world.

We understood one another more by intonation, by facial expressions, mimicry, or by one word or another of the Portuguese they spoke, or by one word or another of the Yiddish we spoke that was lost in some idiomatic expression.

For better or for worse the problem of communication with my parents resolved itself. The greatest difficulty was to establish a bond of awareness and understanding with my sisters, for they were silent more than simply introverted. In permanent congress with themselves, they built a barrier to the outside world, not even allowing it to hear their voices, scorning any of its activities within the neighborhood, the school, or the family. They expressed themselves through their minister of foreign relations: the firstborn, the fattest one who topped her amphibian body with the expressive and sincere visage of a frog, she, the historian. Ambassador of misunderstanding, prizing only her own advice, she managed the thinking and behavior of her sisters, hating me for escaping from her claws.

My mother, who only left the kitchen to go to sleep, never using the living room, not even to receive visitors, would honor whoever penetrated the holy sanctuary of her home with onion and the greasy aromas of Polish cooking, accompanied with exclamations of impatience in her moribund language.

For a long time she had lost hope for her daughters, dedicating herself fastidiously to her culinary tasks more to forget the girls than to taste her specialties. While she was busy with the stove and the pots and pans, life didn't seem so bitter.

The heat of the tropics, the abundance of the sun and rain, which makes everything grow with vigor, filling the world with life, seem to have the opposite effect in some cases where one only sees the effect of decrepitude. At home she witnessed, besides the withering of her parents and their language, the burial of a culture that manifested itself less with each passing day, as in the way my mother forgot the recipe of typical dishes and in the way her conversation with her elders introduced more and more words in Portuguese.

After the construction of the Home for Elder Israelites, I saw myself like all the inhabitants of the neighborhood, involved in the old folks' conspiracy to die in gold. They knew they were the last ones who loved and prayed in Yiddish, the very last to read Sholem Aleichem and Peretz in the original.

There are people who cry and remain inconsolable with the death of a beloved being; others contract professional mourners; others manifest their pain by arranging for a first-class funeral, with flowers and orators. There are populations who sing and party at death, the inexorable and final friend. But the inhabitants of the Home knew that something more was dying than a person or a determined number of people. So they decided to leave in their passage to the other world a reserve of gold.

The remembrance of words in the moribund language evokes the aroma of meals at a set table, strangely blended in one's memory: life and death.

Life at home revolved around the dinner table; rectangular temple, altar of grandeur, locale where one manifested preferences, arena of heated debates and eloquent silences. In the same way it is impossible to speak about our neighborhood without mentioning the Home, it is impossible to speak about our home without referring to our dinner table and its place of honor occupied by an ethereal figure like the angels, but whose presence was certain at meal time: the Radio Announcer whose program *The Third Testament* was aimed at the stubborn tribe of the last speakers of Yiddish. Just like the prophet Elijah, who in the custom of the Hebrew Passover shared the holy wine in each home, the Radio Announcer's voice materialized with the magic turn of the knob of the radio.

On Sundays the luncheon table was enriched by a curious character, white hair, clipped very short, in the style of the soccer player 'Prince' Danilo, deep and melancholy blue eyes, sighing as if he had just lost something very valuable. He would walk around shaking his head sometimes affirmatively, sometimes negatively, looking obliquely at the walls and the floor in an incessant and silent debate, closed off to the rest of the mortals, who, if they wanted to participate, would be treated with an expression of disdain.

At the only meal he had with the family during the whole week, Father would get dressed in his best suit and sit at the table with tie and jacket; he'd put on a mild lavender cologne and, with his back erect, would preside over the luncheon. Seeing him like that, self-possessed and tranquil, and Mother in her fuss to serve, her cries, her soiled apron, one had the impression of watching two films at the same time. The only concession he made to the torrid city of Saint Sebastian of Rio de Janeiro was a small handkerchief he used to meticulously wipe the perspiration from his brow.

On the other hand, the impeccable elegance exhibited in front of the family wasn't a sign of vanity or the mania of being different; it was his way of blessing the home. Just like the high priest in Solomon's temple, dressed in his best clothes during the ceremonies, in the same way by wearing his best vestments, Father transmitted to his children that the holy ground began in one's own home, where profane occurrences could not be avoided but must be in some way elevated. He knew that his children, brought up in a Catholic neighborhood, did not have the comfort of a church where the priest separated so well the sacred from the profane, the permitted from the not permitted, the good from the bad. Therefore, his ideal was to make of our residence, at the same time, home and temple. He had never brought home his business problems, outside annoyances, and he never allowed us to speak badly about people or the government. For him the president, just like a king in antiquity, administrated the country with divine blessings. Each of my father's gestures, to wash, to dry, to tie his shoes, was a ritual, as if heaven were incessantly contemplating him. To sit down at the table, to turn on the radio, tuning in to *The Third Testament*, was the crowning moment of the liturgy.

He earned his living by peddling jewels on installment, transported in his suitcase of alligator skin, an animal that, despite it not being cited by name in Genesis, had undoubtedly been a passenger on Noah's ark, and at the same time it represented the Brazilian jungle; my father did not hide his pride in carrying his suitcase, which made him feel integrated into the national landscape, a link between the Bible and Brazil.

Incapable of informing the family about the progress of his business, on the other hand, he was a marvel at praising his clientele, the ladies of the Southern Zone of the highest society, who received him in their living rooms and behaved respectfully for hours, choosing, selecting the most elegant pieces. Despite the distinctive ladies' habits of delaying in their payment, which created bitterness on Mother's part, for she saw the amount of household goods from the street fair diminish, he was incapable of condemning them. Not even when he learned from the actual fiscal agent who extorted him, almost leaving him penniless, and who had started the trouble on account of the accusation made by one of his genteel clients, did he allow himself to be bitter; he didn't even allow anybody to say one word against such behavior.

## 3

On Sundays the radio program The Third Testament was dedicated to the 'founding fathers' and their grandiose institutions, men who in their tireless labor, their incomparable dedication in the fulfillment of the duties they proposed, influenced, in a decisive fashion, events that changed for the better the course of history. The program was subdivided into the following parts:

First: Reaffirmation of the Judeo-Christian fellowship, a fellowship as ancient as history itself, especially after the pope had forgiven the Jews for killing God and had concluded that after death the souls of the Jews are not necessarily going to hell. Finally, after almost two thousand years of heated debates and no less heated autos-da-fé, when they vaporized the ashes of the recalcitrant souls, the Catholic theologians reached the conclusion that the Jews were not the ones who killed Christ.

Then who did?

Nobody.

What do you mean nobody?

By chance, do the testimonies of the Evangelists, the Jerusalemites, and other elderly people who saw him suffer on the cross, and which so many generations considered worthy of faith, no longer mean anything?

It so happened that he suffered to fulfill his destiny, expiate the sins of the mortals, but no one was given the power to kill him. If he died, wouldn't creation also die? And with creation ending, who would tell his story?

Second: Conspiracies between Gamal Abdel Nasser and Satan. The president of Egypt who founded the United Arab Republics (UAR), giving new breath to Arab nationalism, and who jointly with Nehru of India and Tito of Yugoslavia established the organization of the nonaligned countries, or rather, nonaligned neither with the USSR, nor with the USA, nor with themselves. Besides that, he was heir to Hitler, who founded the Reich of a thousand years that lasted twelve in his desire to exterminate the Jews, in a long line of postulants and extirpators who descended from Haman, minister of the state of Ciro, the founder of the Persian Empire, knowingly frustrated by Queen Esther, founder of our Purim festival, ancestral to our carnival. This history of iniquity goes from the Inquisition, which through its Holy Office of persecuting alchemists (founders of chemistry), sorceresses (founders of feminism), Moors (founders of the oil countries), heretics (founders of the opposition blocs and in the most extreme cases of subversive movements), had a predilection for the Jews (founders of capitalism, communism, Christianity, and according to some fanatics, of Judaism itself), this Holy Office therefore not being democratic in its inquisitorial distribution of torture (the church, for all that, took note of this injustice by establishing the Jesuit order, which began to distribute castigation and punishments with greater equanimity). This history of iniquity continued up to the modern pharaoh of Egypt who nationalized the Suez Canal by blocking it, in this way renewing the millennial tradition established by Moses of opening and closing the waterways of the Middle East.

Third: A moment of silence in memory of the recent death, less than three thousand years ago, of the general counsel Gideon, who founded the science of economy, of maximizing the potential of his army by diminishing the number of soldiers to three hundred and with this very small contingent gained a spectacular victory over the powerful Midianites, establishing the tactics of guerrilla warfare, so that until today Fidel Castro and his Cubans do not forgive him for usurping the 'press' prize for originality.

The Radio Announcer took advantage of the moment of silence to summon the listeners to pray aloud, thanking God for not making Gideon appear in the Koran, as opposed to Abraham, Moses, and Jesus, so that the Arab leaders will remain in complete ignorance about his existence; in this way they will always be defeated in war by the Israelites.

Fourth: The scientific and cultural hour in which the great Hebrew scientists, humane benefactors, such as Einstein (discoverer of relativity), Freud (discoverer of psychoanalysis), Marx (discoverer of communism), Sabin (discoverer of the polio vaccine), Nathan Grinberg (founder of the Retail House, South America, the largest shopping center of textiles and notions in Latin America with headquarters on Lavradio Street), Aaron Cozer (founder of the chain of appliances, 'Emperor of Sound,' who has the honor of serving 72.18 percent of the Carioca population), incidentally the last two being supporters of the radio program, and many others whose heroic and philanthropic lives benefited so many. These founding fathers are compared only to Brazilians of equal stature, but with the aggravating circumstance of the Brazilians being unjustly wronged due to general neglect, such as Santos Dumont (founder of the airways without which one cannot reach the Holy Land in periods of time that are becoming shorter and shorter), José de Alencar (invented the heroic treatment of the Indians, forcing all of Brazil to be proud of its tribal past), Marechal Rondon (founder of the Amazonian telegraph poles, which enable the Nambiquara Indians to send telegrams to all the corners of the homeland), Noel Nutels (who established the treatment of the Indians as Jews and the Jews as Indians, thereby being received in both conditions by His Excellency the president of the Republic, Getúlio Vargas), Sumé (established, even at the time of Jesus, the first Brazil-Palestine cultural agreement), and finally Filinto Cruz, Aaron Cozer's partner in the appliance business, complete proof that Christians and Jews can get along well, as long as there are good deals to be made.

Fifth: The Radio Announcer is aware that science is a double-edged sword; if, on the one hand, it increases our comfort, life expectancy, and leisure, on the other, it increases our anguish and creates spiritual crises; after all, what we believe today to be right and truthful, tomorrow can very well be something passé and folkloric; therefore it's important to release tension created by progress as much for its scientific side as well as for its social, economic, and political aspects, lest the listeners turn against the institutions of the founding fathers. This is the reason why the Radio Announcer created this last part of the program, to close it with this golden nugget. The serious events of the other sections of the program became lighter here due to the refreshing news of the social column.

The Radio Announcer, besides pioneering other inventions, was one of those responsible for introducing the social column on the radio. And what must be understood as the social column? Weddings? Baptisms? Graduations? Coming-out parties? Coming-of-age parties? Even though these daily news items might have some importance for those honored and their beloved, they did not carry as much weight as the last social occurrence. No matter how brilliant a certain man's life might be, nothing would be capable of overshadowing his final hour. Everything is transitory, joys, sadness, persecutions, satisfactions, sufferings, and humiliations. Man comes from dust and to dust he shall return; of what value are the fancy apartments in Copacabana and Ipanema or the luxurious mansions in Teresópolis, if the definitive resting place is in the community cemetery of Vila Rosali, in humble proximity to the proletariat town of São João de Meriti?

The last part of the program very conveniently dealt with the funerals and wakes of the deceased, even though the end of the program was not made up solely of trivialities—what is more trivial than death, the constant companion? At this point the Radio Announcer would take advantage of the moment to complain about the disregard in the conservation of the gravestones and maintenance of the cemetery.

The Radio Announcer now demonstrated his mastery and experience in the art of the narrative; his voice would go down a few octaves, become less hurried, accentuating each syllable in order to reinforce the importance of what was being said. The climax of *The Third Testament* was simultaneously the joy of sharing the pain of the family and the deceased's friends and the opportunity to meditate on fate, on the real life, and to judge our previous actions in this world as changing forms and illusory ideas.

The name of the most recently deceased was repeated three times. First in a forceful manner, then in a normal tone, and finally in an almost inaudible whisper, for man is contained in his name: he is born, grows, and dies like the word, which vanishes into the air.

Next would come the short biography of the deceased, an abbreviated curriculum vitae, relating the most important events of his life, now extinguished, or the name of the hospital where he lay dying, for how long, the illness that mowed him down, and the name of the doctor who signed the death certificate.

The family hypnotized, amid sighs and the shaking of their heads, would listen to the Radio Announcer, the guest of honor, who to the sound of the funeral march would finalize the program just in time for dessert. At the table the two sides of the coin: the delicacies of the palate and the coldness of death, apple tart and rigor mortis, chocolate cream puff and the decomposition of the dead.

# Eliezer Levin

Eliezer Levin was born in the southern colony of Baron Hirsch in 1930 but at the age of five moved to the city of São Paulo, where he remained the rest of his life. An engineer by profession as well as a businessman and author, Levin wrote for the Jewish press of São Paulo and centered most of his narratives in the Jewish neighborhood of Bom Retiro. Levin's writing spans the bridge between chronicle and fiction, but for the most part takes the form of vignettes, tableaux, anecdotes, and stories. His three novels, Bom Retiro: O bairro da infância (1972) (Bom Retiro: Childhood Neighborhood); Sessão corrida: Que me dizes avozinho? (1982) (Run-on Session: What Do You Have to Say, Grandpa?); and Adeus, Iossl (1994) (Good-bye, Joseph), manifest this episodic format. His two collections of story/chronicles, Crônicas do meu bairro (1987) (Chronicles of My Neighborhood) and Nossas outras vidas (1989) (Our Other Lives), capture Jewish alterity and the ethnic's sense of duality. In the five stories/chronicles translated here, Levin in a simple and direct style conveys the humor and tribulations of Brazilian Jews in Brazil and elsewhere, as in 'New York, New York,' a diasporic tale of Jewish ubiquity. The other stories are told from the viewpoint of the young adult Jew looking sardonically at the many characters who populate his world.

Eliezer Levin

# New York, New York

Everybody who goes to New York always has something to relate. I wouldn't be the exception, even though it wasn't exactly what one might have foreseen.

Right on my first afternoon, it being the anniversary of my mother's death, I tried to discover where I could find an Orthodox synagogue for the afternoon and evening services of Minchah and Maariv. Naturally there were many.

Given that, according to what I was told, there was one right in the vicinity of Central Park, near the hotel where I was staying, I set out on foot. I was walking up Fifth Avenue in no rush; I had plenty of time. The late afternoon sun was still glistening in the windows of the stores and the skyscrapers of Manhattan, this disconcerting Babylonia, where, it is known, live and labor thousands of our race.

To my surprise the synagogue was closed. On a plaque at the entrance, I could read the schedule for services; I had a whole hour to kill wandering about before the first service. Standing next to me, studying the plaque, a middle-aged man, or perhaps older, displayed the same disappointment. By his manner, hat placed on his head, nose slightly hooked, I didn't have the least doubt that he was a coreligionist. He looked ostensibly at the clock on the facade and made a face.

With all that spare time, I decided to cross the avenue and went to look for a bench in the landscaped square facing me, where with some comfort one could enjoy the passersby. I noticed that the little man accompanied me some steps behind, and when he caught sight of the first free bench, occupied merely by an elderly lady who was taking in the sun, he ran over in order to sit down right next to me.

The old man was wearing a tweed sport coat, a bit démondé, a large necktie loosened at the knot, filled with colors, and he had a prank-ish air spread all over his face. The first impression I had was that the man was getting ready to knife me. However, he started with an introduction. He began telling me that he was from Chicago, where he lived alone, and he had come to spend a few days in New York at his sister's home.

'Her grandchildren are to me like my own,' he informed me, in an English that left no doubts as to his origin.

Without a doubt the man had class. Being in a good mood, I decided to play his game.

'So you are from Chicago?' I asked, naturally thinking, without being able to avoid it, about this city's long history with its gangsters, the clashes between its gangs, and all that gross atmosphere of crime. As if in a movie screen of my memory, there loomed up before me the well-known faces of Edward G. Robinson and Paul Muni.

'Yes, I live in Chicago, since the Prohibition. Have you in Brazil heard of the Prohibition?'

'Of course,' I answered, half smiling, each time more engaged in his scheme.

'I was a gangster in one of the gangs that fought against Al Capone. Today I am retired.'

The man hadn't as yet knifed me, but I was expecting it any minute. I decided to make things easy for him.

'And how is your income going today?'

'From time to time I pick up some change at the roulette table in Las Vegas. It's enough to live on, and I even bring back some dough for my sister.'

Nice play, I thought to myself, he is still getting ready for the kill. Smiling, just like a tourist but by now a bit suspicious, I asked: 'Do you regularly attend services at the synagogue?'

'No, I am not fanatical about religion. Sometimes, I get nostalgic and there I go.'

From that cue he began to speak to me about his deceased parents, his life in Russia, and even about the heder he had attended as a child.

'I would go to shul everyday with my father. Do you want to hear some parts of the chazones?' he asked me, and without waiting for an answer, he began to hum some niggunim.

The man really had a lot of class, and I thought that I had done more than enough to merit his knifing. It was at that point that we were interrupted by the old lady who had been sitting next to us, keeping quiet the whole time.

'Yes, I remember! I remember it well,' she exclaimed impetuously, with a heavy Russian accent. 'That's how they sang. These were the sad melodies that rang out in their temples.'

We both looked at her with astonishment. Despite her old clothes, her wrinkled face, she curiously exhibited the manners and air of someone out of the ordinary.

'Who are you, lady?' my partner asked, slightly irked.

'I belong to the family of the czar; I am a Russian princess,' she declared in a weak but natural voice, without any hesitation.

Afterward she awarded us with a smile that seemed to me (I could swear) to be that of an authentic aristocrat. And this time, finishing off our surprise, she chanted in a low voice the old *niggun* of the Kol Nidre.

What occurred to me at that moment was that it would be very difficult for me to get away unscathed if I were to tell this story to my friends in Brazil. To tell them that I was in New York City, seated on a park bench, on the one side with a Jewish gangster and on the other with a Russian princess, would be just too much. At the least they would call me a daydreamer.

# Eliezer Levin

# A Schoolmaster's Requiem

Schoolmaster José, an old friend of my father, expired at nine o'clock in the morning on a Friday, in the old folks' home where he had been living for some time. He was a little more than seventy years old, widowed, without children, and was accompanied to the Butantã Cemetery by four people. Two of them sent by the home to handle the funeral bier, and there were also myself and my wife. The funeral was done hastily, since it was the eve of Shabbat and because it was raining—a fine and persistent rain. There were neither speeches nor a waste of time on prayers, except for the strictly necessary ones.

Facing the open grave, while the lumps of wet soil were being thrown in, I kept thinking about what that man's life had been. Had it been worthwhile? I am certain that, if we could have heard his opinion, he would have said yes. He was the type of man who spent his life laughing about everything.

Of the teachers who got together at night in my father's home to discuss matters about the teaching profession, perhaps he was the most modest of all. He was merely the *melamed* of the primary-school level who transmitted the *alef-bet* to the children, nothing more than that. When discussion dealt with the plea to raise salaries or to establish new directives for the teaching of Jewish subjects in the schools, there would be inflamed speeches, radical opinions would clash in the air, but he was the only one to remain silent. Everybody tried to put in their two cents' worth. That's why, in the heat of the debates, at times somebody would overdo it, letting escape, as it naturally happens, some absurd rhetoric or even some real nonsense. It was only at this point that he made himself known: 'Coo . . . coooo . . . coo . . . coooo.'

Everybody would laugh, and serenity would again prevail. After all, they were respectable teachers and not uncivilized children. Debates, yes; discussions, yes; freedom of expression, yes; but not without due respect.

That 'coo . . . coooo' of schoolmaster José was also known by his students—six- and seven-year-old boys. He tried to put into those thick little heads the Hebraic alphabet, but when the situation got really difficult to the point of exploding the patience of any other teacher, he would let out a laugh and in front of the perplexed eyes of the frightened little boy, he would let out his happy 'coo-coooo,' which made the boy smile again.

His colleagues didn't take him very seriously, but they treated him nicely, albeit with a certain degree of paternalism. After all, he was one of them. A funny class of people were those Jewish teachers of that period. They considered themselves to be the cream of intellectuality, they quoted poets and philosophers, they employed a stilted style, they spoke loudly among themselves, but when they had to face their employers, they lost a little of their attitude and ended up accepting the small salaries that were imposed on them. Given the failure of their class, they would go back to meeting among themselves. In one way or another, all of them had their excuses and tried, by means of comments and more inflamed speeches, to hide their bitter humiliation. In the midst of the noisy racket that took place, overriding the entanglement of voices, the curious aside would be heard: 'Coo . . . coooo . . . coo . . . coooo.'

Some of them would react: 'He's a child! Did you ever?'

Others laughed and slapped him on the back, as if approving of his opinion, because, that 'Coo-coooo,' in reality, as they had already suspected for some time, represented an opinion like any other.

Ever since I was a child, there at home, I got used to the happy and jovial presence of schoolmaster José, who came to talk with my father, not only with regard to problems at school but also about Judaism, about what was going on in the world, about the polemical articles in the Yiddish press, about books in general, about Talmudic questions (he was the official reader of the Torah and the megilloth in one of our synagogues). But the big topic, without a doubt, invariably revolved around the educational work to which he had always been committed.

'You know, Jossel,' my father would say to him, 'we Jewish teachers have the mania of delving into our occupation as if it were the most sacred thing in the world. We give of ourselves body and soul. All our energy goes into this task, and nothing is left for us, except diseases of the heart and gastric ulcers. That's your problem, Jossel.'

'And is yours very different than mine? Coo-coooo.'

They would both end up laughing. The teachers of that period were just like that. I wonder if they're still like that.

'It's too bad he never had children,' my wife says to me in a whisper, as if guessing my thoughts.

'That's where you're wrong; he had hundreds of children.'

'Are you referring to his students? And where are they now?'

'There's the absurdity of it all; we all end up being forgotten.'

'That's no consolation for anybody.'

'And who's looking for consolation?' Trying to give her a more convincing response: 'I believe what's most important of all is our own calling.'

'But what calling is that?'

'In schoolmaster José's case, it's likely that, a little before he closed his eyes, he performed his great calling: Yankel, Moishele, Berele, Shloimele . . . And from each of these invoked figures, he must have distinctly heard: Present, Moré; present, Moré; present, Moré.'

We again became silent. At the last thud of earth that struck against the wood of the coffin, now totally covered, a small bird detached itself from the tree branch, flapped its wings, and flew far away, leaving in the air the solitary chirp: 'Coo-coooo.'

# Eliezer Levin

# The Seed from Safed

I met Dona Esther by accident, an old friend of my mother's, at one of those watering-hole resorts where I was spending a short spell. Despite her seventy-some-odd years, I found her to be hale and hearty and even somewhat loquacious, as in the old times. Pleased to see me, she riddled me with questions about the family, wanting to know about everything. At her invitation we sat down in front of a large drinking fountain on that late afternoon, and for at least an hour, I stayed listening to her. I must say that few people possess Dona Esther's knowledge about events that take place within our community. What she doesn't know, nobody knows.

I don't exactly remember what caused her to begin the story that made such an impression on me and which I will try to summarize here, using more or less her own words. I believe it was when she happened to mention the city of Safed, where she was born, the one which, besides being a mystical city, cradle of the cabala, is also recognized for the quality of its pure mountain air.

'In general the inhabitants of Safed are not happy when they leave to reside in other centers,' Dona Esther told me. 'For example that was the case with the Lilenblum family. Did you know that they come from Safed?'

I admitted not only that I was unaware of that fact but that I didn't know a lot about that family. She showed surprise. Between one gulp or another of mineral water, which she patiently gathered into a small plastic cup, she then told me the odyssey of that family whom she had known since she was a little girl.

'Well, the elder Azriel Choihet, the patriarch of the Lilenblum, enjoyed a high reputation in Safed, alongside our rebbe. In fact, everybody over there respected him as an erudite scholar. Just imagine, that kind of esteem from a city like Safed. In order for you to have an idea who he was, even the rebbe himself didn't hesitate to consult him whenever he had doubts about some complicated issues related to our religious laws. In that sense Azriel Choihet had a golden head, a logical mind capable of deciphering any halakhah, no matter how difficult it might be. He would have been a genius of a legal counselor, my father (may he be with G——d) used to say, if he had followed that career. But above all Azriel Choihet was a humble man, devout and a conscientious observer of Jewish law, in accordance with the traditions deeply rooted in the men of our city.

'Who would have imagined, then, that his eldest son, Betzalel, one day had to leave Safed and depart for the Americas? Many others, pressured by the misery of those times of English rule, needed to emigrate. By coincidence he and my father, with their respective families, journeyed together on the same ship. Here in São Paulo they maintained a long friendship, even though in time Betzalel Lilenblum ended up following a more liberal lifestyle, diverging on this issue from my father.

'To prove how much a seed from Safed is unhappy and suffers when being transplanted to other terrains, I am going to tell you the experience that happened to him a few years later. During the time of the Second World War, scarce was the news we received about relatives who had stayed behind on the other side of the world, especially from our small city of Safed. Therefore, when my father learned about the death of the elder Azriel Choihet, he was upset, and the first thing he did was to direct himself to his friend's house. To his astonishment and shock, instead of finding him sitting shivah, as Jewish law dictates, he found him behind his desk, busy with work. Betzalel came out with this remark: I am not sitting shivah for my father, because I am not worthy of him! . . . That's how it is! The seed from Safed was deteriorating!

'Years passed and Betzalel's oldest son, Alexander, whom we knew as Senderl, graduated from the São Francisco Law School. Although young, in little time he distinguished himself as one of the most brilliant criminal lawyers in the courts. The newspapers reported his accomplishments. In dealing with the law, he had the same logical mind as his grandfather, Azriel Choihet, about whom I already spoke. So, again, to prove that the seed from Safed in fact does not function well outside its territory, that Alexander followed a strange course. The news fell on us like a bomb: he got married in the traditional Church of the Consolation, to a young girl from high society, in the full light of day of Yom Kippur, I don't know if by chance or on purpose.'

On that point Dona Esther paused, took one more gulp from her plastic cup, gave a sigh, and looked me straight in the eye. I wouldn't know how to tell if she was exaggerating or not.

'Don't think, my dear, that the scandal ended there, no. The story goes on. Alexander Lilenblum had a daughter, educated like all the young girls from a good family, within the non-Jewish society that surrounded her. I presume they even enrolled her in a high school run by nuns. She neither knew her grandfather, Betzalel (he had died of a heart attack), nor had ever heard speak of her great-grandfather, the elder Azriel Choihet, from Safed, whose name was never mentioned in her presence. She also graduated in law and had a brilliant career: the family's hallmark. Her father, Alexander Lilenblum, they say, divorced and married a second time. In the meantime, as for her, who had no more connection with Judaism—as though to prove that a seed from Safed, even though unhappy in other climates, always continues to be a seed from Safed—this great-granddaughter of Azriel Choihet suddenly returned to the bosom of Judaism; she converted according to the Orthodox laws and, changing her name of Maria, today flaunts the name of Ruth.'

Since it was already getting dark, Dona Esther said goodbye hurriedly, promising, however, to see me on the next day, in the same place, in front of the water fountain. Who knows, with a more interesting story or, at least, a more joyful one.

# Eliezer Levin

# The Tenth Man

Max didn't have a good reputation in our community, but to me his stories were very entertaining. He had dropped his studies early on in order to be able to work, since his father, a victim of an accident, had become an invalid. Due to his business activities, which were numerous, he ended up knowing most of the small cities in the interior of the state of São Paulo, where he circulated, selling just about everything: costume jewelry, clothes, pictures of saints, umbrellas. Very short (one meter and a half at the most), lisping speech, leading-man looks, he was a very communicative guy, which without a doubt was favorable to his business. On the other hand, with the same facility he had for earning money, he ended up squandering it. Turned on by elegance, he liked to buy stylish clothes; he used brilliantine in his hair and overdid it with the colognes. Moreover, a rascal, bohemian soul, frequenting the waterholes of ruffians and prostitutes, he attributed to himself the not very Orthodox vocation of poet, philosopher, and above all, Casanova.

It's obvious that a guy like that would not be well looked upon by our community. I myself tried to give him some advice, but he would listen smiling, as if mocking the rest of the community.

'After all, what's your purpose in life, Max?' I told him with all the frankness I could muster.

One time, however, setting aside the indifference he customarily applied to my affirmations, he retorted: 'That's where you're wrong, my dear friend! For I'm going to tell you about the experience that happened to me a few days ago and which, in some way, disproves the opinion you have of me.'

'One more of your stories, Max?'

Nevertheless, this time I am forced to admit that this story he narrated touched me and left me a bit perplexed. For want of better words of explanation, I will relate it in the same way I heard it.

Returning from his last business trip, already late in the day, Max was driving in his old Buick down a narrow dirt road, a few kilometers from the main highway, when a wild storm came crashing down. The wind that began to blow was so violent he was forced to shift into low gear. Fortunately, a short distance from the road, he noticed an old house, solitary and big, which he tried to reach. Under the eaves, next to the gate, to his surprise, there was an old man with a black beard and a hat on his head who waved to him to enter. Since the downpour was intensifying, he turned off the engine and ran to the house.

'We were waiting for you,' the old man said to him.

'That's a good one! Waiting for what?'

'You, sir, are the man who was missing to complete our minyan: the tenth man.'

'You're of our flock?!'

'Of course.'

'I didn't know that there was a synagogue around here!'

'Please, come in. We're already late, and we can't delay the evening services any longer.'

Max was astonished. The man gave him a yarmulke and, opening the door, invited him to go inside. The atmosphere was cozy, albeit poorly lit. An old copper chandelier hung from the ceiling, throwing shadows all over the enclosed room. Actually, it seemed like the modest interior of a synagogue: the bimah, right in the middle, covered with a velvet cloth; up against the back wall, side by side, the Sacred Ark and the cantor's music stand, where a wax candle was burning, definitely in memory of someone; next to the side walls, on each side, a long bench and a long wooden table with old books strewn about.

Upon Max's entrance, a small assembly of old men, occupying the table to the right, stopped talking and turned their eyes in his direction.

'Yes, now we can begin,' said one of them, getting up and extending his open hand. 'Ah, my dear brother, how we needed you!'

Max was becoming more and more amazed. The eyes of that man sparkled with joy, as if they were resting on a long-awaited illustrious figure.

'Thanks to you we will be able finally to carry out our services,' he repeated, with eyes overflowing with gratitude. 'Therefore, in your honor, in the interval between Minchah and Maariv prayers, we will study a verse by Pirkei Avot.'

The little old men got up from the bench and, one by one, greeted him effusively. Afterward, stationing themselves in the direction of the Sacred Ark, they began to pray. Outside, from the view one had from the window, the tempestuous storm was shaking the trees, and the sky was filled with lightening.

Once the 'eighteen prayers' were finished, the same little old man whom the others called rebbe, began to speak:

'Brothers, let's hear what Rabbi Hillel has to say: "Neither distance yourself from the community, nor depend upon yourself until the day you die; and do not judge your neighbor without finding yourself in his position." What does this mean, my brothers? What are our masters saying?'

Max, for as many years as he might live, according to what he finally said, would never forget all that he had heard in that quarter of an hour. Once the service was over, as if by enchantment, the storm had ceased. As he was taking his leave from the nine little old men, he couldn't control himself.

'How did you know that I would come?'

'We never had the slightest doubt. The tenth man always appears, and you are our tenth man,' the rebbe replied impassively.

Deeply moved, Max could not sleep that night. On the following morning he returned to the locale to see in the light of day that which had seemed to him to be a dream.

'Believe me,' he insisted, as he reached that point in the story, 'there no longer was any synagogue in that area. In its place, merely dense woods.'

'Of course, Max! Even if I don't believe everything in your story, it's not without its edifying moments; that's undeniable,' I pointed out to him with all the endearment inside me.

'Well, I declare that it's all true,' he retorted, winking at me.

Eliezer Levin

# Mr. Samuel

It was one Sunday morning, very early, when I received that phone call
from Mr. Samuel. Although he was an old neighbor of my father, I only
knew him superficially. When both of them, almost within the same
period of time, became widowers, they began to visit each other and
took long walks together through the Garden of Light neighborhood.
Later, when he became sick, my Dad came to live with us, and the
relationship between them was reduced to one phone call or another.
And afterward, not even that. With so much time having gone by, I
barely remembered him.

'Mr. Samuel?! Do you want to speak with Dad?'

'No, I really want to talk to you.'

'Are you okay, Mr. Samuel?'

'Things are pretty bad for me.'

'What's the problem?'

'I'm going to be thrown out of the apartment where I have been
living . . .' His voice was tremulous, and I could sense right away the
drama that was going on at the other end of the line.

'These matters are not so quickly acted upon like that. Nobody is
going to put you out on the street, Mr. Samuel. There is always a long
process ahead.'

'On Friday an officer of the court came here to give me notice. He
told me that I have only two weeks' time to defend myself.'

'And what about your son?' I asked in astonishment, reminding
myself of the only son he had.

'He is in Europe, traveling; he'll only be back within a month,' he
answered me in a whisper.

The worry and the fear that sprang from that lonely man's voice
were very palpable. Therefore, I didn't think twice.

'Let's do the following, Mr. Samuel: I will come by your apartment

to pick you up, and you will come and have lunch with us. There's no
need to worry; my lawyer will take care of everything.

'When will you show up?'

'In a little while, OK?'

'Should I wait downstairs?'

'No need, I'll ring the buzzer.'

I found him on the street, waiting for me; a little short guy, white
hair, wearing a suit and tie. In his hand he had a thick portfolio. Seeing
me, he burst into a big smile. I placed him in the car, and during the
ride I heard him repeat several times that story about being evicted
without giving me time to say anything. I only managed to tell him:
'Don't worry, leave it to me.' And afterward, to change the subject:
'You know, Dad is very anxious to see you again.'

'How is he?'

'He's still recuperating.'

'Did he stop smoking?'

'A long time ago.'

'I always told him to stop with the cigarettes.'

I asked him about his son: 'Have you already received a postcard
from him?'

'Not yet. Jossel must by now be traveling with his wife and children
to Israel. Do you know my grandchildren?'

'I never had the pleasure.'

'Ah, they're marvelous kids! Do you want to see a picture of them?'

I was moved when I saw my father and Mr. Samuel embrace and,
afterward, recall old memories. The lunch was joyous, even more due
to the bottle of red wine we opened to commemorate their reunion.
After that, since it was natural for people over seventy, I thought that
they might want to rest a bit. For that reason I said to our guest: 'Now
I'm going to arrange a bed for you to take a good nap.'

'No, thank you; I prefer that you take me home.'

He said good-bye to his friend, and when the car left, he still kept waving from a distance with his handkerchief. He kept quiet during the ride
home; I noticed, however, that a shadow still hovered over his face.

'Did you already telephone your lawyer?' he asked me suddenly.

The question took me by surprise. I answered him seriously: 'It's
Sunday; nothing can be done today, Mr. Samuel. Early tomorrow
morning, I will send him all your papers.'

'I am going to confess something to you: ever since I received that damn notice, I have been so nervous that I can't even sleep.'

'Well, now you can sleep without worrying. Believe me, it's a long process. In any event with the strategy we're going to take, there will be plenty of time for your son to personally follow the case.'

Seeing him more at ease, I also became more calm. Since I wanted to redirect his thinking, I asked: 'By the way, how is your own health, Mr. Samuel?'

'I'm well, thank you. Do you know how old I am? Eighty-six. But I'm in excellent health, as you can see. How old is your father?'

'Seventy-five.'

'So young!' he exclaimed. 'However, he is a bit worn out, isn't he? I think he should take more walks, as we used to do in the past.'

From Monday on, as much on this day as on the rest of the days of the week, I began to receive phone calls from him, one in the morning and the other in the afternoon, wanting to know how his case was coming along. I did what I could to calm him down. My lawyer worked quickly, trying to get the defense case going as early as possible.

When I thought I had finally managed to calm him down, I received a new type of phone call.

'Forgive me for bothering you,' he began, with his tremulous voice. 'I couldn't sleep the last few nights.'

'What happened, Mr. Samuel?'

Loosing his control, in a tearful voice, he cried out: 'Until now I haven't received a single card from my Jossel. I am very worried.'

At night it was my turn to call him.

'I located your son in the Hotel Dan in Tel Aviv. I spoke to him, by phone. He's very well. Your daughter-in-law and your grandchildren send hugs and kisses. They are having a fabulous trip.'

Ah, blessed lies!

'Did you tell him about the eviction?'

'No, I didn't say anything.'

'That's a good one! They're having a good time while here I am dying of worry!'

# Paulo Jacob

Paulo Jacob was born in Manaus, Amazonas, where he studied and later graduated from law school. He began his career as magistrate, a judge of judicial law, in the district of Canutama on the Purus River in 1952. In this capacity he traveled on the Amazon River and its tributaries for ten years, becoming acquainted with its people and the region. During the 1960s he was appointed as a judge to the court of appeals in the Amazon's Court of Justice in the city of Manaus. He was a member of the Amazon Institute of History and Geography and the Amazon Academy of Letters. The recipient of various literary prizes, he won the Walmap Prize in 1967 for his novel *Chuva branca* (White Rain). Among his works, which include ten novels, he also published in 1985 *The Dictionary of Popular Language of the Amazon*. Besides his major theme of man against the jungle, Jacob's works harbor an ecological aspect in his respect for the rich resources and cultures of that exotic region and its Indians. In a dense style, recreating the language of the region, his prose conveys the beauty and sonority of the Amazonian idiom. As an erudite connoisseur of Jewish and regional traditions, Jacob is not Jewish, according to scholar Regina Igel. But his Jewish novel *Um pedaço da lua caía na mata* (1990) (A Patch of Moonlight Fell on the Jungle) suggests otherwise with its detailed knowledge of Jewish customs and religion. Nevertheless, this Jewish novel tells the story of the family of Salomão Farah, a Sephardic Jew who struggles to maintain his Jewish culture for his family amid the encroaching cultural ambience of the Amazon. The novel is a series of vignettes portraying anti-Semitism and the condition of the Jews in the tiny Jewish community of Parintins, Amazonas. Salomão's struggle with the land and the jungle is comparable to his resistance against the powerful social and cultural forces of assimilation. The excerpts translated here dramatize Salomão's attempts to maintain Jewish culture for his son Jacob and his relationship with the local clergy and towns people. Paulo Jacob died in the city of Manaus in 2003.

# Paulo Jacob

EXCERPTS FROM *A Patch of*
## Moonlight Fell on the Jungle

## Tishah b'Av

Tishah b'Av, ninth day of the Jewish month of Av. Remembrance of
the destruction of the temples of Jerusalem. A date of much suffering
for the Jews. The first temple crushed by Nebuchadnezzar in 586 BC.
The other destroyed by Titus in 770 AD. The holy Beth Hamikdash
ravaged with much disrespect to the sanctuary. Fasting like on Yom
Kippur. The holy day begins before sundown. Ending on the next day
after the sun disappears. To remove the parokheth from the front of
the Ark. To light candles at nightfall. To listen to the reading of the
religious services. The Jews seated on the floor, beside the bottom
of the benches. The benches turned upside down. Not to use leather
shoes. On these sanctified days, no wine at all, and no meat. At the
beginning of the evening, to listen to the *kinot*, hymns and prayers of
mourning. Work is permitted. Not to shave or to have sexual relations.
The study of the Torah prohibited, for being a pleasant activity. *Assara
b'tevet*, the beginning of the siege of Jerusalem by Nebuchadnezzar.
God offers good tidings. And man cannot refuse a legitimate pleasure.
Refusing, he commits a sin. For having spurned what God offers. *Ha-
yoshev b'taanit nikra choteh*. He who fasts due to torture is called a sinner.
One mustn't refuse what God offers willingly. Today my son arrives
home. Teacher Nicota always says. Sir Solomon knew how to bring
up Jacob. He treats the teachers with respect. Yes, ma'am, yes ma'am.
Need chalk, I'll get it. Need the ruler, the inkwell, the pencil, the same
thing. On the day of no water, he took a can and went to fetch some in
the river. And on top of it all he still asked, Don't you need more water?
Afterward the water carrier pours more. Teodoro always lacking in
his duty. Sometimes not enough water even to drink. Very foolish of
Teodoro. Puts the money in his pocket, disappears from work.

'What ya're thinkin', Jacob?'

'Want to talk more with ya', Pa.'

'So talk.'

'I need adult clothin', pants and jacket.'

'Why didn't ya' ask?'

'Thought Pa didn't have the money for that spendin'.'

'Go over to Moses's place and pick the cloth.'

'Can I go right away?'

'Yes, ya' can.'

'And who's goin' to make the suit, Pa?'

'Cid Cabral works the sewin' machine pretty good.'

'Thanks, Pa.'

Son is right. Man size, legs stickin' out. And there's goin' to be another party at the Araújo Filho School. Buy two suits, two shirts, two ties. My son needs to make a good impression. And hadn't noticed that yet. Short pants, hairy legs showin'. Feelin' annoyed, ashamed even more 'cause of the girls. The pair of shoes with half a sole almost like new. A little shoe polish, and it'll shine. Only one year of use. A hole again and have to buy another pair. For the time being it'll hold. No use in spendin' foolishly. Solomon needs to hide his money. Jacob is goin' to study in Belém. Either buy a house, put him in a boardinghouse, or in the house of someone from here. To stop studyin', not allowed.

'Solomon, distracted, thinkin' about money.'

'Thinkin' about Jacob's studies.'

'Didja hear the latest?'

'What happened, Presépio? Tell Solomon right away.'

'Ladislau was fired.'

'What in the heck, Ladislau as well?'

'He got into a fight with Odri 'cause of some papers he needed.'

'Who'd think a thing like that could happen? Odri's best friend kicked out on the street.'

'And he says he's goin' over to the opposition party.'

'No way. He's Odri's friend.'

'Politics has these surprises, Solomon. When one least expects it, the politician changes his coat and his party.'

'And isn't Odri goin' to be kicked out on the street?'

'Some final arrangements have yet to be made. The boss is goin' to speak again with the governor.'

'Who's goin' to believe in those dirty politics?'

'Why all this lack of faith, Solomon?'

'It's only rumor and more rumors. Just yesterday Gimica said that Odri was at political headquarters for hours. And when is it all goin' to end? No way of telling up to now.'

'Politics is patience; it's a game; ya' have to know how to play. To put yar cards on the table. It seems like ya' really don't like Odri.'

'Solomon doesn't like or dislike anybody. God save us from such a thing. Jews mixed up in politics.'

'But ya' always leaned toward the opposition. Ya' tend to be on Sir Chico Bento's side.'

'Don't speak so loud; people may be listenin'. Solomon pays his taxes, he's a Jew; he can't be against the government.'

'Ya're Brazilian like everybody else. Ya' can speak what ya' believe.'

'Don't ya' know? Solomon is a Jew.'

'I'm goin' over there to talk with Bottle-in-the-Water. I'll come right back with the latest news.'

'And did the telegraph operator get the newspaper from Manaus?'

'Better yet. He has the telegraph.'

Dirty telegraph operator. Meddler in everybody else's business. Got a telegram. And the people know right away what it says. On account of that, a lot of money lost. Soon as he learned the quotation of the prices, he went out and spread the word. Took a little money, his tongue is waggin'. And there's no one who'll fire the bastard. He's backed by politicians. Father André wasn't showin' up, 'cause of givin' people in the interior the sacraments to be free of obligation. And he went to Manaus several times. And he was almost transferred. Weren't for Sir Chico Bento, he'd already be posted on the River Madeira. He swore never to be against the man. He even said it at Mass. A good man, helps the Holy Mother Church a great deal. It was that act that excused the priest. The certificate of transfer already approved. The bishop handed it over to Sir Bento; he could tear it up. As proof of our friendship. He kissed the bishop's ring. He really thanked him for the favor.

'Take this little bit of money for the church.'

And take a look at this 'little money,' a note of a thousand. The bishop put the money in the pocket of his cassock. Made the sign of the cross. May this seed always come to us. For the eternal greatness of our kingdom. Holy God, Holy God. Amen! Amen!

'Father André, you haven't been around.'

'Some trouble about freeing people of obligation. But afterward I went to Manaus to break up a little scheme. They had filled the bishop's ears with lies. Thank God everything ended in peace.'

'And what did they do with ya', Holy Father?'

'Only stupid things, you don't need to know. See if you can dig up a little money for the church.'

'Things are goin' from bad to worse. There hasn't been one bit of profit this month. So I think yar prayers didn't help.'

Rotten chestnuts were bought, spoiled tonka beans. All 'cause of Jauaperi's not takin' notice. When Jacob realized it, everythin' was already lost. No one knows who sold the spoiled product. Solomon never missed helpin' the church. In case business goes bad. Today's frugality, may not even be enough for lunch. Merchandise at a very high price. Even flour went up in value. Products of the land shouldn't cost so much like that.

'Solomon cries with his mouth full. You sent hundreds of liters of chestnuts by the ship *Ajudante*. Tonka beans were also shipped in large quantity. Where did you put all this money?'

'But the payment will only come in two months.'

The prayers didn't work. God did not come through for Solomon, the sinner. But he helped the Jew's son. He got the diploma of a good student. So isn't that a miracle? He stopped helpin' Solomon 'cause of his many sins. God's help is late, but it eventually comes. If you have faith, life soon gets better. Just as true as the church is goin' to end up collapsin'. Killin' his friend Father André. The ceilin' ruined; the walls corroded; the paint chipped away. The bats shittin', pissin', ruinin' everythin'. Afterward not to feel remorse. The church caved in, drove a stake right through his friend Father André. Poor priest. Such a good person, to die like that so randomly. All the money put aside he spent on the church. Another like him is not goin' to be found. After his death they may even call him a dirty thief. The bats are eating the church. They even shit on the heads of the saints. With that greatest lack of respect for holy things. On the following day the dung beetles increased. Bugs with shitty assholes like hell. But Solomon never slighted Father André. Even a small donation he always managed. Like before only thing now is to cover up.

'And the money for the charity, for the sacraments?'

'Do you think I'd spend holy money on myself?'

'Heaven forbid. I spoke 'cause I remembered.'

'To be deceitful with a priest. That's a punishment to send you to the depths of hell. To suspect a minister of God, very inconsiderate. Solomon, confess, you want God's forgiveness. To doubt a priest, a big mortal sin. The money was spent on this and that. The bishop demanded a little bit. He needed to take care of a few repairs at the cathedral. How can one stop helping the mother church of Manaus? And Solomon slandering his friend.'

'What is this, Father André! It was never a question of doubtin' yar word.'

'But you asked where I had put the money for charity, for the sacraments.'

'Foolishness of a Jew. Forgive Solomon, Father.'

'I forgive you in the name of the Father, the Son, and the Holy Ghost.'

'Don't do that, Father! Usin' a sacrament of the Catholic Church with a Jew.'

'Don't talk back to me, Missus Veríssima. You take care of your chickens, your ducks; I'll take care of my sheep.'

'And so it's not a sacrilege?'

'Sacrilege is to let the church go to pieces, without asking the Jew's help.'

'Don't get mad, Father. Here, take these coins for the church.'

'I really knew that Solomon wasn't going to disappoint his friend.'

Solomon speaks nonsense. The priest got angry for good reason. What did he have to do with the money put aside. A lot of nerve of the Jew. He is never goin' to pray for Solomon. He even got exasperated with Missus Veríssima. With his son the prayers helped. It was a matter of Jacob studyin' a lot. If he helped, it was just a little. It was worth overcomin' other people's anger. To confer a prize on a little Jew. Let it be as God wishes. Because everythin' he does, he does very well.

[. . .]

# Kiddush Ha-Shem

All day long the same insults. Castrated Jew, wandering Jew. Drinks the blood of Catholics. Drove Christ out and killed him on the cross. Jewess has a horizontal vagina. That's what happened around the time of the fight. From now on nobody acts pigheaded anymore. He complained to Dona Anita Freitas. The teacher didn't make anything of it. With Dona Nicota the same thing happened. Much trouble falls upon Jacob. And the boy doesn't pick on anybody. Killed Jesus; put him on the cross. I dunno how many more things. Jacob, quiet, studious, it takes a lot to rile him. And my son still has a lot to learn. It won't be long before he heads for Belém. To enter the university, to be a Jew of much learning. The teachers praising him. Jacob is going to go far. He passes on the first admissions test for high school. He knows arithmetic well, Portuguese. Composition well written, dictation without any mistakes. The picture of Chiquinho feeding corn to the turkey, he described with such beauty. He deserved 100 percent with honors. He never gets less than 80 on his tests. That little kid is going to be somebody important. As I kept on teaching him. *Kiddush ha-Shem*, that's really the same as martyrdom, divine sanctification. To die like a martyr, preserving the Jewish faith, the word of Elohim. That's how the pitiful priest is seen. Thin, *hermá*, ragged, and worn-out. From the looks of things he got to be like that as soon as he caught tuberculosis. Bad diet from those peregrinations on the river. Which is what in fact also happened to Father André. Skin and bones just like a consumptive.

'Is Father André sick?'

'He caught dysentery.'

'And how did that happen?'

The people don't help the Holy Mother Church. It's their way of leaving without obligation. To receive a small duck here, a chicken there, a little piece of Amazon fish further on. A dozen eggs there up ahead. That was the case of his catching the runs. *Puxuri* fruit didn't work. The shitter only plugged himself up with the rind of the river guava. Quite an embarrassing case. The priest feeling desperate, looking for a latrine. And backwoodsmen 'magine priests to be saints. And saints are plugged up; they don't shit. To go out running, almost staining his

cassock. And to clean up with his shit all watery. To wipe his behind
with cornhusks. One can well see the priest's sacrificial lot. And there
are still many louts who keep on saying: That one lives well just like a
priest. He has plenty of food; he has women for free. And look at those
who suffer. All night long awake. The big pestering mosquitoes. Worse
than that, only hell itself. Mosquito was the pest invented by the devil. A
whole night of mosquitoes. You can count on it; you won the kingdom
of heaven. It disobliges you from so much sacrifice. Only to collect fifty
eggs, twenty ducks, thirty chickens, two turkeys, a pail of mush. Our
daily bread growing scarce. As was already said. Christ's blood watered
down, without taste, weakened. Looks more like blood of a famished
poor man. It's disgraceful for a blood of Christ to be so watery like this.
There's no money for the sacred rites. The only way to manage is to put
more water in the wine. The Host wafer is that tiny morsel. Little Host
made of nothing. Christ's body almost doesn't fit. Nobody helps the
Holy Mother Church. Here the Jews are more Catholic than the Catholics. Each day that passes, Christ is becoming less and less. That skinny
little thing, stunted. Tiny holy bread. Also look at the price of wheat.
The church falling to pieces. The local administration doesn't help, the
same with the state. They only want to swipe the people's money. The
church is not going to withstand another winter. Shitty church, stinking
of piss. The saints, may God forgive, pure shit. Much sacrilege like that
goes on. On account of this a bat looks like the devil. With those little
ears exactly the face of the devil himself. The people talking. Tomorrow
there's a wedding at the priest's shitty church. A wedding or a shitting?
A rat even shat on Dona Mundaia. The woman became exasperated.
She really scolded the priest. To call the church shitty, a mortal sin of
these people. Hitting somebody during this kind of talking, smacking
one's fist in the other's face. Christ also flogged the vendors at the door
of the temple. Disrespectful of God's house. That scanty little piece of
Host. The rickety, scrawny Christ. Then the people talking about the
priest. Putting nicknames on holy things. Just like what happened to the
judge. The poor guy with a half-twisted arm, got stuck with the name
of Let's-Take-a-Stroll. The doctor as well taking part in that greatest
of ridicules. Let's-Take-a-Stroll arrived. Let's-Take-a-Stroll traveled to
Manaus. Today there's a wedding presided over by Let's-Take-a-Stroll.
They end up calling the Host needlefish. Wheat at an enormous price.
Reduce the holy bread; it's a way of economizing.

'You should go to Manaus, Father. Take some little tests on those lungs.'

'So you think I'm tubercular? Have some respect for your friend, Solomon.'

'No intention of offending you, Father.'

'Let's get out of here before this conversation falls upon the lips of people. Right away people will begin to say bad things. Like Father André's got tuberculosis.'

'Excuse me. I figured that in this condition you could catch a bit of anemia.'

'And how about a little money for the church.'

'Take all of today's revenue. But don't forget to always pray for your Jewish friend.'

'You don't even have to ask. I do that in all the masses.'

Capable of possibly having caught pulmonary tuberculosis. Feeling sick while administering the sacraments to the faithful. Dry pirarucu Amazon fish, flour, often missing his breakfast. True, he has suffered plenty. If he dies, who's going to pray for Solomon. A good prayer is really worth somethin'. It helped business a little bit. Last month enough money came in. A tiny, persistent, dry cough like that and you can count on pulmonary TB. It's an evil that can finish one in a relatively short time. Solomon will end up losing the blessing of the Catholic Church. He won't die. He's sure of that. During the time of Janoca, he went about in the same way. He lost a few kilos. He got better after drinking celery juice. Living through the greatest discouragement of his body. No will to row down the river the whole day through. That happened after Janoca's departure. The news spread as he was mooring his boat. Janoca moved to Belém for good. Something of a few hours ago. On account of the storm, he arrived a little later. Beautiful night, a patch of moonlight fell upon the jungle. The moon's blessing hadn't yet been given. That's when a supple young woman came to the riverbank.

'Have you already heard the news, Sir Solomon?'

'So, about what?'

'Janoca moved to Belém. The poor girl didn't want to go; her father made her. She began to cry, until her eyes swelled.'

Everything God does, he does well. But to take away a man's woman, that's something very serious. In that way it's wrong. To take away

the Jew's love. And Solomon wanting to get married. That father of
the girl made a big deal of it. He cursed his daughter; he was going
to kill Solomon. He didn't bring up his daughter for her to marry
a wandering Jew. With another person it didn't matter. To marry a
Jew—he preferred to see his daughter dead. And actually dead, really.
Excommunicated by the church of God. To end up in the depths of
hell. He already heard about that heresy, a Jew marrying a Catholic.
Capable of drinking the blood of their children. Jew even pierced the
sacred Host. It was right at the hour when Christ's blood gushed. Live
blood, red. To send Janoca away. And on top of everything else with
lies about the Jew. Shameless, ignorant, half-breed backwoodsman.
He even ordered Solomon killed. The bullet was really made of tough
steel. Just look at the size of the bullet hole in the itinerant's wall. The
bullet passed within an ace of the bedroom. It singed the grip of the
hammock. Very lucky not to have died from this deed. The greatest
sadness came to him. Clear night, beautiful. A patch of moonlight
fell on the jungle. Still water of the river, no turbulence whatsoever. In
that immense quiet of the night, an immense emptiness in the head.
Men also cry. Tears came, his eyes dripping. Sobs lost in the clarity of
the night. Little patches of moonlight falling on the jungle.

# Amália Zeitel

Amália Zeitel was born in Campinas, São Paulo, in 1933 and died in 1992. She graduated in theater in the School of Communication and Arts at the University of São Paulo in 1971 and completed her MA in fine arts at the same university in 1974. As a teacher she offered courses in music, the plastic arts, body expression and modern ballet, dramatic arts, and theater education. At the time of her death she was serving as vice president of the Brazilian Center of the International Institute of Theater (an organ of UNESCO). In 1956 she was an actress in and founder of the theater at the Jewish Brazilian Cultural Institute and in 1982 was a participant in the First International Conference and Festival of Jewish Theater in Israel. As a translator from English to Portuguese, she published translations of several books and plays, including Peter Shaffer's *Equus*. She wrote several plays, including *O sétimo dia* (The Seventh Day; performed in 1970 at the Hebraica Theater in São Paulo and published in 1982). Her first collection of twenty-one stories was *Morangos com chantilly* (1982) (Strawberries with Cream). Told in a detailed yet simple style, these narratives focus on the condition of modern women as mothers, wives, housewives, friends, and professionals. The stories convey aspects of feminine thinking and also deal with the writer in the act of creation. Although the stories are not overtly Jewish, they treat cultural issues familiar to Jews— cross-cultural experiences, exclusion, and alienation. The title story, anthologized here, shows the ravages of cross-cultural marriage and dislocation, leading to marginalization and even madness.

# Amália Zeitel

# Strawberries with Cream

'Hello.'
  'Marilia?'
  'Who is it?'
  'It's me; don't you remember anymore?'
  'Mother of God! Julia! How are you?'
  'It's not Julia; it's Alicia.'
  I had less than a second to pull myself together.
  'Of course, Alicia, I guess I didn't recognize your voice.'
  'Nonsense, you always call me Julia.'
  It's natural, very natural for me to call the Roberts Ricardos, Christina is Cecilia, John is Joseph, Marcia is Carmen; why Alicia is Julia, I don't know.
  'You're right, forgive me, you know I now go around addressing Sheila as Sandra? Old age, you know how it is . . .'
  Alicia laughed. I laughed along with her. I gave her the requested recipe for squash soufflé and faced the onslaught.
  'Let's have lunch on Thursday? Only the two of us, let's? Do you know how long it has been since we last saw each other?'
  'Is that why you forgot my name?'
  I decided to face the music. Certainly not on account of the time that had passed, but also because I knew more or less about certain things.
  'Yes, of course, Alicia, I don't even know what your face looks like anymore.'
  Not on that Thursday but on the following one, we met. I had already eaten a bunch of carrots, peppers, and radishes, thinking that I had been monumentally stood up, when a pale and wrinkled woman approached my table. Her blond hair had faded; she was wearing pretty clothes—a sweater that had some rhinestones, a nicely tailored

coat, and the pocketbook, which she placed on the table, was made of dreamy kid leather. I looked at that old woman and was just about to say, 'It's taken.'

'No!'

'Surprised?'

'Who . . . me? Come now, Alicia, I was distracted.'

'I'm Julia, certainly.'

I gave her a great big hug; I found it wonderful that she displayed some sense of humor; we laughed, and I collapsed into my seat. I gulped down two more carrots until I pulled myself together; I couldn't believe my own eyes: the most beautiful woman I had known, the aura of an angel, a doll's face, still a young girl, was nothing but a hag.

What was going on? I tried to get straight to the point.

'My dear . . . huh . . . what . . . what are you going to order?'

We ate in silence. Eating, in a manner of speaking, for that woman seemed like a little bird pecking with difficulty at one grain here and there. I choked up, my feet feeling ice cold and my face on fire.

Back to my mind came the images that so many times had been the symbols of a lively fairytale. A gorgeous bride, descending from a real carriage, drawn by four, nothing less than four, white horses. Maids of honor—a whole entourage. The air was perfumed, the salons of the castle decorated with flowers I had never seen, but I didn't even see the decorations; I saw the castle. Of course, imagine a Brazilian attending a wedding in a castle in the summertime, in the south of France, of a not-yet-decadent family. Everything was special but too much so. Pheasants and wild boars, a flock of doves in flight—corny, but nonetheless a flock of doves—luminous water fountains, sing-ers, orchestras; I lived a dream that's only in the movies. As a social columnist would say, 'We toasted a bride and groom who inspired everyone. Young, pure, snow-white, beautiful.' Loaded with dough. A somewhat timid French girl, Alicia was in her third year of medi-cal school, a genius, according to some people. He, Brazilian, was accustomed to sailing a yacht there on the Riviera. Going over my memories, I think I allowed a smile. Alicia awakened me.

'Laughing alone?'

'That's right, I was remembering your wedding and how it was that we became acquainted.'

'Don't start again with your complex about being a party crasher, all right? Friends of Jonas are friends of mine, especially you.'

'No, Alicia, nonsense'—and finally, I took aim—'today I feel really guilty.'

She looked at me; she didn't say anything.

'I think I abandoned you.'

I remember well, we both felt bad when Alicia made the decision that she would have to give up her medical studies; her coursework from there had no credit value here in Brazil. I had strongly supported her to begin anew, entrance exam and everything, but her husband opposed what he considered a 'regression,' in addition to his evidently preferring that his wife stay at home. We used to meet quite a lot during those early times; I followed very closely Alicia's enormous difficulty in adapting herself. Surrounded by lots of folks but people who had nothing to say to her. But, on the other hand, they loved each other; who knows? I think I distanced myself when I noticed that they were quarreling too much. Invariably things got tense when she said she was in exile.

'Maybe you did abandon me,' she answered, biting one of her very poorly trimmed fingernails. 'But I doo not blame yooo. Wee became unbearrable peeople . . . I and my hosband.'

I did not fail to notice the heavy accent or the intonation. Albeit poorly adjusted, Alicia had easily learned and mastered her new language. And now this?

'Don't talk like that, my dear. Jonas was such a great guy.' I was being sincere. 'He always loved you very much.'

'That kind of loove I don't weesh on anyone.'

'But, Alicia, listen, I . . . I must tell you something. Many people are not happily married, who knows why, arguments, but I look at you and I can't believe . . . you . . . you seem very depressed. What's going on?'

'Nothing different . . . nothing special . . . nothing new.'

'Well then, excuse me if . . . if I say something foolish, but why . . .'

Calmly, Alicia cut me off.

'Then don't say anytheeng.'

That was Alicia, a woman with character, positive. And now, my God, which approach should I take? It's not easy talking to her . . .

'And the children, are they fine?'

'They are excellent. *Ils sont la meilleure chose de ma vie.*'

And now what's this with the French? We had never spoken in French! I'm going to ask about her medical studies, I thought. Actually I had never accepted that unfortunate decision, but, on the other hand, what an old topic; it'll probably be dead and buried; no, I won't mention it, so I'll talk about the subject we have most in common, the only one. That's it; I'm going to give her my new recipe for chicken with cheese; the children love it. Ridiculous, only now did I realize that years had passed, that our 'everything's fine, everything's fine' was idiotic, and I'll find out that she called me asking for recipes as a way of asking for help.

'Deed you know that next year I weel grraduate from medeecal school?'

'I don't believe it! Is that true?' So that was it. But then my head was already thinking a mile a minute; the woman before me was a mess; anyone who is fulfilling oneself cannot be unkempt in that way. I think I heard wrong. 'Wait a minute, Alicia, what did you say?, I . . . I was distracted.'

'And thee day I grraduate, I am leeving Jonas. Or better, he eeze goeeng to abandon mee and take the keeds. I neverr should have come to thees countree.'

'Hold on, Julia, was it Jonas who said that?'

'Non, hee deed not say eet.'

'Then, who did?'

'I know. Julia, right?'

Without my having had time to become aware of the repeated lapse, Alicia opened her purse, took out her cosmetic case, and began to apply rouge to her face. She said: 'You know, I feel very well being with you.'

But God only knows how I was feeling next to that strange old woman. Her face now had two red spots; could it be that she was making a fool out of me?

'I'm pleased. I also feel . . . but listen here. Forgive me, it's that I'm not understanding, this . . .'

'There eeze notheeng to underrstand. Eef I grraduate, I am not goeeng to get marrried.'

'But you're already married, you already have children, and you can graduate.'

'Vell, that eeze eet. Alicia got marrried, and now Julia eeze goeeng to bee a doctor.'

'Julia? What Julia? Don't kid with me, Alicia; I mean, I made a mistake, okay, but you're joking with me.'

At that moment Alicia's stare was drained of all life; it simply went right through me, and there I was hanging in the balance in front of her, trying to provoke some reaction, but her eyes were like two stones immobilized in space, a very strange faded blue. Did I say something foolish? But by now I did not even remember what I had said. Ah, she had laughed at my 'Julia.' Could it be that I had always called her Julia? Boy, how confusing . . .

'Julia eeze not jokeeng; shee neverr jokes. Alicia, yes, Alicia jokes a lot. Thee fortunetellerr told mee, but I, I saw eet.'

That insane look continued to stare at who knows what in the distance. Insane?

'Alicia, come here.' I took her hands, pulled them closer to me. 'Listen, my friend, don't you like to live here in Brazil just a little?'

'I doo not leeve een Brezeel; I leeve in the medeecal school. You arre verry confused.'

'I am? Ah, I know . . . Well, so you mean that the fortuneteller said that when you graduate, Jonas, in retaliation, is going to take the children away, is that it?'

'Non, but non. Julia eeze goeeng to leeve forreverr een thee school; shee eeze goeeng to bee a doctor over there.'

'Ah, I get it. And what about Alicia?'

'Me? I adore taking care of my kids. And I adore my husband.' Her accent had disappeared just like it had appeared, and I began to see that I had placed myself in a delicate situation.

'Alicia, my dear, it's all right; listen, I called you Julia because of my confusion, do you understand? Julia doesn't exist. Alicia, you, let's have dessert?'

Alicia's eyes rolled around and stared at me. I became even more frightened; they were an intense blue, a hue I had never seen before. And from them tears began to flow.

'Oh, Alicia.' I was still holding her hands. 'You're going to mess up your rouge. Here, take this napkin. Why are you crying?'

Alicia sobbed and looked at me. I, not knowing how to pray, said a prayer to God to give me a bright idea, to give me the intelligence to say something that might help.

'I already know, my dear,' I murmured. 'You want Julia back, don't you? Look, I'm going to confess something from the bottom of my heart: I guarantee that Julia does indeed exist. Do you want to go and find her, together with me?'

Her sad face smiled, more a grimace of pain than a spark of hope, but she sturdily nodded her head.

We devoured the strawberries and cream.

# Esther Largman

Esther Largman was born in Salvador, Bahia, in 1934 and is a historian by profession. She received her BA and MA degrees in geography and history from the Faculty of Philosophy of the Federal University of Brazil in 1955 and in 1956 entered the doctoral program in the history of Brazil. In 1978 she studied cultural anthropology at the Federal University of Rio de Janeiro. Author of several short stories, she also published an article on the Jewish community of Bahia for the magazine Shalom in 1992. She wrote the novel Jovens polacas (1993) (Polish Girls), about Jewish white slavery in Brazil at the beginning of the twentieth century. Since these women portrayed in her novel transgressed the social codes and ethical principles of Judaism, this subject was taboo for many years. In 1997 one of Brazil's foremost playwrights, Miguel Falabella, prepared a proposal for a TV miniseries based on Largman's novel. In 1998 Jovens polacas was adapted for the theater and performed at the famous Maria Della Costa Theater in São Paulo. Largman is also the author of Jan e Nassau: Trajetória de um Índio Cariri na corte holandesa (1996) (Jan and Nassau: Trajectory of a Cariri Indian in the Dutch Court), the novel Tio Kuba nos trópicos (1999) (Uncle Kuba in the Tropics), and the historical study Judeus nos trópicos (2002) (Jews in the Tropics). The excerpt translated here involves the encounter of one 'Polish girl' and her immigrant cousin, who knows nothing about her fate as a prostitute. Here the reader witnesses the intra-ethnic reaction to this social phenomenon. The excerpt concludes with a scene at the brothel, where the 'girls' discuss how they ended up in this tragic situation and also hints at the overarching organization, the Zwi Migdal, that trafficked in this white slavery.

# Esther Largman

EXCERPT FROM *Polish Girls*

It was still November, but summer seemed to have arrived with all its force. It was very hot, the mangos were already ripened, and in the neighbor's yard many of them were lying on the ground, half ripe, half rotten.

Anita swept the broom vigorously, the perspiration running down her back. She was still a young woman, but her heaviness made her look older; she had to be around thirty—not tall, large and round breasts, short and thick legs. The street urchins called her 'pigeon-woman' or 'chesty Ruskie,' but she didn't care. A good-hearted type, calm. Her freckled face, her beautiful black curly hair sometimes gave her an infantile expression.

She took very good care of her home. They lived in the upstairs part of a two-story house on the street they now called Conception, but which already had been Pedreira and Vasco da Gama, near Tiradentes Square. One entered by a side door that, beyond a small corridor, led to a stairway with a carved wooden banister. At the top of the stairs there was another door of paneled wood, which led to the apartment, opening directly onto a large room. There was one more room, a kitchen, and a bathroom, besides a tiny little room in the back and a small bathroom for the maid, but she neither had nor did she want any cleaning help.

'Why do I want more?' she thought. 'Only me and Yankle, God doesn't want to give me children,' . . . Yankle was Jacob, her husband, a Pole she had married in Brazil. They got to know each other in the home of her aunt and uncle, with whom she had come to Brazil from Odessa as a young child, because they didn't have children and they needed help and also because her parents' situation in Russia was very difficult. Anita suffered in silence. She suffered for the absence of the family she left far away; she suffered with the hot climate and now, above all, because she hadn't had children. She had already lost hope, and although she knew her husband loved her, she was afraid of losing him; she struggled to be a dedicated, affectionate wife; she cleaned very well and took very good care of the house and, moreover, cooked as few do. Gefilte fish, the fishcake she learned to make as a little girl with her mother, was the best, Yankle would say. 'He is tender, he provides me with the greatest of comforts, and in bed he is so good . . . It's not possible that he will leave me some day, even though he could, according to our laws . . . 'cause I can't get pregnant.'

While she was thinking as she picked up the trash she had piled in the corner of the room, she heard footsteps coming up the stairs and soon after a knocking on the door. She quickly removed her apron, threw it on the kitchen chair, and went to open the door.

She stepped back in surprise. Facing her a slim and blond young woman with fine features looked at her with a somewhat uncomfortable smile. She was well dressed.

'Sarah? What are you doing in Brazil? When did you arrive?' Anita instinctively spoke in Yiddish, actually because she still spoke little Portuguese and rather poorly at that.

'May I come in, Cousin?' Sarah asked timidly, standing on the threshold.

'Oh, my God, excuse me. I was so surprised that I seem like a crazy person. Of course, come in.' She pulled the young woman by her arm, and next they embraced, kissed, and examined each other.

Silent tears began to run down Sarah's smooth and beautiful face. She and her cousin Anita used to live in the same city, near each other. There was an eight-year difference between them.

'But sit down and tell me everything. Do you want a soft drink?' Anita was excited and happy; she didn't even notice her cousin's sad expression.

Sarah sat down and took off her white kid leather gloves, her French straw hat, and looked around the room: on one side stood the round dark wooden table, with four high-back chairs, the cushioned seats of velvet, wine-colored brocade. On the center of the table an embroidered doily of immaculate whiteness, which served as the base for a crystal-clear vase without flowers. In the other corner two armchairs with matted-straw seats were separated by a small table on which rested a newspaper printed in Yiddish. In the room there were two doors that opened to balconies with wrought-iron latticework. They were closed, despite the heat; Anita forestalled the dust from entering the house; she only opened them when her husband came home—the curtains were tied by a bow made of the same embroidered tulle, one on each side, graceful. The appearance was pleasant and tidy.

'Nu? So?' Anita asked, already somewhat anxious. 'How are our people doing with that war? With that horror . . .'

'Anita, darling, I have already been here for two and a half years,' Sarah interjected.

'But how!? And only now have you come to visit me?'

'I don't know how to tell you . . .'

'Speak up right away, come on, what happened? I'm already worried. Nobody wrote anything to me. How can this happen?' Anita shot her questions in an accelerated rhythm, almost without catching her breath. 'Was there some kind of censorship? Don't they let anybody there write anymore?'

'There was some difficulty with the mail, but that's not it. They didn't say anything because I'm the disgrace of the family. I ran away,' the downcast young girl answered slowly and sadly.

'You ran away?!' She waited a little. 'And with whom? Why?'

'It's a long and painful story. I would very much like you to listen to me and to forgive me; perhaps you may be able to help me. I'm living in such agony . . . Is Jacob going to arrive soon?' she anxiously asked.

'No, he only comes home in the late afternoon; you don't have to worry.' Anita quieted down, somewhat mistrustful, half curious, but already full of pity. Her cousin was very beautiful, so much sadness and paleness, a sickly manner . . .

And Sarah began to tell her story.

Ever since her other uncles and her cousin Anita had emigrated, times had been difficult in Odessa. And they continued to be, without any hope of getting better, especially for the Jews. Her father became ill; they were starving. The first year of the war finished off the family business— the little store, where they sold delicatessen, had to be closed; they were only losing money; her mother was taking care of the house, her younger brothers as well as her father. Fifteen-year-old Sarah decided to quit school and began to work as a dressmaker in a factory. One day a new foreman appeared, a dark young man, very elegant and handsome, Benjamin Tarnow, who began to talk to her, praised her beauty, and after a few weeks, invited her on a date. Little by little Sarah fell in love. Some time afterward they became engaged, and Benjamin announced that they would go to South America, where he had well-to-do relatives with an established business. They would spend their engagement in Odessa and would get married as soon as they arrived. Her mother was against it; she began to cry and to complain, that she was still a young girl, that she was the only one who could help the family, that it was absurd . . . Sarah had her doubts, but the young man, resolute and convincing, even promised to send money each month; then they would send for the whole family—why continue in that land swept by misery and war? So, on a certain crazy day, after writing a letter with a thousand explanations and promises, she ran away. After arriving in France, they boarded a ship for Brazil. She was then seventeen and a half; the war was ending its first year. A macabre anniversary.

Sarah told that story with her head down, her hands folded in her lap. At this point she raised her face and spoke: 'But I always send money home, and they never write to me.'

'Okay, continue, what happened afterward?'

On the ship she noticed that Benjamin was talking with some guys. They seemed to know him and they looked at her with a malicious expression. One day the oldest of the group made a rude remark to her face; Sarah, offended, spoke to her fiancé about it. To her dismay he not only was indifferent but, on top of everything, emphasized the fact that the guys were his friends. When they arrived in Rio de Janeiro, after stopping in Recife, tired and by now a bit sorry, she stayed in a horrible hotel, a hot and dirty hovel. She complained to Beny.

'What did you think, that I was going to live in a palace? First we have to work, and work hard, isn't that so, my princess?' he asked in an irritable and sarcastic manner.

Sarah sighed deeply and said nothing.

'So?' the other woman insisted, already anxious.

'So,' continued Sarah, 'so I caught a glimpse of my hell. I realized that my dream was never going to materialize; I saw that, besides being a liar, Beny was dishonest, crude, and when I reacted, he was direct and cruel: he had brought me to be one of his *curves*, one of his whores!'

'Oh, my God! My holy Lord!' Anita exclaimed, horrified, as she began to wring her chubby hands.

'Anita, darling, I wanted to die of shame.' Sarah spoke softly and emphatically, with her lips puckered. 'But he has experience with that sordid business. He placed me in a room, made me go hungry. There were women who kept an eye on me, day and night, I was insistent about not giving myself to men; I preferred to die. Then he began to beat me. I received many beatings, I became swollen, but I didn't give in. Oy! What a destiny! Remember, Anita? Me of all people, who used to have discussions with my colleagues about Tolstoy's ideas, Pushkin's poetry, Lermontov's style, and Rosa Luxemburg's ideals! . . . I couldn't believe what was happening, that I had fallen into one of those traps. I cried day and night, until I got tired; the tears dried; only revulsion and bitterness were left.'

Anita listened, her eyes wide open, horrified.

Sarah continued: 'Then Beny, that scoundrel, discovered my vulnerable side: he threatened to write and tell my parents. That's when I weakened. I panicked; the shame of having fled was already bad enough, but my parents knowing that I was living in a whorehouse, in a brothel, that would be a complete tragedy! And at that point . . . I gave in.'

The silence in the room was hanging, suspended, waiting for a sigh, a heavier breath. Both women stood with trembling lips, their tears running down their faces.

'The worst,' the girl slowly continued, her blue eyes reddened from crying, 'the worst is that I had a child, a girl, my little Mira. She is beautiful, and is two years old.' Only then did the girl show a proud smile.

Anita became pensive; she took better notice of her cousin's clothes, very chic, better than her party dresses, without a doubt: a wide skirt of beautiful taffeta, a silk blouse all embroidered with fine lace, high-heel shoes. Then she understood where all that extravagance had come from.

'I'm very sorry; I don't even know what to say, dear Sarah,' she said in a whisper. 'This is all very sad for you, and for all of us. I'm going to ask a big favor of you. Don't come back here like this; you know how Jacob hates this and for us it is a . . . ,' uncomfortable, she stopped, 'shame.' I don't want him to know anything about this, promise?'

'I know, I'm a disgrace to everybody, but nobody knows anything; they only know that I ran away,' the girl repeated. 'Now do you know why I didn't look you up until today? I knew your address, but I only got the courage to come for a very strong reason, Anita, and you have to help me. Don't worry; nobody saw me come in; I was very careful.'

Sarah went from the feeling of shame to that of anxiety. She was standing; she walked a little around the room; she stopped; she placed her hands on her face; she threw her head back. She was the picture of agony.

'How can I help you? What can I do?' her dismayed cousin asked.

Sarah opened her elegant purse and took out an embroidered hanky; she wiped her eyes and looked firmly into the other woman's eyes.

'I know that you do not have children, and I wanted you to take care of little Mira.' Facing her perplexed cousin, she continued: 'I will pay for the expenses. All of them. A nanny to care for her and to help out, clothes, food, studies, everything, everything. I only want my daughter to grow up far away from that filth and not to be ashamed of her mother. You know, Anita, I had two other children, but it seems God helped me: they were born dead. My little daughter is the most precious thing I have in the world, she is going to have another future, and you have to help me, please, please,' she softly implored.

After a few seconds she listened to the answer.

'I don't believe that it's possible, you don't know my husband very well, and moreover he's part of the Bund; that's why I told you not to come here anymore. Jacob already fought in his homeland against those kind of people, you know?'

The idea, the novelty in itself had its charm. To raise a child as if it were your own, being a parent, was even a consolation, but Yankle with his hatred for ruffians and brothels . . . He deeply despised the Yiddish pimps and their prostitutes; he called them the enemies of the people, that they attracted hate and anti-Semitism. One time he told her that over there in Poland, already serving in the party, the Bund, he was part of the group that attacked the taverns and the brothels and sometimes yanked the innocent girls from those places. Only that once there was a very ugly ruckus, and the police arrived to protect those dirty people. As a matter of fact, it was known that the impure ones and the police mutually helped each other, even in the suppression of the strikes. It was during that brawl that Yankle was hurt, leaving a scar on his face.

'My cousin,' Sarah said, 'I only came here out of despair. Give it some thought; be calm. Your husband must be a good man. Who knows? Perhaps he may even be able to accept the idea. I promise that I will pay for everything,' she repeated, 'and I will only see my daughter when you want me to. Tell my story, I wasn't to blame, I am a victim of those vile people, and I'm caught, but at least I managed secretly to save a bit of money.'

She took a deep breath and concluded: 'Now I'm going. I don't want to meet Jacob; I wouldn't be able to face him. Here is my address. If you want to, look for me during the day and say that you're my seamstress, that you came to collect your money.'

She got up, handed over the folded paper, grabbed her hat and purse. She stared at her cousin, who was somewhat withdrawn; she didn't know whether to embrace her or not. Slowly she went toward the door; she turned around, gave a sad look, and descended the stairs, her high heels tapping against the wood. Upon reaching the street, she lowered her hat, carefully looked around and turned right, walking beneath the admiring gaze of some men passing by. There were few women on the street; some were quietly leaning out of their ground-floor windows. A Middle-Eastern woman offered her matches. Sarah looked at the ground and did not stop until she turned the corner.

Anita remained standing, her eyes fixed on the door that Sarah had passed through, completely confused. What should she do? She felt afraid to tell her husband and decided, for now, not to say anything; imagine if their friends learned about this stain on the family . . . She picked up the broom, the rag, the schmatte, and went to take a bath. She needed to be clean and fragrant for her husband when he arrived home from work. The tailor shop was beginning to earn some profit, given that at the start it had been difficult, but now he had a good clientele, not Jewish, refined goyim; our men saw no value in a well-cut suit, and, besides, they didn't have money to wear vests, dress shirts with stiff white collars. It's true that the clothes were warm, but the elegant Brazilians liked to follow the Parisian styles, and Yankle understood this very well; he had learned his trade while still in Poland, but afterward he went to live in France for some months before arriving in Brazil. Who knows, she thought, already with her head beneath the strong force of the faucet, some day we will have a beautiful shop of imported fabrics; it will be less tiring, he wouldn't have to go see his customers in this heat, and it should be more lucrative . . . she let the water flow a little bit more, shut the faucet, and began to dry herself, caressing her shoulders, her breasts, her thighs, and she felt aroused. Hopefully he will not take long and come home soon—she smiled to herself, happy. Suddenly she remembered Sarah and felt a tightening in her chest, a severe pain like an omen. Her cousin had arrived to remove her little bit of peace because she, Anita, despite not having children and feeling nostalgic about her homeland, was learning to resign herself, as though it were the only way to be happy, to live serenely with her husband. And suddenly this tenuous peace was torn, a fragment of concern penetrating the equilibrium she had achieved with considerable difficulty since she had left her father's home.

Sarah climbed the stairs of house number 18 on Holy Spirit Street—which from that year on became known as Luis Gama—and entered the large parlor. Her friends were chatting; soon they would be going to dinner. There were various brothels in the red-light district, but the woman who cooked and cleaned for these places was Benedita, a fat and calm mulatta who had once been a whore but the madam thought that she would be of more worth in the kitchen. In the beginning the foreign girls found the food very strange, but they finally got used to it.

Besides herself there were five other prostitutes and the madam, Dona Norma. Fanny Feld was Polish; Elisa Wain, Rumanian; Laura Castilha, a very lively Spaniard who always spoke in a loud voice; Emilia Willer, a very sober and sad English girl—no one would say that she lived in a brothel—and finally, Sara Kolner, a red-haired Austrian; she was older, thirty. The others didn't appear to be more than twenty-five years old.

Sarah had settled in the chair and become self-absorbed, without being part of the group. She hadn't even noticed that the girls were talking, each one relating passages from her life, above all, how she had ended up in a whorehouse. It was already a routine, a diversion; on certain afternoons before dinner, before their clients arrived, they would exchange reminiscences and experiences; many times they cried, but it wasn't uncommon for them to burst out laughing. It did one good; the crying and the laughter cleansed their souls. With the exception of Laura, they were all Jews. They spoke Yiddish, but when the Spanish girl appeared, their precarious Portuguese, completely mutilated, served as the mode of communication, out of respect for their other colleague. And little by little, the goy was grasping one word or another, beginning to understand a little of that very tongue-twisting language.

The one who took care of the house and of them was Norma Kohn, an energetic woman, a very tough procuress who controlled all the comings and goings, the money that came in, their movements; she bought and ordered the making of their dresses as well as the rest of their accessories. But when one of them had a problem, she would solve the situation right away; she tried to help. Also, Sarah rationalized, she had to take good care of them—sick girls could not bring in the profits. And it was also because of this that they were well dressed, in order to attract a better clientele. On the other hand, the clothes were not to Sarah's taste; they were flashy, and so she gave herself the luxury of owning two dresses that were more modest for going on some outing.

Sara Kolner belonged to Jacob Gant. She was talking about how her husband had transformed her. She was young and beautiful; she lived with her parents in Graz, in Austria. Jacob had come from Poland and had courted her. Her parents were delighted, and after a short courtship he decided to marry her, alleging that he had to travel a lot to see his fiancée, since his business dealings were in his homeland. Whatever business this was she did not know, but she imagined that her father understood the situation better. Gant knew how to talk; he had studied and said that his ideal was to go to America or Canada, to work and later to graduate; he wanted to be a doctor of letters. They were married only in the religious ceremony; they wouldn't need to make it official under civil jurisdiction; the religious one was more secure (sad mistake, for Sara learned too late that her would-be husband was married, in the same way, with at least two more girls in his homeland, and had also misled the two of them; although for Jewish girls that kind of wedding was valid, sacred, and for that reason they considered themselves his wives . . .)

Once the marriage had taken place, with a small party in Graz, soon afterward, he decided to go to Argentina, and in spite of Sara having become upset with his decision—it was very far away and she would stay there without seeing her family for a very long time, she imagined—she knew it was her duty to accompany her husband.

Besides, the situation in Graz was very difficult; she had been working as an assistant in a perfumery and earned little, scarcely providing for her own sustenance. And her father was a poor watchmaker.

Just how much she was going to suffer and miss the streets, the squares, her friends, she only came to realize on the other side of the ocean.

'Of course,' she said, 'when I arrived in Buenos Aires, my husband alleged that he wasn't finding any work and took me right away to the brothel on Avellaneda Street, very well known there, and he didn't even prepare me. He spoke right up and told me why he had gotten married, that he did not like to work and that it wouldn't do me any good to rebel. I asked him to let me go away. Do you know what he did? He laughed in my face and said with complete natural-ness and cruelty: "My little darling, your parents have already been informed. Your old man is already in mourning for you. He is sitting shivah. And he went to the rabbi to complain, but our people had a way of placating him. After all, if he insists, he's going to end up sick; I think the threat worked." Can you all imagine how I felt after hearing all that? In a state of shock, completely motionless. I suffered a great deal, I cried, but what good did it do me? I knew neither their language, nor Argentina's, I didn't have any money, and I was so disappointed with Jacob that everything was all the same to me.'

'And how did you come to end up here?' Emilia wanted to know. She spoke in a low and restrained tone.

'I was exploited for years, there in Argentina. Afterward Jacob sold me to another man who had a brothel in Rosario, and afterward I re-turned to the capital. Then, after talking with some other girlfriends, I decided to take a risk, and having saved some money, I was able to flee to Brazil. I wanted to be independent and perhaps, who knows, one day return to see the mountains of my homeland. But my joy lasted only a little while. Having barely arrived at the hotel whose address they had given me, I met a guy who ordered me to stay and wait for my husband. I don't know who betrayed me, maybe Lola, the wretched procuress, but they found out and sent Jacob after me. I was forced to return to work for them; later they decided to send us to Rio and to organize another whorehouse, which is this one.'

'Who are they?' asked Laura with curiosity. 'I didn't know about that detail in your life, *mi querida*.'

A silence hung over the room. The dark Spanish girl looked at one of them, her black eyes sparkling. 'Oh, yes, my hombre told me everything. You're afraid of that Migdal, aren't you?' she asked brazenly.

'It's better not to talk about that,' Fanny hastened to say.

# Bernardo Ajzenberg

Bernardo Ajzenberg was born in 1959 in São Paulo, where he studied in Jewish primary and middle schools before enrolling in 1977 in the University of Campinas, São Paulo (UNICAMP) to study economics. He never completed the program since he soon went to Israel to harvest oranges and later traveled throughout Europe. He returned to Brazil and began working for a newspaper, the *Gazeta Mercantil*, in 1976. Since receiving a degree in journalism from the Fundação Cásper Líbero, he has worked as a journalist and as secretary to the editorial office and ombudsman for the following newspapers and magazines: *Gazeta Mercantil*, *Última Hora*, *Veja*, and *Folha de S. Paulo*. Until recently he was executive coordinator of the Moreira Salles Institute in São Paulo. He is also a translator and the author of five novels: *Carreiras cortadas* (1989) (Careers Cut Short), *Efeito suspensório* (1993) (Suspensory Effect), *Goldstein & Camargo* (1994), and *Variações Goldman* (1998) (Goldman Variations), *A Gaiola de Faraday* (2002) (Faraday's Cage), for which he received the annual prize for fiction from the Brazilian Academy of Letters. Ajzenberg has also published a collection of stories, *Homens com mulheres* (2005) (Men with Women), noted as a finalist for the prestigious Jabuti Prize. *Goldstein & Camargo* and *Variações Goldman* focus on Jewish themes and the city of São Paulo. The excerpt translated here is a *paulista* narrative about a Brazilian lawyer of Jewish descent whose unstable identity in a city of different ethnic groups begins to disintegrate psychologically and professionally. The interethnic ambiance is the background for a dark story of Pirandellian proportions in which different versions of the same drama point to the impossibility of objectivity. Although the novel's title evokes the friendship between a Jew and a non-Jew, the story focuses on family conflict between generations, father and son, and siblings. Filled with Jewish guilt, Goldstein has disappeared and alienated himself from family, friends, and colleagues after deciding to defend his dear childhood friend, Luca Pasquali, who is accused of murder.

# Bernardo Ajzenberg

## EXCERPT FROM Goldstein & Camargo

Early on in life I became one of those callous individuals who doesn't
believe in the existence of platonic love. However much she represses
herself or is repressed, perhaps even due to this, the lay sister who
secretly loves some lad always feels her sex vibrating amid her desires—
or between her legs, to be more exact (excuse my vulgarity!). It can't
be different, neither for her nor for anybody else. And I know today
there is nothing bad about that; after all, no feeling exists as an isolated
phenomenon. Love, yes, love, that business not always lucrative but
always contagious and beautiful called love, to be honest, does not
function without its salacious side—just like the actual human body,
capable of living exactly because it produces excrements, sweats, and
secretions. Everybody knows that without its sewers the city can infect
itself with the plague, that garbage is the other side of *glamour*, and
so on and so forth. Existence is made up of these exchanges, of this
fluctuating fluid, isn't that so? And nevertheless, in spite of all this, in
spite of seeing as obvious these few, risky, and unoriginal ideas, I am
obliged now to ask of myself, in a quasi lament, the following: what's
the use of a concept like this, which I find to be sufficiently healthy,
well conceived, and positive—at least it prepares me at every instant
to bypass inevitable disappointments—if the woman I loved for such
a long time and, therefore, desired in flesh and bone for such a long
time, believed exactly the opposite, or rather, that only the platonic
can exist as true love?

So this was the impasse at which I arrived while looking for Goldstein's parents, trying to understand his disappearance from the office
in order to verify the, I would say accusatory, statements made to me
by Luca Pasquali about my partner.

The only person close to Goldstein I knew was his wife, Rebecca. When I telephoned, I felt in her trembling voice that she was

experiencing complete bewilderment: she hadn't seen him for days; Márcio had only left a note under the door of the apartment, saying that he was going to travel but without clarifying where he was going or for how long. I proposed to her that we have a chat in my office; I needed information; it was imperative that we at least exchange some ideas, I explained. We made an appointment on the same day, and the situation seemed so serious to me that I adopted an unprecedented behavior: making up some excuse, I let Sandra leave early; in fact, I sent her out of the office immediately.

Upon opening the door to let her in, my first sensation was that there was some mistake. Rebecca was totally miniscule: a little more than a meter and a half in height, her head small in diameter and slightly flattened, like an apple, tiny arms, her blond and wavy hair in disarray over her narrow shoulders, I'd say a person almost without any waist, with thin and short legs, her right hand drowning in mine as we greeted. I invited her to come into the office.

In my room at the office, the lead gray skirt down below her knees and the white blouse with the snug collar, in their discretion, reinforced in me the surprising impression that that small woman had nothing to do with Goldstein and his mania for elegance: I was expecting a tall and talkative blond, with too much mascara, decked out in earrings, brooches, and necklaces, her long nails painted with a ruby-colored nail polish. I was expecting someone with fingers adorned with gaudy sapphires or emeralds, or even a lady dressed in a blouse with an audaciously low neckline and an alligator-skin handbag. On the other hand, I admit that I wasn't disappointed. On the contrary, for my purposes, the contrast between the expected and the real was even gratifying, one less problem, since it would be much easier, that is, there would be less interference in getting down to a real conversation, which, after all, had a specific goal, far from any emotional involvement.

One detail attracted me right away to that real Rebecca, almost a pixie having difficulty in adjusting to the leather easy chair in my room: in the absence of any makeup, dominating over dozens of miniscule freckles that gave perfect symmetry to her apple-shaped face, her light-brown eyes, being so sad, loomed saliently, enormously, destructively. I offered her water, and she accepted, timidly.

A short time into the conversation, during which she kept her mouth always open, in the form of an egg, resting horizontally even when she wasn't speaking—an involuntary expression of pain and despair, I figured, an embodied fear, almost the photographic picture of a nervous tick—Rebecca manifested complete ignorance about her husband's life. In the last few years, she had worried not so much about Goldstein's professional activities but rather about some of his strange moods, the frequent hours of total introspection, the absence from the house at unexpected moments, and even his coldness in dealing with his two daughters—which didn't happen at the beginning of their marriage. The constant and rapid alternating state of mind she never managed to understand: one Sunday, for example, Goldstein had awakened in a good mood, and after half an hour, as if some poison had been slipped into his coffee, he already had another face, and then became happy again at lunchtime and then gruff—this is how she described him, using the word 'gruff,' an ingenuous word—a little later, when they decided to go for a walk in Ibirapuera Park. And the most incomprehensible thing is that he liked Ibirapuera Park, she insisted rather superfluously and without surprising me, because many times even I was forced by Márcio to change into my jogging outfit at lunchtime and to go out running through the park like an idiot, without knowing why. 'Professional obligation,' he used to say, and he convinced me.

They had been married for seven years and had known each other for a total of eight. Therefore, only one year of courtship and straightaway to marriage. And soon after, two daughters—Goldstein didn't allow contraceptives, Rebecca explained to me, and she, despite thinking differently and having other plans (she quit studying halfway through medical school), she didn't have the strength to prevail, or she didn't want to prevail; she herself wasn't sure about that. Two daughters and a house to manage without many resources (soon after his marriage Goldstein and I decided to establish our law practice). Seated in the easy chair, Rebecca did not stop talking about her disappointments, and that's how, contrary to my expectations, I was sitting before a fragile woman who evidently loved my partner but didn't exactly know who he was.

Rebecca said, offering yet another example, that Goldstein used to take his daughters horseback riding on weekends. The last two times, however, when they spent a few days in Campos do Jordão, he had asked to go riding alone after leaving the children in the rented chalet. The first time around, Rebecca found this strange—he had never done that—but she wasn't curious about knowing what her husband intended by that behavior. The second time, more intrigued, she arranged a way to follow Goldstein's path from a distance and, astonished, observed him standing still in a shaded spot, caressing the nag, and she made the point of stressing that it wasn't a thorough-bred Arabian or a Mangalarga. So there was Goldstein caressing the horse, incessantly, for more than fifteen minutes, his chest against the animal's neck. Posing like a martyr, Rebecca said, referring to Goldstein caressing the sweaty nag like a beloved friend, as if asking the animal to caress him as well; and soon after he was crying, crying a lot over the horse, it seemed like a convulsion. She thought about going to her husband, to offer him some solace, in short, to play her role as the wife; that's what she said. But she restrained herself. Little by little Márcio recovered himself, dried his eyes on the sleeve of his T-shirt, and returned to the stable, in slow motion. There hadn't been any outing or diversion.

In light of this meeting it was clear to me: I was not going to obtain from Rebecca many explanations about Goldstein's behavior. She was almost like a child consciously experiencing her first big shock; that's how I rationalized the situation as I got up to let her know we should bring the conversation to an end. I sympathized with her bewilderment—I couldn't do much more up to that point. We became friends, it seemed to me, leaving up in the air of the building's corridor the promise—actually, a kind of commitment of intentions—to clear up jointly the teeming number of uncertainties that had surfaced during the last few weeks. As if saving the best strategy for the end, her sad and large eyes, gaining with effort a bit of their luster, Rebecca suggested I seek out Márcio's sister, Miriam Goldstein. They had not kept in touch; the only thing Rebecca knew about Miriam was her address, but she, Miriam, would certainly have much more to tell about the 'missing' partner and husband.

Men and women spend years, even decades, imagining who would be the ideal partner to start a life, perhaps to raise a family. They do everything: go to parties and bars, play games, look into other lifestyles, take mutual risks. When they finally take notice, just like it happens with professions, their ideal partner has been right there, by their side, for some time, and is discovered by accident—in a neighbor, a colleague, or, despite the opposing social codes, in a more or less close relative. All this is foreseeable, customary, and universal. And in this way, actually putting it quite stupidly, men proliferate, isn't that so? From my point of view, however, I find it more stimulating not only to detect this partner in someone whom I already know but also that this decisive encounter occur in different circumstances, even quite opposite to those that propitiated the initial revelation. In that case it's not a matter of neighbors, thus, not just anybody with whom one shares the same environment, but rather via some unimaginable chance encounter, an almost impossible coincidence one could not count upon—these are the most striking factors for reinforcing this, at least that's what I learned for any relationship.

Two days after my meeting with Rebecca, I arrived at a building with only three stories, without an elevator. Miriam's apartment was on the top floor. I had the luck of getting there just at that afternoon hour when a janitor was at work cleaning the hallway; so busy he didn't even bother himself with my entrance—and in cases like the one I was dealing with, it is actually better to arrive unannounced. I reached the third floor panting, regretting once again not getting any pleasure from practicing sports or doing any exercise. Since there was a peephole in the door, I passed a hard comb through my hair—my hair is short and prematurely gray, easy to keep—and I straightened my tie into the Italian-style collar, all this to avoid a possible rejection on account of my appearance. From inside there came a crystalline sound, soothing, a strange music, a melody like a Gregorian chant; it seemed like a church organ. I rang the bell, and the music soon stopped, followed by the darkening of the peephole.

There are those who say that fear makes a pig thinner. I don't know if this is true, but the sensation of losing a few pounds hit me right in the stomach when the door of the apartment opened, despite my not being (I presume!!) a swine. Because who appeared before me was no one more and no one less than Maura Gonçalves, my splendiferous masseuse, my own masseuse, the woman responsible for the few and only hours of relaxation I have managed to spend in many years. I don't know which of us was more astonished.

'Isn't this Miriam Goldstein's home?' I stuttered, as she invited me to enter, excessively polite, just like she would welcome a federal income tax inspector or a TV technician making an estimate. 'It is,' that's just how she answered, without saying anything else, only a smile, which I found to be ironic; the door had already closed. And right away, acting as if she were the owner of the apartment, more relaxed, she offered me a glass of water, which I accepted just as timidly as Rebecca had accepted the glass of water I offered her two days earlier in my office. Inside that apartment I became the awkward pixie Rebecca had been.

My first rationalization was to think that Maura and Miriam were living together; maybe they were even married. I had never imagined that my masseuse might be a lesbian, much less my partner's sister, and even more so the two of them in an exemplary coincidence of being a couple. This made me uneasy as I waited for the glass of water, a feeling certainly based on my prejudices but not only these, because what also came into play was the fact that, to my delight, not inconsiderable were the savored fantasies in my mind about Maura and her hands, the magical hands of a masseuse.

Perhaps it may be important to state here and now, as a kind of clarifying parenthesis: Maura was not a fake masseuse, those that publish ads in the newspapers using the massage only as a pretext for prostitution. She had diplomas from courses taken abroad, especially in the United States and one even in Japan. Her massage technique was extraordinary, really above average. She knew how to rapidly eliminate the stiffness in my muscles, and in such a professional manner that she would decompose, via the actual massage, the small hallucinations, somewhat depraved and not confessable, that I viciously nurtured at the beginning of each session. In this way her skill imposed an absolute respect for her character and profession, in truth always leaving me ashamed for not yet being able to control my own illusions, the residual sparks of an adolescence, I am speculating, for certain, poorly utilized. Still continuing with the open parenthesis, I take the opportunity to clarify that the fact I resort to a masseuse had nothing to do with a search for supposed extraterrestrial solutions; I believe neither in pixies (despite having compared Rebecca and even myself to them out of, let's say, narrative convenience) nor in astrology; I don't want an Indian guru to make me levitate in meditation over the problems of the idiotic life I have been living for years, nor do I look for formulas or herbs to purify my body. In my view massage is a purely physical force, concrete and scientific, a merely compensatory intervention. And that's how it has always been.

There, waiting in the living room of the apartment, probably carried away by some agile defense mechanism, I soon began to think that Maura and Miriam must be two friends, young women full of exuberance sharing an apartment, and not a lesbian couple; it may be more realistic to think this way. At the same time, tired of seeing myself as naive, I reflected that it wasn't wise of me to discard any hypothesis; that's why I attempted to read some titles of the few books sitting in a small bookcase to see if they would give me some indication. However, nothing special: they were all about massages. That's what I was doing, absorbed in these embarrassing speculations, until, having come back into the room, bringing from the kitchen a glass of water, Maura faced me and said smiling—I confess, beautifully: 'I am Miriam Goldstein.'

If it weren't for the water, at that point a providential element, my sudden and stupid pallor would probably have given way to something like a collapse. Seated in a wicker easy chair in front of me—and only then, as incredible as it may seem, did I notice that she had her right foot in a cast—she explained to me that she had used the pseudonym Maura Gonçalves ever since the beginning of her career as a masseuse, six years ago, because she thought her Jewish name likely to jeopardize her getting clients. She was truly ashamed—in this case a feeling, I figure, unjustified, but anyway—of having a complicated name, and on the other hand, she feared discrimination fostered by competing colleagues. While I was listening to this explanation—I don't know why—I myself became ashamed as I suddenly realized that that woman knew my body as few others, the enormous defects of my posture and the imperfections of my skin, my disproportionately salient features.

I hesitated, attracted by a beauty now subject to appreciation—she was before me, close by, deliciously attainable, for the first time without the barrier of the professional relationship between our bodies—and fighting at the same time to placate my own shame, I hesitated to bring up the reason why I was there. I considered if it wouldn't be better to invent some other story and to avoid, in this way, the risk of spoiling, like a film in the cinema, what already seemed to me capable of becoming a beautiful love story, initiated by fate.

I asked her what had happened to her leg. 'Foolishness, nothing special, a slip on the stairs when I was coming home from shopping at the supermarket.' She said because of that she had even left a message for me in my office, canceling our massage sessions for two weeks.

Close by the window I noticed a table filled with glasses—some with more water, others with less, but not a single one empty. I asked Miriam (Maura) if she had given a party last night; it was a way of bringing up a topic, which provoked a maternal smile on her face. Calmly, raising above her elbows the long sleeves of her red T-shirt—there I could see a bandage on her right forearm—her long and straight dark hair, green eyes, huge and round, thick lips holding up two delicate cheeks, a model's body, vividly proportional, limping a little but charmingly, that slender and beautiful body wearing bell-bottom jeans walked up to the table and began to run the tips of her fingers on the rims of those glasses, delicately.

A glass harmonica, she said, was the instrument that was being played while I was standing in the corridor before ringing the doorbell. Now Maura (Miriam) showed it to me, and with it she made sweetly invasive music emerge, extracted semimagically from those glasses that I later learned were made of pure and expensive crystal. Just like her precision-applied massages, for several minutes her long fingers skillfully passed over the fragile pieces, resolute and intelligent fingers of paralyzing lightness—an additional therapy. There, contrary to what Rosangela, Luca Pasquali's sister, and Rebecca, Goldstein's wife, transmitted to me a few days ago, Miriam (Maura) refuted in practice the theories that every woman harbors a melancholy soul even in the full flower of her virtues. There she was sheer happiness, a being in ecstasy during that private concert.

Once the music was over, still unsettled, I timidly offered a silly and solitary applause, while my masseuse returned to the wicker easy chair saying, somewhat didactically, 'A glass harmonica, Paulo, this here is called a glass harmonica, a centuries-old instrument, very popular in Europe during the Middle Ages.' Next, from Maura (Miriam), already resettled in the easy chair, her legs elegantly crossed despite the cast, came the inevitable question, direct and more frightening: 'Well, what are you doing here?'

Then it was her turn to be fidgety, squirming nervously, from one moment to the next, when I said I was there to talk about Márcio Goldstein, who turned out to be not only her older brother but my law partner as well. From that moment on she was Miriam Goldstein and not Maura Gonçalves, which for me was already accepted and established; after all, I was, I explained with a certain irony, the 'Camargo' of the famous firm Goldstein & Camargo. Therefore, surprises for all tastes were evident, one after the other, on that late afternoon, inside the small apartment.

I told her what I knew about Goldstein's situation, his irregular behavior at home, his abandoning the office, adding that for me all this must have some very strong link with the Luca Pasquali case. Miriam didn't know anything about those events and didn't seem to be shocked about the story of the murder committed by Pasquali. On the contrary she forgot about it almost right away, preferring to linger on the problem about her brother, whom she called a 'porcupine,' with an almost malicious emphasis on the first syllable of this word. Then, while she was beginning to talk about Márcio, a strange metamorphosis began to take place in the woman: her dainty hands, her tranquil eyes, her free movements of a short time ago gave way to the gestures of an angry creature, biting her nails, squirming in the easy chair as if I were accusing her of some crime. Her eyes swelled a great deal.

For many years, ever since he was a kid, Miriam said with her hands intertwined, Márcio had succeeded in distancing himself from the family in a deliberate way. 'He bites the hands that feed him,' she said; in fact she ranted, railed at her brother with these words. Goldstein's life had always been a permanent quarrel between him and everybody else. Tranquility had always been limited, whatever the circumstances. Parasite, immature, that's how she classified Márcio right from the start. On the day of his bar mitzvah, for example, therefore at thirteen years old, right after the grand and long-awaited party, paid with the thousands of dollars saved by his parents for many years, Goldstein locked himself in his room and threw out the window, without explanations, several of the presents received throughout the day. That day, however, was a very special day for their parents, Miriam told me, certainly for the whole family, and yet Márcio behaved like an ungrateful brat, in short, reacting in an unwholesome manner. In her

opinion it was therefore right for her father to open the door to his
room with the spare key, after waiting in vain for hours for Márcio to
spontaneously do the same, and to give his son a beating, using as a
weapon the belt he wore for the big party, a biblical thrashing, on the
very day that he reached, at least theoretically, his religious manhood;
an unforgettable day for her, a cursed day, starting in a festive manner
and ending in real disaster.

Goldstein didn't like his own family; he detested his own family;
that was the reality; he only liked his street friends and his schoolmates.
Miriam said this swiftly, her words running over one another. The times
she broke her leg, and coincidentally for a total of five times, always
the same leg, Márcio never went to visit her, except for this last time,
for reasons she couldn't quite understand and which perhaps involved
the Pasquali case. When they had plans together, with diverse groups
of girls and boys at the PIC (the Paulista Israeli Congregation, where
their parents sent their children to obtain, in theory, she explained to
me, some Jewish social companionship), Goldstein was the first to
adopt attitudes that marginalized her, the skunk; for her that's what
he was; he almost ridiculed his sister in front of everybody—that's
what Miriam told me—treating her like an enemy, trying his best to
isolate her from the rest of the children. And yet she, Miriam, had stood
up for him on many embarrassing occasions, inside or outside the
house. She had stood up for him when their parents caught him one
Saturday evening lying on the leather couch in the TV room with the
maid. And that had happened so many other times . . . Yes, they would
watch TV every Saturday night, when their parents went out, and they
were always the same programs, first the *Raggedy Family*, then *Tubby's
Hour*, with that music, which she was now singing sadly to me to the
beat of a military march: 'Tubby, Tubby, now it's time for you to get
in line . . . singing well, you'll be cheered, singing badly, go sing in
your backyard . . . tub, tub tub, Tubby, it's time for you to get in line,'
and her brother rubbing himself on top of the maid to the rhythm of
that stupid music, the shameful bastard, on top of the poor great-
granddaughter of slaves, Miriam was telling me. She had stood up for
him when, at the headquarters of that same PIC, a group of older boys
tried to pull down his pants under the pretext of finding out what he
was carrying inside them, hidden, some pornographic magazines—
which she didn't know, never knew if it was true or not.

But that was the true Márcio, the hypocrite. I know, she said, because his girlfriend at the time told me another story, that he himself
had told her as if it were some great achievement, Miriam said. He
was fifteen years old, the idiot, that's what she used to call him, when
inside a bus an older guy wearing glasses sat next to him, and he
started up a conversation; he said he liked art, theater, those things,
and that he took photographs. Márcio said that he also liked all that,
and the guy then invited him to go to his house, which was at the next
bus stop; all they had to do was to get off at the Ninth of July Avenue,
near 14 Bis Square. So they got off the bus, and the guy took Márcio
to an apartment in one of those crummy buildings, right away showing him above his bed a number of cardboard boxes from which he
took photos, dozens of photos of nude boys, some excited with their
members in full erection, others not so, more docile, some photos
with close-ups of even more intimate parts. The imbecile didn't catch
on, and the guy later asked if he didn't also want to be photographed
like those boys; the photos should come out beautiful; after all he
was a well-endowed boy with nice features. Right after that the guy
invites Márcio to follow him; they go into the bathroom, and seated
on the edge of a tub, the guy asks him to take off his clothes to see
what he was like, just to see if he was photogenic, he said, and, still,
with good humor, being very experienced, he comments, 'Oh, you
are Jewish,' and asks the idiot to come close to him. The guy gently
pulls Márcio by the waist, takes off his glasses, and says: 'Let's see
what you're like with a hard-on (excuse the expression, Miriam said
to me), to see if we'll get some neat photos,' and he begins to suck
my brother, and it's only then that Márcio, your smart partner, only
then, do you believe it? it's only then that he realizes what is happening
. . . 'A minor victimized by sexual abuse,' I said interrupting Miriam
in my judicial lingo. Victim, my foot, no way, she blabbered out; to
be a true victim you have to feel that you're suffering something; but
not him, the wretched little Jew, born in between abortions, because
Goldstein is nothing more than that, she said. It's certain that he then
pushed the guy's head away and apologized for pushing the guy's
head away, for spoiling the guy's pleasure, and said that he didn't
want to continue with that business, that he didn't enjoy that stuff,
that wasn't his thing; even the guy was polite; he didn't push it; he
only begged him to come back another time. But he didn't have to

apologize at all; well, it was the guy who should have done that! But all that shows just what your partner is like: he doesn't know what he wants; he doesn't understand anything that's happening around him, except for what may be of immediate interest to him and to nobody else, the dim-witted egotist that he is.

Getting up from the wicker chair, going around the table where her harmonica of glasses stayed, Miriam also told me what she categorized as her brother's lowdown opportunism when, at eighteen, he took advantage of a trip to Israel, where he would spend one month with a group of volunteers working on a kibbutz, actually in order to accentuate the family's grief, that's how she expressed herself. Do you think that he, the always and complete Narcissus Márcio Goldstein, do you think that he agreed to go over there with the group to proudly help out in the orange harvest, like all the others did? Miriam questioned me with eyes growing bigger, already answering 'no, none of that'; he really went to fuck all the other female volunteers, including those of other countries and even gentiles, that's the truth; he didn't go there to carry irrigation pipes or to gather coconuts up in trees every day, learning a little about farm life, assuming responsibilities, none of that; he actually went there to get to know other idiots, Frenchmen or Italians, who spoke about terrorism, preached communism, had books and manuals, those kinds of things; that's what he went for; not to help Israel out of its difficulties, as the other members of the group did, but rather to try hashish in some campsite, to listen to Bob Dylan and other depraved souls; not to insert some hopeful scrap of paper into the Wailing Wall in Jerusalem, nothing like that. He went there to get to know the Jewish prostitutes of Tel Aviv, that's for sure: he wanted to know what a Jewish prostitute or a prostituted Jewess is like, yes, that's it!

That's why he, Márcio Goldstein, the rusty tin of a cheap ring, she said, didn't return to Brazil on the expected date, preferring to flee on a boat bound for Greece and I don't know where else, six months wandering through Europe without knowing where to go, without a telephone call of more than a minute, without letters, one postcard or other filled hurriedly with the usual formulaic greetings, and after Greece to Yugoslavia (during that time there still existed a Yugoslavia, isn't that right?), Italy, France, Spain, Portugal, I don't know where else; he had played a really great joke on all of us who were waiting

for him in the airport on the day when all the members of the group
arrived with their colorful duffel bags and knapsacks, embracing their
parents, brothers and sisters, bringing small presents, relieved to be
back home, filled with stories to tell about Israel and the difficulties
of the kibbutzim, happy faces, their hands still with calluses from the
agricultural labor, satisfied, matured; but not him, the stupid one,
nothing more than a duffel bag filled with dirty clothes and a note
of two lines announcing, the uppity rascal, that he had decided to
stay around there, the perfect imbecile, crossing strange seas. Israel, nothing of the sort! The scoundrel, better to see other countries,
while his parents spilled their tears over here, without knowing that
he was resting tranquilly inside a sleeping bag, in the bowels of a
church in Venice, that he would be stoned for admiring a strange
statue in Sarajevo, an irresponsible bastard, in short, an ingrate, a
pathological egotist, that's Márcio; Miriam condemned him (yes, it
was a verdict, that torrential rain of words), squirming more and
more in her wicker chair.

And nevertheless, behind that bravado, those daring and distant
glances, for Miriam, Goldstein's biggest problem was always the fact
that he allowed the important steps, the true steps of his destiny, to
be defined by others, not by himself. Those aggressive transgressions
ended up becoming a facade, painful indeed for the family, but nothing more than a facade. In the end a chronic self-indulgence always
prevailed, permanent, the cowardliness of one who degrades himself
for any kind of recognition, according to her, a cowardliness for not
taking on true challenges face-to-face, where they really take place,
thus, close to the people and the places near us; and Goldstein's greatest defense in order to cover up this structural weakness was the most
obvious: not to allow, at any cost, that it become apparent. That way,
on the surface, in his manner of dressing or presenting himself in
public places, or as he had done during that escape through Europe,
he would seem the opposite: full of determination, a style of his own;
in truth, a pretense, according to how Miriam related it with the high
volume of her voice, to cover up the wait for the next mandate coming
from the outside, from the group, from his father (Márcio studied
law because his father ordered him to do so, she said) and, primarily
during his first years, from his neighbor Luca Pasquali.

Goldstein's parents, Miriam said, never had the slightest notion of what was going on, about what passed through their son's head all the time, or even about the personal and professional activities of that son. To her they are not to blame for any of this, not only because Márcio, the human beast, was deliberately distancing himself from them, by his own will, but also due to the fact that they belonged to a sacrificial generation, of a very special type of sacrifice, she said with didactic intonation.

I then learned that their father and their mother are children of immigrants who came to Brazil from Poland at a very young age at the beginning of the century, fleeing from destitution and from the persecutions or the threats of persecutions against the Jews of Eastern Europe at that time. Goldstein's paternal grandfather, Miriam told me, was the son of a chicken merchant who arrived here with the clothes on his back and became a street peddler, selling ties, stockings, and whatever he could, traveling without rest through various cities with a suitcase full of odds and ends. Despite being the son of a merchant with better means than the other grandfather in Poland, his maternal grandfather had to confront the same problems over here—where, by the way, he accidentally arrived, since he intended from the beginning of his voyage to go to Buenos Aires. But he disembarked in the port city of Santos, thinking he was in Argentina—seeing that until his death in the Second World War, his father never accepted his son's decision to leave his native land. He didn't sell the same things as a peddler, but he certainly crossed paths with Márcio's paternal grandfather on many corners of the Bom Retiro Jewish neighborhood.

Goldstein's paternal grandfather managed to establish himself, along with his brother who came to Brazil a few years after him, as one of the most important manufacturers of clothing in that neighborhood. By then his maternal grandfather had become known by selling and repairing large and small clocks and watches. The drama—that's the word she chose—the drama of the generation of her parents, called Milton and Sarah, therefore Márcio's parents as well, was always that of feeling the obligation to match the monstrous effort exerted by their parents (Miriam's, Laura's, and Márcio's grandparents) to recover all that they had lost as exiles. And that effort could only result, even more in Milton's case, in a corresponding social ascendancy, a visible, sensitive ascendancy, gratifying perhaps not as much for them as for their immigrant parents. Ascendancy, in this case, meant, she said, to become at all costs a doctor (whether it be an engineer, a medical doctor, a dentist, or a lawyer) and to do with one's own hands, but to a superior degree, what their parents had done, those pioneer parents who traveled miles and miles alongside dozens of refugees, confronting the high seas in terrible conditions, without the slightest idea about the land they would find at the end of their long journey—as a way of paying them back. It was the dream of the immigrants and the obsession, involuntary or not, of Sarah as much as of Milton.

For this reason Milton became an anesthetist—I don't know if it's what he actually loves to do, but that matters little, Miriam stated. And the guilt would be so great in the event he didn't adhere to the expectations of his parents that his own children—the grandchildren of the immigrants, I can only understand it in this way—would end up becoming, even if this weren't their intention, secondary considerations for their parents; they would in practice be mere subsections listed within a paragraph—to employ a legal analogy unambiguously. In that way Miriam felt the full weight her parents carried on their shoulders, besides the remorse of not being able—that's what she was explaining to me as she walked about the room with difficulty—of not being able to reverse the situation, not being able to give love, to give love to their children, she insisted, as they wanted.

Except for that the Goldsteins' adaptation here, the growth of their children and grandchildren naturally followed a process of assimilation to 'national' life—she was explaining to me already seated in the wicker chair—of integration with non-Jews and of the decalcification of their Jewish identity, which was waning, lamentably, especially in hers and Márcio's generation, an identity more and more difficult to maintain, more and more transformed into a psychological and not a social category; Miriam expressed herself in this essayist tone, as if she had already studied the topic many times, searching soberly for words. Miriam believed that the distance, the lack of real dialogue between Goldstein and his parents, could only be explained in this way.

'To be a Jew, for example. What does this mean to Goldstein? Probably little more than to carry on his back, unconsciously, a melancholia, as heavy and as present as a shell for a turtle. Do you think he is capable of feeling the enormity of the continuing pain behind the numbers tattooed, and today still not extinguished, on the arms of thousands of survivors of the great calamity, right here? Imagine, as if here, instead of this bandage, there only existed a number of various digits. Can you imagine this?' Goldstein was incapable of understanding all the nuances inherited from a millennial history; for that reason he was disturbed, Miriam declared.

Besides all this, Goldstein was also a racist, and she insisted in stating his disparaging classifications in this manner, citing as an example the fact that he hated an ice-cream peddler who worked on the island of Guarujá when they were kids only because the man was black. Miriam said that neither did the death of Laura occur nor was there any sticky mess on her body from some ice-cream peddler on the beach at Guarujá. Her aunt Ilza, whom Márcio also hated—he hated many people, Miriam said—Aunt Ilza was a kind person, in spite of being nervous and quick-tempered, Miriam said. Goldstein invented all that—just like Freud's hysterical women, she said again—in an imbecilic delirium, always repeated, according to her, in order to ac-count for his own anxieties, because he wanted, had always wanted, to have an interesting life, spicier than the tasteless and straight life he had always had. Because, she said, Goldstein never knew how to see or feel any beauty, perhaps a small pleasure, in trivial things. For him, as for many other people, Miriam said, by now recovering a bit of control over her own nervousness, for him there exists no pleasure without pain—that was his biggest problem.

For her, then, Márcio never knew how to see in people what they really were; he always sees in the person the father of this same person, who thus ceases to exist with his own, autonomous will, in short, as a person. Only the fathers of people exist; that's what she said was Márcio's opinion; every person is his own father until the latter dies, Goldstein thought, according to his sister, because, in truth, even he, Márcio himself, always saw himself only like this in the mirror, his father's own face, the same faults, the same lamentably sad and melancholy gaze—and down deep he dreaded seeing himself like this in the mirror, without a future, Miriam said, because that meant, of course, his own annihilation.

The clarity and intensity of my masseuse's discourse were so great that, for some moments, I reasoned that I was in the company of a sick person—beautiful, it's true, but above all sick. Her words came out of her without intermissions, machine-gun bullets stored for years, that's for sure; in fact, I thought, for many years she must have had the desire to tell these things to somebody but never found the right audience. And, suddenly, here was a candidate, dropped by chance into her living room, ready for the sacrifice of being her target. And I explain why 'target': it's that Miriam addressed me as if I were Márcio Goldstein himself, perhaps making me responsible for being his partner, perhaps because in this way she could manage to speak more openly, in the aggressive manner she adopted, having buried the gentleness that had captivated me a few moments ago, when she was playing her glass harmonica with a sanctified expression—I came to see her eyes explode.

In fact, Goldstein always hated his sisters, Miriam continued in her interminable recital of accusations, and particularly he always wanted to see his oldest sister, Laura, imprisoned, as unhappy as possible, even dead. Márcio in fact was jealous of Luca Pasquali, she thought, because he had never had the courage to do to somebody, precisely Laura, for example, the same that his childhood friend had done to his wife. According to her, it was actually due to that hostility that Laura had decided to change countries a few years ago, to live in Warsaw, in Poland, as a professional photographer, in her grandparents' native land, near the tombs of her ancestors but far away from Márcio, that prototype of a beast.

Miriam saw—and her hands were moving around as she spoke to me—on a certain afternoon when she returned home from school, Laura surprised by Márcio at the gate of the house, her brother telling her that the family dog was dead, dead in the dining room with its eyes open. And Laura, the closest to the dog, then went into the house shaking, in tears, to find out right away that in fact the dog was merely sleeping with its eyes open, which often happens with dogs, just that, and the movement of its respiration was so vigorous that not even a crazy person would think it was dead. Or then, the times when her brother, that deceitful bastard, as she called him, played tricks even on her, Miriam, when they were running up the stairs to get into the house to see who would be the one to first reach the television set, since—that was the family rule—whoever turned on the television would be the one to command the change of channels. Small things, said my masseuse, but many, and accumulated and repeated end-lessly, maliciously, in all sorts of ways and variations, in childhood, adolescence, and even after, therefore uninterruptedly, composing a history of terrorism, true family terrorism practiced by Márcio against his two sisters, against his whole family, to tell the truth.

Do you know what Goldstein's greatest pleasure was? Miriam asked, continuing on (I was beginning to feel sick, sweaty, not knowing how far those indefatigable attacks would continue): to afflict others with the sufferings and pains that he bears and cannot forget, a kind of macabre sport common to so many maladjusted people, Miriam commented. 'Go look for him and ask him to repeat all that about the ice-cream peddler's sticky mess on my body at the beach on Guarujá, about Laura's death, toppling from the veranda; look here at a recent photo of her in Warsaw (she was pointing to a picture frame in the bookcase and I in fact saw a young woman smiling with a camera hanging from her neck). Is that a dead person? Go look for him again and ask him to repeat, looking straight into your eyes, to see if he has the courage, to see if something comes out of him. Nothing comes out of that dirty mouth; he crumbles, because it's sheer madness.'

Huddled on the sofa, my glass of water empty, squeezed between my hands, there I was a humbled person facing a monster. And even worse: she was a captivating monster, a kind of reverse Don Juan, moving me with each word. Looking into my eyes as one who emits a historic maxim at the end of a long discourse, Miriam said with dramatic intonation, in a synthetic and threatening way: 'Paulo, I am going to put an end to Márcio, know this, and now I already know how, because before I didn't know. And the stage is going to be set by Márcio himself, via Luca Pasquali's trial.'

Miriam got up, took from me the glass I was squeezing between my hands, and went into the kitchen. Upon returning, more calmly, she already seemed at this point, again, the woman of the glass harmonica, managing even to smile. She told me that she could no longer do massages for me; from now on she wouldn't feel right after having said all that about her brother, my partner after all. I couldn't do anything beyond acquiescing and thanking her for her stories; they would be very useful, I added, for Luca Pasquali's trial. I didn't pay attention to the threat she had made about Luca Pasquali's trial, interpreting it as more bravado than a real objective—at least it was more comforting to think like that. We said good-bye in the hallway. Shaking hands, I couldn't hold on: I gave her my business card with my address and telephone; I wished her a speedy recovery with her leg and her arm and said that I would like to see her again, not as a masseuse but as Miriam Goldstein, a wonderful, I dared to say, woman. She merely smiled; she didn't answer yes or no. Her eyes no longer swollen, she turned around and closed the door.

I slowly descended the stairs in the direction of the sidewalk, remembering a passage from a book I had read, a sad book, which said that the exact moment we stop loving our parents and our brothers and sisters and begin to hate them, that moment, we cannot define precisely and, as a matter of fact, we do not force ourselves to recapture that exact moment because down deep we are afraid to do so. It's terrible, but I don't believe that those words are very far from the truth.

In spite of that, already in the car, on the way back to the office, I began to think that maybe all that hatred of Miriam for her brother could also have another explanation. Maybe there wasn't any truth to her stories; after all, maybe she herself was trying to erase from her memory her own conflicts, traumas, whatever, and in reality was a woman in love with her own brother—that's what I was thinking— therefore being jealous for years, almost insane, due to this clearly taboo passion. A reasoning that led me next to think, having stopped at a red light, of that business about the impossibility of platonic love. And still more, ideas and stories being linked together, I began to think about another possibility, already the green light, who knows more complicated: the platonic love for her brother, in which she was submerged, trying to deny it every minute to the point of even calling Márcio a 'porcupine,' why couldn't she at that point exchange that love for another love, but this time a real love, or rather, love for me, I dreamed, a love for me, an available man, literally ensnared in that space by his ex-masseuse, after a little more than one hour of conversation?

# Roney Cytrynowicz

Roney Cytrynowicz was born in São Paulo in 1964. He studied economics and received his doctorate in history from the University of São Paulo.
He has worked as copyeditor for the daily *Folha de São Paulo* and also
editor for the Jewish magazine *Shalom*. In 1990 he published *Memória
da barbárie* (Memory of Barbarism), a journalistic and memorialist account of the genocide of the Jews during World War II. As a historian,
Cytrynowicz has published several studies, including *Guerra sem guerra:
A mobilização e o cotidiano em São Paulo durante a Segunda Guerra Mundial*
(2000) (War without War: Mobilization and Daily Life in São Paulo
during World War II). *A vida secreta dos relógios e outras histórias* (1994)
(The Secret Life of the Clocks and Other Stories) is his first work of
fiction. This collection of stories received the Nascente Prize from Abril
Publishing House and a prize from the National Competition on the
Short Story organized by the Paraná State Secretariat of Culture. This
volume is the first in a series organized by the publishing house Scritta
and dedicated to new Brazilian novelists. Cytrynowicz's stories serve
as a fine example of the new generation of Brazilian Jewish writers.
While these stories bring the reader to a universe of pain, memory, and
humor, they also evoke the memory of the Holocaust, a trauma not
lived by the author but engrained in his Jewish sense of self. Cytrynowicz's work illustrates the long-range impact of the Holocaust on the
Jews of Brazil. The collection pivots upon the tonality of memory, and
these two stories reveal how the pain of memory does not disappear
with the distance of time and space. The title story's focus on clocks
underscores the indissoluble link between time and Judaism. 'Shed
II' catapults the reader into the past terror of the Holocaust and into
its present horror in Brazil.

Roney Cytrynowicz

# The Secret Life of the Clocks

It has been many years since I last slept at my grandfather's house. I haven't seen him for many years. When I enter his home, everything seems familiar to me, as if I had lived there the same amount of time as he did. I am overcome by a feeling of tranquility, by the security of an affection more ancient than remembrance. Each piece of furniture in the house has a story that my grandfather narrates as a family story. It is different with the clocks. It took years to choose the best ones, to clean the mechanisms, to set the time, to orchestrate the concert. I see my grandfather winding a grandfather clock; he does so with dedication and patience, as if he were investing in a long experiment, as if this ritual demanded all his wisdom. My grandfather and the clocks. It is necessary to become familiar with their mechanisms in order to understand the intimacy of this relationship.

In the bedroom made up for me, as in the rest of the house, there are dozens of clocks; I never managed to count them all. In the passing of one night, clocks appear and disappear. Or they change places (I believe that my grandfather does not entirely control them). In the kitchen, a cuckoo. The little door is open, the cuckoo has stopped, and its gaze descends obliquely in the direction of whoever enters. It may be watching out for my grandfather. Or it may be that my grandfather is the one who is suspicious and left it quarantined. A half hour is a long interval to leave it alone, locked up in its house. The secret life of the clocks. I think this could be the title of the great novel about my grandfather's life.

His home seems like a room of machinery. The room of the machinery of the universe. My grandfather says that if one single tic sounds different, even during his sleep, he wakes up and goes to see what is wrong. But what can be wrong if each clock tells a different time, if they're not there to tell the right time? My grandfather fixes them.

What, exactly? Repair. Remedy. In Hebrew *tikkun olam*, reparation of the world, cosmic redemption, messianic times. Each erroneous *tic* may be a defect in the room of machinery of the universe. Jewish tradition says that a single erroneous letter can compromise the world's existence. My grandfather knows. He looks after four letters combined within two words: *tic-toc*. This is his mission in life. Four letters that need to be repeated in a symphony, in which each fraction of a second is vital. Because the seconds of the clocks are not synchronized. That's the way the days differentiate themselves. The delay of a thousandth of a second in a clock changes the symphony, the order of the universe. The delays of seconds unleash revolutions. My grandfather watches over them so that the balance is not broken. It's like when I see him running through the house, ignoring the docile step of his slipper, which never disturbs the life of the clocks.

It's nighttime in my grandfather's house, it's hot, and I'm sleepy. But it's impossible to sleep. At each instant the passage of time breaks the silence. I have come for a short stay. Soon I will no longer be there; soon he will no longer be. The heat disfigures the fractions of time, dulls the sharpness of the *tic* and prolongs them as warm and sticky. The seconds become heavy. My grandfather likes the heat. The clocks work better; it is a time of happiness.

For many years he has been offering clocks as gifts to his children and grandchildren. To share in the administration of the house of machinery is useless. Nobody will know how to listen to the *tics* as he does; nobody will go about the house during the night finding the remedy that will guarantee the infinite fractionation of time. Four letters combined in two words will be lost in the universe awaiting a new repair. My grandfather had a pacemaker installed, which also has a *tic-toc*. He asks me to place my ear to his heart. I claim I hear nothing. Only the clocks can listen, he says.

Before saying good-bye, for the last time, I'm given another time-piece, a stopwatch. For the passage of short periods of time that do not lose themselves, they merely flee a little in order to go back to the beginning. The stopwatch always goes back to zero, the zero degree of time. I receive the stopwatch with an emotion that no other timepiece had aroused. I test it, perfect. The meaning now is clear: between us time will go on for only a few seconds, small, necessary runs. In order to always return to zero. The hour of departure is our zero time. Our timepiece will always be a stopwatch. The tic-toc will be stored for small explosions of time, small explosions of nostalgic memory.

I descend from the building; I'm going away. I wait for the car; I start the stopwatch. I look up to my grandfather's window. There he is; it's the first time I see him like this, as if he were finally surrendering to the emotion of departure. Condensed in that image. I stop the watch; I interrupt the passage of time. It is necessary to return to the beginning. Zero time. The image in the window. We will always be together.

Roney Cytrynowicz

# Shed II

Stefan made Mlotek's acquaintance five days before the surgery. 'I want a new face,' he said. 'You will have one,' he heard, during the longest dialogue of the consultation. Stefan did not notice a tiny movement on Mlotek's face, his eyes opening in order to augment his angle of perception, his eyebrow raised by his forehead. One of his lovers, right after the war, had confidentially revealed to Mlotek that when his lips began the movement of separating one from the other to articulate some sentence, his eyes had already disclosed a 'briefing' of what he essentially wanted to say. On Mlotek's face that movement was something like a supplementary network of nerves that linked brain, eyes, and mouth, articulating thought and speech in an entirely personal manner. When his eyebrow reached the maximum height on his face, the slow movement that transformed his antiseptic indifference into suspicion ended. It was Stefan's '*sehr gut*,' practically inaudible, between hiding any trace that might reveal his identity and his cry of salvation expressed in the only language he felt comfortable speaking. Stefan did not explore Mlotek's countenance. The transitory aspect of his own face made the impulse to register his interlocutor's facial features unimportant, and so Stefan backed away, confident of the meticulous gaze Mlotek was casting upon him. For one moment he looked at the palms of his hands and thought about changing his fingerprints. Stefan did not think this would constitute a relearning of the world, his hands having to touch and recognize objects all over again; for him his hands were merely mechanical arms of his brain, the world made up of objects and realities, not textures and cloth. 'It's going to be good,' he repeated to himself, '*sehr gut*.'

The sudden pain in Mlotek's tooth was the first sign. Next the terror he felt after each surgery, making his body a mere collage of tissues suspended by the bloody stream. This was the camp's code; that tooth was the key of memory. Every time it was pressed, a long battle began: pain versus memory. War of nerves. Chemical war. The shards in his head now seemed to compress themselves and crush his brain. Mlotek understood it was necessary to identify the man before the surgery, before he himself crossed out the marks of that face and destroyed forever the possibility of stopping the pain.

The tooth twinged a second time. A pang of memory banned forty-five years ago had been reset in motion. The pain demanded the settlement of memory's debt. Pain and memory equipped their armies, cellular microbattles being resolved within a few seconds. Forty-five years of suffering irrupted, imploding a vast network of lines of resistance and phobias that protected the core of memory, a sealed capsule, shielded by nervous impulses that the most remote reminder would detonate.

Mlotek did not prepare himself for the reencounter; he grabbed the pistol and kept it in his coat pocket. It was the first time they would be facing each other as equals. The first battle had ended in a tie. The second one was now beginning.

Shed II of the camp, Mr. Stefan, does this name remind you of something?

What did you do to me?

Shed II of the camp, Mr. Stefan?

Who are you?

I was in Shed II, Mr. Stefan.

What do you want from me?

You were the doctor in Shed II, Mr. Stefan, weren't you?

That was almost fifty years ago.

I was a boy, five years old. At that age, one saves everything, memory stays in one's bones. Bones grow and so does the memory inside them. Even after death memory stays.

Tell me, what do you want?

I had a twin brother, Mr. Stefan. You preferred twins.

I don't remember anything.

You wanted to know why we were so alike, isn't that so, Mr. Stefan?

I did that for science.

Science!

Science! When he heard that word, Mlotek squeezed the pistol inside his pocket until he assured himself that he was grabbing it, the barrel pointing to his own body; not being sure whether the shot would go off in another direction. His forehead raised his eyebrow to the maximum height permitted by his muscles. Science! Forty-years after, the same arrogance, damned murderer! It would be easier to settle everything. Why prolong the conversation? Why give him the right to respond? Why ask questions?

After the camps, all his family dead, Mlotek studied medicine. He now was one of the most reputable specialists in his field, known within a small circle for operating on changes of identity: political refugees, fires, horrible accidents, birthmarks, scars, small defects, criminals. Mlotek never asked questions. Two or three times the police had made some inquiries, rummaging through his file cards; he'd merely change the subject. For Mlotek the body was a complete world, with its own fluxes, governing organs, policing cells, moral systems, and so forth. He believed each body had its own economy of matter and values; his job was to operate on periodic readjustments in order to restore tensions that could be disturbing the order of things, to take a little from here and place it there, small reallocations. Sometimes Mlotek felt a slightly terrifying emotion, and associated it with usurping bodily functions, as if he were at the point of changing the substance of lives; at those moments he would withdraw his scalpel and reset the matter in its original place. The body was his religion, with its taboos and sacred zones. While he was operating on Stefan, Mlotek felt he was touching on one of the universe's nervous systems, not mere adjustment but performing serious surgery on creation itself.

For Mlotek each operation was an attempt to bring his brother back from Shed II. When he began to unravel the gauze from the face of his patients, his fingers felt their way trying to recognize the texture of his brother's face. Mlotek imagined that the lines of his fingers and those of his brother's forehead would recognize themselves immediately, as if their identities had been merged within the textures of their skin. Mlotek was partly himself, partly his brother, a body with two lives; one already dead. Inside his body there were skin and bones of the other; part of Mlotek had died with his brother, skin and bones. Forty-five years later how to know which was one and which was the other? His body had absorbed his brother; it had killed the pieces that refused to accept the new body. Mlotek squeezed the gun in his pocket, but he seemed to insist on pointing the barrel at his own body.

When he discovered who Stefan was, Mlotek could not help himself. To mold that face into his brother's image was revenge for two lives. The army of memory released from the sealed capsule small impulses that permitted Mlotek to sculpt his brother's face. When the surgery was over, for the first time since he had gotten out of Shed II, Mlotek felt himself entirely whole.

Money, you want money?

Do you remember, Mr. Stefan, of having fused skin and bones between me and my brother?

How much, say it!

Taking a good look, Mr. Stefan, I see that you don't exactly look like my brother. Fortunately I did not succeed. It's not possible to take God's place, even when he's absent, Mr. Stefan. Medicine is imperfect, very imperfect.

One million, okay?

Your evilness is inside my bones, Mr. Stefan. I keep your mark, the mark of your murderous mind inside my body, Mr. Stefan.

Then, two million?

My brother died right away. He was more courageous than I was, but perhaps that may have caused him to experience a greater shock. Courage was of no use in helping one survive Shed II, isn't that so, Mr. Stefan? Many times I saw the strongest die first. They were not able to bear that absolute fall into hell. Only the weak could live in that world.

I was a doctor. It was my job. For the good of science!

Science! Mlotek began to sweat uncontrollably. The perspiration ran down into his eyes, and he realized he was beginning to lose his senses. His blurred eyes seemed to block the movement of his lips, and sentences came out like tiny bubbles of soap, disintegrating at the first contact with the air.

His ear began to ring. Mlotek believed he had heard an internal explosion, the memory capsule irrigating the body with the registered past of cosmic fear, as when he saw himself facing that man for the first time, a five-year-old boy, tied to the bed, and the executioner, a white apron manipulating surgical instruments in his direction. That terror had never been codified, the registered memories immediately sealed in the capsule. The irrigation of memory now searched the means for bringing the registered past up to date into a body forty-five years older. I have to be strong, thought Mlotek. But his voice came out like a five-year-old boy. Five years, Lublin, the teacher at the heder, used to say each match lit re-creates the original light of creation, as if, a little each day, God were dividing the responsibility of life with us. But the match's fire soon extinguishes itself, explained the teacher, like the light of the universe, each one in its own time; it's important to put out the match at the right time, without burning one's fingers, but without squandering those few seconds that can prolong our permanence in the universe. Mlotek also remembered those conversations about the fireflies, batteries of the universe recharged every second, the teacher used to say. Different from the light of matches, which represented a small chance for man to redeem himself, the fireflies replenished that original spark billions of times every day, without any effort. They are like the eyes of God, the teacher would say, the pronunciation of a magical formula, their lanterns roaming through the night of the universe, illuminating other susceptible worlds of creation.

What to do with the man in front of him? A five-year-old boy and a fifty-year-old man faced each other in a battle that seemed to decide the world's destiny. The five-year-old boy was asking for vengeance, a blind and annihilating vengeance, capable of destroying everything. The fifty-year-old man was trying to reason and to postpone that unrestrained destruction for a more lasting vengeance. The fifty-year-old man understood that there wouldn't be only one death.

Mlotek was looking at that figure in front of him and no longer understood who he was. His brother was stronger, but he died before him; he would never forgive him for that; he was always the winner. His brother was there; he had come to settle accounts. The strongest died; this was wrong; it didn't fit the logic of things. After years of confinement inside another body, the brother was now in a body all his own. He had managed to expel him, and now he was turning against him, the man in the white apron, as if it were forty-five years ago. The memory capsule read: the battle was won, the detonation of the last electrical core was discharged. So that he could die the death that he did not die when he was five.

What do you want from me, after all?
  Murderer!
  Say it, what do you want?
  You, you killed my brother!
  I am your brother!
  Don't you ever repeat that! I'm going to kill you!
  You don't have the courage to kill your brother!
  Shut up! I'll kill the both of you!

Mlotek felt his body explode. He squeezed the trigger. Five bullets. Five years. Fifty years. Two deaths. Three lives and everything finally over.

The nurse heard the blast of the shots and ran to the room. She saw the two bodies stretched out on the floor. She looked at one. Then to the other. Her bewilderment surpassed the horror on the floor. She phoned the police. Who was that man? No document identified him. No record. Nothing. The police decided, for obvious reasons, that it was Dr. Mlotek's twin brother. That's all it could be. He had returned. He was stronger.

The rabbis still argued whether it had been suicide. The police inquest had left a margin of doubt. The Kaddish was brief. The burial was simple. Four men lowered the coffins of the two brothers. The community insisted that they be buried side by side. In order to facilitate their reconciliation in the next life.

# Samuel Reibscheid

Samuel Reibscheid was born in São Paulo into a family of immigrants from Galicia who arrived in Brazil in 1925; he grew up speaking Polish, German, and Yiddish. Reibscheid is a medical doctor and professor. He has published numerous studies and books in his field of specialization. Medicine has taken him to Marseilles, Paris, Jerusalem, Haifa, and Malmö, and as a result the locales of his travels permeate his stories. The story collection *Breve fantasia* (1995) (Brief Fantasy) is his first published work of fiction. Reibscheid has also completed a manuscript of short stories titled *Retratos em preto e branco ou super Judeu* (Portraits in Black and White or Super Jew) and published a novel, *Memorial de um herege* (2000) (A Heretic's Memorial), based on Jewish history and documents that relate a Kafkaesque story of persecution, prejudice, and intolerance. In his first collection some of the stories take place in the old Jewish neighborhood of Bom Retiro in São Paulo. Memories of childhood spent in that neighborhood, a gallery of funny characters as well as ironic and comedic Jewish situations related to, for example, the circumcision ritual, make this collection an entertaining read. From daily incidents to such themes as the Holocaust and anti-Semitism, these stories also tackle the big questions related to twentieth-century Jewish history and culture. With humor at times reminiscent of Sholem Aleichem, the tales often use mockery as the basis for telling a story, thereby calling to mind a staple of Yiddish literature. The story 'Meu nome é Jó' (My Name Is Job) incorporates Reibscheid's use of dark Jewish humor, his ongoing dialogue with the Bible, and his experience as a medical doctor. The story underscores the inscrutability of the Jewish God and man's frustration at not being able to understand.

# Samuel Reibscheid

# My Name Is Job

My name is Job. In a family that chooses only biblical names out of habit, from time to time someone is called Job. I was born in São Paulo; I live in São Paulo. My parents came from Poland more than fifty years ago. They established themselves here, began their lives anew, procreated children, and paid taxes.

But the name they gave me . . . It could have been Elias or Moses or Isaac or even David.

I was condemned to repetition. One's name is a second skin, deeper and more ingrained. Except for the original Cain, nobody gets his name anymore. Oedipus? Only one. Adolph! How absurd! But I know a large number of Abels. How would it be if I were called Oswald?

Ever since I was a child, I have felt like a prisoner of some grand scheme/game. Always a yes and afterward a no. Everything and then, nothing. Wealth, followed by misery. Day and night. Like Job. Heaven, then hell!

Now I am in hell. In intensive care. I am the patient in bed number 4, known as bed 4. This is what I hear: 'Give this to bed 4! Visit bed 4!' I no longer have a name—so much the better! I am an old octopus, worn out by wear and tear, filled with plastic tentacles. I serve to demonstrate the principle of connecting vessels. Filled with tubes that go in and out. Their function is of great importance. Above me: tubes going in. Below: tubes going out. The secretions are measured, and the liquids are replaced. In the veins, in an artery. Liquids and salts go in. Into the stomach, into the bladder. Remains and secretions go out.

Good and bad actions are placed on the scale of the Final Judgment. Angels, choirmasters, residents, and nurses attend and boo, applaud, or beg 'encore.' If the result is negative, the doctor gives me liquids. If positive, he doesn't give me anything and waits for me to waste away. A tube with oxygen dehydrating my mucus. Wires connect me to monitors, and each time I move myself an alarm goes off. The nurse or the doctor or who-knows-who looks at me crossly; after all I am disturbing universal peace. A young female student contemplates me with a look of pity and through the tubes I say: 'You nincompoop, your day will come! You're going to feel pity for your rear end!'

She comments to somebody: 'He's delirious again.'

In bed 6, in front of mine, a young mitral valve with reddish cheeks. Change of valves, somebody says it's the third operation. She has a thoracic drain; she shakes every time she breathes. Dyed blond hair, one can see the black roots near her skull. A pretty girl! Bed 8, a bullet wound to the brain, a vegetable, with respirator and everything else. A plant, a dracaena. Terminal cancer, bed 1. It's Mr. Metastasis; it makes one think seriously about euthanasia. Movement. Nurses, doctors, interns, cleaning ladies. The only things missing are popcorn and hot-dog vendors. An attendant smuggles in cigarettes, and the coronary patients who can move about go smoke in the toilet.

Visiting hours between 2:00 and 2:30 in the afternoon. Familial sobbing! Smeared creams for the skin. Feelings. Tons of feelings. They spill onto the varnished floor. Out of loss and out of guilt. They contemplate the beds, and they shed tears. Noses dripping. A goo. Fogged-up glasses. Traces of caterpillars in the hairs of his forearm . . .

Curly hairs inside his underpants. Tired cheeks. I foresee kisses and caresses smelling of bologna sausage. A bath in bed. I am nothing more than a head of lettuce. A bunch of watercress leaves. Talcum powder. Perfume. A young physiotherapist massages my thorax. A Japanese or Chinese Brazilian with slanted eyes asks me if I am in pain. 'I'm only going to feel pain when you stop feeling it. Don't ever stop!' She laughs nervously. A young girl. I feel as if I'm in a Thai brothel. A eunuch wearing Ali Baba clothes and carrying an enormous scimitar snatches the last dollars from each frightened client and kicks each one in the ass . . . Behind him are continuous projections of super pornographic videos—she with a dog, she with women, he with men, she and he with a donkey—as well as pathological cine-angio-coronary x-rays showing complete obstructions of all the arteries from this and other worlds. I am a character from the silent movies. Mashed potatoes. A rancid smoked sausage drooling with fat. I kick the sheets up in the air, and they end up hanging from a light fixture above the bed. I am naked in the middle of visiting hours. The attendant becomes hysterical and shouts. The morphine and the Valium give me an incredible sense of well-being, and I am caring less and less about anything.

I received my diploma many years ago. A gala affair. Speeches. Champagne. Bestowal of the degree and taking oaths. Photograph in cap and gown. Master's degree. Doctoral degree. Marriage. Daughter. Work, much work. Internships. Money. Sons. Circumcisions. Trips. Congresses and classes. An apartment, afterward a beach house. More work. Material acquisitions. More apartments. Investments. Properties. Gems. Paintings. Children grow up. My daughter marries a degenerate, a boob, a fortune-hunter. She was warned . . . 'Get away from that guy!' . . . After three months she comes back home, blaming everybody for her unfortunate choice. She was beat up by her husband, a tyrant who still managed to end up with a car and the furniture given to the couple. What could have happened? She refuses to say a word. The fellow peed in bed? He had a colostomy and never let anybody know? He dove on top of her from the top of the wardrobe? She never told me what really happened. As a matter of fact she never again spoke to me. Since then she watches television the whole day long and eats pastry and candy. Astronomical quantities. She devoted herself to gaining weight. She grew so fat that she looks like a stuffed pig. A Strasbourg goose ready to become pâté de foie gras. She rolls around the house, blaming me for everything. My sons accuse me of not being sufficiently rich. They want to go to Europe at the end of each year. They want imported cars. They look at me with scorn. One is a specialist in computerized orgasm, and the other dedicates himself to spiritual studies. A specialist in pyramids. He studies the void. I complain about such absurd professions, and their mother says: 'Leave them in peace! One is young only once in life! Don't be bossy!' I shut up; it's difficult to say anything at all. And everybody begins to get disgusted with everybody. Little by little.

One more television. Stereo-schmereo. Color and three-dimensional. Penta-dimensional.

One more coat. More cars. But my name is Job. I do not forget. One can't forget.

It's no longer necessary for the devil to challenge God in order to tempt, lose, and test me. That had already been done once, and since then the program was set. In between gulps of camel's milk, a scribe detailed everything into chapters and verses. It's in the Bible for all to read.

The programming was reset in motion when they called me Job. How could they think of this name while they contemplated an undefended and uncircumcised baby? Could it be that I was crying because I was cold? Was I jaundiced? Chafed? Impetigo? My wife goes away with the pharmacist. Being so fat, my daughter no longer walks and spends her days giving interviews to television networks, stretched out on a reinforced couch. The Female Barrel. The Fattest Female in Latin America. The Bloated Bride. The Marriage that Turned into Fat. Fame! Glory! She helps out on TV news programs. Each day they announce her weight alongside the quotations of the stock market and the dollar. She is weighed with the help of a crane, and everybody exclaims: 'Oh!' It's hard to get inside my house, for I trip over journalists and jars of fruit preserves. My ex-son-in-law, the degenerate, I learned he got married two more times and dissipated two more fortunes. He telephones me and asks: 'And so how goes it there, old man! Satisfied? How is the elephant doing?' My sons sought refuge in Machu Picchu, residing in a center for transcendental companionship. They alleged it was impossible to achieve familial companionship. They play the flute the whole day long and practice esoteric doctrines of the Incas. They consume what the land gives, or to be more specific, kale, grass, and sown cannabis leaves . . . In the last letter they sent, years ago, they said they had found peace and were living in communion with Nature, and so on.

My mother-in-law laughs when she passes by me and whispers with her friends without any pretense. She puts on high red boots with spurs, even in the summer, and looks like a sadomasochistic Cossack. If she were not Jewish, she'd be anti-Semitic, a capo from a concentration camp. She has a denture implant with vampiresque eyeteeth, and when she smiles, I automatically protect my jugular veins. When the doctor announced the birth of my daughter, my father-in-law furtively commented that I had weak sperm and that's why a boy wasn't born! When the boys were born, he affirmed that everybody knows who the mother is. But the father . . . Is it possible to listen to a thing like that? My business went down the drain, and I no longer have any possessions. The money ended. My clothes drawer was green on account of the bills it held. Today it contains only old socks and shirts. Expired passports. Old 3 x 4 photos. Guarantees for electronic appliances that no longer exist. I have nothing else.

It was all so foreseeable! Why this name? Why Job? Why not David or Solomon? Why not feel the possibility of glory when one thinks of one's own name?

What's the use of rebelling? Against whom? And what for? The immediate problem is the catheter, an intolerable thing. I yank it out with care.

A priest comes to visit the patients in the unit. A chat. An extreme unction. The male nurse who takes care of me is a believer and wants to convert me. In between an anticoagulant and a Valium he says that salvation is in Christ. I went into a fit of laughter when he spoke about this, and in order not to offend him, I decided to receive the priest, a good friend of his. 'I see that your name is Job,' says Father Cartofle. He's Dutch, fat, and ruddy cheeked, like a roasted potato. He lived among the Venezuelan Indians for ten years and now, semiretired, dedicates himself to the hospital. 'You must know what your fate will be! With that name you're surely going to lose everything—if you haven't already—and for sure, if you don't rebel against the Creator, you will gain everything back, perhaps twofold . . .'

My doctor arrives, Dr. Isaac Yarosgarten, and he becomes livid when he comes across Father Cartofle. 'Father, hadn't we decided that you would not converse with the patients of other faiths? Can it be that Christian patients are not enough for you?' Without checking with me, he calls for a rabbi. I manage to yank out the gastric probe. Progress. Rabbi Varénheques tells me seriously: 'Brother! Your name says it all! You had everything and lost everything. But if you have faith, you will recuperate everything and maybe even more.' He talks for a little while; I discover he is Galician and appreciates a glass of vodka. The rabbi is the son and grandson of rabbis and says that rabbinism is in the blood. Who will come next? A pastor with a previous stay in Africa? A voodoo priest with little dolls and pins?

I am discharged from the hospital. I see things and people I didn't even know how to keep in my memory. Visions. Certainly caused by all the medicines. I dream continuously. My world is oneiric. A pendulum. I go back and forth. Virtual reality. I am not thirsty, and I drink three glasses of water. I have just awakened, and I fall asleep. I put on my clothes, and I become naked. I don't undress; I drop my clothes. I catch a glimpse of male and female acquaintances. Always in the pose of some old black-and-white photograph, in white frames, irregularly scalloped at the edges. Things are obviously pictorial but with expression, lively . . . biblical characters, but only those who appear in the illustrations, drawings in pen point . . . Joseph was an imbecile . . . he should have slept with Potifar's wife—a thin young man keeping away from a woman who gets beaten by her husband while the pharaoh laughs to himself, seated on an immense marble throne where voluptuous Batsheva stands—a King David with a satyr's shaped beard plays a lyre while he covetously contemplates an olive-skinned girl, a cheap striptease artist covered with whiplash scars on her fat rump . . . the sea is deep, a row of Jews, all parched; mother heroines carrying bags of sandwiches, juices, towels, and sunscreen lotions—and Moses-Mao declares that in order to cross the Red Sea one just has to take the first step. Or the first stroke. Athos sodom-izes Portus, who sodomizes Aramis, who sodomizes D'Artagnan. All homos! One active, one passive, and two promiscuous bisexuals! The illustration shows the four of them playing at being a choo-choo train, but all want to be the engine. What is it, and what is it not?

After a month I go for a check-up.

'Dr. Isaac, my body weighs upon me; my head is throbbing; I have difficulty breathing. My bones hurt, and my joints have hardened. My prick is only good for peeing and has turned into a ridiculous appendage.'

He answers ironically: 'I don't even have that pleasure anymore, such is the difficulty I feel urinating on account of an enlarged pros-tate. Take advantage and pee to your heart's content. Pee while you can! What memories!'

Suddenly everything I do turns out right. Definitely in keeping with the program outlined by the scribe who lived in tent number 13 in the Sinai desert. Isaac Ben Yakov Ben Ezequiel Ben . . . Bureau of Proper Names. Wait to be called. The only tariff: a dry tamarind. An easy-to-find tent. To the left of the eighth palm tree. Right over there where they are composing the Book.

Any business I engage in is guaranteed success! My friends want to buy lottery tickets together with me, such is the fortune that follows me! One who is blessed. In the supermarket women touch me. To bring them luck. To make them pregnant. To stop them from getting pregnant. Down deep, down deep I must be a believer . . .

I'm in heaven. In a barbecue steakhouse. Back to normal. Without probes, drains, or electric cables. My limits go as far as those of my skin. A fellow like anybody else. This is happiness. Nirvana. I chew meat until my jawbones ache. Liquids and solids enter where they should enter. Male and female friends! Words. Sounds from childhood. Laughs. We discuss and chat. I comment: 'I am Job, there's no use in escaping this. I had everything, I lost everything! Once again I won everything back and a little bit more! Health returned. Now I harbor a secret fear. It doesn't pay to consult the Book, for it is remiss. Is everything going to be repeated again? Am I going to end up again without anything? Another wife and children who are going to want to put me into a jug of vinegar? Sickness again? Intensive care? Is it possible? What game is this?'

There is no answer, and so I order dessert.

# Moacyr Scliar

Moacyr Scliar was born in 1937 in Porto Alegre, a city with the third largest Jewish community in Brazil, in the southern state of Rio Grande do Sul, noted for its *gaúcho* regional and folkloric culture of cattle raising and farming. Indelibly marked by his Jewish Russian heritage, Scliar considers himself a cultural hybrid. He took his degree in 1962 at the Faculty of Medicine in Porto Alegre and was a practicing physician and administrator in public health from 1969 to 1987. His early schooling was at Porto Alegre's 'Yiddish' college, the School of Education and Culture. His secondary studies were in a Catholic school. Scliar began his literary career in 1968 with the publication of his allegorical story collection *O carnaval dos animais* (1968) (*The Carnival of Animals*, 1985). Since then he has produced more than 125 stories and approximately twenty novels. His most famous novels are *A guerra no Bom Fim* (1972) (*The War in Bom Fim*); *O exército de um homem só* (1973) (*The One-Man Army*, 1985); *Os deuses de Raquel* (1975) (*The Gods of Rachel*, 1986); *O centauro no jardim* (1980) (*The Centaur in the Garden*, 1984); *A estranha nação de Rafael Mendes* (1983) (*The Strange Nation of Rafael Mendes*, 1987); *Sonhos tropicais* (1992) (*Tropical Dreams*); *A majestade do Xingu* (1996) (*The Majesty of the Xingu*); *A mulher que escreveu a Bíblia* (2000) (*The Woman Who Wrote the Bible*); *Éden-Brasil* (2002); and *Os vendilhões do templo* (2006) (*The Moneychangers of the Temple*). Among his six story collections are *A balada do falso messias* (1976) (*The Ballad of the False Messiah*, 1987); *O olho enigmático: Contos* (1986) (*The Enigmatic Eye: Stories*, 1989); and *A orelha de Van Gogh* (1989) (*Van Gogh's Ear*). *The Collected Stories of Moacyr Scliar* appeared in English translation in 1999. As the most notable contemporary Brazilian Jewish writer, Scliar writes tragicomic, allegorical, political, fantastic, enigmatic, and humorous parables that capture the diasporic spirit and the different tribal allegiances of Brazilian Jews. Representative of Scliar's contribution to fantastic realism, the stories anthologized here from *Contos reunidos* (1996) transmit the spiritualist and inscrutable aspects of life where redemption is always yet to come.

# Moacyr Scliar

# In the Bosom of Abraham

Life was excellent in the bosom of Abraham, according to the report our grandfather periodically sent us from there, availing himself of a medium who lived on our street and who charged a small fortune for this service. But we all agreed that we would do anything to receive news from such a good and charming man. We paid in dollars.

Our grandfather would go on at length about the description of the place where he had been taken thanks to thousands of good deeds. This here is immense, he used to say, very excited (immensity was important for a man who had spent the greatest part of his existence confined to a miniscule room in his son's house). It's immense, one can walk for hours and days, and afterward one can rest, and it is so soft, so nice and warm. The warmth was particularly important to my grandfather, who suffered from rheumatism and especially from the cold.

We used to ask what he did all day long; my cousin, a student of administration, wanted to know if there was some program of activities. No, answered my grandfather, there wasn't any damn program (that he used obscenities, ah, that he did) or scheduled activities. He would spend his time ('time' wasn't exactly the term, when dealing with eternity, but after all) conversing with other honorable souls, some of them even acquaintances, like the owner of the corner bar, who frequently had let him charge his drinks, and who had died tragically, run over by a public sanitation truck. At times angels passed by, chanting melodies, but my grandfather didn't pay much attention: he didn't like music. He preferred to walk.

His excursions, however, were limited to the left breast, of the two, the least abundant. The right breast, larger, was so far away that my grandfather could barely see it (it's true that his sight wasn't the best; before dying he always spoke about changing his glasses, which he ended up not doing: the obsession of postponing, postponing). In order to get there he would have to descend that valley existing between the gigantic breasts (mountains, real mountains) and walk, walk without stopping. There was yet an additional difficulty. Like many Abraham had a hairy chest, a real thicket. My grandfather was afraid, on top of everything else, to unwillingly pull one of those gray hairs.

That he would like to go to the other breast, that he would like to do. That's where the widow Janeta was to be found. This upstanding woman, already dead for some time, had been his great love. They were from the same village in Eastern Europe; brought up together, they were inseparable, and everything indicated that they would come to be married, for the joy of their parents and everybody else's. But when he was eighteen my grandfather decided to visit the city nearby; there he met a young woman, the daughter of a rich merchant. Without delay they got married; at the time many people said that my grandfather had acted out of monetary interest, but it couldn't be so. Greedy he wasn't, so much so that he often gave to charity; besides, how is one to explain his going to the bosom of Abraham? No, he wasn't the perfidious person people said; he was a good man. In fact it was kindness that ruined him: everybody asked to borrow money from him; everybody exploited him. He and his wife ended up emigrating. They wanted to begin a new life in the New World, which is what they actually did, but he never forgot the sweet Janeta. He received sporadic news about her; on the day he learned about her death, he wept a great deal but consoled himself, saying: I'm going to meet up with her in the bosom of Abraham. Which is what could have happened. If not for it being so far. If not for the thicket of hairs.

Not managing to reach his love, my grandfather kept on staring into the distance. There were many people in the right breast, millions of upstanding people; but my grandfather believed, at least that's what he told us, he could see his Janeta there in the distance. As always she continues to be beautiful, he sighed. He wanted to communicate with her via the medium, in a kind of telepathic triangulation, but the man told us that it was impossible, unless we wanted to pay an extra fee, very high. We didn't agree on this matter, however; we didn't have anything against this Janeta, but, after all, she wasn't our grandmother, and we couldn't encourage a spurious passion, especially in the bosom of Abraham. Despondent, my grandfather kept on strolling around the enormous mammilla.

Imagine this thing here spouting out milk, he would say, much to the consternation of the medium, who saw himself obliged to transmit word for word these crude jokes. The worst is that with this kind of talk our grandfather forced us to imagine a geyser of lukewarm milk, creating an honest-to-goodness torrent. One day, we thought, our grandfather will be pushed away by the torrent, and we will be able to do nothing more for him. Life in the bosom of Abraham is not without its risks.

# Moacyr Scliar

# The Children of the Androgyne

In childhood we suffered a great deal with that home situation. On the
rare occasions we went out into the street (always together and holding
hands: we felt more protected like that), the neighbors would point to
us, laughing and sneering: look at the children of the androgyne. And
we were perfectly normal, the boys as well as the girls; we answered
back (we yelled; sometimes in despair, we yelled), we are normal, we
are normal. They didn't believe it: normal, my eye. Normal, a stick up
your ass. And they dared us: pull down your pants! Lift up your skirts!
Always holding hands, we left, running at full speed. We were timid,
so says tradition, like the children of androgynes. Also timid was that
person who had procreated us and whom we called 'father,' because
he looked like a man with his short hair and his relatively deep voice—
besides this, he wore masculine clothes, except for when he wanted
to get comfortable (to watch TV, for example),then he would opt for
an old, flowery dress. We never saw him or her nude. We knew nothing of his genitalia; we had to imagine it or then turn to the books he
had collected on the topic in his extensive library: at a certain point
in time he had decided to inform himself about his condition and
had read everything that had fallen into his hands. He had become so
informed that he and the surgeons could have discussions as equals.
The professionals said an operation could resolve his case, but this
wasn't the problem: the problem was that he couldn't decide whether
he wanted to become a man or a woman. Contrary to others who saw
within this duality a wild mistake of nature, he considered himself
to be a superior being: I'm enough for myself; I'm sufficient unto
myself, he used to say, and he was never wrong. He had developed a
technique, a secret he never revealed to anyone and which had allowed
him to fulfill the dream of many of his breed: autocoitus. Which he
rarely practiced. Actually because the act apparently demanded of

him long psychological preparation. Weeks before this act, he was already acting distant, reserved, even a little perturbed; we felt he was focusing his energies on the big moment: one night he would communicate to us his inclination to go to bed early, alleging indisposition or something similar.

As soon as he shut himself up in his room, we ran to glue our ears to the door (the hole in the lock was, of course, blocked). Given the thickness of the wood, what we heard was very little: some sighs, some laughing, some exclamations—I love you, I love you—sometimes in his usual masculine voice, sometimes in falsetto. The oldest child, a boy who later would become a teacher, observed in a low voice that the expression was incorrect; the right one would be I love me, I love me. The youngest was already showing her vocation as a future psychologist by retorting, with disdain, that language was not the best way to understand androgynes. The discussion ceased when the door was abruptly opened, and he appeared—not relieved, but irritated; he had guessed our presence in the hallway. To avoid a reprimand, we fled, some laughing, others in tears.

He took precautions to avoid an unwanted pregnancy. Even so, we believe we had once seen him pregnant. He had a hard time; occasionally he would vomit a lot, partly due to anxiety: at the time he had a good job, the pregnancy could mean dismissal pure and simple. He must have aborted because he spent a few days in the hospital, and when he came home, he cried a lot, in secret. A rough ordeal, according to Dr. Raimundo, his doctor.

We also went through rough ordeals, and it wasn't only on the street, or in school, or at the club. TV people would constantly besiege us, and more than once we were approached on the street by young adults in whose pockets we noticed, ever so badly hidden, a portable tape recorder. All that trouble, however, was compensated by his extraordinary capacity to give affection. When we became sick, he would take us in his arms; we could then feel, under his polyester shirt, the small breasts, always hard, despite the years (and despite the fact of having nursed all of us). That inside his pants his big penis also bulged out, mattered very little to us. We were with our father, we were with our mother, and this was all that we wanted.

# Moacyr Scliar

# The Necrologists

One doesn't come to this art by chance, wrote the necrologist Kurt in one of his autonecrologies (he composed one per day, upon waking: it's an exercise, he declared, equivalent to other people's jogging). The term 'art' seemed a bit strong for the necrologist Everaldo, who modestly considered himself to be a laborer of necrologies, but the necrologist Pierre was categorical: the obituary, he said more than once, is a literary form like any other. He felt offended when he noticed that people reacted to such a declaration with a barely disguised smile; because of this he had a book published (leather bound, beautiful illustrations), his *Complete Necrologies*, with which he competed for more than one literary prize. He never won, so he himself created an award with his own name. He died before the submission date was closed, which saved him from a disappointment: there wasn't even one candidate. The necrologist Jean, who wrote his colleague's necrology, omitted those facts, which, according to him, represented a blot on the history of necrology.

'The first necrology,' said the necrologist Oswaldo, 'is like your first girlfriend: you never forget.' The necrologist Raul carried in his wallet his first necrology: 'Wherever I may be,' he used to say, 'I always read it. I read it in the morning and at night, when I get up and when I go to bed, in joy and in pain. I read it to have an encounter with my true self.'

'Contrary to what many people think and to what certain dictionaries state,' affirmed the necrologist Sandro, 'necrology isn't necessarily a eulogy for the deceased. I am friend to Caesar, but I am a better friend to truth. If Cromwell, the great Cromwell, demanded to be pictured with the wart that made him ugly, why shouldn't a dead person—who by the way is in no condition to discuss the subject—be pictured in the most honest way possible?' The owner of the newspaper where

he was employed did not agree; the business was in financial difficulties; he didn't want to know about any confusing matters. In order
not to renounce his principles, the necrologist Sandro always wrote
two necrologies: one, complimentary, that was published; another,
truthful, remained locked in his safe: 'The deceased was known as a
cynical, overbearing, Machiavellian person. His fortune was in part
the result of unbridled financial speculation, in part due to pure and
simple theft . . .' In his moments of bitterness, the necrologist Sandro
confided in his friends, 'I go back over these necrologies and I find
in their authenticity true refuge, consolation, and the reaffirmation
of my dignity' (however, when one of those necrologies mysteriously
disappeared, he spent many sleepless nights fearing it would fall into
the hands of the deceased's influential family. He accused the cleaning lady, who defended herself: 'I don't know what you are talking
about, I don't want anything to do with the dead, and what's more
I'm illiterate'). Because of those occurrences, the necrologist Salles,
embittered, used to speak about the 'death of the necrology.' 'It's an
art going into extinction,' he used to say, 'the young only want to know
about rock 'n roll.' 'Very well,' retorted the necrologist Simon, 'the
necrology is in crisis, but that's the natural consequence of historical
evolution: we live in an age that denies death, that puts makeup on
cadavers, that cremates bodies, that throws human ashes into the
sea; consequently we have to adapt, we have to produce necrologies
compatible with this new reality—in the form of cartoons, on video,
on CDs.' 'None of that,' protested the necrologist Alan, who saw in
the necrology the supreme test for the written word. 'It's a text that
challenges the writer, demanding of him a great capacity for synthesis
and formal style.' The necrologist Abigail headed a feminist current
within the field of necrology: she not only protested against the low
percentage of women in the obituary section of the newspapers but
also wanted to prohibit male journalists from writing necrologies about
women, alleging that only a woman, even a dead one, can speak to
another woman. The necrologist David traveled to London on a tour,
but instead of following the schedule for visiting the tourist attrac-
tions, he would spend his days in the British Museum looking at the
mummies and writing necrologies of the pharaohs—which at night in
the two-star hotel (but with breakfast included) he would read to the
other travelers. Which generated various complaints; an old widow

who had spent all her savings on the trip objected, yelling loudly: 'I am not obliged to listen to this maniac speaking of dead people about whom he knows nothing.' The tour guide tried to convince the necrologist David to give up necrologies; not being successful, he decided to move him to another hotel (four stars but breakfast not included—which the necrologist, in any event, did without: he would wake up anxious to meet what he called 'his mummies,' and he didn't want to lose any time).

The necrologist Waldemar was being pursued by a recently graduated lawyer who wanted his help in perfecting his curriculum vitae for an important job. 'I don't know anything about that,' he complained. 'I only know how to speak about the dead.' 'But,' retorted the young advocate, 'if you write such a good résumé of the life and work of the dead, why not try it with the living?' The necrologist Waldemar gave in and did his CV request, but—in the habit of his craft—he put the verbs in the past tense. Once corrected, the lawyer submitted the document to the employer—but was turned down. 'The idea of death permeates my work,' the necrologist Waldemar said, and not without some pleasure.

The necrologist Ivan was looking for the palindrome necrology that could be read backward and forward. Everyone found this obsession very strange, and he himself was disturbed by it, until he realized the symbolism involved in this quest: he was, in truth, searching for a new form of expression that, nullifying the traditional idea of beginning, middle, end, would make the permanent reversibility viable, the eternal return. But that, he concluded, was only within God's reach. He returned to the traditional necrology, at which he wasn't so bad, according to his own evaluation.

At the Third World Conference of Necrology, in Malaga, Spain, the necrologist Wilfred presented a paper titled: 'Necrology: History, Basic Concepts, Formal Classification.' He pointed out the following types of necrology: strictly speaking laudatory, laudatory *cum grano salis* (discreetly ironic), laudatory-informative, purely informative, lyrical, informative-lyrical, epic, epic-informative, epic-lyrical-informative. The necrologist Wilfred also wanted the profession to be standardized in the various signatory countries of the Necrological Document of Malaga; but the proposal was defeated, according to the necrologist Wilfred, on account of the feelings of guilt and inferiority that torment all who work with death. All the same the conference in itself was very exciting, thanks to two parallel events. The first was the costumed ball, where everybody came dressed as ghosts. The second was the competition for 'The Best Necrology on Napoleon,' which was to have on the panel of judges a female descendent of the emperor and which was a great success, though a bit diminished by the absence of the invited descendent, who simply did not appear. 'The only thing I wanted was to write the necrology of that lady,' shouted the necrologist Harald. 'Honest to God, it's the only thing I wanted.' 'Why,' asked the necrologist George in the hallway, 'can't we use the necrology to transform the world, inclusively and primarily in a surreptitious way?' He gave some examples: on the death of a cruel and inhumane manager, his necrologist would say: 'Thousands of cruel laborers will nostalgically remember their charitable boss.' Reading this text the laborers would realize the farce they were living, and so they would rebel and take over the factory. No one took the necrologist George seriously, who, so they say, had gone to Spain only to remember his father, a member of the International Brigade during the Civil War. The necrologist Phillip, concerned about his colleagues' low income, had the idea for the necrology stamp: each time an important person died, the post office would print for the family in mourning stamps with small texts about the life of the deceased to be used for the thank-you cards. The necrologist Ramires was more practical: on All Souls Day he'd put up some kind of stall at the entrance to the cemetery. There, amid the flower sellers (who complained about the under-handed competition), he'd offer to work out prospective necrologies. People could obtain that text, furnishing some personal details and listing the great accomplishments they foresaw in their future. The price was practically symbolic; 'I charge because I'm against doing things for free,' he used to say. 'It's a question of principle, not of money, and it's a pedagogical attitude: it's important to give value to the necrology.' The idea wasn't bad, and the timing was actually very good (on what other occasion would such a large number of people think about death?), but the necrologist Ramires, without an auto-mobile to enable him to get to the more-distant cemeteries, where the rich were buried, had to be content with C- and D-class clienteles. 'But what newspaper would publish my necrology?' was the question humble widows asked him. To prevent that nuisance, the necrologist

Ramires came up with the idea for a publication called *Necro News* dedicated only to necrologies. He was depending on the support of funeral homes and morgues, but he wasn't successful.

One man requested from the necrologist Tomás a necrology for his recently amputated right arm. 'An arm, even the right arm of an agile person, is not an autonomous being,' argued the necrologist Tomás. 'The arm had a funeral I paid for,' replied the man, 'and if there was a funeral, why not a necrology?' 'The arm now beneath the ground,' he continued, 'was the arm that carried my school books, the arm that embraced my first girlfriend.' The necrologist Tomás, who, unemployed, was anxious to compose a necrology, any necrology, ended up agreeing and wrote a very beautiful necrology, in his opinion, describing the emotion of a man who separates himself from the member that accompanied him all his life. The necrologist Leo, his friend, didn't like anything about the story. 'And if it were a hand? A finger? A fingernail? If a crazy man asked you to write a necrology for the fingernail he had just cut, would you write it? For the hair cut from your head, would you write it? For the hairs trimmed from your beard by your razor, would you write it?' 'Yes,' the necrologist Tomás said sadly, 'I would write all those necrologies; after all the fingernail that falls to the ground precedes the death of the body of which it was a part, in the same way as the hairs cut by the barber. They are modest parts of our very selves which advance toward extinction in the form of the vanguard, like a charging battalion.'

'But fingernails . . .' exclaimed the necrologist Leo.

'The fingernails! The fingernails!' shouted the necrologist Tomás furiously. 'Yes, the fingernails! I know, colleague, that fingernails are seen by many as a symbol of evil because they are similar to claws, because the scratches left on the backs of lovers serve as proof of infidelity for betrayed wives. But I ask: what do the fingernails have to be blamed for if they look like claws? Why should they be blamed for marriages that end in divorce? Wasn't it only hypocrisy that held such precarious unions together? No, colleague, no. We cannot manifest such injustice with the fingernails. If they're worth being cared for by manicurists, if they are worthy of tons of nail polish produced for them daily by manufacturers of cosmetics, if they justify the production of scissors, nail files, nail clippers (all of these packaged in elegant leather cases, authentic or not), and also the brand of nail cutters called Trim, then they also deserve necrologies.'

At that point in the rationale of the necrologist Tomás, a great student of history, he remembered that the Inquisition had accused many people of being practitioners of Judaism, based on the fact that the suspects saved the fingernail clippings of the dead. And he pondered: if New Christians had to face the Holy Office on account of fingernails, shouldn't necrologists face with equal courage the jeers of modern inquisitors? The necrologist Leo shut up without any arguments.

The necrologist Lucas defended the idea that the necrology, like any other journalistic material, should translate the existential experience of its author. 'How can I speak of the dead,' he asked his colleagues, 'if I do not know what it is to die?' One time he spent twenty-four hours inside a coffin and only got out because the funeral director needed that coffin for a bier. 'If God were to appear in my dreams,' the necrologist Roaldo anxiously asked himself, 'and were to say: "Necrologist Roaldo, I will only allow into heaven those whom your necrologies absolved," do you think I would continue on in this activity? Do you think I could stand such a great responsibility?'

There exists a real self-conceit in the necrologist, maintained the necrologist Michelle. 'We believe,' she said, 'that, because we can give a résumé of the lives of important people in a few lines, we have the power to decide what is important and what is not in human existence.' In order to neutralize this feeling, she, a beautiful woman, filled her bedroom with reproductions of the *Dance of Death*, by Dürer, plastic skulls, and a large banner that said: 'Vanity of vanities, all is vanity.' Immediately the necrologist Frank, according to his own words, took on any challenge: 'Pride is something I threw away in the trash a long time ago,' he affirmed. He was much sought after by many people who wanted necrologies for their animal house pets; and he even went so far as to take a trip to Paris specifically to familiarize himself with the epitaphs in the cemetery for dogs and cats that existed over there. His necrologies were good but a bit recherché: 'Yesterday the heartfelt and loyal Doberman Caesar emitted his last bark . . .' Or then he would resort to rather dubious humor: 'The rats of the São Pedro neighborhood are happy: yesterday one of their most tenacious enemies, the cat Chan, died, property of Madam Ruth . . .' His colleagues decided to put his vocation to the test, and one of them decided to request a necrology for a snake. The necrologist Frank refused: he loathed ophidians. Unmasked, he had to renounce his trade. He bought a chicken coop. Daily and without any remorse, he supervised the slaughter of thousands of chickens; for the memory of those creatures he never wrote a line.

'Formal aspects of the necrology': this was the title of the master's thesis submitted by the necrologist Milton. To develop his valiant work (400 pages, 312 bibliographic references), he interviewed dozens of colleagues, asking them about their aesthetic criteria. In this way he learned that the necrologist Armando was against exclamation points ('They make an attempt against the sobriety of a text, which must be characterized by containment') and ellipses ('Our affirmations must be definite'); but he dreamed about ending a necrology with a question mark, symbolizing our doubts about death and eternity. The necrologist Vitor had a mathematical formula for calculating the number of words in a necrology. In the numerator: the age of the deceased, the number of children, grandchildren, and great-grandchildren (applied to each case a factor of variables, because having children is not the same as having grandchildren), income verified by a copy of the statement made to the Federal Income Tax Office, of the number of clubs the deceased was a member. In the denominator, amid other data, his weight. Thin, the necrologist Victor did not excuse obese people: 'The body mass,' he used to say, in an exalted manner, 'is nothing more than the expression of the egotistical activity of eating, or rather, of removing from circulation the nutrients other people perhaps needed more.' A computer program facilitated the processing of these statistics, but it would not provide the final text. That was achieved by the necrologist Howard, who programmed his laptop to emit instantaneous necrologies according to the deceased's profession. All one had to do was type 'Executive,' for example, and on the screen would appear the statement: 'A brilliant career in the business world has just come to a close.' But this easy technique had a price; it was not without some anxiety when the necrologist Howard pressed 'Enter': when the words disappeared from the screen in a flash, he was overcome by depressive thoughts about the fleeting nature of life. The necrologist Herbert didn't run this risk; since he was poor and did not have access to a computer, he did have a bank of adjectives, a small file whose entries contained qualifiers and synonyms. In this way he could vary his eulogies without fear of repeating himself.

For a fan of crossword puzzles, the necrologist Rebecca wrote a special necrology, imitating exactly that, crossword puzzles. The reader would have to solve them with the information furnished by the necrologist Rebecca. In the horizontal spaces the nouns that characterized the deceased; in the vertical ones the verbs that described his or her multiple activities in life. The necrologist Byron wrote, perhaps due to his name, necrologies in verse—the sonnet was his favorite form, but when the owner of a large alcoholic beverage distributing company died, he wrote a long epic poem. He was well compensated: a bottle of scotch for each verse. Unfortunately, it wasn't his favorite brand of scotch. The necrologist Walter worked with acrostics: each letter of the deceased's name led to the beginning of a verse. He was overjoyed with long names, but one time when he was invited to write the necrology of a Chinese man call Li Chu, he refused with scorn (which by the way resulted in his being tried for racism; he had to prove that the accusation was unfounded).

The necrologist Emma had a real dread of the exaggerated eulogy. 'It is an error we cannot make,' she used to say. 'But,' she would anxiously ask herself, 'how does one know when a eulogy is exaggerated? Is "wise" a qualifying adjective more praiseworthy than "intelligent"? Is "dynamic" better than "energetic"? And what is more worthy of praise, to be "charitable" or to be "fair"?' She decided to proceed with that evaluation by way of a laboratory experiment. She would select a group of volunteers in a good state of psychic health; to each one she would say, for example: 'You are enterprising' and afterward 'You are daring.' She would measure, as one does with lie detectors, the physiological alterations of her subjects: pulse, blood pressure, temperature, and—very important—degree of blushing, comparing the manifestation of color to the person's skin with a scale of reddish tones. The idea was the following: the more praiseworthy the attribute, the more a person would blush. The problem is that she could only use these criteria on white people, which would be an intolerable example of discrimination, and moreover, only on live people, since the dead do not blush. Which would always leave a question up in the air: is it possible that the dead value eulogies in the same way as living people do?

The necrologist Santino hated his rival Bernardo, also a necrologist, so much that he began to send him through the mail anonymous necrologies, made at a clandestine printing shop: 'Yesterday the necrologist Bernardo died . . .' With that practice he hoped to cause a heart attack in his enemy. The necrologist Bernardo really died but of lung cancer—he smoked too much. Just to frustrate the necrologist Santino, he left his own necrology completed. 'Too bad,' sighed the necrologist Santino. 'He could have taken advantage of one of the texts I wrote; it would have been an opportunity for a reconciliation—posthumous, but nonetheless a reconciliation.' The necrologist Smith so hated the small city where he lived that he began to compose the necrology of all the inhabitants, beginning with the outstanding people in the community; he had the secret hope that some catastrophe would destroy the place—when all the necrologies would then be published simultaneously, representing not only a necrological tour de force but his final vengeance. The necrologist Ernest, who was also a psychologist, did not share in these negative feelings. The necrologist used to say, 'It is an act of love.' He asked his patients to compose their own necrologies, in this way counting on their improving their self-esteem.

'If there were to be a planetary war,' asked the necrologist Bader, 'and the Earth destroyed, who would write the necrology of humanity?' That thought bothered him, but not very much; he kept imagining what a great necrology that would be, the necrology of the whole human species. A necrologist's dreams are like that: they don't fit into the short space of a lifetime.

# Jaime Lerner

Jaime Lerner was born in São Paulo in 1959. At the age of seven he, along with his family, emigrated to Israel, where he studied and later graduated from the Academy of Cinema and TV, Beit Zvi. While living in London, he completed a master's degree in film in 1984 and produced the short film *Jon Watchin' Time*. In 1985 he returned to Brazil and participated in the first FestRio film festival. The prestigious Film Festival of Gramado brought him to Rio Grande do Sul, where he now lives. He offers courses in film at the Catholic University of Rio Grande do Sul and works in film advertising. Other films he has produced are *A festa* (The Party) and *Mazel Tov*, the latter a short on the beginning of the Jewish colonization in Rio Grande do Sul. Lerner recently participated in the Festival of Jewish Contemporary Film in Rio Grande do Sul and has produced several sociopolitical documentaries. His first book, *Grupo de risco* (1990) (Group at Risk), is a novella about the fear of AIDS. His first collection of stories, *Entre quatro paredes* (Between Four Walls), appeared in 1995; according to scholar Regina Zilberman, these stories are narratives about the insecurity of our times as well as a commentary on being imprisoned within the four walls of a repressive society. The story anthologized here, 'Herança' (Legacy), points to the insidious prejudices beneath the social surface of a multicultural and multiracial society struggling with equality for all. In this story Lerner dramatizes the feelings of alienation and exclusion experienced by a Jew, a mulatto, and a black woman. As a unique and daring racial trinity, the three represent a newly formed friendship that may confound certain societies. The old Jew imagines what it would be like for the three of them to parade down a street in modern-day Germany. His 'legacy' becomes a lesson about true racial democracy.

# Jaime Lerner

# Legacy

Hirsch cast his eyes on his new companion and was filled with affection. I like him, he thought, reminding himself he rarely erred in these first impressions of his. The man smiled at him while being introduced; he hesitated a little and finally extended his hand, bowing a bit. Hirsch's son invented some excuse and left them alone; he was always a very busy man, sometimes out of sheer habit, sometimes because he really had something to do. Hirsch made a sign for João to sit down. This would be his last gesture of kindness toward the young man.

I like him, he thought, again observing the big mulatto seated somewhat awkwardly in the designated armchair. I like him, and at the same time I feel immensely sorry for him. What turn of fate forces a strong young man, full of life and health, plans and potential, to push a wheelchair occupied by an old man like me already at the end of his career? It was arduous work, practically without any time off, twenty-four hours a day of intense proximity between the two of them. Hirsch knew it was need that obliged João to accept the position. If he were to be kind to the youth, he knew he would end up letting it show how much he felt sorry for him and thus wouldn't be able to avoid hurting his pride. That would certainly make the job abominable; it would also make João an unhappy companion. For the youth's own well-being, he decided to treat him rudely, put on a mask of arrogance, and let him be very free to hate the old man whom he had to carry around from one place to another. This would be what his know-it-all son was in the habit of calling 'transference.' Instead of detesting the condition that tied him to a job like this, João would detest the incarnation of this job: old man Hirsch. He never made a point of being loved by people, and therefore, it would merely be a small sacrifice to make João a little more happy.

João also liked the old man. We could say it was mutual affection at first sight. He felt relieved when the man's son left the room, as if a wall of ice had been removed. He was not affected by his patient's cantankerous manner; he could very well understand it. He could see by Hirsch's features that he was not a man to be chained to a wheelchair, dependent on someone in order to move about, to take a bath, and so on. He didn't have the details, but he did know that the old man had arrived in the country destitute and all alone; without knowing anything or anybody, he had built a small empire. The man seemed to possess an infinite amount of energy incrusted in his personality. He couldn't stop from being bitter about his new situation. João understood poor Hirsch; he knew the old man's disdain wasn't directed at him but rather at his condition as invalid, and therefore, he wasn't offended by his employer's manner. However, he knew he couldn't react to his patient's gruffness with sensitivity, showing understanding. That would only make him appear to be superior in Hirsch's eyes; it would emphasize even more the dependence he was subjected to; it would remind the old man of his situation in a very cruel way.

Hirsch, consequently, greeted João with a reserved look on his face; he would point to an object or a direction to take without saying a word; he'd grunt his orders and observations. João made an effort to treat him in the same manner; he executed his duties without a smile; he'd grind out his answers between his teeth and every now and then would show a pouting look of indignation he had learned from his mother.

As time went by the intimacy between the two increased, and it was no longer rare to see them exchange insults, digs, to disagree on any subject. They seemed like those couples who are together for centuries and nobody understands why. In this case the relationship was about deep affection.

Salomão Hirsch was born in Germany in 1920. It's enough to know a bit of history and a minimum of mathematics to understand what this means. At thirteen years of age, when young boys of Hirsch's religion go through the ritual that leads them to manhood, his country decided to hate him. The hatred toward Hirsch was the law; it was the word of command, the reigning ideology. Hirsch wasn't able to understand why a whole nation hated him, him as well as his family, his brothers, and relatives. The country dedicated itself to perpetrating this hatred with so much fervor, ingenuity, and fierceness. Those who did not share in the hate shared in the fear, and certainly this wasn't a consolation to anybody. From thirteen to twenty-five years of age, Hirsch specialized in the art of survival. He soon perceived that he could neither lose any time nor waste his strength trying to understand, refusing to believe. The deal was to keep himself alive, to face only the present. He began to live clandestinely on the streets of Berlin. When the military siege tightened, he tried to flee to the hinterland and was caught; he completed his postgraduate work in the camp at Dachau. He survived from day to day and from minute to minute; he survived the slave labor, the hunger, the winter, the number tattooed on his arm, the sight of the smoke rising from the chimneys of the crematoriums, the idea that there was nothing left to survive for. When the camp was taken by the Allies and the awareness that everything was really over managed to penetrate his head, Hirsch decided that he would go very far away. He wanted to begin a new era, to get back to living as if nothing had happened, to forget all these years, above everything else. He came to Brazil, and at the train station in Porto Alegre, he was approached by a man accompanied by an exotic woman.

'Are you a Jew?' the man asked him in Yiddish, and before Hirsch could respond, the man shoved his suitcase at him, wished him good luck, and with the woman jumped inside the passenger car. In the suitcase there were the most varied types of cloth, and for a moment Hirsch thought that they were stolen goods. The next morning he learned about the scandal that put the whole Jewish community into a flurry: Yankel had abandoned his family to run away with a goy, who on top of everything else had Indian blood in her veins. Hirsch became irate when he heard the comments about Yankel's lover. Up until now his life had instilled in him an immense aversion to racism, and he could not accept this type of attitude, much less coming from his own brethren. He tried to remember the features of the woman he had seen getting rapidly on the train. He felt an overwhelming affinity with her. He also felt an affinity with Yankel, who was embarking on a new life and had the generosity to give Hirsch, an unknown, his vendor's suitcase filled with wares.

Hirsch believed that Yankel's suitcase brought him luck, and the facts only came to corroborate this superstition. He traveled through the backlands; he got to know all types of people and sold as no other peddler managed to sell. It was a miracle: Hirsch could barely speak the language, he didn't smile, he made no effort to please, and yet he always returned with an empty suitcase, his little notebook filled with orders. Soon he had to buy one more suitcase and even thought of hiring a helper. However, he decided to forego the idea; he preferred to enjoy this new life of his alone. Besides the suitcases and the wares and the little notebook of orders, Hirsch carried one more burden with him. The people saw him bend over under its weight, even though there seemed to be nothing on his shoulders. Hirsch tried to free himself of this burden, to leave it on the train, to abandon it in some distant place, only to reencounter it soon afterward. Suddenly it would return, to stick on his heel, climb up his spine, lodge itself in his head, neck, and back. No matter how much he tried, Salomão Hirsch could not manage to forget his twelve years of survival in Nazi Germany and one day understood that a human being never would be able to forget.

He then reconsidered and decided that he wouldn't devote himself anymore to wiping out that period in his life. He was going to build his new life on the foundations of the old one, using his wounds as a source of courage and learning. He would have a family, sons, friends, and would not hide his long-suffering past from any one of them. He considered it dead and buried. However, it was essential that they build a sepulcher for it and never stop remembering. In this way at least, it would be more difficult for the past to be repeated.

João had arrived in Brazil in 1548 in the form of a chromosome harbored in the blood of a slave woman, on the first slave ship that landed on Brazilian land. Therefore, João was a four hundredth, direct lineage of those who arrived on the *Mayflower* of our antihistory. His ancestors did not suffer cold or hunger, as was Hirsch's case—it was never a question of eliminating them—since they were property and had to be kept alive for production and procreation. However, none of them had the opportunity to overcome their past, to bury it with their own hands. Like Hirsch they were yanked from their homes, badly treated, scorned, packed into unsanitary housing. They planted for the white man to reap, cooked for him to eat, built for him to inhabit, cleaned for him to dirty. João experienced this reality in his own home, since his mother supported, cooked, and cleaned for his father, and when there was time left she also took a beating from the man. João left home knowing that a better fate awaited him, and with this awareness he managed to get around the pitfalls of the street. One night he awoke with a strange noise by his side. He opened his eyes and found the eyes of a policeman who was putting on a hood. He fled, running from the viaduct where he slept with the other street urchins; he heard the shots and the pain and the terror and the moans and the complicit silence of the night. He didn't stop running until he crossed half the country and ended up in Rio Grande do Sul. He got a job, had a few sidelines, had hard times, until he finally managed to enroll in a nurse's aid course, where he distinguished himself through hard work. He and Hirsch were survivors, and therefore, something deeper than personal appeal united them from the first moment. The pact between them was so strong that nobody could imagine it. Not even themselves.

Rita was the daughter of Dona Clotilde's maid. When she went out into the street, she would walk as if she were taking her little breasts out for a stroll. Fifteen years old, a certain charm, energy, much luster, and a pair of little tits that seemed to have a life of their own. Upright, frisky, provocative, they paraded around the park or through the streets, trying to call attention from underneath the girl's T-shirt. They seemed like those young cubs that sniff everything around them, jump from one side to the other, shake their tails, wiggle their ears, filled with curiosity. Rita could not pass by unnoticed as she went to and fro on her forays to get milk, bread, and many other things. Hirsch noticed João's eyes following the girl each time she passed by them, generally in the park, during the afternoon outing. One day Hirsch called her, asked her to come closer. João folded his arms, discontented. Hirsch asked some questions, introduced himself, introduced his companion, showed some interest, and that was enough to win over the girl. The old man knew it was merely an excuse, Rita's true interest was João, and he, in his wheelchair, was nothing more than a broadcasting antenna. But that was exactly what made him happy. Gradually they became friends. Hirsch and João had to abandon their rudeness in the presence of the young girl, and pretending to be kind to each other out of consideration for her, they could stop pretending to hate each other for a few minutes during the day.

In this way a trio was formed, which restored in Hirsch a little bit of the happiness of being alive. He manipulated the relationship of his two 'children' (after all, he felt himself closer to them than to his blood relatives) and still spent time being amused by the girl's naiveté, by João's playful charm. However, he wanted to provide them with something more than the moments spent in the park, which, due to her tardiness, forced poor Rita to listen to the most righteous of sermons back home. He thought about hiring the girl as a helper in the house, but he gave up the idea since her family would not give her any time off. Maybe as João's assistant, rendering services only to him. He imagined the conversation with his son, the arguments and the counterarguments, and got tired just thinking about it all. He made a thousand plans, projects, programs. He saw himself in church, accompanying the two to the altar; he tried to guess which would be the most honorable of gifts he could give them. He knew more than anyone else that in life there do not exist fairies, gnomes, goblins. However, it didn't cost anything to fool oneself from time to time.

It was when he heard João describe to Rita the strength of his idol, 'Black Hook,' who next week would be boxing against a shameless Argentine, that he got the idea: the three of them would go to the boxing match, and it would be a surprise for the two young ones. Hirsch executed his plan astutely, so much so that it left João's mouth wide open as they approached the gymnasium and even more so when they met up with Rita. She had received a mysterious note along with the ticket of admission to the boxing match. As Hirsch had foreseen, nothing stopped her from showing up. Down deep the old man almost started to regret his good deed. People were coming from all sides; they shouted, argued, causing a bewildering hum. Their seats were in the middle of the gymnasium, very close to the ring. They had to elbow themselves for some time through the crowd. The air was dead; it seemed as if there was not enough for breathing. The smoke from the cigarettes rose high up, taking form in the light of the reflectors.

João was dazzled; never had he seen a live boxing match. While they moved toward the rows, he protected old man Hirsch as if he were a mother. He felt Rita's beating heart glued to his back. As she was taking in the smell of sweat, the masculine hormone being exhaled through the men's pores, her nostrils were expanding out of fear and excitement. Finally they made themselves comfortable. Rita and João on the end seats, Salomão alongside them, sitting on the permanent vehicle that substituted for his feet. It's true; ever since the stroke he hadn't felt like this, in danger, but now it was a different danger that was worth confronting. The preliminary fight started; a red-haired woman in a bikini strutted around the ring indicating the number of the round. João felt Rita's attentive eye; he took on an expression of not being affected by this. Hirsch smiled; he was sure that for him the redhead's struts around the ring would be the best part of the fight. He didn't understand how his companion could get excited seeing one man hitting another, the two hugging, facing each other in a venomous manner, praying for the moment when the adversary would fall flat on the canvas. But there's no accounting for taste, the Talmud had already stated, and besides João hundreds of mouths roared, shouted names, yelled, and howled, merely warming up for the main event.

By the time the main fight began, Hirsch was already feeling bad. He closed his eyes, tried to mask his discomfort so as not to spoil the occasion he himself had arranged. He tried to imagine himself in a better place, in the company of his 'children' on a long voyage. This was it, he smiled; he would go with the two of them to Germany, fifty years after having fled far away. He thought about the conversation he would have with his son before departing. He knew he wouldn't understand; he wouldn't have the depth of soul to fathom the situation. He's an idiot, he thought, grinding his teeth forcefully at the moment when the miserable Argentine delivered a dirty blow to 'Hook.' João looked at the old man with admiration. Hirsch recuperated from his anger, while in the ring the black man came back with an upper hook, defending himself by taking the blows of the boxer from Buenos Aires. He knew that once he made up his mind, his son could yell and complain to his heart's content. He would go to Germany with João and Rita; the three of them would get satisfaction by parading around the streets of Berlin. An old Jew, a proud mulatto, a voluptuous black girl without any inferiority complex to show. After leaving the Aryans flabbergasted, they would go into Dachau, Hirsch holding up with difficulty, telling the two what was possible to tell, showing the places, remembering the dates, the faces, the uniforms. Rita would grab onto João's arm; her sobs would get old man Salomão to cry again. The mulatto would attempt to maintain his composure, he would make that pouting face he had learned from his mother, but he couldn't really fool anybody. The three would feel the same pain, the same indignation, the same bewilderment. The three would at the same time think how fragile was the shell that hid inside man the most foul of creatures, the most horrendous facet of a being living on the face of the earth. They would understand it wasn't merely about a particular case, a single accident in the history of humankind, an episode dead and buried. This would be Hirsch's legacy, the most important inheritance he had to pass on. Maybe it wouldn't make life any easier for either of them, probably the opposite. But that didn't matter; this wasn't the real objective of a legacy; it wasn't the criterion for measuring its value. He knew that the two would grasp its meaning, they would know how to take full advantage, and thus they were worthy of receiving such a gift. Hirsch felt relieved. He felt grateful for the inspiration that gave light to his ideas; he felt proud of these two beings who shared with him that same sensation. It was a legacy he was passing on while alive; he had to be present to transfer it personally in order to give it validity. For this reason it would never be forgotten, neither the legacy nor the circumstances of its transmission. Contrary to the great fortunes, the more it was used, divided, shared, the greater it would become.

This was what the old invalid and survivor Salomão Mansfeld Hirsch was thinking as he closed his eyes never to open them again, at the exact moment when the South American Spaniard hit the canvas and the crowd jumped out of their seats, cheering, counting in time with the referee.

# Cíntia Moscovich

Cíntia Moscovich was born in Porto Alegre, Rio Grande do Sul, in 1958 and graduated from the School of Communications at the Catholic University of Rio Grande do Sul with a major in journalism; she received her master's degree in literary theory from the same university. She works as a press advisor, journalist, teacher, and translator of English, French, and Spanish. The recipient of many literary awards for her stories, she received first place in the Guimarães Rosa Short Story Contest in 1995, which drew over a thousand contestants worldwide. Her first collection of stories, O reino das cebolas (The Kingdom of Onions), which deals primarily with family relations, was published in 1996, followed by her first novel, Duas iguais (1998) (Two Alike), about a lesbian love affair. Since then she has published two collections of short stories: Anotações durante o incêndio (2000) (Notes during a Fire) and Arquitetura do arco-íris (2004) (Architecture of the Rainbow). In 2006 she published another novel, Por que sou gorda, Mamãe? (Mother, Why Am I Fat?). Although she writes about both genders, most of her protagonists are women from different walks of life—housewives, a photographer, Jews, an elevator operator, and so on. With an incisive look at the disenchanted condition of women, Moscovich writes stories devoid of feminist jargon and propaganda. Using humor and irony in a direct style that also captures the colloquial with verve, Moscovich also challenges the reader's sensitivity regarding the small daily things that harbor unexpected dimensions. The story anthologized here, 'Sheine Meidale' (Yiddish for 'pretty girl'), from her first collection, is one of the stories about Jews. A coming-of-age narrative, the story focuses on a Jewish girl's loss of sexual innocence, her family's Jewish frame of reference, and her consciousness of sexual and ethnic differences.

Cíntia Moscovich

# Sheine Meidale

It was in the late sixties. I am absolutely sure because I remember
everybody piled up in the living room of our apartment, Mother popping corn in the kitchen, the Philips TV screen blinking in black and
white and there, in the monochrome image, Man stepping on the
moon for the very first time. The conquest of space had been initiated, so extolled my father, and my mother, standing still at the door
with the big, fragrant bowl resting on her stomach, mouth wide open
for having seen the future happening in her own living room, barely
noticed that the popcorn was getting cold. We, the children and visitors, also didn't notice. To see the things that were not yet a reality had
always been, and would always be, my father's prerogative. On that
night I, my two brothers, the twins from the first floor, and Luiz, the
caretaker's son, made plans, many of them, celebrating the things
bound to happen and not even knowing what they would be.

But while the new times were not escaping from inside the television
set, we made our lives right there. Our side of Ramiro Barcelos Street,
the new part, was situated in that limbo space between the old Jewish
neighborhood of Bom Fim and the Rio Branco district; there the street
already had two lanes, both coming down from Independence Avenue,
separated by a cemented divider of red sand. Propelled by the decline
the cars whizzed by, peeling rubber against the cobblestones, and
because of the traffic, we had to make an obligatory and anxious rest
stop on the divider before crossing the second lane and way before
reaching the little soccer field. The little soccer field was nothing more than
the land where the blue and diagonal Clinical Hospital was erected,
its structure occupying something less than half the total area; the
remainder was taken up by a sparse pasture, filled with rocks and
mounds, and used for the soccer games over which I presided. If
you really think about it, the rank of captain of the team was a right

acquired by sheer force: I was the oldest and, therefore, the strongest, so much stronger that there never was anybody who would question my authority without getting an 'I'll-getcha-kid.' As if my physical superiority weren't enough, I had managed to buy an official soccer ball with my monthly allowance, which had cost me a week without candy, without matinées at the Rio Branco movie theater, without comic books, without the little marbles from the grocery store Aço Verde, and, most painful, without the sardine sandwiches from Dona Frida's luncheonette at school. An atrocity of sacrifices, and I flaunted them from Calvary's beaten path. That whole story made the soccer ball mine more than any other thing in the world, and it had the power to make my father respect, and make others respect, my sense of ownership—even though he was appalled at the neglect I paid to dolls and to playing house. Day after day, he reminded me that when I reached womanhood, the business with the soccer ball would have to stop. Ah, but reaching womanhood would still take time; my mother always kept repeating that her first menstruation had not happened until she was fifteen years old, still, some three years more than I was. In this sense the things that would make me more than a young girl would still take time, and I was free to play soccer with the kids. Very well. Besides me my team was composed of my two brothers and the twins from the first floor. The herd of opponents did not have assigned positions that were fixed, but it was always headed by Luiz, the caretaker's son, one year younger than I was and, I would later discover, infinitely more foolhardy. Every day, after having finished his obligatory chore, there in the underground garage, of incinerating the garbage in the furnace that was dangerously stationed alongside my father's tail-fin Fairlane, Luiz would climb the stairwell that accessed the building and ring the doorbell two times. It was the signal for me to go out, hugging my ball, followed by my brothers shouting, 'Wait up.' Many, innumerable times, I managed to burn my father up with my pouting face, my lower lip extended. 'It was only a little game of soccer, Father, what's wrong with that?'

'Look here.'

Man had already stepped on the moon, had already returned, and no other transformation more dramatic than the change of seasons had occurred in our lives. Therefore, it was just one more January afternoon, rancid and sticky as the summer afternoons are in Porto

Alegre. Luiz had come over to my house right after lunch, and we installed ourselves in the coolness of the servants' work area to play pick-up-sticks. My brothers were who knows where, and my mother was in the kitchen finishing up washing the luncheon dishes. That's when it happened.

Of course, I was already used to seeing pricks. Therefore, when I responded to Luiz's request, and I looked—it wouldn't be me if I didn't look—I came upon a pretty familiar appendage. The only thing was that my brothers' pricks didn't have that thing on there. 'What thing?' he wanted to know. 'That over there,' I answered, already bending my body over and coming close to the object in question. Luiz didn't like my index finger, with anatomical interest, nuzzling his unblemished foreskin. 'No, they really didn't,' I exclaimed, after having finished my examination. Why did his prick have that thing? When I repeated the question, I thought about Jankiel, my brother, the youngest, and of that special day.

Right away in the early morning, my mother dressed us up with going-out clothes, tying my hair in a ponytail, the worst torture a girl with frizzy hair can endure. I looked at myself in the mirror, embittered by the cute little dress with embroidered bodice and collar and with the monumental bow up high on my neck; on my feet my sneakers were replaced by black patent-leather shoes, irritatingly tight at the ankles. *Sheine meidale*, my father dubbed me, when he saw me, in the eternal exclamation of pleasure, which he always repeated when he cast his eyes upon the pretty girl I had turned out to be. The ceremony would take place there at home, no doubt about it; the door had remained open since the early morning. The relatives kept coming, pinching my cheeks with the satanic pleasure they were authorized to exert due to blood ties. Platchek, the mohel, in charge of the Brith, arrived close to noon with his grimy beard, his large felt hat shadowing his features even more, the nail of his small finger larger than all the others. Platchek's fingernail was, by itself, a startling authority and, as such, scratched out orders in midair, organizing social functions. That the women take leave. I left, dragged by my mother, in the anguish of leaving my brother screaming, tied to the satin pillow by the folded swaddling band. I was taken to the kitchen, and I grabbed on to a glass of guarana soda. I raised the glass, and through its translucence I tried to filter the images and snuff out the sounds. I was not successful. My middle brother was also ousted and came to find refuge amid the feminine flank. I placed my arm on Hersh's shoulders and tried to calm him down with the glass of soda. There we stayed, seeing our uncles and cousins gathered around in a noisy circle, their heads protected by the colorfulness of their yarmulkes, and their bodies moving in a single rhythm forward and backward. One day, this I also remember, I asked my father why all the men, during prayer, swayed that way. My father laughed in such a loud manner that I could see his shiny gold molar, the same laughter as when I asked any intelligent question, followed by a look of approval that filled me with vanity and comfort. And like all the other times, he cast upon me the kindliest eyes in the whole universe, as are the eyes of fathers, and explained to me, trying to guess my pace of comprehension, that the body glowed like a flaming candle because, during prayer, the soul insisted on escaping. That's how I understood that, in order to reach God, both soul and body struggle in a furious clash of wills. Later I would understand that the soul only rests when the flesh tires. But that would be only much later. In that way there they were, the men of our family reunited, their souls wanting to begin some flight, the prayers rising in Yiddish, my not understanding very much. My brother yelled louder, much more; it was all over. My mother placed her fingers on her mouth, poor thing, poor thing. Hersh grabbed me, and I grabbed on to my mother's legs. I should calm down, my father was safely holding Jankiel, and nothing was going to happen, she assured me, and so that I would trust what she told me, she rhythmically tapped the top of my head with the palm of her hand, it's okay, it's okay. I hugged Hersh more forcefully against my breast. He had already buried his face in the lacy yoke of my dress, and I repeated the kind gesture on his back, it's okay, it's okay, and his desperation lessened slowly. The three of us clung to one another, the body of a family, while the youngest went through the first sacrifice, reactivating the covenant with God. Suddenly everybody yelled, 'Mazel tov'; my father smiled, embraced by my uncles, and we knew that everything was done. The pillow and my brother were passed around to everybody's arms. My mother was delighted upon receiving her son; she lowered herself and showed us the little one. Horrible. The poor thing was red from so much crying, the wine hadn't done much good, and if that wasn't enough, Platchek had covered part of his legs and waist with the most-yellow sulfate he could find. My father came to us, only happiness on his face, and, wetting his baby finger in the chalice of wine, spilled a few drops of wine in the mouth of the recently circumcised boy. Finally Jankiel fell asleep, and everybody attacked the smoked herring and the strudels. Although everything indicated the opposite, that was a party. The party of the primary alliance, of the divorce between the prepuce and the glans.

While I was deep in silent thought, thinking about the things that had been, Luiz dove into the panic of possibilities.

'You're not going to tell your mother, are you?'

Luiz was taking me from that other day in the past and was bringing me back to his drooping and wilted prick. No, I wouldn't tell; he could calm down. Didn't I feel like holding his prick? I did; of course I did. I held it, and it began to grow, dilating, swelling in my fingers. I felt a delicious warmth coming from in between my legs.

'Kiss it,' he asked.

'Yah, and I'm going to kiss peepee?' I refused, disgusted.

He tried to convince me that his prick didn't have the taste of pee-pee. Of course it did, I reacted. He gave in; if I didn't want to kiss it, that was okay, but just one thing: 'It's not a prick; it's a penis. Only children have little pricks.'

I pondered that idea. Could be, sure, his prick was a penis. He asked me to show him my pussy. No, only my panties; my mother had told me that I should never show my pussy to anybody, only on my wedding day. He understood and began his mating call.

'Do you want to be my girlfriend?'

And the question came out like this, rasping, nervous. Yes, I wanted to, I answered, even without being very sure of loving him. To love, really love, I loved Márcio, a classmate who had never paid attention to me. But if Luiz wanted to, why not be his girlfriend? Therefore, because we were sweethearts, he stood up and clung to me, sticking his prick in between my legs, deliciously rubbing my pussy. Paradise. I lowered my polyester shorts, and I let him lean against the cotton fabric of little bears covering my private parts. I know that we stayed a long time in that coming and going, that hard thing, prick or penis, it didn't matter, giving me pleasure, our arms tied to our bodies, and suddenly, I felt a relief, while he shuddered when he asked that I not press so much because it was already hurting. All right, I was no longer pressing. He withdrew his swelled member, kissed my cheek, and told me he had to go incinerate the garbage. I accompanied him to the door, and I felt very, very anxious. We agreed that we wouldn't tell anything to anybody; it was our secret, wasn't it? It was, yes it was, and, kissing me once again on the cheek, he shot through the corridor. I stayed there, braced against the door, and an infinite sadness weighed over me. It's that I was sure that my father would kill me if I dated a goy. How could I marry Luiz?

Classes at school would begin in March, within a week. The English classes would also begin in the Cultural Center, downtown. Notebooks, pencils, erasers, Magic Markers, everything new. My grandmother gave me a white wrinkle-free shirt, and my mother replaced my crummy flats with a better pair of shoes. I was becoming a young woman; I couldn't go around so unkempt. We also went to Petipá to buy the little tie for the school uniform and, to my distress, a pair of gym shorts, those made of heavy cotton with elastic tightening around the legs and the waist. I protested and protested against the damn shorts; I looked like a head of cabbage. I think my mother agreed, but she said I needed to wear them during gym class. I was consoled only when I remembered Luiz would never see me wearing those things. My courtship with the boy was going very well. The most recent discovery had been the building's rooftop, up until then the exclusive territory of the caretaker. We used to spend tranquil afternoons, watching Police Hill, the crawling traffic of Protásio Alves Avenue, and the houses suspended far off in Petropolis. Thick hairs in the armpits and on the calves of my boyfriend began to appear. In a short time his legs became longer, so much so that he seemed to me a lanky doll. Luiz became angry with my direct observations. 'What's the big deal,' I responded. Right, there was nothing to it, even though I had told him that his prick was getting big. It really was, in such a way that it was already occupying almost all of the palm of my hand. By now the prepuce had receded a little and the glans was already showing itself, glorious and red. On many different occasions I had to control myself so as not to give in to Luiz's pleas. He insisted on putting, just a little bit, of his business inside my pussy. Nothing doing, I controlled myself, knowing that was the part I had to preserve. We had developed a more elaborate method of being together: we would take off our clothes—except for my underpants, never these, of course—and we would kiss each other's body real slow. I loved it when he would linger over my breasts; these, like his prick, had also grown. As for me, I had lost all my revulsion, I had begun to feel pleasure in kissing him, and I rewarded myself because I knew he was going to rub his hand so much in the middle of my legs that I would soon 'come.' Yes, 'to come' was also a new term. And there was another: 'masturbate.' Luiz liked me to masturbate him so he would come. Now, from the hole where he peed, some drops of a half-white liquid came out, and he would tell me that was the way men came. And, nobody had to tell me, I understood that was the way women got pregnant. The soccer ball games followed, but to my father's joy these were already getting rarer due to the absolute lack of time. One thing tormented him: what was I doing spending so much time with the caretaker's son? Gee whiz, couldn't one play anymore?

The classes at school demanded I be disciplined in my studies, and they took up the time I dedicated, at least up until those circumstances, to my playing and going out with Luiz. As if the mountainous stack of dates and equations were not enough to memorize, the phys-ed classes now took place in schedules and places outside school time. As if two whole afternoons stuck in those horrible shorts weren't enough, the English classes at the Cultural Center had started. And as if all this weren't enough, my father took it into his head that I had to learn ballet. Oh, no, anything but that. When was I going to find time to play soccer? My father looked at me very seriously, very, in that way of his of putting me in my place. I better pay attention, he would only say it once, I was becoming a young woman, and when I became a young woman, which was not going to take long, the business about the soccer ball would be finished; there would be no more talk about the subject, understood? No, I didn't understand; I didn't want to understand. I ran to my bedroom, threw myself on the cotton napped bedspread. Rage, rage. And that body of mine, why didn't it obey me? Why did my waist insist on slimming down? Why did my pussy acquire hairs? Why did my breasts stick up in the air? How could I play soccer with all that stuff bouncing around? A bra, Mother had bought me a bra, advising me that I should use it; otherwise my breasts would end up falling down. Besides, that was a very delicate part of a woman's constitution; it had to be protected.

I went to the armoire and opened the drawer. There it was, the bra. I stuck my arms through the straps, but I couldn't reach the clasp on the back. I turned it way around, which is what I always saw my mother do, first buttoning the part in the back and, with both hands, turning the elastic around to its proper place. I tightened the straps on my shoulders. In the mirror my breasts filled the cups; the little flower buds were growing in size, molded into curving shapes. Young woman, yes, I was almost a young woman.

On that afternoon, like all Tuesdays, I had come home exhausted from the phys-ed class. My plans were for a great bath and afterward a quick get-together with Luiz before dinner. Neither my brothers nor my father had arrived; the house remained in saintly order after a good cleaning. My mother was in the kitchen, and given the smell coming from the frying pan, I gathered that we would be having steak with onions. Mother and her onions. I went into the kitchen, and said hi and stole a piece of fried cassava. I got a scolding, and I obeyed; I really needed to take a bath. I went to the bathroom, took off my sweatpants, the cabbagelike shorts, and I sat down on the toilet basin to pee. When I lowered my panties, I couldn't hold back the scream.

I had always hated rare meat. I balked. You don't like it, but you have to, my father said curtly, pretending to be strict. No, I didn't have to; I wouldn't eat that crap. My mother said it was expected; I was irritated because I was sick. Sick, not at all. Becoming a young woman was that. I didn't understand my father's proud face, my mother's undisguised satisfaction. Even my brothers seemed happy. Stupid, everybody stupid, my father, my mother, my brothers. Stupid mankind.

Young woman. So it had happened, without warning, without a threat, without anything. I had transformed myself into a young woman before supper, after having swiped a fried cassava. Wouldn't that have been punishment for having stolen food before going to the table? And I knew that. The thing happened the moment I was peeing, before the bath: it only took the lowering of my panties, and the danger was there, the bright red stain. It was the most agonizing scream of my life. My mother came to my rescue, frightened by the hullabaloo. Not even waiting for me to pee, she already was laying her hands on my neck, kissing me, rubbing me: 'Look at that, how beautiful, it's your menstruation.' Menstruation. I couldn't even manage to cry. I took

my bath with revulsion. How could that have happened? If I hadn't
jumped so much during gym maybe that disaster would not have been
consummated, who could know? My mother stayed there, on duty in
the bathroom. She handed me a sanitary napkin. And what was I to
do with that? I discovered that my mother had greater patience than
I could imagine: 'Like this, my girl, place it right in the middle of the
lining; it holds with your panties, take care not to leak'; if I wanted,
she could buy me a waistband to hold the padding. Never, I would
never use a waistband. Was it going to go on bleeding for a long time?
For about three days, and one shouldn't speak about it in front of my
father and the youngsters. That was private to me. Yes, private to me
alone. I was still getting used to walking with that clog between my legs
when my father arrived. My mother ran to him, whispered in his ear;
the two of them laughed; they looked at me. My privacy was violated.
My brothers arrived; my father called the two of them; he whispered
to them; the three of them looked at me. My public privacy.

After dinner, the plate of fried cassava savagely devoured, I asked to
be excused, and I locked myself in my room. Some years ago I perfectly
remember my mother having given me a book with a boring blue cover.
She recommended I read with attention, and if there were any doubts,
I shouldn't hesitate to ask. Of course, I knew that in those pages the
danger of things to come was waiting for me. I considered destiny as
something not so unavoidable, and escaping what was waiting for me, I
threw the book into the mess of albums of pasted soccer-player pictures.
A pain in the ass, that story about the future. Now, however, it was there,
in the middle of my legs, the immediate reason that motivated me to
find that book. Where had I thrown it? When I was able to behold the
celestial blue cover—after having spilled on the parquet floor bottle
caps, decals, a goalie's glove, two rolls of tape, a piece of dainty ribbon,
and the whole collection of *Natural World*—a dizzy spell massacred my
head. Finally, the future. I tenderly placed the spine of the book in the
palm of my hand, my fingers holding up the hard cover. *Where do babies
come from?* and the bottle shaped letters repeated the question. As part
of my ritual I turned on the bedside light and leaned against the pillow.
So was that it? No big news after all, except for the fallopian tubes and
other things equally strange. The scrotal sack, for example. In half an
hour I was schooled in the subject.

'Now I'm a young woman.'

Luiz opened wide his brown eyes. What did that mean? It meant that the menstruation had come; I could already have children; didn't he know about such things? He did know; he had read something. Was it possible to see my menstruation? Not even if the world came to an end, I summed up. He sat down on the steps, rested his arms on his knees. And if I got pregnant? Dummy, how could I get pregnant if we didn't have sexual relations?

'Of course we have sexual relations,' he said irritably, banging his fist against his scrawny thigh.

I tried to calm him down. We had never technically spoken about the subject, and I thought he knew about the facts of life. He didn't know; I had to tell him everything, the story about the little seed, the whole bla-bla-bla. It was unbelievable, but my boyfriend was not informed about where babies came from. Even less he wasn't informed about the more specific details. I left him there, seated on the steps, lost amid vaginas, ovules, ejaculations, and spermatozoids. A dull-witted youngster. I went to sleep. After all, I was a young woman.

In school I only told the news to Clô, my classmate who sat next to me and who managed to glimpse a sanitary napkin in the middle of my notebooks. From her I couldn't hide a thing; it would be betrayal. At recess time I discovered that Clô didn't know how to keep a secret, and soon afterward my classmates surrounded me, forming a boisterous circle. So I had become menstruated? Could a menstruated woman wash her hair? I didn't really know, I had always heard a list of things that women in that state couldn't do: whip mayonnaise, drink something cold, ride on horseback, and, above everything else—according to my father—play soccer. I was the first one in my class to suffer the assault of things that were to be. I told them the little that was to tell, spreading the proper panic in relation to the gym classes, and for the first time since the hullabaloo had begun, I understood that it really was something very important. From day to night my hips grew, and in proportion my waistline took shape even more; my breasts filled out, my nipples grew, and the hairs of my armpits thickened. No, the recent events didn't drive me to despair as I thought they could. That's because, above all else, Márcio, my secret love, came up to me at the school exit and invited me to go to the Saturday matinée at the Guarany Cinema. Of course, I accepted. So it was arranged; on Saturday he would pass by the house. My heart trembled with joy, and my body exploded with excitement. I followed the boy while he went down the stairs that led to the school, handsome, his hair flowing, the blue and white uniform ruffled, the black briefcase hanging from his hand. Márcio, Márcio. Could it be that he wanted to be my boyfriend?

On that afternoon, walking down Protásio Alves on my way home, I took a short cut, turning onto a sandpit that led to the soccer field. There was Luiz, kicking the ball with the twins from the first floor. Shriveled, skeletal. What had I seen in him? But he was nice, a hard-working kid; yes, okay, he was a goy, and if I decided to marry him the world would stop turning. But why would I marry Luiz? I felt very responsible; I didn't like him; therefore I shouldn't encourage false hopes; my destiny was with Márcio, I was sure. I filled my soul with courage and signaled him to walk with me. He came running, flying. I said I needed to speak with him very seriously, was that all right? He consented, pacing his step alongside mine. I made him sit down in the upholstered easy chair and informed him I would bring some Q-juice for us to drink. I came into the room, step by step, balancing the glasses on the silver tray. He found it odd, the fussy use of the saucer and even more the crocheted napkin. He didn't understand my sudden hospitality and understood even less when I insinuated that I was already a young woman and everything would be changing. Well, he already knew my father didn't like the soccer games; he saw no problem in lessening the trips to the soccer field. Luiz also knew that my father didn't very much like my spending the whole time with him. What if the two of them had a talk, the man-to-man business; he wanted to court me seriously; my brothers were on our side, he was sure. I figured that subtleties were not his forte. I also thought I had to be very careful in dealing with other people's feelings.

'Luiz, it's over. I no longer like you.'

He despaired, shouted, cried, threatened to tell everything to my father. Everything? I became a little frightened but figured that fear wouldn't be of any use at all. If he wanted to tell my father, let him go there, tell him. I was going to deny it, negate everything to my death. Afterward he knew very well that my father believed much more in me than in him. He wanted to try? Dummy.

'Sheine meidale,' and my father became completely proud, satisfied at seeing the beautiful young woman that I had become.

I had taken a bath, covered myself with Ross talcum powder, and put on the best clothes I had been able to find. I was all fixed up, my dress matching the ribbon on top of my head. Afterward I appeared in the living room for my father's approval, the definitive one. It had come out right, despite my knowing he detested the idea of a boy taking me to the movies. Well, it was only the movies; what harm was there?

Márcio arrived five minutes early, smelling of a recent bath, his hair parted on the left. He sat down on the sofa next to the easy chair where my father sat. I kept observing what could become a disaster. I prayed to God and to my guardian angel. Fortunately, contrary to what I expected, my father lowered the paper and brought up a subject: wasn't he the son of Jacob, the doctor? He was. I sighed because I knew my father liked familiar references. My mother came from the kitchen with a silver tray and served everybody guarana soda. When the topic of conversation wore out, Márcio remembered we had to go. We left.

Until today I cannot remember the film we saw. I do remember his taking my hand as soon as the lights dimmed; we remained that way for a pretty long time. I also remember his face covering my vision, his breath of Ping-Pong Chiclets, and that tongue in my mouth. It was a kiss, a real kiss, finally. He put his arm around me, and although the position was a bit uncomfortable, I let it be. More, many more kisses followed; his hand slid without shame over my breasts and my legs. I was happy, very happy. When the movie was over, we went over to the Public Marketplace holding hands and took a bus that stopped in front of the Clinical Hospital. Oswaldo Aranha Avenue had never seemed so big; Redemption Avenue had never looked so green. We said good-bye at the door of my building, and I kept watching my boyfriend cross the first lane of Ramiro Barcelos Street. On the sandy street divider, he half-turned, smiled, and shouted that he liked me a lot.

On the soccer field Luiz, the twins from the first floor, and my brothers were playing a crummy soccer game with the trophy that had been mine and which I insisted on giving to Hersh. Márcio passed by them and gave a kick to the ball, which had swerved away from the field. A perfect shot with the instep of his foot. Luiz caught the pass, stopped the game, and, placing the ball under his arm, followed with his eyes the boy who was moving away, skipping, his two hands inserted in the pockets of his pants.

# Acknowledgments

All translations from the Portuguese are by Nelson H. Vieira.

Marcos Iolovitch, excerpts from *Numa clara manhã de Abril*, 2nd ed. (Porto Alegre: Editora Movimento/Instituto Cultural Judaico Marc Chagall). © 1987 by Marcos Iolovitch. Used by permission of Léo Iolovitch.

Clarice Lispector, 'Trecho,' first published in *Vamos Ler*, September 1, 1941. © 1941 by Clarice Lispector. Used by permission of Agência Literária Carmen Balcells.

Clarice Lispector, 'Eu e Jimmy,' first published in *Folha de Minas Gerais*, December 24, 1944. © 1944 by Clarice Lispector. Used by permission of Agência Literária Carmen Balcells.

Elisa Lispector, excerpt from *No exílio*, 2nd ed. (Brasília: Editora de Brasília/ EBRASA). © 1971 by Elisa Lispector. Used by permission of Tânia Kaufman.

Elisa Lispector, 'Por puro desespero,' in *Tigre de Bengala* (Rio de Janeiro: José Olympio Editora). © 1985 by Elisa Lispector. Used by permission of Tânia Kaufman.

Jacó Guinsburg, 'Miriam.' © 1954 by Jacó Guinsburg. Used by permission of the author.

Jacó Guinsburg, 'Figuras na sombra,' first published in *CULT: Revista Brasileira de Literatura* 3, no. 32 (March). © 2000 by Jacó Guinsburg. Used by permission of the author.

Samuel Rawet, 'Natal sem Cristo,' in *Diálogo* (Rio de Janeiro: Edições GRD). © 1963 by Samuel Rawet. Used by permission of Clara Rawet Apelbaum. English translation reprinted with minor revisions from *The Prophet and Other Stories* (Albuquerque: University of New Mexico Press). © 1998 by Nelson H. Vieira.

Samuel Rawet, 'Moira,' in *Que os mortos enterrem seus mortos* (São Paulo: Vertente). © 1981 by Samuel Rawet. Used by permission of Clara Rawet Apelbaum.

Rosa Palatnik, 'Duas mães,' translated from the Yiddish by José Steinberg, in *Dois dos justos: Contos* (Rio de Janeiro: Gráfica Editora Itambé). Translated from the Portuguese by Nelson H. Vieira. © 1975 by Rosa Palatnik. Used by permission of Ida Szafran.

Judith Grossmann, 'A Sra. Büchern em Lebenswald,' in *A noite estrelada: Estórias do ínterim* (Rio de Janeiro: Francisco Alves). © 1977 by Judith Grossmann. Used by permission of the author.

Alberto Dines, excerpts from *Morte no paraíso: A tragédia de Stefan Zweig* (Rio de Janeiro: Nova Fronteira). © 1981 by Alberto Dines. Used by permission of the author.

Sônia Rosenblatt, excerpts from *Lembranças enevoadas* (Recife). © 1984 by Sônia Rosenblatt. Used by permission of Izaias Rosenblatt.

Samuel Malamud, excerpt from *Escalas no tempo* (Rio de Janeiro: Editora Record). © 1986 by Samuel Malamud. Used by permission of Ilana Strozenberg.

Francisco Dzialovsky, excerpt from *O terceiro testamento* (Rio de Janeiro: Editora Anima). © 1987 by Francisco Dzialovsky. Used by permission of the author.

Eliezer Levin, 'Nova Iorque, Nova Iorque,' 'Réquiem de um mestre-escola,' 'A semente de Safed,' 'O décimo homem,' and 'Seu Samuel,' in *Nossas outras vidas* (São Paulo: Editora Perspectiva). © 1989 by Eliezer Levin. Used by permission of Editora Perspectiva.

Paulo Jacob, excerpts from *Um pedaço de lua caía na mata* (Rio de Janeiro: Nórdica). © 1990 by Paulo Jacob. Used by permission of the author.

Amália Zeitel, 'Morangos com chantilly,' in *Morangos com chantilly* (São Paulo: Editora Perspectiva). © 1992 by Amália Zeitel. Used by permission of Editora Perspectiva.

Esther Largman, excerpt from *Jovens polacas*, 2nd ed. (Rio de Janeiro: Rosa dos Tempos). © 1993 by Esther Regina Largman. Used by permission of the author.

Bernardo Ajzenberg, excerpt from *Goldstein & Camargo* (Rio de Janeiro: Imago). © 1994 by Bernardo Ajzenberg. Used by permission of the author.

Roney Cytrynowicz, 'A vida secreta dos relógios' and 'Shed II,' in *A vida secreta dos relógios e outras histórias* (São Paulo: Scritta). © 1994 by Roney Cytrynowicz. Used by permission of the author.

Samuel Reibscheid, 'Meu nome é Jó,' in *Breve fantasia* (São Paulo: Scritta). © 1995 by Samuel Reibscheid. Used by permission of the author.

Moacyr Scliar, 'No seio de Abraão,' 'Os filhos do andrógino,' and 'Os necrologistas,' in *Contos reunidos* (São Paulo: Companhia das Letras). © 1995 by Moacyr Scliar. Used by permission of the author.

Jaime Lerner, 'Herança,' in *Entre quatro paredes: Contos* (Porto Alegre: Secretaria Municipal de Cultura/Fumproarte). © 1995 by Jaime Lerner. Used by permission of the author.

Cíntia Moscovich, 'Sheine meidale,' in *O reino das cebolas* (Porto Alegre: Prefeitura Municipal de Porto Alegre/Fumproarte/Mercado Aberto). © 1996 by Cíntia Moscovich. Used by permission of the author.

In the *Jewish Writing in the Contemporary World* series

*Contemporary Jewish Writing in Austria*
An Anthology
Edited by Dagmar C. G. Lorenz

*Contemporary Jewish Writing in Brazil*
An Anthology
Edited and translated by Nelson H. Vieira

*Contemporary Jewish Writing in Britain and Ireland*
An Anthology
Edited by Bryan Cheyette

*Contemporary Jewish Writing in Canada*
An Anthology
Edited by Michael Greenstein

*Contemporary Jewish Writing in Germany*
An Anthology
Edited by Leslie Morris and Karen Remmler

*Contemporary Jewish Writing in Hungary*
An Anthology
Edited by Susan Rubin Suleiman and Éva Forgács

*Contemporary Jewish Writing in Poland*
An Anthology
Edited by Antony Polonsky and Monika Adamczyk-Garbowska

*Contemporary Jewish Writing in South Africa*
An Anthology
Edited by Claudia Bathsheba Braude

*Contemporary Jewish Writing in Sweden*
An Anthology
Edited by Peter Stenberg

*Contemporary Jewish Writing in Switzerland*
An Anthology
Edited by Rafaël Newman

To order or obtain more information on these or other University of Nebraska Press titles, visit www.nebraskapress.unl.edu.

LaVergne, TN USA
05 November 2009
163112LV00003B/1/P